Educational Investment

in an Urban Society

EDUCATIONAL INVESTMENT IN AN URBAN SOCIETY

Costs, Benefits, and Public Policy

EDITED BY

Melvin R. Levin

Director, Division of Urban Studies
Boston University

AND

Alan Shank

Assistant Professor of Government
Boston University

Teachers College Press

Teachers College, Columbia University, New York

© 1970 by Teachers College, Columbia University
Library of Congress Catalog Card Number: 70-110397

Manufactured in the United States of America

For

John Holmes

1921-1949

PREFACE

This book of readings, together with a rather lengthy introduction, represents a venture onto spongy ground, replete with quicksand and other traps for the unwary. But, like other explorations of forbidding territory, there are good reasons for the excursion.

We are now witnessing, on a gigantic scale, an international game of "I doubt it," which calls into question allocations for even the most sacrosanct of institutions, not excluding the church and the U.S. military. More to the point, the days of almost automatic incremental budgetary increases for education may be nearing an end. Certain simple, devastating questions are beginning to be asked and noble but essentially silly answers are no longer safe from searching criticism. More people want to know the precise nature of the output yielded by past and present programs and the basis for assuming that additional expenditures for one or another alternative programs will yield relatively greater returns. Equally uncomfortable questions are beginning to be asked about our whole approach to the problem, not if more money for teaching machines can bring greater results than more money for teachers but whether expanded funds for health programs could generate greater payoffs than more money pumped into school systems. And then there are the deadly questions regarding goals and values in a pluralistic society: education by whom and for what and who is to sit in judgment and by what right?

This book will not provide definitive answers to these questions. In a society such as ours, perhaps no book has that capability. But the reader who follows the trail to the end is guaranteed a modest amount of expertise, mingled with respect for the intellectual quality and the humility of the pioneers who are blazing the new trails.

M. R. L.
Boston
December 1969

CONTENTS

INTRODUCTION

The purpose of this book is to examine the application of a technique that has been long used in such fields as water resources to the field of education. Cost-benefit analysis in educational policy is relatively new. The modern foundations were laid as recently as the early 1950's and it is only in the past half dozen years that the approach has been put to systematic and rigorous use. The readings in this volume cover the historic background of cost-benefit analysis together with some of its potentials and limitations for the field of education.

SOME BASIC DEFINITIONS

Cost-benefit analysis is generally defined as a measurement technique in which the total costs of a given project or program are compared with the probable total benefits. The result is a numerical ratio, which is widely accepted as a guide for investments in (or rejections of) project proposals. Theoretically, the totals on both sides of the ledger include indirect as well as direct cost and benefits. For example, student income lost during training periods in school might be added to instructional costs, whereas a reduction in delinquency as reflected in lower correctional costs might be included in second-round benefits attributable to a training program. Although cost-benefit techniques attempt to take intangible factors into account, such as actual or probable effects on citizen morale or aesthetics, this measurement instrument in practice relies heavily on quantifiable, tangible elements.

A variation of cost-benefit, known as cost-effectiveness, was applied with alleged success in the U.S. Department of Defense dur-

1

ing the recent administration of Secretary Robert McNamara. Cost-effectiveness measures attempt to place less emphasis on estimating returns from investments and more on correlating alternative monetary allocations to achievement of specified goals. Whereas cost-benefit analysis tends to focus on quantification of total inputs and outputs in monetary terms, cost-effectiveness analysis can retain an output variable in a "raw" form without converting it to dollar values. In pentagonese, for example, the input side of a cost-effectiveness calculation may be ten billion dollars for a given weapons system, which can be translated not into dollar returns but into a hypothetical number of dead Russians or Chinese. Measured objectives might range, for example, from a reduction in Vietnamese insurgency to achieving lower rates of illiteracy in core cities. For this reason, the cost-effectiveness approach permits considerably more latitude in program planning than traditional cost-benefit techniques, which concentrate almost exclusively on measures of economic efficiency.

A more sophisticated refinement of cost-effectiveness is Planning-Programming-Budgeting (PPB).[1] PPB starts with goals and works back. It attempts to juxtapose alternative choices of program elements within broad program categories (e.g., on-the-job training vs. institutional or classroom training). By analyzing the probable costs and benefits of the alternatives against the yardstick of overall program goals (e.g., reducing the unemployment rate among the teenage unemployed), PPB allegedly permits a more rational structuring of expenditures.

It should be noted, however, that each of the three general analytical measurement approaches rests heavily on various judgmental factors, each of which is vulnerable to manipulation to produce desired results, and, taken together or separately, they offer guidelines rather than precise blueprints for action. In other words, various cost-benefit techniques can be used to support either desired or undesired public policy goals.

THE ELEMENTS OF COST-BENEFIT ANALYSIS IN EDUCATION

The basic literature of cost-benefit analysis and allied techniques indicates the problems and prospects of evaluating and identifying national educational priorities and policies. The relevant literature reveals six major areas of cost-benefit considerations: human capital and education, educational expenditures and worker productivity, benefits and costs of education, PPBS, social indicators, and cost-benefit in action.

Human Capital and Education

During the late 1950's, several economists discovered that investments in human capital are closely associated with traditional concepts used to explain economic growth rates. Theodore W. Schultz, Gary S. Becker, and Burton A. Weisbrod (Articles 1-3) found that investments aimed at improving labor capability, primarily through education, accounted for a major share of economic expansion.[2] Weisbrod discovered that public acceptance of the value of education is reflected in long-term changes in public expenditure patterns: In 1900, total expenditures for education in the U.S. represented only 9% of total investment in plant and equipment; by the early 1960's, the proportion had climbed to 37%. Denison found that increased education has had a profound impact on improved incomes in the labor force.[3] More education has resulted in higher economic productivity.

This new emphasis on human capital represented, in part, a rediscovery of concepts developed by the founding father of modern economics, Adam Smith. He included "all of the acquired and useful abilities of a country as a part of capital"[4]—a breadth of vision that contrasts sharply with the narrow concentration on reproducible goods characteristic of many of his successors. Schultz discovered that it is not easy to identify with precision the full contribution of education, which is so fundamentally important to a nation's social well-being and political stability as well as to its economic fabric. Nor is it possible to develop a complete inventory of costs since so many of these are hidden costs and since most of the educational function is the responsibility of public agencies that do not have the measurable profit-and-loss characteristics of the private firm.

There are two ways of looking at educational costs-benefits— from the standpoint of the individual and from the perspective of public policy. The two perspectives are often identical because higher personal incomes are usually closely correlated with greater national output and a larger tax base. On the other hand, an individual may make a great deal of money by putting his education to anti-social uses. He may use his schooling to raise his income by using illegal, quasi-legal, or unethical means. And he may carry these activities so far as to pay less than his proportionate share of taxes so that the public benefits from his shady dealings are minimal or actually negative. Assuming that those who engage in such practices are a small minority, Thomas I. Ribich (Article 9) has made careful calculations of the personal monetary benefits associated with given amounts of education. He suggests that the return-on-investment from college graduation averages out to something in excess of 10% (including foregone income as part of the investment). Apparently the payoff from education at lower levels is even greater: The average return from completion of elementary school is estimated at from 35% to over 50%.[5]

Some of the basis for Ribich's estimates can be seen in Table 1, although the figures are for men and therefore tend to be overstated for the general population. The 1966 data point to very significant jumps in lifetime income from age 18 to death—less than an eighth grade education vs. completion of elementary school (about $60,000), one to three years of high school vs. completion of high school (almost $60,000), and high school graduation vs. one to three years of college (over $50,000). The largest single increment (almost $114,000) accrues to the completion of college when compared to one to three years of college education.

One important qualification that has significant implications for educational policy should be added to the concept of investment in human capital. Becker found that there is much more success in identifying and measuring quantitative than qualitative differences. Program investments can be assessed on the basis of their quantitative results, but, in practical terms, it is far from simple to develop accurate measurements of the relative quality of education programs.

There are also a number of geographic, racial, and other factors which bear on the concept of investment in human capital. The returns from education tend to be lower in most categories in the economically distressed parts of the nation; returns usually are lower for women as well as for Negroes and other groups subject to occupational discrimination. If marketplace reasoning is followed and the objective is to maximize economic returns, it is likely that greater returns could be achieved by betting on the winners; present patterns of geographic, sex, and racial discrimination would be intensified and the application of cost-benefit results would exacerbate existing inequalities.

As a practical matter cost-benefit reasoning has not been, and probably never will be, the sole criterion in public policy. In the field of education, for example, it has long been recognized that public investment has great social value as well as an impact on the personal and national economy. Public schools have been a principal method for instilling in highly diverse ethnic and racial stocks a common bond of citizenship and a common cultural base. Education also has important military implications. Maintaining a high

TABLE 1

Lifetime Income in 1956 and 1966
Based on Arithmetic Means for Men in Selected Age Groups,
by Years of School Completed, for the United States
(in 1966 Dollars)

Years of School Completed and Selected Age Group		1966	1956
INCOME FROM AGE 18 TO DEATH			
Total		$320,698	$249,716
Elementary:	Less than 8 years	188,659	157,027
	8 years	246,525	213,559
High School:	1 to 3 years	283,718	241,129
	4 years	340,520	291,706
College:	1 to 3 years	393,969	332,410
	4 years or more	541,911	445,214
	4 years	507,818	(NA)
	5 years or more	586,905	(NA)
INCOME FROM AGE 18 to 64			
Total		$292,038	$225,668
Elementary:	Less than 8 years	169,538	139,505
	8 years	221,759	190,172
High School:	1 to 3 years	253,881	214,511
	4 years	303,284	257,796
College:	1 to 3 years	346,988	290,243
	4 years or more	473,292	388,621
	4 years	452,596	(NA)
	5 years or more	500,368	(NA)

NA-Not Available

Source: U. S. Department of Commerce, Current Population Reports Series P-60, No. 56, August 14, 1968, *Consumer Income: Annual Mean Income, Lifetime Income and Education Attainment of Men in the United States. For Selected Years, 1956 to 1966.*

level of public investment in education is increasingly crucial in an era in which enormous amounts of time, money, and talent are devoted to technological innovations in warfare and a highly-trained base is needed to support a sustained military effort.

There are other benefits that may have only an indirect relationship to maximizing monetary returns from public expenditures. Expenditures for avocational education, especially for the aged, are difficult to justify on purely economic grounds. Similarly, investments allocated for "advanced" education for housewives and for members of disadvantaged minorities could conceivably yield greater returns if they were instead channeled to education for gifted children and adults. The inference is clear: Cost-benefit approaches applied to public investment in education cannot be limited to monetary rates of return; considerations of justice, morality, and equity[6]—and national defense—somehow must also be entered into the decision-making equation.

Educational Expenditures and Worker Productivity

One of the principal objectives of educational policy, particularly in the past few years, is the equalization of educational opportunity. Although public education below the college level remains strongly influenced by local preferences under the present system of administrative fragmentation, the trend is very much in the direction of enlarged state and federal participation and standard-setting. According to Jerry Miner (Article 4), this shift toward greater intervention by state and federal governments partially reflects a mounting fiscal crisis in many municipalities, but it is also linked with social objectives (such as racial integration, assisting distressed areas, and helping disadvantaged people) that are only indirectly associated with maximization of economic returns from educational investment.

In educational programs for the underprivileged, efforts in recent years have leaned heavily on attempts to bring opportunity to the hard-core jobless through on-the-job advancement. There is a critical argument in favor of a comprehensive educational-training approach—the almost immediate payoff from this kind of educational investment, a fact that helps to generate interest in such programs among both the adult poor and the Congress, which must vote the necessary funds. This almost immediate payoff from vocationally-oriented continuing education differs radically from the situation of elementary and secondary education. In the latter case, one generation sacrifices part of its income to educate the next, with perhaps a ten- or twenty-year wait for the investment to yield dollar returns.

Charles S. Benson (Article 5) indicates that although there is an observable relationship between literacy training programs (particularly if combined with on-the-job training) and personal and societal gains, it is much more difficult to establish a direct, scientifically plausible, causal relationship between an extra year or two of high school and measurable gains in economic productivity. Some students of manpower problems suggest, moreover, that we have created a "credentials trap" in which diplomas rather than demonstrable skills are a job prerequisite.[7] It is alleged that much of the labor force is over-educated for relatively simple tasks, which are normally learned informally or formally in the first few weeks of employment.

S. M. Miller and Frank Riessman describe the present educational system as a "new guild system of credentials, licenses and certificates—largely built on the basis of education—which keeps people out of many occupational channels."[8] For many occupations they suggest that one must start young, and there are no second chances. The schools help to sort people out at an early age, much as did England's notorious "11+" examination, which consigned most of the population to the working class on the basis of examination performance before the age of 12. Miller and Riessman stress the need for a range of second chances for people who have stepped off the educational ladder.

The fact that years of formal education beyond elementary schooling are not inseparably connected with job performance— especially if occupational and job prerequisites can be realistically restructured—is closely related to recent efforts to employ hard-core unemployed in civilian and military jobs and to the "new careers" concept. New careers involve a reordering of job specifications at the bottom end of the job ladder to stimulate the creation of subprofessional aides with a minimum of schooling to assist teachers, police, social workers, and other staff serving the community.[9]

The argument, however, that much of the nation's labor force has more education than is absolutely necessary to hold a job ignores three important factors. The first concerns the rapid increase both in the numbers and proportions of professional and technical jobs in the labor force, which has not only made it imperative for more workers to have more education but also makes adult education a necessity to keep skills competitive and up-to-date. Secondly, the argument does not take sufficient account of the effect of education on citizenship and cultural patterns and on personal and family morale and motivation. Finally, there is evidence to suggest that continuing education can have substantial benefits by capitalizing on past educational experience; the payoff from additional education beyond the high school level seems to be particularly pronounced.

Another controversy concerns the problem of weighing the value of schooling against wages lost while attending school. Investments in public education, as well as in other types of schooling, must take into account the concept of foregone earnings. If a young person were not attending high school or college, he would presumably be employed; in effect, he gives up the opportunity for earnings in favor of attending school. Based on comparisons of earnings of comparable young people already at work, Theodore Schultz (Article 6) found that, in 1956, the cost of these foregone earnings is estimated to represent over 60% of the total costs of high school and college education.[10] In the case of certain post-high school educational programs, however, there is usually no interruption in the flow of earnings. In some recent programs, new work-training courses generate a flow of earnings—and taxes. Thus, if foregone earnings are accepted as a major component of educational costs, programs of continuing education appear to have a striking cost advantage over investments in schooling that require abstention or withdrawal from the labor force. There is, moreover, an obvious advantage from the standpoint of the student: no lost "opportunity costs" are normally involved because he is not giving up opportunities for employment while he is continuing his education.

The fact that decisions affecting educational investments rarely reflect close attention to cost-benefit approaches is only partially attributable to skepticism concerning the utility of the technique in its present, early stages of development. Even with its current imperfections, cost-benefits analysis can be an extremely useful tool, but its potential has been badly neglected. Schultz charges, for example, that far too little attention is given to efficiency criteria for saving the time of students or teachers. Student time is treated as costless.[11] This assumption may be feasible for children and adolescents, but it is dangerous for mature adults, many of whom tend to be hypersensitive about wasting time in apparently useless schooling. Some of the problem with dropouts at all levels is a pervasive sense of unease regarding the possibility that schooling may be insufficiently related to the student's needs. This disquiet is exacerbated by the fear that not enough systematic attention is being given to prospective demand for skills and knowledge in an institutional setting too often characterized by slow, fragmented responses to even the most urgent issues. In short, partly because of past disillusionment, the mature adult has his doubts that the present system will deliver the goods for him.

Consideration of the economic costs of education leads to another, related conclusion. With few exceptions, students in high school (and perhaps in much of post-high school education) pursue their schooling without a clear idea of how it is to be used over the next three or four decades of their working lives. To a great extent, adolescence is a time of discovery, and school experience itself opens up career horizons. Thus, from kindergarten through high school, the student, his family, and government are investing in ten to twelve years of education that is to be used over a work span of three decades.

Since the pace of technological change is accelerating and the future, even with scholarly crystal-ball gazing, is unpredictable, the recent graduate embarks on his career with a store of accumulated knowledge that is certain to become partially obsolete fairly quickly. Thus, investment in education must continue beyond years spent in public schools in order to have an adequately skilled and up-to-date labor force.

Benefits and Costs of Education

Theodore Schultz estimated that, in terms of 1956 dollar values, the total public and private capital investment in education per member of the labor force rose from just over $2,200 in 1900 to almost $7,600 in 1957.[12] Asssuming a continuation of the 1950-1957 rate of $200 annual increase in this investment, in 1969 the educational per capita investment figure (in 1956 dollars) probably exceeds $10,000. There are those who maintain that part of this investment is "wasted," as in the case of a female college graduate who marries at a young age and withdraws from the labor market never to return to gainful employment. On the other hand, it seems clear that there is serious underinvestment at the elementary school level; Schultz suggests that "anything less than 8 years of schooling"[13] represents just such a case.

It is noteworthy that virtually all of the discussion and analysis in the U. S. respecting the economic value of education to the individual and to the nation rest on the implicit assumption that this is essentially a classless, open, expanding society. It is assumed that economic growth helps to create chronic shortages of skilled manpower and that the numerous job openings reinforce an ideology that maintains that advancement is, or should be, primarily based on merit. In older, class- and caste-ridden societies there are almost insuperable barriers to mobility via education: the very low percentages of offspring of working class parents enrolled in colleges and universities is one of the principal causes of student unrest in France, Italy, and other nations. Social and economic barriers are not unknown in the U. S., however, as attested by the disproportionately small percentages of Negro, Latin American, and working class children attending institutions of higher education.

Were caste and class barriers in the U. S. as rigid as some maintain, there would be little object in educating a restive, frustrated corps of graduates (like those in India) who are more likely to find outlets in menial labor or radical politics than in positions commensurate with their schooling. Until recent years, it was not unusual to find Negro college graduates employed in low status white collar jobs. (This is no longer the case; in fact, educated Negroes and Latin Americans are much sought after, even though a great problem still exists for the undereducated in minority and racial groups.) At present, the removal of remaining barriers for the obviously qualified is less an issue than schooling and training for the poor. Much of the thrust of various educational programs emphasizes uplifting the less educated, minority groups into the mainstream of the labor market and the society.

One of the principal problems of minority group employment involves motivating and training the adolescent and adult who are unemployed or underemployed. Unlike the problem of job discrimination against the well-educated member of the minority group, this clearly goes to the core of the new emphasis in continuing education on training and educating the disadvantaged.

The obvious benefits to the jobless person who completes a course of training and finds a gainful job are simple enough to measure. But once the focus is widened beyond the student's earning power, such calculations become much more complicated. One of the difficulties in establishing an effective correlation between educational investment and returns relates to the nature of the educational process. There are substantial benefits over and above those which can be added up in the student's greater earnings. Burton A. Weisbrod (Article 8) lists among the educational beneficiaries

the student's future children, who will receive informal education in the home . . . the neighbors who may be affected favorably by the social values developed in children by the schools . . . employers seeking a trained labor force . . . the society at large by developing the basis for an informed electorate.

Weisbrod indicates that there are also other benefits to the student, which are difficult to assess in monetary terms. These include the possibility of exercising an option to use previously completed education to obtain more schooling; broadened career choices; and "hedging" against the hazards of technological change. There is an inverse relationship between education and prolonged periods of unemployment.

Two external benefits are more directly related to continuing education for the poor. The first is the preventive value of reduced welfare caseloads and unemployment rates and the associated reduction of civil disorder. This involves what may be termed avoidance benefits. The second is the positive value of a relatively well-educated, taxpaying stratum of society, which may avoid the necessity of costly public programs of public safety and law enforcement, for example.

There are also certain indirect monetary benefits which are often overlooked. In addition to their principal functions, schools act as babysitters, thereby permitting the gainful employment of millions of women. Weisbrod estimated that in the mid-1950's the value of the nation's school day "child care" services to 3.5 million working mothers with children between 6 and 11 years of age amounted to $2 billion a year.

Although this research and discussion are concerned with real entities, many such entities are hard to measure. In fact, even if the quantification process is limited to the student himself, statistical exercises relating to the economic value of education are often difficult to defend. This discussion is directly applicable to continuing education. Although it is easy to claim that a six-month evening course in computer programming costing $1,000 is responsible for a $3,000 annual increase in earnings, the balance sheet is far more complicated. What has actually occured is the addition of one highly lucrative rung to an educational ladder stretching over 12 years or more. Continuing education often has a very large payoff because it capitalizes on many years of previous training.

Cost-benefit calculations that focus on the time and cost expended for continuing education must give due weight to the fact that this type of education is a means to improve upon—or to safeguard from obsolescence—large, accumulated public and private investments in human resources. The payoff is real enough, and there is every incentive to accord it high priority, but it must be viewed as an essential stage in a continuing process of education in which the rewards for each additional stage tend to be increasingly larger than the previous increment of investment.

Continuing education is an important component of human re-source development. John Vaizey (Article 7) points out that, of the economist's trinity of land, labor, and capital, labor "is equivalent to manpower, *plus* its skills, plus the huge stock of ideas and pro-ductive talent locked up, for instance in libraries and the family." Continuing education, in many instances, is the key that opens the essential lock; this may be particularly true for the disadvantaged who, by reason of a lack of motivation or environmental and family circumstances, failed as children and adolescents to take full advan-tage of elementary and secondary schooling. (The educational sys-tem itself may have been faulty, lacking in quality and relevance.) Grown to maturity, perhaps with military service and a few years of distasteful menial labor and periods of joblessness behind them, with the help of life experience the adult may have developed the incentive and wider horizons necessary to profit from education and training useful to his needs.

The War on Poverty is one of the principal stimuli for an in-creased emphasis on investment in education. There is increasing recognition that poor education and low family incomes are often closely linked and the present educational system in the existing slum milieu seems to reinforce present problems rather than to remove much of the slum population from poverty. Many hope that a combination of relevant education and manpower training for mature breadwinners can lift whole families out of poverty—perma-nently.

Thus, although efforts to improve school and pre-school educa-tion are much in evidence, there is also increasing attention to a component of the educational spectrum that tends to be overlooked by cost-benefit researchers—continuing education for adults at the sub-professional level. Continuing education may provide the miss-ing diploma, license, or certificate, which has become increasingly necessary for entry or advancement.

The wide income disparities in annual and lifetime earnings as-sociated with different educational levels have already been al-luded to and will be discussed at greater length below. Walter Fogel[14] examined educational disparities based on race, class, and area to determine if levels of income rise with completion of addi-tional years of schooling. He concluded that such disadvantaged groups as Negroes, American Indians, and Puerto Ricans are forced to endure frustratingly long waiting periods before attaining in-comes appropriate to educational levels, in comparison with other groups in society.

Herman Miller's data reveal that, proportionately, five times as many children from well-off families (over $10,000 income in 1959) as children from poor families (under $5,000 income in 1959) attend college. There is, moreover, much carryover from one generation to the next, particularly with respect to the level of education attained by the father. Completion of high school can result in a dramatic improvement not only in the earning power of the parent but in the likelihood that his children will have a better future. This generational "rub-off" is another strong argument for placing more emphasis on continuing education as a poverty preventive for the next generation.

A 1968 Census Bureau report estimated that the average lifetime earnings of a U. S. elementary school dropout will be $150,000 below the lifetime earnings of the average high school graduate and $300,000 below those of the average college graduate. The differential is shown graphically in Figure 1. Two implications of Figure 1 are clear. First, the earnings gap between the ill-educated and the well-educated seems to be widening. The estimated lifetime earnings differential between elementary school graduates and high school graduates was just under $75,000 in 1956 but had widened to over $90,000 in 1966. Second, there is a clear-cut implication for adult education, especially for adult basic education and high school equivalency programs, in these enormous earnings differentials.

The figures presented in Table 2 indicate that nationally, employed males in the U.S. who had completed the eighth grade (but had not gone beyond that level) averaged over $1,300 a year more in earnings than men with less than an eighth grade education, and almost $58,000 more in estimated lifetime income. The differentials are roughly the same for men with 1-3 years of high school as compared to high school graduates.

It would be an error to restrict the discussion of education to the completion of a given quantity of schooling. Numerous studies have disclosed that the educational skills of the poor may have little relationship to years of school completed. The "cumulative deficit" in New York City's schools[15] is apparent in other parts of the nation. Social differentials in education are also closely associated with area and region. Writing about his native Appalachia, Harry Caudill relates the bitter experience of a Kentucky father whose sacrifice to keep his son in high school seemingly proved valueless when the boy failed an achievement examination given by an aerospace corporation that mistrusted high school diplomas issued by Kentucky, Arkansas, and Mississippi schools.[16]

FIGURE 1

Estimated Lifetime Income in Constant 1966 Dollars Based on Income and Life Expectancy Experience of 1966 and 1956, by Educational Attainment of Men 25 Years Old and Over, for the United States

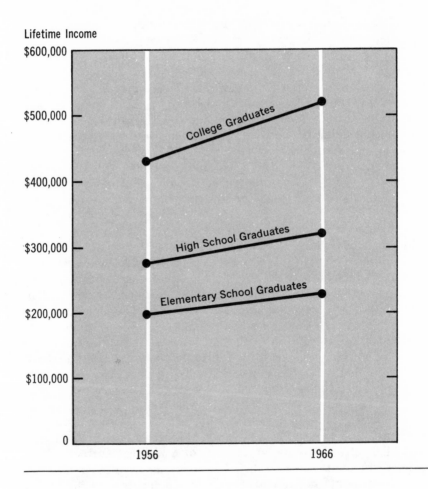

Source: Current Population Reports Series P-60, No. 56, August 14, 1968.

TABLE 2

**Mean Income in 1966 of Men 25 Years Old and Over,
and Estimated Lifetime Income for Men by Years
of School Completed, for the United States**

	Annual Earnings	Annual Differential	Lifetime Earnings	Lifetime Differential
Elementary				
Less than 8 years	$3,520	$1,347	$188,659	$57,866
8 years	$4,867		$246,525	
High School				
1 to 3 years	$6,294	$1,200	$283,718	$56,802
4 years	$7,494		$340,520	

Source: Tables A and F, Current Population Reports Series P-60, No. 56, August 14, 1968, *Annual Mean Income, Lifetime Income, and Educational Attainment of Men in the United States. For Selected Years 1956 to 1966.* U.S. Department of Commerce, Bureau of the Census.

There is, however, evidence to support the belief that the steady barrage of propaganda urging poor children to stay in school has begun to bear fruit. In 1968, it was estimated that about three-fourths of poor youths in the nation between the ages of 16 and 21 were attending school or had completed high school, whereas over half of their parents had no high school education. Yet a substantial education gap remains: the comparable figure for youths from better-off families was 90%.[17] Even more important, as has been indicated, much of the schooling available to the poor is of inferior quality. This recognition has been reflected in considerable new legislation.

Since 1964 a number of federal programs have been initiated in accordance with the pursuit of two educational objectives:

An opportunity for the best education which the Nation can offer each individual, suited to his abilities and interests and without regard to his family income, race or place of residence.

An improvement in the quality of education through experimentation with new materials and methods, new ways of using and training personnel, and new organizations designed to ensure regeneration and renewal of the Nation's schools and colleges.[18]

The more significant of these educational programs include: Operation Headstart, which provides preschool education, nutrition, health, and related services to children from poverty families and is designed to raise achievement to normal levels and to ensure chances for success in school; Title I of the 1965 Elementary and Secondary Education Act, which is directed toward improving the quality of education for poor children from kindergarten through the 12th grade; and the 1968 Vocational Education Amendments, which place special emphasis on the training needs of poor youths and adults and the handicapped. These amendments also eliminate the old categories of training for specific occupational areas in order to relate training to the actual job market demand in each area of the country and seek to bring business and labor expertise closer to the schools in order to develop more relevant courses. Continuing education for teenage dropouts and potential dropouts has also received a good deal of attention, most notably through the Job Corps and Neighborhood Youth Corps (NYC). The NYC provides part-time subsidized work during the school year and full-time work during the summer, along with counseling for needy students of high school age who feel financial pressure to quit school, and similar work experience and related services for poor youth who have already left school and are unemployed. Job Corps provides training, supportive services, and allowances in residential centers to help school dropouts become employable. These federal manpower training efforts on the poverty front had been preceded by two earlier pieces of legislation, the 1961 Area Redevelopment Act and the 1962 Manpower Development and Training Act. Both contained provisions for a combination of vocational training (classroom and on-the-job) and monetary allowances.

An evaluation of the results of educational programs designed to assist the disadvantaged tentatively suggests that the costs of special programs of enrichment, counseling, and motivation development may come close to or may exceed anticipated monetary benefits. In contrast, there seems to be much more assurance of a substantial payoff from programs designed to provide additional education, particularly beyond the high school level. Thomas Ribich (Article 9) suggests that veterans' educational allowances, scholarship programs, and similar efforts yield high returns precisely because they rely on voluntarism and a significant degree of student motivation.[19] Similarly favorable experience was encountered in the MDTA program, which worked smoothly and at low cost during the earlier years when it engaged in "creaming" well-motivated candidates but ran into much difficulty when Congress required that it reach out to the hard-core unemployed.

The special problems posed by the application of traditional educational approaches to slum populations has led to a variety of remedial recommendations of which community control of public schools is the most recent. Two proposals relating to the alleviation of poverty should be noted since they have a direct bearing on the relationship between continuing education and poverty. The first involves "new careers for the poor," a restructuring of present occupational patterns to create hundreds of thousands of such subprofessional jobs as teacher's aides and other public service positions.[20] The present stratified job ladder is to be altered to a continuum which permits the motivated and talented poor to advance from low skill entry jobs to any station available to the more favored members of society.[21] Over time, this approach will obviously impose new training tasks on the continuing education function. In cost-benefit terms, Riessman and Pearl hypothesize that the smaller classes and personal attention permitted by an increase in instructional staff would result in great benefits by helping to reach the estimated 7.5 million youths who otherwise might be expected each decade to drop out before completing high school. Riessman and Pearl call for "rigorous examination" of this hypothesis, suggesting that if the use of large numbers of teaching aides does not "pay off" as expected, available manpower should be deployed elsewhere.[22]

Another line of action that would involve new challenges for assisting the poor in education programs is the attempt to get mothers in the Aid to Families with Dependent Children (AFDC) program "off the welfare rolls and onto payrolls." The actual cost of establishing the beginnings of a requisite system of low-cost day care centers to permit large scale training or employment of mothers with dependent children has not yet been determined.[23] Nor have the possible social costs been determined. It is not yet known, for instance, whether dependent children are better off with their mothers or in nurseries during the working day.

Before proceeding with an examination of specific examples in the use of cost-benefit techniques as an aid in program evaluation, it is useful to review some scholarly assessments, which are based on the past 25 years of theory and practice.[24] In summary, it appears that there are at least six major problems associated with cost-benefit analysis in education:

1. Education has hard-to-measure, non-monetary, as well as monetary, objectives and consequences.
2. Education must be weighed against alternative uses of time, e.g., loss of leisure.

3. Education for minority ethnic and racial groups must take into account the higher cost of programs for those with few skills and with other handicaps.

4. Education and economic expansion are closely related. Justification for some educational programs must be sought on non-monetary grounds, e.g., achievement of equal opportunity, social justice, etc..

5. Completion of years of school is linked to factors other than public investment, including family background, individual ability, motivation, etc..

6. Educational returns are usually calculated on the basis of prior trends, which may not be reliable for predictive purposes.

It would be fair to say that there are many unanswered questions, which suggests that extreme care is needed in appraising the results. One economist concluded in late 1967:

Adding up the situation as of the present, there have been brave beginnings in benefit/cost valuations, but that is all. Thus far we have made only limited empirical applications of our theoretical arsenal, we have used blunt instruments on frail data. But crude as they may be, these pilot efforts point the way to bigger, better and more pertinent research endeavors.[25]

In reviewing the current state-of-the-art, a number of economists raise various issues that have plagued cost-benefit analysis almost from its inception. Jack Wiseman (Article 10) reminds us that education serves important non-monetary ends and that concentration on economic implications tends to create confusion for policy-making. Education is a major element in the growth and formation of culture, personality, and civilization. In focussing on the visible tip of the iceberg—numerical calculations of dollar returns—the major benefits from educational investments may be concealed.

Another problem of cost-benefit analysis in education concerns the use of leisure time. It was suggested earlier that education for adults has the economic merit of interfering little, if at all, with the production process. If leisure time, in which continuing education takes place, is assigned a value either in monetary terms or as "psychic income," the balance sheet might be altered significantly. Obviously, many Americans assign less value to leisure time than to money. In 1966, about one worker in 20 in the U. S.—3.6 million —held two or more jobs.[26] It is also obvious, though, that foregoing any significant amount of leisure in favor of more education would be looked upon as a deprivation by many, possibly most, adults.

Wiseman argues convincingly that cost-benefit studies should not be divorced from the broader institutional setting. The fact that Negro high school graduates earn less than white high school drop-outs (and that similar statistics are available for other deprived groups) adds support to the notion that there is a permanent "underclass" composed of roughly 20% of U. S. families. Poverty and poverty-related conditions are closely associated with underachievement in education. The prospects for those at the bottom of the ladder are increasingly dismal since technological changes have made a large supply of low cost, unskilled labor increasingly redundant; this is in sharp contrast to the experiences of earlier minority groups, who came to America and found many unskilled jobs available. Now, however, there are few opportunities for upward mobility—to move from pick and shovel, to foreman, to contractor. Under present circumstances, education is the key to upward mobility; and all types of educational programs are necessarily assigned a critical role in opening up opportunities for the disadvantaged. But education and training for the disadvantaged tend to be expensive and this raises important questions. What cost calculations can be built on such social values as equality, justice, and freedom of choice? Is it necessary to prove that costly education and manpower training help to prevent riots and diminish crime, before such programs can be instituted? How do dollar costs of motivating and educating the disadvantaged and of breaking down institutional barriers to their mobility compare to anticipated moral, as well as monetary benefits?

Obviously, major reliance must be placed on prospects for economic expansion. A growing economy is a prerequisite not only to provide tax revenues for training and educational programs but to offer some assurance to job incumbents that there is no danger that new entrants will threaten their hard-won job status. Without steady expansion of the economy, the possibilities of effecting much change in the prospects of a major segment of the market—the disadvantaged—are slim indeed.

William G. Bowen [27] indicates that the influence of institutional barriers on the problem of calculating educational payoffs for the disadvantaged is certainly present. This is reflected in criticisms of estimates of educational benefits on the ground that differences in intelligence, ambition, family connections, geographic location, and other factors may have been more significant than completion of a given number of years of schooling. The fact that the educational returns for Negroes are lower than for whites indicates that we are dealing with complex human equations rather than simple, measurable investments in stocks and bonds. Attempts to develop comparative data for control groups in which class, race, and location are constants and education is the only variable have not been wholly successful. It is particularly difficult to assess differences in individual ability or motivation or to isolate the special circumstances (such as family connections) which may have an important bearing on jobs and earnings.

Another problem in cost-benefit calculations arises from wage and earnings structures. Some jobs vital to society are traditionally low-paying, whereas others of much less real value yield substantially more income. Gunnar Myrdal observed, with some surprise in the early 1940's, that despite the importance attached to education in America, teachers were relatively poorly remunerated in money, status, and tenure.[28] Nurses, social workers, and clergymen have also been traditionally poorly paid, whereas some sleazy offshoots of private enterprise that verge on confidence games award very large returns to their practitioners. Simple calculations of returns on educational investment would award higher marks to the operator of a phony "charm" school, to cite an obvious example, than to a nurse or a teacher.

The real question is whether the market place is to provide the principal criterion for public policy. Unless non-market factors are brought into play, the outlook for some types of education as well as other public policy (e.g., conservation) may be cloudy.

One aspect of the non-monetary side of education relates to perceptions of relative occupational status. There is a definite prejudice among many slum residents against the "dirty" jobs even though these jobs may pay higher wages than "clean" jobs. For example, manpower agencies have encountered more opposition in ghetto areas to training for relatively high-paying jobs in auto mechanics than for lower wage jobs in television repair. Sentiments of this type not only affect cost-benefit calculations but also alter the demand for education programs. In this sense, the vocational elements in educational policy must not only be clearly related to the job restructuring process in the economy but also to the changes that have resulted, for example, in the near-disappearance of domestic servants and their partial replacement by commercial service firms, which offer mechanized, better-paid jobs.

This change in attitudes applies to broader currents of American society. In the late 1960's, there is obviously a growing public sentiment that the corrupting effects of poverty and the present welfare system on the individual and on the society at large cannot be tolerated. For this reason, more strenuous and expensive efforts can be anticipated, which will be aimed at replacing a "handout" with a "hand up," to cite the political shorthand. As suggested earlier, programs to penetrate the hard core poverty population tend to be extremely costly and may well require judgments that go beyond simple rates of return to individuals to justify their existence.

A final problem in estimating the probable returns from educational investment is that calculations must be based on an extrapolation of past trends. But the past may not necessarily be a satisfactory guide to the future; unforeseeable events equivalent in impact to the escalation in Vietnam are likely to have major, unanticipated effects on both the cost and benefit sides of the educational balance sheet.

Perhaps the most fitting conclusion which can be offered at this time with respect to the contribution of cost-benefit techniques to policy formulation is that there is enough evidence to show that when the approach is properly used it can be of considerable value. In effect, cost-benefit has not gone very much beyond reinforcing common sense. Education, up to the limits of one's talents, pays off rather nicely in the context of a growing America. After completing a penetrating review of past research, William Bowen sums up the matter succinctly:

Almost without exception, the persons who have actually done the kinds of research described above have been commendably modest in describing their success—and well they should be, for there is certainly much that is unknown.

Nonetheless, the results obtained for the U. S. economy do offer rather consistent (some might say surprisingly consistent) support for the notion that education, on the average, has paid significant financial as well as nonfinancial rewards. The evidence is quite strong that individuals with the requisite ability have been well advised to continue their education through university level—and there is no reason to think that this pattern will not continue.[29]

PPBS

Some economists and fiscal experts have applied cost-benefit analysis to the so-called Planning and Programming Budget System. The tentative nature of so much of the cost-benefit research after a quarter of a century of application and analysis points toward two conclusions. First, new approaches to government policy require a long period of maturation before they can be considered effective instruments; second, innovations take a long time to percolate through governmental machinery. The diffusion process can be greatly accelerated, however, if the innovation is or appears to be a natural evolution from present practices and if there is a powerful executive thrust behind it.

Considering the numerous problems associated with cost-benefit analysis, Aaron Wildavsky (Article 11) notes that various economists and fiscal experts have moved toward developing two new analytical techniques: the planning-programming-budgeting system (PPBS), and use of social indicators to establish priorities for domestic programs.

PPBS and social indicators have been topics of serious discussion at the federal level for only half a dozen years. It now appears that the process of exploration and debate is accelerating and in another few years, perhaps by the early 1970's, PPBS and social indicators will be in general use throughout the federal establishment and in sophisticated states and municipalities.

Before proceeding further, it is useful at this point to consider the nature and objectives of PPBS. One of the best short descriptions of this approach is found in Selma Mushkin and Brian Herman's study of state-local finances:

Program analysis essentially involves a reduction of complex problems into their component segments so that each can be studied. Questions of fact can thus be subjected to the test of observed experience. Those aspects of the problem that involve value judgments can be separately identified and the basis of judgment made explicit. The analysis of concern is the cost and effectiveness of alternative ways of meeting the problem(s). The alternatives may be in the form of different programs or different levels of programs, or both.

The basic elements of analysis include:

... A clear definition of the problem.

... Identification of the basic governmental objectives involved.

... Identification and description of the key features of the alternatives available in attempting to meet the problems.

... Selection of criteria or measures of effectiveness which will permit estimation of the progress made toward satisfying the basic objectives.

... Estimates of the full cost implications—future as well as immediate—of each alternative.

... A clear presentation of the trade-offs among alternatives, having regard for the *relative* cost and effectiveness.

... Identification of the major uncertainties involved in cost and effectiveness estimation and the quantification of those uncertainties to the extent possible.

... Identification of the major assumptions made so as to spell out the degree to which the measured program effectiveness or cost may be sensitive to these assumptions.

... Documentation of the study findings to permit others to understand and evaluate what has been done.[30]

The Mushkin-Herman analytical framework underscores some of

the potential benefits that can be derived from a good PPBS system. It suggests that simply by asking for alternative ways of satisfying program objectives, PPBS helps to generate ideas and raises hard questions regarding simple justifications of year-to-year incremental budget requests. With its inescapable emphasis on costs, PPBS brings into consideration the possible wider application of user charges and public fees for public services and special assessments for various public programs.[31]

PPBS allegedly achieved highly satisfactory results in the Department of Defense during the early 1960's. President Johnson announced in August 1965 that he was asking the heads of all federal agencies to introduce PPBS to define agency goals and to devise efficient, and least costly, means of reaching these goals through the use of program analysis. By early 1966, the Bureau of the Budget had issued appropriate instructions to the federal executive departments. PPBS was to be applied immediately in the 21 largest agencies and 18 other federal agencies were encouraged to follow suit.[32] For a variety of reasons, though, progress in adopting PPBS remains slow, not only at the state and local levels, where an impasse is expected, but also in the federal establishment. Reasons for this leisurely pace are not hard to find. There is more than enough room in every agency for long and inconclusive dispute at every stage of the PPBS process. Factions can argue over proper goals and priorities, over performance criteria, over who is to judge performance, and over "trade-offs"—what is worth surrendering in return for other gains. It is a well-known fact that data can be manipulated at will to yield desirable outcomes.

PPBS offers many of the same attractions and disadvantages of the cost-benefit approach for educational policy. The emphasis on achieving specific goals (for example, elimination of illiteracy by a given date) may modify the emphasis on monetary goals, however. The heavy emphasis on dollar values makes the cost-benefit approach vulnerable to attack by those who feel that more than marketplace economics and efficiency criteria should go into policy formulation. In spite of this recognition, social intangibles may suffer from the same kind of neglect under PPBS as in cost-benefit analysis if only because of the constant temptation to demand that dollar inputs be realized in measurable dollar outputs.

Despite this caveat, PPBS, in Aaron Wildavsky's terms (Article 11), poses a "direct challenge to the general decision-making machinery of government." On the other hand, Wildavsky suggests that cost-benefit analysis tends to be far more confined, sharpening choices within the limits of the system.

Some of the potential limitations of PPBS are summarized by Wildavsky as overcentralization, restriction on the future freedom of maneuver of the chief executive, and a tendency to oversell the advantages of a management tool at the cost of political rationality. Melvin Levin (Article 12) underscores the problem of relating PPBS to accepted goals in a fragmented society, which is often in sharp disagreement over ends as well as means. Furthermore, it may be some time, he suggests, before the necessary talent is generally available to devise budget systems to the point at which bureaucrats of ordinary competence can operate an acceptable program.

PPBS is still too new to have generated much intensive work in the field of educational policy, but there have been initial speculations that raise serious questions. Werner Hirsch, for example, presents some tentative conclusions to the effect that if the nation decides that two years of education beyond the high school level are desirable, post-high school education through summer courses has a far greater payoff than the junior college. There are, he suggests, "less expensive alternatives for the junior college program."[33] His results are strongly influenced by the capital costs involved in constructing new educational facilities rather than using existing buildings and instructional staff during evening and vacation periods. Cost comparisons of this sort obviously do not take into consideration the qualitative and environmental factors which have major impacts on the educational process. This is perhaps the major reason for viewing PPBS—like cost-benefit—as a management tool, useful for information and preliminary guidance, but by no means to be used indiscriminately in policy formulation as a replacement for experience and judgment.

One's reservations concerning PPBS are reinforced by a series of research papers on the topic published in the *Public Administration Review* in early 1969, a little more than two years after the *Review's* 1966 issue on PPBS. Aaron Wildavsky (Article 13) argues that the Defense Department model is a poor one since DOD operates in a universe in which large margins of error are apparently acceptable. Policy analysis, Wildavsky feels, is still largely an art form. For this reason and others, he warns against overselling PPBS, particularly as an instrument of grand policy. Wildavsky feels it is far better to limit intensive analysis to a few major issues related to the direct requirements of top management. In a final statement, the author concludes that the climate for new ideas is propitious and that we must go beyond the fashionable pretense of PPBS into the heart of policy analysis for public policy.

Werner Hirsch (Article 14) focuses on some of the implications of PPBS for educational policy. He raises the most basic issues (e.g., whether more should be allocated for education than for space exploration or defense) and proceeds to the equally thorny problem of optimum educational program mix. Should less be allocated to elementary and secondary schools than to higher education? It is not surprising that Hirsch's answers are more "simple yardsticks" and "partial answers" than definitive conclusions.

Social Indicators

Proponents of the PPBS and cost-benefit approaches recommend across-the-board adoption of these techniques by all types of agencies. The movement to create a Federal Council of Social Advisors, on the other hand, includes a very different phenomenon. Such a Board would be established to perform in the social sphere —health, education, welfare, housing, etc.—the kind of task that the Council of Economic Advisors has been doing in the economic sector. The Council would formulate social indicators to measure the nation's progress in alleviating social ills and generally to chart advances toward—or retreats from—the achievement of social goals relating to the quality of life in an affluent, post-industrial society. Whereas the Council of Economic Advisors is largely concerned with economic changes in dollars and goods, the proposed Council of Social Advisors would concentrate on broader, societal factors. Like their economic counterparts, the Social Advisors would serve as guides as well as barometers. The Council would evaluate general strategies, identify shortcomings, and recommend alternative actions. And it is quite conceivable that, following the pattern of the economic advisors, similar boards of social advisors could be created by the states and their metropolitan areas.

Much of the data needed for a social advisory operation are on hand. Many indices of social change are already available, including crime and welfare rates, employment and unemployment data, education statistics, and information on health and housing conditions. What tends to be left out are underlying causal factors, a feeling for morale, personal and collective satisfaction, loyalties, and alienation. There is a danger, then, as with other forms of quantification, that impressive-looking numbers may conceal or distort reality.

Criticisms of present, or more accurately, proposed social indicators, must be tempered by the recognition that the concept, in its current form, is quite new. Even more youthful than PPBS, the recent discussion of a proposed Federal social advisory council dates back only to the mid-1960's.[34] Despite its newness, the proposal has generated considerable interest, so much so that an entire volume of high quality essays has already been published on the topic. In that book of essays, Bertram Gross[35] discusses the evaluation of social indicators as well as the many unanswered questions relating to proposed design and use. He concludes that much vitally-needed data are currently not available. More important, considering the sensitivity of the issues, are problems concerning the biases of the designers of indicators. Some researchers have long criticized intelligence tests and school scoring systems for their middle class orientation, which allegedly leads to discrimination against members of minority and working class groups.

A preliminary attempt to lay the foundation for a federal system of social indicators was completed by the Department of Health, Education and Welfare (Article 15) just before the Nixon administration took office. Even in its tentative state, the study is worth examining. The report begins to present the kind of balance sheet on education and other areas of social progress that is likely to become increasingly familiar. Wilbur Cohen's analysis of social indicators for education (Article 16) points out that the nation's "learning force," the total number of people involved in formal learning activities, exceeded the number of persons in the labor force as early as 1960. By the mid-1970's, the learning force may reach 150 million whereas the labor force may not yet approach the 100 million level. Cohen foresees the total expenditures for all levels of government for education reaching 8% of the nation's gross national product by 1975 (vs. 6.7% in 1965). His article calls for a sweeping inquiry of ends and means—including the production of meaningful data for performance evaluation.

When and if a viable system of social indicators is devised and functioning Councils are in operation, the end product is likely to be of considerable value in formulating educational policy. Hopefully, a national Council of Social Advisors can furnish a useful framework for broad analysis. By translating broad social goals into valid indices, critiques, and policy recommendations, a Council of Social Advisors could provide an overall structure for program planning. In a sense, the Council could evolve into an accepted oracle, an authoritative agency whose judgments and recommendations would serve both as a base for agency program planning and as leverage for securing the necessary support to achieve accepted, specific goals.

Cost-Benefit In Action

The preceding sections of this chapter have been devoted primarily to a review of concepts and hypotheses in cost-benefit analysis as they seem to relate to the public policy goals of education. Lesser amounts of attention were given to two newer and relatively untried approaches, PPBS and social indicators. The remainder of this chapter is concerned with the relevant experience of cost-benefit analysis and allied approaches, rather than with conceptualization. It considers a number of full-scale case histories and fragmentary pieces of evidence that bear on educational policy.

Cost-Benefits and OEO Budget Justification

One of the primary uses of various forms of cost-benefit analysis is as an instrument of persuasion. It is useful in this connection to consider the experience of the federal Office of Economic Opportunity as a harbinger of things to come, a warning to the unwary, and a pioneering effort in the application of cost-benefit reasoning. The Office of Economic Opportunity, because of staff orientation and as a response to vitriolic Congressional and press criticism, has been unusually active in sponsoring in-house and external evaluations (including cost-benefit analysis) of its program.

At the 1968 Congressional hearings on appropriations, OEO officials employed a number of cost-benefit ratios to justify their funding requests. OEO's Research and Evaluation Office maintained that $1 invested in Upward Bound, a program designed to permit poor high school students to prepare themselves more adequately for college, "is worth $1.65 to $2.78."[36] The return per dollar from the Family Planning Program was said to be much higher, ranging from $4.69 to $26.83. (Family planning under OEO auspices, for which the annual appropriation increased from $9.6 million in 1968 to a still modest $13 million in 1969, is a euphemism for birth control. It should be noted, however, that family planning activities of the U.S. Department of Health, Education and Welfare increased from $29.2 million to $47.3 million during this same period and HEW is requesting $69.1 million for this purpose for 1970.[37]) Strangely, OEO's claims for benefits that result from increased expenditures for family planning did *not* include long-range reductions in welfare, crime, and other costs as well as benefits to the individual, the family, and the community.[38] The program request was remarkably minuscule in view of the enormous payoff from family planning and the allegation that current family planning efforts are reaching only a small proportion of the poor. It was estimated that only one-seventh of the women of child-bearing age who live in low income areas and who need family planning services obtained such services in 1967.[39] The expanded budget for the program would still meet only a fraction of the estimated need.

In addition to these cost-benefit ratios, other types of meaningful relationships between OEO program allocations and costs were presented at the 1968 Hearings. These included the claim that the poor receive at least $3 in self-help services from local agencies and other federal agencies for each dollar expended in the Community Action Program.[40] It was maintained that "where alternative services exist, CAP delivery costs are substantially lower."[41] In the case of legal services, CAP's unit cost per case was cited as $49 as compared to $101 for purchasing the same services from outside lawyers. "The annual cost of providing medical care to needy poor people averages $140 while equivalent care would cost $262."[42] In both instances, however, comparisons may be misleading since, as the OEO statement suggests, the realistic alternative to CAP legal and medical services is little or no service. Finally, a cost-benefit analysis of the VISTA program in Columbus, Ohio, showed a benefit-cost ratio of 5.4:1.0.[43] Closer observation of the OEO claim that the benefits of VISTA exceeded costs by 443% indicates, however, that 60% of the so-called benefits consisted of wages received by clients who were placed by VISTA, "the assumption apparently being that they would have had no income in the absence of VISTA."[44]

In summary, OEO expended a total of $15.4 million for its program evaluation activities in fiscal 1968—a doubling of the amount expended for the previous year. This constituted less than 1% of total OEO expenditures and the most strenuous Congressional prodding was required to force OEO to engage in evaluative efforts of even this magnitude. The lessons of OEO's experience with evaluation is that sizable and sophisticated efforts are required to do a thorough job in this field. Much of OEO's data may be temporarily useful for budgetary justification purposes but are obviously suspect to skeptical professionals. Quite probably, other agencies at every level of government will be forced to provide more plausible justification for budgetary requests—including cost-benefit data—than simple additions to last year's budget. In that event, all agencies will be forced to set aside a significant fraction of program funds for program planning and evaluation to provide plausible, technically defensible justifications for their budget requests.

Perhaps as a harbinger of future program research, Werner Hirsch has developed a tentative program budget to rationalize and otherwise improve federal education policy. In his contribution to a volume on program budgeting, Hirsch (Article 14) tends to be optimistic. In his opinion, program budgeting can be employed to help select the proper mix between education and defense, for example, and on the second level it can help to determine the best mix of different education programs. Finally, he sees program budgeting as particularly useful in making low-level decisions involving cost and output factors.

Manpower Training Programs

In the past few years, various Manpower Training Programs have been analyzed by cost-benefit techniques. Much of the research is associated with evaluations of the War on Poverty, a program which has been subjected to more searching scrutiny than almost any in U. S. history. To a degree, however, such cost-benefit analysis should be viewed in larger perspective, as part of the growing governmental and academic concern with discovering why costly efforts are not as productive as originally anticipated. In particular, training activities funded under the Manpower Development and Training Act of 1962 and the Area Redevelopment Act of 1961 had displayed convincing evidence of a tremendous payoff—as long as programs concentrated on the readily employable. The same findings did not seem to apply to manpower training programs funded under OEO, which concentrated much more on the costly-to-service hard-core poor. There is a direct parallel here in education. Middle class children are less expensive to educate, as is evidenced by the fact that per pupil costs in some suburbs with well-regarded schools are less than in such ghettos as New York's Harlem. When suburban costs are relatively high it is usually because of elaborate enrichment programs.

Manpower training research has dealt with a basic problem in aggregation: Why haven't manpower programs made more of a dent in the poverty problem? The answer apparently lies in two major areas: (1) many poor people have so little background and preparation for employment that it is hard to reach them and agencies haven't put enough effort into the search; and (2) many poor people are likely to remain outside the labor force by virtue of age, illness, child-rearing responsibilities, or other incapacities.

One scholar has concluded that

. . . later and more sober analysis indicated that a major proportion of the poverty problem could not be solved by human capital programs. Large numbers of people were simply outside of the productive labor force and could only be brought into the productive labor force at prohibitive costs.[45]

The great difficulty and substantial expense involved in bringing such persons into the productive mainstream accounts in part for the fact that, until fairly recently and then only by virtue of Presidential directive, manpower training agencies tended to concentrate most of their efforts on the more responsive, reachable, low risk, motivated person who was likely to make the agency's efforts productive within its limited budget. It was not surprising that one close observer could assert that "most of those most in need of job training tend not to benefit from the program that Congress has enacted."[46]

TABLE 3

Estimated Characteristics of Enrollees
by Approach in 1968
(in percent)

Approach	Poor	Less Than High School	Non-White	21 or Younger	Male	Welfare Recipient
OJT	53	50	41	30	68	8
Institutional	80	68	63	57	62	19
Rehabilitation	68	58	23	22	56	12
Work Support:						
In-School	98	98	50	100	56	28
Post-School	99	80	52	55	50	45
TOTAL	86	80	44	64	57	23

Source: Special Analyses, Budget of the United States, Fiscal 1970, p. 146.

This conclusion may be somewhat outdated by recent changes in manpower training programs. In 1967, 86% of participants in the manpower training programs were classified as "poor," whereas only 11% of the nation's labor force was in this category. 23% of the manpower program enrollees were welfare recipients compared to only 1% of the general labor force.[47] As indicated in Table 3, the proportion of poor was highest in work support programs and lowest in on-the-job-training and rehabilitation programs. "OJT enrollees were similar to rehabilitation clients because the OJT programs reached those most job ready."[48]

The Special Budget Analyses point toward further changes in manpower programs in favor of training the more disadvantaged.

Costs for such programs as the Job Corps and the slum area Concentrated Employment Program tend to be high because they provide intensive supportive services. Man-year costs for work support
programs are high because of the living allowances provided for
trainees.

TABLE 4

1970 Participant and Man-Year Unit Cost°

Approach	Man-Year Cost Est.	Participant Cost Est.	Estimated Distribution of Participant Cost by Percent		
			Allowances	Education and Training	Other
On-the-job Training	$2,500	$1,300	14	10	76
Institutional Training	4,750	2,100	34	31	35
Disability Rehabilitation	1,200	1,300	32	32	58
Work Support:					
In-School	1,550	450	85	2	13
Post-School	2,300	1,000	51	16	33

° Includes State and local cost sharing.

Source: Special Analyses, Budget of the United States, Fiscal 1970, p. 144.

The figures presented in Table 4 have considerable bearing on
educational policy. Assuming that one of the principal functions of
education is the alleviation of poverty problems through such activities as remedial education and high school equivalency training,
the federal programs offer the possibility of doing more with relatively little additional expense. Many states confronted by serious
fiscal problems can ride on the coattails of costly federal efforts,
directing their own limited allocations to areas likely to increase the
return and supplement from federal programs. This underscores a
fundamental fact in public policy: for a number of reasons, many of
them related to lack of money, the states are often in the position
of designing efforts within and around the framework of federal
policy, rather than initiating massive, pioneering programs of their
own. From the standpoint of state policy, one dimension of the
cost-benefit approach relates to attacking as many state and local
problems as possible with maximum use of federal funds, using
scarce state funds for non-federally aided programs only when absolutely necessary.

THE JOB CORPS   The Job Corps was a prime target of the wave of performance evaluation studies which followed Congressional probing of the anti-poverty program during the latter part of the 1960's. The Job Corps, which provides education and training for disadvantaged youngsters at a number of residential centers, was a particularly vulnerable target for Congressional critics. This was due in part to the strained relations between corpsmen and local residents near some centers and in part to allegations of overall program mismanagement. But most important was the high cost per trainee ($8,000 or more per year, including subsistence payments).

In a critique of the initial OEO-sponsored evaluation studies, Sar Levitan (Article 17) indicates that such efforts were designed to provide ammunition for continued funding of the Job Corps program. OEO attempted to justify continuation of the Job Corps by arguing that trainees gained an average of 1.6 grades in reading ability and 2 grades in arithmetic comprehension for nine months spent in a center. An OEO-sponsored study concluded that the realistic ratio of benefits over costs for trainees ranged from 1.05 to 1.65. Levitan also found that another OEO evaluation study arbitrarily assumed that corpsmen who spent one month in a Job Corps Center learned as much as corpsmen who completed the full nine-month program. He argues that this assumption affected the validity of the OEO findings, since only one corpsman in three remained through the nine-month period.

Unaccountably, the OEO calculation also failed to take into consideration a fortuitous rise in federal minimum wages, a fact which may be partly responsible for the corpsmen's higher wages vs. the "no shows." The research was based on 48 more years of working life for corpsmen, a span which Levitan feels is too long. And, perhaps equally important, the calculations left out probable beneficial but unmeasurable side effects of the Job Corps experience in the way of improved social development and family stability. Summarizing his conclusions in 1967, Levitan wrote that the case for the Job Corps has not been established especially since "alternative, less costly, alternatives are available."[49] In late 1968, using unpublished new data, Levitan pointed out that the average educational advancement for trainees was actually only half as great as originally claimed by the Job Corps. On this basis, he states that "no conclusive case has yet been established to justify the Job Corps on the basis of past performance."[50] The phasing out of the Job Corps by the Nixon administration reflects, in part, an agreement with this conclusion.

VOCATIONAL VS. ACADEMIC SECONDARY SCHOOLS The preceding analysis has been devoted to specific federal programs. Another type of evaluation is one which deals with such broad alternatives as, for example, vocational high schools versus academic high schools. Graduates of full-time vocational schools have a relatively better employment record than students from academic high schools in communities where vocational high schools seem to be selective in their choice of students. This indeed is the conclusion of the study prepared by Jacob Kaufman and others (Article 18) for the U. S. Department of Health, Education and Welfare. The findings would have been very different in communities that use the vocational high schools as a dumping ground for substandard students. What this all suggests is that cost-benefit, along with other aspects of program design and program evaluation, must probe into the context of the educational system, including a common-sense examination of attitudes, leadership, staffing, clientele, and selection process. Few meaningful conclusions can be drawn without an adequate knowledge of the background situation.

Kaufman and his colleagues conclude that, based on higher earnings over a six-year period, investment in the vocational-technical curriculum "is an economically efficient investment" and that public "funds should be shifted from the academic toward the vocational-technical curriculum." These conclusions are based on a comparison of post-high school earnings of a sample of academic and vocational graduates for the school years 1956-7 through 1959-60 who did not go on to college. Over the six years, vocational school graduates earned an average of $54 per month or $644 per year more than their academic counterparts. The earnings differential seems to diminish year by year, however; the level of academic and vocational earnings tends to converge approximately six years beyond graduation. Reviewing available cost-benefit research in vocational education, Garth Mangum concludes that "for those not continuing beyond high school, preparation for employment is better than no preparation for employment."[51]

CONCLUSIONS

As is often the case, a mountain—or perhaps more accurately, a hillock—of research on the costs and benefits of education lends support to accepted popular belief. There may be contention over just how much profit education returns to the individual and to the society at large, but laymen and economists agree that the balance sheet is usually favorable.

Up to the present, analysis of some portions of the educational spectrum (e.g., continuing education) has been as much neglected by cost-benefit researchers as by legislators. This is not wholly understandable because, on the basis of accepted cost-benefit criteria, continuing education programs tend to cost relatively little and to pay off rather well for several reasons: (1) Continuing education does not interrupt the flow of production and paychecks (hence its popularity in such industrially mobilized nations as the USSR and China) and there are no foregone student earnings to add to total costs. (2) Costs also tend to be low because continuing education makes fuller use of existing facilities, rather than requiring large capital outlays as is the case with other types of education. (3) Equally important, continuing education offers a relatively inexpensive opportunity to exploit and to capitalize on many years of previous education and experience; significant results may be achieved at relatively low cost.

One particularly difficult problem in the measurement of educational costs and benefits concerns the assessment of program quality. The text has discussed this at some length. In these final comments, it may only be necessary to reiterate that boxes on organization charts tell us nothing about the quality of administration and operations, and that purchasing units of education is not equivalent to buying quantities of steel ingots. Of all the problems that afflict the researcher, measurement of performance quality is perhaps the most frustrating—a fact that should not be forgotten.

The emphasis on monetary returns from public outlays must not be permitted to obscure other issues in educational policy that go to the heart of the values of American society. Progress toward racial equality, the reduction of economic and social disparities, the quality of governmental services, and perhaps the strengthening of a frayed social fabric are closely linked to various aspects of education. Cost-benefit and related techniques can be extremely helpful in choosing between program alternatives and in upgrading government operations, but there is more to public policy than the simple rules of the marketplace. It is easy to determine that public investment in gifted students is highly profitable. But educators who work with the aged, with the handicapped, with the disadvantaged, or with other groups for whom education is likely to cost more in public investment than is returned to the Gross National Product should be extremely wary of indulging in cost-benefit exercises. The experience with the Job Corps can easily be repeated; programs that can be fully justified on equitable and moral grounds can be terribly vulnerable to profit-and-loss bookkeeping.

Economists who have worked in the cost-benefit vineyard are deservedly apologetic for the narrowness of an accounting system in which it is difficult or impossible to take into account many of the most important aspects of the programs being measured. It is not surprising to find that the crucial non-monetary facets of these programs are advanced as debating points to secure favorable publicity rather than as subjects suitable for rigorous comparisons of viable alternatives. Favorable results can be secured by comparing items in which the relationship may be tenuous, but the contrast between stark alternatives possesses political drama. In foreign affairs the reduction of the U. S. commitment in a given nation may be said to lead to a chain of unfavorable consequences as, for example, when a setback in one country is alleged to pave the way for a series of defeats culminating in nuclear holocaust. The net result of failing to fund educational or manpower training programs does not lend itself to visions of such an apocalypse. But it has been suggested that the alternatives to a concentrated drive to train and employ the disadvantaged could be extremely costly.

It costs $25,000 to arrest a youth, try him, and commit him to prison. A subsistence level of public aid will cost a State an estimated $100,000 to deal with his unemployability between ages 19 and 65. Nor can one ignore the expense of the rapidly rising per capita tax dollars spent on police, fire, and health services. The price for police in run-down areas is two and one-half times that in more respectable areas; welfare costs are four times higher. In contrast, a training program of under a year together with a job will repay its cost twice over in taxes alone in less than two years.[52]

It should be, of course, unnecessary to justify on purely financial grounds programs that may be absolutely vital from the standpoint of the public welfare. An uncritical adherence to cost-benefit reasoning would lead to funds being channeled exclusively to persons who could demonstrate potential either for great contributions to the national economy or, conversely, for causing provable and avoidable damage as, for example, future rioters, inmates of prisons or mental institutions, or hard-core welfare cases. Yet, if the health of the society—including the next generation—is truly taken into account, there can be little question that increased efforts in education can play a vital role not only in terms of cash payout but also in achieving social goals—some of which may require more investment than they are likely to return in quantifiable "profits."

One difficulty with attempting to broaden the focus of such approaches as cost-benefit and PPBS, which are deeply committed to manipulating comparable, observable data, is that although most of the costs are painfully visible to the harassed taxpayer, most of the benefits may be hidden. To reiterate: The fact that benefits cannot be statistically quantified does not mean that they may not be critically important. In the past two decades, bitter experience with the developing nations has revealed all too clearly the importance of an education system, which in the U. S. tends to be as taken for granted as part of the landscape.

Cost-benefit techniques, most likely as a component of PPBS, are likely to be applied to an increasingly broad range of programs. Comfortable agency habits in which a year-to-year funding increment can be counted on may not hold true in the future. New, unsettling horizons will open up when programs are systematically assessed and evaluated on a more rigorous basis than is presently the case and when it becomes normal to give serious consideration to alternatives for existing policy. Quite possibly, however, the principal results of PPBS will be tighter control over agency and unit operations, rather than a truly searching, time-consuming, and costly sweeping reassessment of basic policy and program mixes. The chief obstacle to wholesale adoption of advanced budget techniques seems to be the crucial shortage of talented PPBS designers, although there is obviously much-foot dragging at all levels of government.

The reader should be aware that cost-benefit and PPBS are partly matters of perspective. Most of the literature focuses on costs and returns to the individual and to the federal government. The administrator involved in formulating policy for municipal or state government soon discovers that much of his task is to devise methods of achieving maximum results at minimum cost to financially hard-pressed communities and states. There is then a kind of cost-benefit that may be termed public entrepreneurship, in which the objective is to finance programs using a maximum of other governmental financial resources. In short, cost-benefit is partly a matter of perspectives: the individual rarely fails to show a personal profit from public investment, whereas the federal government can show a profit or loss. State and local governments, under our existing tax system, tend to view federal or private investment as costless. They tend to measure costs and benefits on the basis of whether a particular program will add to their financial burdens.

Finally, the reader will observe that, although there are significant areas of controversy, the experts are pretty much in agreement on essentials—that much more research is needed before we can reach definitive conclusions, and that the present state-of-the-art offers general guidelines, useful hypotheses, and interesting speculations rather than an acceptable blueprint for policy. Cost-benefit and PPBS can be extremely valuable adjuncts to decision-making (not excluding promoting programs with the public and legislators), but they must be handled with prudence and intelligence or they can be dangerous to the user. Education has greatly benefited from a broad and deep faith in its moral and practical utility, but, unless great care is taken, placing all or part of it on the accounting block is not only likely to weaken public support by rendering its claims vulnerable to sharp-eyed auditors, but may also diminish the support for vital programs that cannot be made to appear profitable in monetary terms.

NOTES

[1] For further examples, see the symposium of articles in the *Public Administration Review,* Vol. XXVI, No. 4 (December 1966), in particular the article by Allen Schick, "The Road to PPB," pp. 243-258.

[2] This was even observable in Japan and various devastated European nations, which experienced remarkable economic recoveries in the post-World War II period. The rebuilding of the industrial base and new city development were both, in large measure, a result of the economic power of accumulated and accumulating knowledge.

[3] Edward F. Denison, *The Sources of Economic Growth in the United States and the Alternatives Before Us* (New York: Committee for Economic Development, 1962), pp. 67-79.

[4] Theodore W. Schultz, *The Economic Value of Education* (New York: Columbia University Press, 1963), pp. vii-xii.

[5] See Thomas I. Ribich, *Education and Poverty* (Washington, D.C.: The Brookings Institution, 1968), p. 9. Substantial extracts from this book are presented as Article 9.

[6] See Burton A. Weisbrod, "Expenditures on Human Resources: Investment Redistribution or What," *Federal Programs for the Development of Human Resources.* A Compendium of Papers Submitted to the Subcommittee on Economic Progress, Joint Economic Committee, Vol. 1 (Washington, D.C.: U. S. Government Printing Office, 1968), pp. 80-83.

[7] The phrase is used by S. M. Miller and Frank Riessman, *Social Class and Social Policy* (New York: Basic Books, 1968), Chapter 5.

[8] *Ibid.,* p. 70.

[9] See Arthur Pearl and Frank Riessman, *New Careers for the Poor* (New York: The Free Press, 1965), especially Chapter I.

[10] It should be noted that the foregone earnings factor is considered mythical by at least one authority, who suggests that inclusion of housewives and others who forego gainful employment indicates that this type of calculation can be pushed to the point of absurdity and beyond. See John Vaizey, *The Economics of Education* (New York: The Free Press, 1962), pp. 42-43.

[11]Schultz, *op. cit.*, pp. 49-50.

[12]*Ibid.*

[13]*Ibid.*, p. 47.

[14]Walter Fogel, "The Effect of Low Educational Attainment on Incomes," *Journal of Human Resources*, Vol. 1, No. 2 (Fall 1966), pp. 22-40.

[15]This phrase refers to the tendency of slum children to fall farther and farther behind as they progress through the school system. A reading difference of six months in the second grade between Negro and white children in New York may widen to 2½ years by the seventh grade. Roger R. Woock, "Community Operated Schools, A Way Out?," in *Man Against Poverty: World War III: A Reader on the World's Most Crucial Issue*, Arthur I. Blaustein and Roger R. Woock, eds. (New York: Vintage Books, 1968), p. 250.

[16]Harry M. Caudill, *Night Comes to the Cumberlands: A Biography of A Depressed Area* (Boston: Little, Brown and Company, 1962), pp. 337-338.

[17]*Economic Report of the President*, Transmitted to the Congress January, 1969, 91st Congress, 1st Session, House Document No. 28 (Washington, D.C.: U. S. Government Printing Office, 1969), p. 162.

[18]*Special Analyses, Budget of the United States, Fiscal Year 1970* (Washington, D.C.: U. S. Government Printing Office, 1969), p. 114.

[19]See Part VI, Cost-Benefit in Action.

[20]Frank Riessman and Arthur Pearl, "Poverty and New Careers for Non-Professionals," in Blaustein and Woock, *op. cit.*, pp. 216, 228.

[21]*Ibid.*, pp. 221-222.

[22]*Ibid.*, p. 219.

[23]In 1967 there were over four million working mothers with children under six. This total is expected to increase to over five million by 1980. See U. S. Department of Labor, Wage and Labor Standards Administration, Women's Bureau, *Working Mothers and the Need for Child Care Services* (June 1968).

[24]For a lengthier discussion of the principal author's views in this field, see Melvin R. Levin, "Costs, Benefits and Social Indicators," in *Community and Regional Planning: Issues in Public Policy* (New York: Frederick A. Praeger, 1969), pp. 64-82.

[25]Mary Jean Bowman, "Decisions for Vocational Education: An Economist's View," *Vocational-Technical Education, A Prospectus for Change*, Carl J. Schaefer and Jacob J. Kaufman, eds. (Boston: Massachusetts Advisory Council on Education, 1968), pp. 69-70.

[26]*Statistical Abstract of the United States, 1967*, U.S. Department of Commerce (Washington, D.C.: U.S. Government Printing Office, 1967), Table No. 319, p. 224.

[27]William G. Bowen, *Economic Aspects of Education* (Princeton, N.J.: Princeton University Press, 1964), pp. 13-38.

[28]Gunnar Myrdal, *An American Dilemma: The Negro Problem and Modern*

Democracy (New York: Harper and Brothers, 1944), p. 885.

[29]Bowen, *op. cit.,* p. 38.

[30]Selma Mushkin and Brian Herman, *The Search for Alternatives: Program Options in a PPB System,* State-Local Finances Project (Washington, D.C.: The George Washington University, October 1968), pp. 3-4.

[31]*Ibid.,* pp. 5-6.

[32]U.S. Bureau of the Budget, Bulletin No. 66-3, *Planning-Programming-Budgeting,* October 12, 1965, and *Supplement to Bulletin No. 66-3,* February 21, 1966.

[33]Werner Z. Hirsch, "Toward Federal Program Budgeting," *Public Administration Review,* Vol. XXVI, No. 4 (December 1966), p. 266.

[34]See Daniel Bell, "The Idea of a Social Report," *The Public Interest,* No. 15 (Spring 1969), pp. 72-84.

[35]See Bertram Gross, "A Historical Note on Social Indicators," in Raymond A. Bauer, ed., *Social Indicators* (Cambridge, Mass.: The M.I.T. Press, 1966), pp. ix-xviii.

[36]Statement of Theodore M. Berry, Assistant Director for Community Action Programs of the CAP-OEO, *Departments of Labor and Health, Education and Welfare Appropriations for 1969.* Hearings before a Subcommittee of the Committee on Appropriations, House of Representatives, Ninetieth Congress, Second Session, Part 6, Office of Economic Opportunity (Washington, D.C.: U.S. Government Printing Office, 1968), p. 219.

[37]*Special Analyses, Budget of the United States, Fiscal Year 1970, op. cit.,* Table L-14, p. 167.

[38]*Hearings of the Departments of Labor and Health, Education and Welfare Appropriations for 1969, op. cit.,* p. 219.

[39]*Ibid.,* p. 238.

[40]*Ibid.,* p. 209.

[41]*Ibid.,* p. 212.

[42]*Ibid.*

[43]*Ibid.,* p. 495.

[44]Sar A. Levitan, "VISTA—The Great Society's Domestic Volunteers," *Poverty and Human Resources Abstracts,* Vol. III, No. 5 (September-October 1968), p. 18.

[45]Lester Thurow, "Raising Incomes Through Manpower Training Programs," *Contributions to the Analysis of Urban Problems,* A Selection of Papers from the Rand Workshop on Urban Problems, December 18, 1967-January 12, 1968, Anthony H. Pascal, ed. (Santa Monica, Calif.: The Rand Corporation, 1968), p. 92.

[46]Alvin Schorr, *Explorations in Social Policy* (New York: Basic Books, 1968), p. 266.

[47]*Special Analyses, Budget of the United States, Fiscal Year 1970, op. cit.,* p. 145.

[48]*Ibid.,* p. 146.

[49]Sar A. Levitan, "An Evaluator's Second Thoughts," *Poverty and Human Resources Abstracts,* Vol. III, No. 5 (September-October 1968), p. 19.

[50]Sar A. Levitan, *Antipoverty Work and Training Efforts: Goals and Reality,* Policy Papers in Human Resources and Industrial Relations, No. 3, a joint publication of the Institute of Labor and Industrial Relations, The University of Michigan at Ann Arbor, Wayne State University at Detroit, and the National Manpower Policy Task Force, Washington, D.C. (August 1967), p. 37.

[51]Garth L. Mangum, *Reorienting Vocational Education,* a joint publication of the Institute of Labor and Industrial Relations, The University of Michigan at Ann Arbor, Wayne State University at Detroit, and the National Manpower Policy Task Force, Washington, D.C. (May 1968), p. 36.

[52]Frank H. Cassell, *The Public Employment Service: Organization in Change* (Ann Arbor: Academic Publications, 1968), p. 100.

Part I

Human Capital
and Education

1

INVESTMENT IN HUMAN CAPITAL

by Theodore W. Schultz

In his landmark studies, Professor Schultz has played a major role in developing the concept of investment in human capital as a subject for serious economic study. Schultz suggests reasons why economists have tended to neglect this field and offers cogent arguments for intensive research as a guide for public policy.

Although it is obvious that people acquire useful skills and knowledge, it is not obvious that these skills and knowledge are a form of capital, that this capital is in substantial part a product of deliberate investment, that it has grown in Western societies at a much faster rate than conventional (nonhuman) capital, and that its growth may well be the most distinctive feature of the economic system. It has been widely observed that increases in national output have been large compared with the increases of land, man-hours, and physical reproducible capital. Investment in human capital is probably the major explanation for this difference.

Much of what we call consumption constitutes investment in human capital. Direct expenditures on education, health, and internal migration to take advantage of better job opportunities are clear examples. Earnings foregone by mature students attending school

Reprinted from Theodore W. Schultz, "Investment in Human Capital," *The American Economic Review,* Vol. 51, No. 1 (March 1961), pp. 1-17. Reprinted by permission of the publisher and author.

and by workers acquiring on-the-job training are equally clear examples. Yet nowhere do these enter into our national accounts. The use of leisure time to improve skills and knowledge is widespread and it too is unrecorded. In these and similar ways the *quality* of human effort can be greatly improved and its productivity enhanced. I shall contend that such investment in human capital accounts for most of the impressive rise in the real earnings per worker.

I shall comment, first, on the reasons why economists have shied away from the explicit analysis of investment in human capital, and then, on the capacity of such investment to explain many a puzzle about economic growth. Mainly, however, I shall concentrate on the scope and substance of human capital and its formation. In closing I shall consider some social and policy implications.

I. SHYING AWAY FROM INVESTMENT IN MAN

Economists have long known that people are an important part of the wealth of nations. Measured by what labor contributes to output, the productive capacity of human beings is now vastly larger than all other forms of wealth taken together. What economists have not stressed is the simple truth that people invest in themselves and that these investments are very large. Although economists are seldom timid in entering on abstract analysis and are often proud of being impractical, they have not been bold in coming to grips with this form of investment. Whenever they come even close, they proceed gingerly as if they were stepping into deep water. No doubt there are reasons for being wary. Deep-seated moral and philosophical issues are ever present. Free men are first and foremost the end to be served by economic endeavor; they are not property or marketable assets. And not least, it has been all too convenient in marginal productivity analysis to treat labor as if it were a unique bundle of innate abilities that are wholly free of capital.

The mere thought of investment in human beings is offensive to some among us.[1] Our values and beliefs inhibit us from looking upon human beings as capital goods, except in slavery, and this we abhor. We are not unaffected by the long struggle to rid society of indentured service and to evolve political and legal institutions to keep men free from bondage. These are achievements that we prize highly. Hence, to treat human beings as wealth that can be augmented by investment runs counter to deeply held values. It seems to reduce man once again to a mere material component, to something akin to property. And for man to look upon himself as a capital good, even if it did not impair his freedom, may seem to debase him. No less a person than J. S. Mill at one time insisted that the people of a country should not be looked upon as wealth because wealth existed only for the sake of people.[2] But surely Mill was wrong; there is nothing in the concept of human wealth contrary to his idea that it exists only for the advantage of people. By investing in themselves, people can enlarge the range of choice available to them. It is one way free men can enhance their welfare.

Among the few who have looked upon human beings as capital, there are three distinguished names. The philosopher-economist Adam Smith boldly included all of the acquired and useful abilities of all of the inhabitants of a country as a part of capital. So did H. von Thünen, who then went on to argue that the concept of capital applied to man did not degrade him or impair his freedom and dignity, but on the contrary that the failure to apply the concept was especially pernicious in wars; " . . . for here . . . one will sacrifice in a battle a hundred human beings in the prime of their lives without a thought in order to save one gun." The reason is that," . . . the purchase of a cannon causes an outlay of public funds, whereas human beings are to be had for nothing by means of a mere conscription decree."[3] Irving Fisher[4] also clearly and cogently presented an all-inclusive concept of capital. Yet the main stream of thought has held that it is neither appropriate nor practical to apply the concept of capital to human beings. Marshall,[5] whose great prestige goes far to explain why this view was accepted, held that while human beings are incontestably capital from an abstract and mathematical point of view, it would be out of touch with the market place to treat them as capital in practical analyses. Investment in human beings has accordingly seldom been incorporated in the formal core of economics, even though many economists, including Marshall, have seen its relevance at one point or another in what they have written.

The failure to treat human resources explicitly as a form of capital, as a produced means of production, as the product of investment, has fostered the retention of the classical notion of labor as a capacity to do manual work requiring little knowledge and skill, a capacity with which, according to this notion, laborers are endowed about equally. This notion of labor was wrong in the classical period and it is patently wrong now. Counting individuals who can and want to work and treating such a count as a measure of the quantity of an economic factor is no more meaningful than it would be to count the number of all manner of machines to determine their economic importance either as a stock of capital or as a flow of productive services.

Laborers have become capitalists not from a diffusion of the ownership of corporation stocks, as folklore would have it, but from the acquisition of knowledge and skill that have economic value.[6] This knowledge and skill are in great part the product of investment and, combined with other human investment, predominantly account for the productive superiority of the technically advanced countries. To omit them in studying economic growth is like trying to explain Soviet ideology without Marx.

II. ECONOMIC GROWTH FROM HUMAN CAPITAL

Many paradoxes and puzzles about our dynamic, growing economy can be resolved once human investment is taken into account. Let me begin by sketching some that are minor though not trivial.

When farm people take nonfarm jobs they earn substantially less than industrial workers of the same race, age, and sex. Similarly nonwhite urban males earn much less than white males even after allowance is made for the effects of differences in unemployment, age, city size and region.[7] Because these differentials in earnings correspond closely to corresponding differentials in education, they strongly suggest that the one is a consequence of the other. Negroes who operate farms, whether as tenants or as owners, earn much less than whites on comparable farms.[8] Fortunately, crops and livestock are not vulnerable to the blight of discrimination. The large differences in earnings seem rather to reflect mainly the differences in health and education. Workers in the South on the average earn appreciably less than in the North or West and they also have on the average less education. Most migratory farm workers earn very little indeed by comparison with other workers. Many of them have virtually no schooling, are in poor health, are unskilled, and have little ability to do useful work. To urge that the differences in the amount of human investment may explain these differences in earnings seems elementary. Of more recent vintage are observations showing younger workers at a competitive advantage; for example, young men entering the labor force are said to have an advantage over unemployed older workers in obtaining satisfactory jobs. Most of these young people possess twelve years of school, most of the older workers six years or less. The observed advantage of these younger workers may therefore result not from inflexibilities in social security or in retirement programs, or from sociological preference of employers, but from real differences in productivity connected with one form of human investment, i.e., education. And yet another example, the curve relating income to age tends to be steeper for skilled than for unskilled persons. Investment in on-the-job training seems a likely explanation, as I shall note later.

Economic growth requires much internal migration of workers to adjust to changing job opportunities.[9] Young men and women move more readily than older workers. Surely this makes economic sense when one recognizes that the costs of such migration are a form of human investment. Young people have more years ahead of them than older workers during which they can realize on such an investment. Hence it takes less of a wage differential to make it economically advantageous for them to move, or, to put it differently, young people can expect a higher return on their investment in migration than older people. This differential may explain selective migration without requiring an appeal to sociological differences between young and old people.

The examples so far given are for investment in human beings that yield a return over a long period. This is true equally of investment in education, training, and migration of young people. Not all investments in human beings are of this kind; some are more nearly akin to current inputs as for example expenditures on food and shelter in some countries where work is mainly the application of brute human force, calling for energy and stamina, and where the intake of food is far from enough to do a full day's work. On the "hungry" steppes and in the teeming valleys of Asia, millions of adult males have so meager a diet that they cannot do more than a few hours of hard work. To call them underemployed does not seem pertinent. Under such circumstances it is certainly meaningful to treat food partly as consumption and partly as a current "producer good," as some Indian economists have done.[10] Let us not forget that Western economists during the early decades of industrialization and even in the time of Marshall and Pigou often connected additional food for workers with increases in labor productivity.

Let me now pass on to three major perplexing questions closely connected with the riddle of economic growth. First, consider the long-period behavior of the capital-income ratio. We were taught that a country which amassed more reproducible capital relative to its land and labor would employ such capital in greater "depth" because of its growing abundance and cheapness. But apparently this is not what happens. On the contrary, the estimates now available show that less of such capital tends to be employed relative to income as economic growth proceeds. Are we to infer that the ratio of capital to income has no relevance in explaining either poverty or opulence? Or that a rise of this ratio is not a prerequisite to economic growth? These questions raise fundamental issues bearing on motives and preferences for holding wealth as well as on the motives for particular investments and the stock of capital thereby accumulated. For my purpose all that needs to be said is that these estimates of capital-income ratios refer to only a part of all capital. They exclude in particular, and most unfortunately, any human capital. Yet human capital has surely been increasing at a rate substantially greater than reproducible (nonhuman) capital. We cannot, therefore, infer from these estimates that the stock of *all* capital has been decreasing relative to income. On the contrary, if we accept the not implausible assumption that the motives and preferences of people, the technical opportunities open to them, and the uncertainty associated with economic growth during particular periods were leading people to maintain roughly a constant ratio between *all* capital and income, the decline in the estimated capital-income ratio[11] is simply a signal that human capital has been increasing relatively not only to conventional capital but also to income.

The bumper crop of estimates that show national income increasing faster than national resources raises a second and not unrelated puzzle. The income of the United States has been increasing at a much higher rate than the combined amount of land, man-hours worked and the stock of reproducible capital used to produce the income. Moreover, the discrepancy between the two rates has become larger from one business cycle to the next during recent decades.[12] To call this discrepancy a measure of "resource productivity" gives a name to our ignorance but does not dispel it. If we accept these estimates, the connections between national resources and national income have become loose and tenuous over time. Unless this discrepancy can be resolved, received theory of production applied to inputs and outputs as currently measured is a toy and not a tool for studying economic growth.

Two sets of forces probably account for the discrepancy, if we neglect entirely the index number and aggregation problems that bedevil all estimates of such global aggregates as total output and total input. One is returns to scale; the second, the large improvements in the quality of inputs that have occurred but have been omitted from the input estimates. Our economy has undoubtedly been experiencing increasing returns to scale at some points offset by decreasing returns at others. If we can succeed in identifying and measuring the net gains, they may turn out to have been substantial. The improvements in the quality of inputs that have not been adequately allowed for are no doubt partly in material (nonhuman) capital. My own conception, however, is that both this defect and the omission of economies of scale are minor sources of discrepancy between the rates of growth of inputs and outputs compared to the improvements in human capacity that have been omitted.

A small step takes us from these two puzzles raised by existing estimates to a third which brings us to the heart of the matter, namely the essentially unexplained large increase in real earnings of workers. Can this be a windfall? Or a quasirent pending the adjustment in the supply of labor? Or, a pure rent reflecting the fixed amount of labor? It seems far more reasonable that it represents rather a return to the investment that has been made in human beings. The observed growth in productivity per unit of labor is simply a consequence of holding the unit of labor constant over time although in fact this unit of labor has been increasing as a result of a steadily growing amount of human capital per worker. As I read our record, the human capital component has become very large as a consequence of human investment.

Another aspect of the same basic question, which admits of the same resolution, is the rapid postwar recovery of countries that had suffered severe destruction of plant and equipment during the war. The toll from bombing was all too visible in the factories laid flat, the railroad yards, bridges, and harbors wrecked, and the cities in ruin. Structures, equipment and inventories were all heaps of rubble. Not so visible, yet large, was the toll from the wartime depletion of the physical plant that escaped destruction by bombs. Economists were called upon to assess the implications of these wartime losses for recovery. In retrospect, it it clear that they overestimated the prospective retarding effects of these losses. Having had a small hand in this effort, I have had a special reason for looking back and wondering why the judgments that we formed soon after the war proved to be so far from the mark. The explanation that now is clear is that we gave altogether too much weight to nonhuman capital in making these assessments. We fell into this error, I am convinced, because we did not have a concept of *all* capital and, therefore, failed to take account of human capital and the important part that it plays in production in a modern economy.

Let me close this section with a comment on poor countries, for which there are virtually no solid estimates. I have been impressed by repeatedly expressed judgments, especially by those who have a responsibility in making capital available to poor countries, about the low rate at which these countries can absorb additional capital. New capital from outside can be put to good use, it is said, only when it is added "slowly and gradually." But this experience is at variance with the widely held impression that countries are poor fundamentally because they are starved for capital and that additional capital is truly the key to their more rapid economic growth. The reconciliation is again, I believe, to be found in emphasis on particular forms of capital. The new capital available to these countries from outside as a rule goes into the formation of structures, equipment and sometimes also into inventories. But it is generally not available for additional investment in man. Consequently, human capabilities do not stay abreast of physical capital, and they do become limiting factors in economic growth. It should come as no surprise, therefore, that the absorption rate of capital to augment only particular nonhuman resources is necessarily low. The Horvat[13] formulation of the optimum rate of investment which treats knowledge and skill as a critical investment variable in determining the rate of economic growth is both relevant and important.

III. SCOPE AND SUBSTANCE OF THESE INVESTMENTS

What are human investments? Can they be distinguished from consumption? Is it at all feasible to identify and measure them? What do they contribute to income? Granted that they seem amorphous compared to brick and mortar, and hard to get at compared to the investment accounts of corporations, they assuredly are not a fragment; they are rather like the contents of Pandora's box, full of difficulties and hope.

Human resources obviously have both quantitative and qualitative dimensions. The number of people, the proportion who enter upon useful work, and hours worked are essentially quantitative characteristics. To make my task tolerably manageable, I shall neglect these and consider only such quality components as skill, knowledge, and similar attributes that affect particular human capabilities to do productive work. In so far as expenditures to enhance such capabilities also increase the value productivity of human effort (labor), they will yield a positive rate of return.[14]

How can we estimate the magnitude of human investment? The practice followed in connection with physical capital goods is to estimate the magnitude of capital formation by expenditures made to produce the capital goods. This practice would suffice also for the formation of human capital. However, for human capital there is an additional problem that is less pressing for physical capital goods: how to distinguish between expenditures for consumption and for investment. This distinction bristles with both conceptual and practical difficulties. We can think of three classes of expenditures: expenditures that satisfy consumer preferences and in no way enhance the capabilities under discussion—these represent pure consumption; expenditures that enhance capabilities and do not satisfy any preferences underlying consumption—these represent pure investment; and expenditures that have both effects. Most relevant activities clearly are in the third class, partly consumption and partly investment, which is why the task of identifying each component is so formidable and why the measurement of capital formation by expenditures is less useful for human investment than for investment in physical goods. In principle there is an alternative method for estimating human investment, namely by its yield rather than by its cost. While any capability produced by human investment becomes a part of the human agent and hence cannot be sold; it is nevertheless "in touch with the market place" by affecting the wages and salaries the human agent can earn. The resulting increase in earnings is the yield on the investment.[15]

Despite the difficulty of exact measurement at this stage of our understanding of human investment, many insights can be gained by examining some of the more important activities that improve human capabilities. I shall concentrate on five major categories: (1) health facilities and services, broadly conceived to include all expenditures that affect the life expectancy, strength and stamina, and the vigor and vitality of a people; (2) on-the-job training, including old-style apprenticeship organized by firms; (3) formally organized education at the elementary, secondary, and higher levels; (4) study programs for adults that are not organized by firms, including extension programs notably in agriculture; (5) migration of individuals and families to adjust to changing job opportunities. Except for education, not much is known about these activities that is germane here. I shall refrain from commenting on study programs for adults, although in agriculture the extension services of the several states play an important role in transmitting new knowledge and in developing skills of farmers.[16] Nor shall I elaborate further on internal migration related to economic growth.

Health activities have both quantity and quality implications. Such speculations as economists have engaged in about the effects of improvements in health,[17] has been predominantly in connection with population growth, which is to say with quantity. But surely health measures also enhance the quality of human resources. So also may additional food and better shelter, especially in underdeveloped countries.

The change in the role of food as people become richer sheds light on one of the conceptual problems already referred to. I have pointed out that extra food in some poor countries has the attribute of a "producer good." This attribute of food, however, diminishes as the consumption of food rises, and there comes a point at which any further increase in food becomes pure consumption.[18] Clothing, housing and perhaps medical services may be similar.

My comment about on-the-job training will consist of a conjecture on the amount of such training, a note on the decline of apprenticeship, and then a useful economic theorem on who bears the costs of such training. Surprisingly little is known about on-the-job training in modern industry. About all that can be said is that the expansion of education has not eliminated it. It seems likely, however, that some of the training formerly undertaken by firms has been discontinued and other training programs have been instituted to adjust both to the rise in the education of workers and to changes in the demands for new skills. The amount invested annually in such training can only be a guess. H. F. Clark places it near to equal to the amount spent on formal education.[19] Even if it were only one-half as large, it would represent currently an annual gross investment of about $15 billion. Elsewhere, too, it is thought to be important. For example, some observers have been impressed by the amount of such training under way in plants in the Soviet Union.[20] Meanwhile, apprenticeship has all but disappeared, partly because it is now inefficient and partly because schools now perform many of its functions. Its disappearance has been hastened no doubt by the difficulty of enforcing apprenticeship agreements. Legally they have come to smack of indentured service. The underlying economic factors and behavior are clear enough. The apprentice is prepared to serve during the initial period when his productivity is less than the cost of his keep and of his training. Later, however, unless he is legally restrained, he will seek other employment when his productivity begins to exceed the cost of keep and training, which is the period during which a master would expect to recoup on his earlier outlay.

To study on-the-job training Gary Becker[21] advances the theorem that in competitive markets employees pay all the costs of their training and none of these costs are ultimately borne by the firm. Becker points out several implications. The notion that expenditures on training by a firm generate external economies for other firms is not consistent with this theorem. The theorem also indicates one force favoring the transfer from on-the-job training to attending school. Since on-the-job training reduces the net earnings of workers at the beginning and raises them later on, this theorem also provides an explanation for the "steeper slope of the curve relating income to age," for skilled than unskilled workers, referred to earlier.[22] What all this adds up to is that the stage is set to undertake meaningful economic studies of on-the-job training.

Happily we reach firmer ground in regard to education. Investment in education has risen at a rapid rate and by itself may well account for a substantial part of the otherwise unexplained rise in earnings. I shall do no more than summarize some preliminary results about the total costs of education including income foregone by students, the apparent relation of these costs to consumer income and to alternative investments, the rise of the stock of education in the labor force, returns to education, and the contribution that the increase in the stock of education may have made to earnings and to national income.

It is not difficult to estimate the conventional costs of education consisting of the costs of the services of teachers, librarians, administrators, of maintaining and operating the educational plant, and interest on the capital embodied in the educational plant. It is far more difficult to estimate another component of total cost, the income foregone by students. Yet this component should be included and it is far from negligible. In the United States, for example, well over half of the costs of higher education consists of income foregone by students. As early as 1900, this income foregone accounted for about one-fourth of the total costs of elementary, secondary and higher education. By 1956, it represented over two-fifths of all costs. The rising significance of foregone income has been a major factor in the marked upward trend in the total real costs of education which, measured in current prices, increased from $400 million in 1900 to $28.7 billion in 1956.[23] The percentage rise in educational costs was about three and a half times as large as in consumer income, which would imply a high income elasticity of the demand for education, if education were regarded as pure consumption.[24] Educational costs also rose about three and a half times as rapidly as did the gross formation of physical capital in dollars. If we were to treat education as pure investment this result would suggest that the returns to education were relatively more attractive than those to nonhuman capital.[25]

Much schooling is acquired by persons who are not treated as income earners in most economic analysis, particularly, of course women. To analyze the effect of growth in schooling on earnings, it is therefore necessary to distinguish between the stock of education in the population and the amount in the labor force. Years of school completed are far from satisfactory as a measure because of the marked increases that have taken place in the number of days of school attendance of enrolled students and because much more of the education of workers consists of high school and higher education than formerly. My preliminary estimates suggest that the stock of education in the labor force rose about eight and a half times between 1900 and 1956, whereas the stock of reproducible capital rose four and a half times, both in 1956 prices. These estimates are, of course, subject to many qualifications.[26] Nevertheless, both the magnitude and the rate of increase of this form of human capital have been such that they could be an important key to the riddle of economic growth.[27]

The exciting work under way is on the return to education. In spite of the flood of high school and college graduates, the return has not become trivial. Even the lower limits of the estimates show that the return to such education has been in the neighborhood of the return to nonhuman capital. This is what most of these estimates show when they treat as costs all of the public and private expenditures on education and also the income foregone while attending school, and when they treat all of these costs as investment, allocating none to consumption.[28] But surely a part of these costs are consumption in the sense that education creates a form of consumer capital[29] which has the attribute of improving the taste and the quality of consumption of students throughout the rest of their lives. If one were to allocate a substantial fraction of the total costs of this education to consumption, say one-half, this would, of course, double the observed rate of return to what would then become the investment component in education that enhances the productivity of man.

Fortunately, the problem of allocating the costs of education in the labor force between consumption and investment does not arise to plague us when we turn to the contribution that education makes to earnings and to national income because a change in allocation only alters the rate of return, not the total return. I noted at the outset that the unexplained increases in U.S. national income have been especially large in recent decades. On one set of assumptions, the unexplained part amounts to nearly three-fifths of the total increase between 1929 and 1956.[30] How much of this unexplained increase in income represents a return to education in the labor force? A lower limit suggests that about three-tenths of it, and an upper limit does not rule out that more than one-half of it came from this source.[31] These estimates also imply that between 36 and 70 per cent of the hitherto unexplained rise in the earnings of labor is explained by returns to the additional education of workers.

IV. A CONCLUDING NOTE ON POLICY

One proceeds at his own peril in discussing social implications and policy. The conventional hedge is to camouflage one's values and to wear the mantle of academic innocence. Let me proceed unprotected!

1. Our tax laws everywhere discriminate against human capital. Although the stock of such capital has become large and even though it is obvious that human capital, like other forms of reproducible capital, depreciates, becomes obsolete, and entails maintenance, our tax laws are all but blind on these matters.

2. Human capital deteriorates when it is idle because unemployment impairs the skills that workers have acquired. Losses in earnings can be cushioned by appropriate payments but these do not keep idleness from taking its toll from human capital.

3. There are many hindrances to the free choice of professions. Racial discrimination and religious discrimination are still widespread. Professional associations and governmental bodies also hinder entry; for example, into medicine. Such purposeful interference keeps the investment in this form of human capital substantially below its optimum.[32]

4. It is indeed elementary to stress the greater imperfections of the capital market in providing funds for investment in human beings than for investment in physical goods. Much could be done to reduce these imperfections by reforms in tax and banking laws and by changes in banking practices. Long-term private and public loans to students are warranted.

5. Internal migration, notably the movement of farm people into industry, made necessary by the dynamics of our economic progress, requires substantial investments. In general, families in which the husbands and wives are already in the late thirties cannot afford to make these investments because the remaining payoff period for them is too short. Yet society would gain if more of them would pull stakes and move because, in addition to the increase in productivity currently, the children of these families would be better located for employment when they were ready to enter the labor market. The case for making some of these investments on public account is by no means weak. Our farm programs have failed miserably these

many years in not coming to grips with the costs and returns from off-farm migration.

6. The low earnings of particular people have long been a matter of public concern. Policy all too frequently concentrates only on the effects, ignoring the causes. No small part of the low earnings of many Negroes, Puerto Ricans, Mexican nationals, indigenous migratory farm workers, poor farm people and some of our older workers, reflects the failure to have invested in their health and education. Past mistakes are, of course, bygones, but for the sake of the next generation we can ill afford to continue making the same mistakes over again.

7. Is there a substantial underinvestment in human beings other than in these depressed groups?[33] This is an important question for economists. The evidence at hand is fragmentary. Nor will the answer be easily won. There undoubtedly have been overinvestments in some skills, for example, too many locomotive firemen and engineers, too many people trained to be farmers, and too many agricultural economists! Our schools are not free of loafers and some students lack the necessary talents. Nevertheless, underinvestment in knowledge and skill, relative to the amounts invested in nonhuman capital would appear to be the rule and not the exception for a number of reasons. The strong and increasing demands for this knowledge and skill in laborers are of fairly recent origin and it takes time to respond to them. In responding to these demands, we are heavily dependent upon cultural and political processes, and these are slow and the lags are long compared to the behavior of markets serving the formation of nonhuman capital. Where the capital market does serve human investments, it is subject to more imperfections than in financing physical capital. I have already stressed the fact that our tax laws discriminate in favor of nonhuman capital. Then, too, many individuals face serious uncertainty in assessing their innate talents when it comes to investing in themselves, especially through higher education. Nor is it easy either for public decisions or private behavior to untangle and properly assess the consumption and the investment components. The fact that the return to high school and to higher education has been about as large as the return to conventional forms of capital when all of the costs of such education including income foregone by students are allocated to the investment component, creates a strong presumption that there has been underinvestment since, surely, much education is cultural and in that sense it is consumption. It is no wonder, in view of these circumstances, that there should be substantial underinvestment in human beings, even though we take

pride, and properly so, in the support that we have given to education and to other activities that contribute to such investments.

8. Should the returns from public investment in human capital accrue to the individuals in whom it is made?[34] The policy issues implicit in this question run deep and they are full of perplexities pertaining both to resource allocation and to welfare. Physical capital that is formed by public investment is not transferred as a rule to particular individuals as a gift. It would greatly simplify the allocative process if public investment in human capital were placed on the same footing. What then is the logical basis for treating public investment in human capital differently? Presumably it turns on ideas about welfare. A strong welfare goal of our community is to reduce the unequal distribution of personal income among individuals and families. Our community has relied heavily on progressive income and inheritance taxation. Given public revenue from these sources, it may well be true that public investment in human capital, notably that entering into general education, is an effective and efficient set of expenditures for attaining this goal. Let me stress, however, that the state of knowledge about these issues is woefully meager.

9. My last policy comment is on assistance to underdeveloped countries to help them achieve economic growth. Here, even more than in domestic affairs, investment in human beings is likely to be underrated and neglected. It is inherent in the intellectual climate in which leaders and spokesmen of many of these countries find themselves. Our export of growth doctrines has contributed. These typically assign the stellar role to the formation of nonhuman capital, and take as an obvious fact the superabundance of human resources. Steel mills are the real symbol of industrialization. After all, the early industrialization of England did not depend on investments in the labor force. New funds and agencies are being authorized to transfer capital for physical goods to these countries. The World Bank and our Export-Import Bank have already had much experience. Then, too, measures have been taken to pave the way for the investment of more private (nonhuman) capital abroad. This one-sided effort is under way in spite of the fact that the knowledge and skills required to take on and use efficiently the superior techniques of production, the most valuable resource that we could make available to them, is in very short supply in these underdeveloped countries. Some growth of course can be had from the increase in more conventional capital even though the labor that is available is lacking both in skill and knowledge. But the rate of growth will be seriously limited. It simply is not possible to have

the fruits of a modern agriculture and the abundance of modern industry without making large investments in human beings.

Truly, the most distinctive feature of our economic system is the growth in human capital. Without it there would be only hard, manual work and poverty except for those who have income from property. There is an early morning scene in Faulkner's *Intruder in the Dust*, of a poor, solitary cultivator at work in a field. Let me paraphrase that line, "The man without skills and knowledge leaning terrifically against nothing."

NOTES

[1] T. W. Schultz, "Investment in Man: An Economist's View," *Soc. Serv. Rev.*, June 1959, *33*, 109-17.

[2] J. S. Nicholson, "The Living Capital of the United Kingdom," *Econ. Jour.*, Mar. 1891, *1*, 95; see J. S. Mill, *Principles of Political Economy*, ed. W. J. Ashley, London 1909, p. 8.

[3] H. von Thünen, *Der isolierte Staat*, 3rd ed., Vol. 2, Pt. 2, 1875, transl. by B. F. Hoselitz, reproduced by the Comp. Educ. Center, Univ. Chicago, pp. 140-52.

[4] Irving Fisher, *The Nature of Capital and Income*. New York 1906.

[5] Alfred Marshall, *Principles of Economics*, 8th ed. London 1930. App. E, pp. 787-88.

[6] H. G. Johnson, "The Political Economy of Opulence," *Can. Jour. Econ. and Pol. Sci.*, Nov. 1960, *26*, 552-64.

[7] Morton Zeman, *A Quantitative Analysis of White-Nonwhite Income Differentials in the United States*. Unpublished doctoral dissertation, Univ. Chicago, 1955.

[8] Based on unpublished preliminary results obtained by Joseph Willett in his Ph.D. research at the University of Chicago.

[9] Simon Kuznets, *Income and Wealth in the United States*. Cambridge, England 1952. Sec. IV, Distribution by Industrial Origin.

[10] P. R. Brahmanand and C. N. Vakil, *Planning for an Expanding Economy*. Bombay 1956.

[11] I leave aside here the difficulties inherent in identifying and measuring both the nonhuman capital and the income entering into estimates of this ratio. There are index number and aggregation problems aplenty, and not all improvements in the quality of this capital have been accounted for, as I shall note later.

[12] Solomon Fabricant, *Basic Facts on Productivity Change*, Nat. Bur. Econ. Research, Occas. Paper 63. New York 1959. Table 5.

[13] B. Horvat, "The Optimum Rate of Investment," *Econ. Jour.*, Dec. 1958, *68*, 747-67.

[14] Even so, our *observed* return can be either negative, zero or positive because our observations are drawn from a world where there is uncer-

tainty and imperfect knowledge and where there are windfall gains and losses and mistakes aplenty.

[15]In principle, the value of the investment can be determined by discounting the additional future earnings it yields just as the value of a physical capital good can be determined by discounting its income stream.

[16]T. W. Schultz, "Agriculture and the Application of Knowledge," *A Look to the Future*, W. K. Kellogg Foundation, Battle Creek, 1956, 54-78.

[17]Health economics is in its infancy; there are two medical journals with "economics" in their titles, two bureaus for economic research in private associations (one in the American Medical and the other in the American Dental Association), and not a few studies and papers by outside scholars. Selma Mushkin's survey is very useful with its pertinent economic insights, though she may have underestimated somewhat the influence of the economic behavior of people in striving for health. See S. J. Mushkin, "Toward a Definition of Health Economics," *Public Health Reports*, U.S. Dept. of Health, Educ. and Welfare, Sept. 1958, *73*, 785-93.

[18]For instance, the income elasticity of the demand for food continues to be positive even after the point is reached where additional food no longer has the attribute of a "producer good."

[19]Based on comments made by Harold F. Clark at the Merrill Center for Economics summer 1959; also, see [4].

[20]Based on observations made by a team of U. S. economists of which I was a member; see *Saturday Rev.*, Jan. 21, 1961.

[21]G. S. Becker, preliminary draft of study undertaken for Nat. Bur. Econ. Research. New York 1960.

[22]Becker has also noted still another implication arising out of the fact that the income and capital investment aspects of on-the-job training are tied together, which gives rise to "permanent" and "transitory" income effects that may have substantial explanatory value.

[23]T. W. Schultz, "Capital Formation by Education," *Jour. Pol. Econ.*, Dec. 1960, *68*, Tables 3 through 7.

[24]Had other things stayed constant this suggests an income elasticity of 3.5. Among the things that did change, the prices of educational services rose relative to other consumer prices, perhaps offset in part by improvements in the quality of educational services.

[25]This of course assumes among other things that the relationship between gross and net have not changed or have changed in the same proportion. Estimates are from my essay, "Education and Economic Growth." See T. W. Schultz, "Education and Economic Growth," *Social Forces Influencing American Education*, H. G. Richey, ed. Chicago 1961.

[26]*Ibid.*, Sec. 4. These estimates of the stock of education are tentative and incomplete. They are incomplete in that they do not take into account fully the increase in the average life of this form of human capital arising out of the fact that relatively more of this education is held by younger people in the labor force than was true in earlier years; and, they are incomplete because no adjustment has been made for the improvements

in education over time, increasing the quality of a year of school in ways other than those related to changes in the proportions represented by elementary, high school and higher education. Even so the stock of this form of human capital rose 8.5 times between 1900 and 1956 while the stock of reproducible nonhuman capital increased only 4.5 times, both in constant 1956 prices.

[27]In value terms this stock of education was only 22 per cent as large as the stock of reproducible physical capital in 1900, whereas in 1956 it already had become 42 per cent as large.

[28]Several comments are called for here. (1) The return to high school education appears to have declined substantially between the late 'thirties and early 'fifties and since then has leveled off, perhaps even risen somewhat, indicating a rate of return toward the end of the 'fifties about as high as that to higher education. (2) The return to college education seems to have risen somewhat since the late 'thirties in spite of the rapid influx of college-trained individuals into the labor force. (3) Becker's estimates based on the difference in income between high school and college graduates based on urban males adjusted for ability, race, unemployment and mortality show a return of 9 per cent to total college costs including both earnings foregone and conventional college costs, public and private and with none of these costs allocated to consumption (see his paper given at the American Economic Association meeting, December 1959). (4) The returns to this education in the case of nonwhite urban males, of rural males, and of females in the labor force may have been somewhat lower. (5) My own estimates, admittedly less complete than those of Becker and thus subject to additional qualifications, based mainly on lifetime income estimates of Herman P. Miller, lead to a return of about 11 per cent to both high school and college education as of 1958.

Whether the consumption component in education will ultimately dominate, in the sense that the investment component in education will diminish as these expenditures increase and a point will be reached where additional expenditures for education will be pure consumption (a zero return on however small a part one might treat as an investment), is an interesting speculation. This may come to pass, as it has in the case of food and shelter, but that eventuality appears very remote presently in view of the prevailing investment value of education and the new demands for knowledge and skill inherent in the nature of our technical and economic progress.

[29]The returns on this consumer capital will not appear in the wages and salaries that people earn.

[30]Real income doubled, rising from $150 to $302 billion in 1956 prices. Eighty-nine billions of the increase in real income is taken to be unexplained, or about 59 per cent of the total increase. The stock of education in the labor force rose by $355 billion of which $69 billion is here allocated to the growth in the labor force to keep the per-worker stock

of education constant, and $286 billion represents the increase in the level of this stock.

[31]In per cent, the lower estimate came out to 29 per cent and the upper estimate to 56 per cent.

[32]Milton Friedman and Simon Kuznets, *Income from Independent Professional Practice*, Nat. Bur. Econ. Research. New York 1945.

[33]G. S. Becker, "Underinvestment in College Education?," *Proc., Am. Econ. Rev.*, May 1960, *50*, 346-54.

[34]I am indebted to Milton Friedman for bringing this issue to the fore in his comments on an early draft of this paper. See also Jacob Mincer's pioneering paper: Jacob Mincer, "Investment in Human Capital and Personal Income Distribution," *Jour. Pol. Econ.*, Aug. 1958, *66*, 281-302.

2

THE CONCEPT OF HUMAN CAPITAL

by Gary S. Becker

*Becker is among the half dozen scholars who have estab-
lished the theoretical and practical relationships among
investments in education, medical care, and other forms of
"people-oriented" programs. This article summarizes
Becker's analysis of various types of returns from educational investments to the individual and society.*

Some activities primarily affect future well-being; the main impact
of others is in the present. Some affect money income and others
psychic income, that is, consumption. Sailing primarily affects consumption, on-the-job training primarily affects money income, and
a college education could affect both. These effects may operate
either through physical resources or through human resources. This
study is concerned with activities that influence future monetary
and psychic income by increasing the resources in people. These
activities are called investments in human capital.

The many forms of such investments include schooling, on-the-
job training, medical care, migration, and searching for information
about prices and incomes. They differ in their effects on earnings
and consumption, in the amounts typically invested, in the size of

Reprinted from Gary S. Becker, *Human Capital: A Theoretical and Empirical
Analysis with Special Reference to Education.* New York: National Bureau of Economic Research, 1964. Distributed by Columbia University Press. Pp. 102, 153-159.
Copyright by the National Bureau of Economic Research. Reprinted by permission
of the publisher.

returns, and in the extent to which the connection between investment and return is perceived. But all these investments improve
skills, knowledge, or health, and thereby raise money or psychic
incomes.

Recent years have witnessed intensive concern with and research on investment in human capital, much of it contributed or
stimulated by T. W. Schultz. The main motivating factor has probably been a realization that the growth of physical capital, at least as
conventionally measured, explains a relatively small part of the
growth of income in most countries. The search for better explanations has led to improved measures of physical capital and to an
interest in less tangible entities, such as technological change and
human capital. Also behind this concern is the strong dependence
of modern military technology on education and skills, the rapid
growth in expenditures on education and health, the age-old quest
for an understanding of the personal distribution of income, the
recent growth in unemployment in the United States, the Leontief
scarce-factor paradox, and several other important economic problems.

The result has been the accumulation of a tremendous amount of
circumstantial evidence testifying to the economic importance of
human capital, especially of education. Probably the most impressive piece of evidence is that more highly educated and skilled
persons almost always tend to earn more than others. This is true
of developed countries as different as the United States and the
Soviet Union, of underdeveloped countries as different as India and
Cuba, and of the United States one hundred years ago as well as
today. Moreover, few, if any, countries have achieved a sustained
period of economic development without having invested substantial amounts in their labor force, and most studies that have attempted quantitative assessments of contributions to growth have
assigned an important role to investment in human capital. Again,
inequality in the distribution of earnings and income is generally
positively related to inequality in education and other training. To
take a final example, unemployment tends to be strongly related,
usually inversely, to education.

Passions are easily aroused on this subject and even people who
are generally in favor of education, medical care, and the like often
dislike the phrase "human capital" and still more any emphasis on
its economic effects. They are often the people who launch the
most bitter attacks on research on human capital, partly because
they fear that emphasis on the "material" effects of human capital
detracts from its "cultural" effects, which to them are more impor-

tant. Those denying the economic importance of education and other investments in human capital have attacked the circumstantial evidence in its favor. They argue that the correlation between earnings and investment in human capital is due to a correlation between ability and investment in human capital, or to the singling out of the most favorable groups, such as white male college graduates, and to the consequent neglect of women, drop-outs, nonwhites, or high-school graduates. They consider the true correlation to be very weak, and, therefore, a poor guide and of little help to people investing in human capital. The association between education and economic development or between inequality in education and income is attributed to the effect of income on education, considering education as a consumption good, and hence of no greater causal significance than the association between automobile ownership and economic development or between the inequality in ownership and incomes. . . .

1. SUMMARY

Most investments in human capital—e.g., formal education, on-the-job training, or migration—raise observed earnings at older ages, because returns are part of earnings then, and lower them at younger ages, because costs are deducted from earnings at that time. Since these common effects are produced by very different kinds of investment in human capital, a basis is provided for a unified and comprehensive theory. The analysis in Part One starts with a discussion of specific kinds of human capital, with the most attention paid to on-the-job training, because the latter clearly illustrates and emphasizes the common effects. This leads to a general theory applying to any kind of human capital.

The general theory has a wide variety of important applications. It helps to explain such diverse phenomena as interpersonal and interarea differences in earnings, the shape of age-earnings profiles —the relation between age and earnings—and the effect of specialization on skill. For example, because observed earnings are gross of the return on human capital, some persons earn more than others simply because they invest more in themselves. Because "abler" persons tend to invest more than others, the distribution of earnings would be very unequal and skewed even if "ability" were symmetrically and not too unequally distributed. Further, the conventional practice of adding returns to and subtracting costs from earnings serves to steepen age-earnings profiles and to increase their concavity as investment in human capital increases. Still another example, learning on and off the job has the same kind of effects on observed earnings as formal education, training, and other recognized investments in human capital, and can be considered one way to invest in human capital. Because all such activities have similar effects on earnings, the total amount invested in human capital, and rates of return on this investment can, on certain reasonable assumptions, be estimated from information on observed earnings alone.

Some investments in human capital do not affect earnings because costs are paid and returns are collected not by the persons involved but by the firms, industries, or countries employing them. These investments, which are called "specific" investments, range from hiring costs to executive training and are of considerable importance. They help to explain the well-known fact that unemployment is greater among unskilled than skilled workers in the United States, for more specific capital is invested in the latter and employers have special incentive to continue them on the payroll. Similarly, incompletely vested pension plans may be used because they help to insure firms against a loss on their specific investment. The analysis further suggests that this type of investment is relatively more important in monopsonistic than in competitive firms.

Part Two investigates empirically the effect of one kind of human capital—formal education—on earnings and productivity in the United States. The basic technique used is to adjust data on the earnings or incomes of persons with different amounts of education for other relevant differences between them. Chapter IV determines the relation in recent years between earnings and college education, considering, among other things, college costs and the greater "ability" of college persons. The rate of return to an average college entrant is considerable, of the order of 10 or 12 per cent per annum; the rate is higher to urban, white, male college graduates and lower to college drop-outs, nonwhites, women, and rural persons. Differences in the relative number of, say, white and nonwhite or urban and rural high-school graduates who go to college are consistent with the differences in their rates of return.

General observation indicates that college graduates tend to be more "able" than high-school graduates, apart from the effect of college education. This is indicated also by information gathered on I.Q., rank in class, father's education or income, physical health, ability to communicate, and several other distinguishing characteristics. A few studies permit some assessment of the relative importance of ability and education in explaining earning differentials between college and high-school persons. By and large, it appears, ability explains only a relatively small part of the differentials and college education explains the larger part. Apparently, moreover, the rate of return from college is positively related to the level of ability since there is evidence that ability plays a larger part in determining the earnings of college than high-school persons.

Gains from college education vary not only between groups, like men and women, but also substantially within given groups. Indeed, some calculations in Chapter IV indicate that the dispersion of rates of return among white male college graduates is as large as, and perhaps larger than, the very considerable dispersion in the returns per dollar of capital among smaller corporate manufacturing firms. A large dispersion makes it difficult for any individual to anticipate his gain from education, a difficulty that is compounded by a pay-off period of some twenty to twenty-five years. This long pay-off period provides an economic justification for flexible or "liberal" education since most of the benefits would be received when the economic environment was greatly different from that prevailing at the time of entry into the labor force.

In Chapter V attention is focused on the social gain from college education as measured by its effects on national productivity. The major difficulty here, one that always plagues economists, is in measuring the benefits and costs to society that are not captured or borne by college-educated persons. All that could be done was to derive—on the basis of crude information—lower and what is best labeled "possible" upper limits to the social rates of return, limits that unfortunately are wide apart. The more reliable lower limits thus derived do not differ much from the private rates of return, but the upper levels are almost double the latter. In the same chapter it is shown that private rates of return on college education exceed those on business capital. The evidence is insufficient to decide whether this, or the converse, is true of the social rates.

Chapter VI estimates private rates of return from high-school education. Before adjusting for differential ability, these private rates from high-school turn out to be greater than those from college. But the "true" rates, after adjustment for ability, may not be, for ability apparently differs more between high-school and elementary-school students than between college and high-school students. A similar qualification applies to the crude evidence indicating that rates on elementary-school education are the highest of all.

A traditional view among economists—certainly the dominant one when I was a graduate student—is that changes in educational attainments have been largely autonomous, and that the secular increase in education has caused a decline in earning differentials and rates of return on education. Such evidence as there is, presented in Chapter VI, suggests indeed that the relative position of high-school and college graduates probably declined during the first forty years of the century under the impact of increases in their numbers. But the evidence is scattered and much less reliable than the information available for the past twenty years. The latter, presented in the same chapter, indicates that the rapid growth in the number of high-school and college graduates has not reduced their economic position. An alternative view, supported by this evidence, has therefore gained many adherents in recent years; namely, that educational attainments in good part adjust to, as well as influence, the demands of the economic system.

Chapter VII shows that investment in education in fact steepens and increases the concavity of age-earnings profiles, as predicted by the theory in Part One. Partly as an aside, the discussion also includes a critical examination of the common belief that earnings tend to turn down when persons reach their late forties or fifties; this belief is shown to be founded on an illusion, for it is based on data that do not take economic progress into account. The same chapter shows that the steepness of age-wealth profiles—the relation between age and the discounted value of subsequent earnings —is also increased by investment in education and other human capital. It is suggested that the apparent large secular increase in the peak wealth age in the United States resulted from a secular increase in the amount invested in such capital. The chapter concludes with some applications of these profiles, especially to life-cycle changes in savings, indebtedness, and consumption.

2. FUTURE RESEARCH

I have no illusions that this study has more than scratched the surface of the research required on the economic effects of education and other investments in human capital. There is need for additional research on many different aspects of the gain from education and on other implications of the theoretical analysis in Part One. A few examples of possible research will be briefly mentioned.

Economists have been surprisingly ignorant of the quantitative effects of different kinds of ability on earnings and productivity, yet such knowledge is essential in estimating the gains from investment in human capital (and in resolving many other problems as well). The surveys utilized in this study show the feasibility and importance of determining these effects, and many more such attempts should be made in the future.

Only a limited amount could be said about the social gains from education because of ignorance about the external effects. This ignorance is closely connected with ignorance about the "residual" in calculations of the contribution of various factors to growth. Little progress can be achieved, therefore, in improving the estimation of these social gains until methods are discovered for reducing the residual.

To many underdeveloped countries the gains from education in the United States fifty years ago may be more relevant than the gains today because this country was much poorer then and many fewer persons were educated. The evidence available indicates a decline in the private gain from high-school and college education in the first forty years of the century, but a much more intensive study is required because this evidence is not very reliable. Fortunately, Albert Fishlow has already begun a study for the National Bureau of historical changes in the demand for and supply of educated persons in the United States, and his study will throw considerably more light on trends in the gains from education.

I have not tried to estimate gains to persons taking specialized programs in high school and college. Some literature is already available on the gains to various professionals, such as doctors, lawyers, engineers, or scientists,[1] and additional comparisons can and should be made between persons with B.A., M.A., or Ph.D. degrees, liberal arts or more specialized college majors, commerical or academic high-school programs, and so on. My estimates of the average gains to high-school and college persons would be useful as a yardstick to determine when gains were unusually large or small; for example, since average gains are large, the gains from particular specialties would have to be very large before they could be considered "excessive."[2]

There has been persistent interest, if little success, in measuring the differences in quality among high schools and colleges. One way to measure quality within an economic context is to relate expenditures on students and other variables in different schools to the (ability-adjusted) incomes of their graduates.[3] Such studies have already been undertaken on a small sample basis,[4] and, with sufficient persistence, additional information could be collected to expand the samples considerably.

Chapter VII presents empirical work dealing with other implications of the theory outlined in Part One, such as the shape of age-earnings and age-wealth profiles, differential unemployment, turnover of military personnel, differential pay of school teachers, and estimates of the amount invested in human capital. The theory is so rich in implications that many more could be investigated, and empirical work has already begun relating human capital to the turnover in employment of women, comparative advantage and United States exports, the elasticity of substitution between labor and physical capital, and several other problems.

Probably the most important application is to differences in incomes between regions and countries, either over time or cross-sectionally at a moment in time. The estimates presented here of the gains from education could be used to improve Denison's estimates of the contribution of education to economic growth in the United States. The major improvement, however, must await additional work on the external effects of education, work that, I fear, will be rather slow in coming.

A more immediate, and also important, application is to the personal distribution of incomes. This field has been afflicted with numerous theories that scarcely go beyond the skewness in the over-all distribution of incomes although substantial empirical material on the anatomy of income distribution has been accumulated. The theory developed in section 3 of Chapter III combines the effects of investment in human capital and differential ability, and, unlike other theories, contains many implications about income distribution. The empirical work of Mincer, referred to earlier, as well as the fact that at least three-fifths of earnings are attributable either to investment in human capital or to differential ability,[5] is suggestive of the promise offered by this approach. I hope to present further work along these lines in the not too distant future.

3. CONCLUDING COMMENTS

In recent years the outpouring of work on education and other types of human capital has reached such a level that some persons have scornfully rejected it as simply another fad, while others have been repelled by a few reckless applications and by its use to justify all kinds of public policies. To those who believe in the great value of the concept, the excesses have been most unfortunate, although perhaps unavoidable. Probably no important development has ever sailed smoothly into the mainstream of economic thought.

One might, nevertheless, get discouraged were it not for the fact that peoples of the world differ enormously in productivity, that these differences are in turn largely related to environmental factors, and that the latter are in turn related to the accumulation of knowledge and the maintenance of health. The concept of investment in human capital simply organizes and stresses these basic truths. Perhaps they are obvious, but obvious truths can be extremely important. Indeed, I would venture the judgment that human capital is going to be an important part of the thinking about development, income distribution, labor turnover, and many other problems for a long time to come.

NOTES

[1]See, for example, M. Friedman and S. Kuznets, *Income from Independent Professional Practice,* New York, NBER, 1945; G. J. Stigler and D. Blank, *The Demand and Supply of Scientific Personnel,* New York, NBER, 1957; or W. L. Hansen, "The 'Shortage' of Engineers," *Review of Economics and Statistics,* August 1961.

[2]This yardstick has been applied by H. G. Lewis to the medical profession with extremely interesting and surprising results: the rate of return to doctors (on their additional training compared to dentists) has apparently been no higher and perhaps lower than that to all college graduates. See his *Unionism and Relative Wages in the United States: An Empirical Inquiry,* Chicago, 1963.

[3]Another approach is from the cost side, and relates differences in expenditures to differences in curriculum, size, teaching staff, and other "real" inputs; in technical language, this approach in effect constructs "hedonic" cost indexes. An interesting initial study along these lines has been made by R. Calkins, "The Unit Costs of Programs in Higher Education," unpublished Ph.D. dissertation, Columbia University, 1963.

[4]See, e.g., the study by S. Hunt discussed in Chapter IV, "Income Determinants for College Graduates and the Return to Educational Investments," unpublished PhD. dissertation, Yale University, 1963.

[5]Estimated by taking one minus the ratio of the average earnings of persons with no education to the average earnings of all persons.

3

INVESTING IN HUMAN CAPITAL
by Burton A. Weisbrod

*Professor Weisbrod has done pioneer work in quantifying
investments and returns from various types of programs
relating to human resources. While he concentrates on tangible returns from investments in health and education, he
also points out the need to consider intangible benefits to
the society from such factors as a better-informed electorate. He recommends reconsideration of public policy to
offer greater incentives for investments in human resources, including revision of tax legislation.*

I. INTRODUCTION

This paper is about people. It is also about productivity and growth
of an economy. And it is about the proper role of government in a
society devoted to using its limited physical and human resources
wisely for the economic and social well-being of its people.

A nation's output of goods and services, and thus its capacity to
raise living standards, is limited by its resources and by the state of
technological knowledge regarding how to utilize them. Of the traditional triumvirate of resources—land, labor, and capital—only
capital has been thought of generally as subject to significant and

Reprinted from Burton A. Weisbrod, "Investing in Human Capital," *The Journal
of Human Resources,* Vol. I, No. 1 (Summer 1966) (© 1966 by the Regents of the
University of Wisconsin), pp. 5-21. Reprinted by permission of the publisher and
author.

appropriate social control. Land is given by nature, while population and hence the labor supply have been considered to be determined by forces outside the economic system.

The state of technological knowledge, too, has been considered to be determined largely outside the economic system, except to the extent that resources were directed toward research and development. Moreover, knowledge is significant largely to the extent that it becomes embodied in resources—in the form of man-made capital.

With society's supply of land and labor and the state of the technological arts being largely beyond its control, society's ability to escape from mass poverty and to achieve wealth depends critically upon its success in accumulating capital—machinery, equipment, plant, and other man-made producers goods. If the stock of capital can be increased sufficiently, output and living standards can rise despite growing pressure of population on the fixed supply of land.

The trouble with this conventional if somewhat caricatured explanation of the economic growth process is that it fails to explain the growth in United States output in this century. Students of U.S. economic development have consistently concluded that increases in the stock of reproducible physical capital account for only half or less of the growth of our per capita output during this century. What accounts for the remainder?

There are a number of possible answers. Economies of scale may have permitted output to rise proportionately more than the increases in resources. *Improvements in the quality of capital goods* may have occurred without being reflected in prices. *Improvements in techniques of organizing production,* which increased productive efficiency, may have taken place.

But an alternative and possibly the principal answer may be that the stock of total capital has grown much more rapidly than our conventional measures indicate. Capital may exist in intangible form, as well as in the tangible, traditional forms of factories and machines. Intangible capital may be embodied in people—in labor resources. This would constitute a hybrid class of productive resources—a combination of labor and capital which might be called "human capital." Studies of the sources of economic growth that have measured only changes in the stock of *physical* capital (plant and equipment) have been incomplete; they have neglected the growing investment in *human* capital.

The concept of human capital is actually an old one in which interest has been revived within the last decade. What may have been the first reference to the social value of a person as a special kind of capital asset was made by Sir William Petty in 1687. Concerned about the economic losses from the London plagues, Petty estimated the value of an Englishman's production, the extra probability of his death if he remained in London, and the cost of transportation from the city. He then concluded that an expenditure to move people—and thereby to save lives—would indeed be a financially wise investment. The return would be eighty-four-fold!

Neither Petty then nor any of us now—even if *no* payoff had been found—would have advocated public disregard of health hazards. Yet the knowledge that an expenditure on relocation would actually be a profitable investment in human resources may reinforce the social resolve to take appropriate action.

Human capital represents resources which man has utilized to augment his personal productivity. Expenditures on information, labor mobility, health, education, and training all are capable of enhancing the productive capacity of a worker—his human capital. I would regard health and education as the two principal forms of expenditures on human capital, and I shall give attention to each. However, the discussion of health expenditures will be abbreviated, so that I can devote primary attention to education. For education is the area of human resource development in which we face today the most pressing issues of public policy, the greatest and most rapidly climbing demands upon the public purse, and the most challenging opportunities for farsighted social leadership.

In sections II and III, I will analyze private and social, monetary and non-monetary benefits from health and educational investments in human capital. Section IV will then draw some implications from the analysis—for over-all public policy with respect to investments in people, and particularly for investments in their education.

II. HEALTH AS AN INVESTMENT

A healthier worker is a more productive worker—absent less from the job and more productive and creative while on it. Substantial resources have been devoted in Canada and in the United States to improvements in health, and these have brought into being— among other benefits—a more effective labor force.

In the United States, total public and private expenditures on health and medical care have nearly doubled in the last eight years —soaring from less than $18 billion in 1955 to $34 billion in 1963. This represented an increase in the share of Gross National Product devoted to health from 4.7 percent to 6.0 percent.

The rate of increase in Canada has been even more rapid. Between 1955 and 1961, the latest year for which I have located Canadian data, expenditures on health and medical care rose 90 percent, while in the United States they rose 63 percent. In the short space of those six years, Canada increased spending on health from 3.2 percent to 4.5 percent of its growing gross national product.

Life expectancies continue to inch upward, responding in part to these health expenditures. In Canada, life expectancy at birth is nearly five years greater today than it was only twenty years ago.

Thus, whereas we have traditionally referred to *expenditures* on health, we now must recognize that a substantial fraction of those expenditures are truly *investments*—in increased longevity and lifetime labor productivity, as well as in increased human happiness and decreased suffering. Moreover, *preventive* health expenditures can be doubly valuable investments. Not only may they reduce the incidence and production-cutting effects of disease, but by liberating labor and capital resources that are now devoted to *caring* for the victims of disease, they may permit these resources to add to the production of other goods and services.

Let me illustrate in specific terms the investment character of health expenditures. A half-dozen years ago I estimated the dollar value of productivity losses resulting from polio in the United States; it ran to at least $46 million per year.[1] This included production lost from the victims of the disease, as well as the cost of resources devoted to treating and caring for them. More recently I have estimated the cost of preventing these economic losses by immunizing everyone in the United States under age 35, and then immunizing the newborn each year. This massive attack would cost only some $27 million per year—a small price to pay for an annual return of $46 million.

At the aggregate level, data from the United States National Health Survey permit us to make a crude estimate of the potential production being lost because of ill health, and this loss is the as-yet-unrealized payoff from additional public or private investment in medical research and disease prevention, cure, and treatment. In the year ended June 30, 1962, approximately 400 million workdays were lost by employed people because of illness or injury, or six days per worker. This is a loss of more than 2 percent of total manpower available to the economy. And it takes no account of either premature deaths or the debilitating effects of illness and accidents for those who remain on the job, but with impaired efficiency.

I do not suggest that public policy decisions on whether to embark on health programs should rest solely on their narrow economic "profitability" or contribution to economic growth. They should not. The point to be emphasized is that health programs may contribute handsomely to economic progress, *as well as* to the broader aspects of mankind's welfare. My research indicates that the United States has been paying a price of more than $700 million per year in economic costs of tuberculosis and over $2 billion per year in costs of cancer.[2] Better health often is very good business. The fact that national income accounts show essentially no health services under "investment" indicates the re-thinking of conventional practices that is needed.

TABLE 1

Sources of Funds for Medical and Health-Related Research,
United States, Selected Years, 1940-1970

Years	Total, in millions of dollars	Share of Federal Government	
		In millions of dollars	Percentage
1940	45	3	7
1947	88	28	32
1957	397	186	47
1960	715	380	53
1970	2,300	1,610	70

Sources: 1940-60 are from U.S. Senate, Committee of Consultants on Medical Research to the Subcommittee on the Department of Labor and Health, Education, and Welfare of the Committee on Appropriations, *Federal Support of Medical Research* (May 1960), p. 24; 1970 data are from unpublished projections developed for the Rockefeller Foundation Exploratory Study Report of the Ad Hoc Committee to Study Voluntary Health and Welfare Agencies. The federal government estimate of $1.6 billion is consistent with the Bureau of the Budget projections for 1970 expenditures by the National Institutes of Health: low estimate—$1.2 billion; medium—$1.3 billion; high—$2.0 billion. U.S. Bureau of the Budget, Special Study, *Ten-Year Projection of Federal Budget Expenditures* (1961), p. 48.

While much of the benefit from improved health accrues directly to the persons affected, there are also important benefits to others in society. In the jargon of economists, there are "external" benefits. Such external effects are particularly clear when contagious diseases are involved, for then the health of one person affects the health of others. They also exist in the form of benefits to employers, for whom a healthier labor force means less absenteeism and enhanced on-the-job productivity. And they exist in the form of benefits to taxpayers generally; for them a healthier population means, among other things, reduced needs for welfare payments to those whose illness has brought poverty. For all these reasons, there is a national stake in medical research too. New methods for disease prevention, and for treatment, cure, and rehabilitation of the ill, will often spread benefits throughout the society.

To some extent, the investment aspect of improved health is reflected through growing governmental support for medical and health-related research (see Table 1). There are, however, many and complex reasons for this support, only one of which is that better health "pays." Yet, when health program policies are being debated at high government levels, the economic aspects of improved health as an investment in human resources is playing an increasingly prominent role—a role which would be still greater, I would judge, if economists had contributed more to an understanding of the magnitudes of benefits from specific health programs. Nevertheless, the mere recognition of an investment component to health expenditures is itself a major step toward rational government decision-making.

III. EDUCATION AS AN INVESTMENT

Better health—resulting from expenditures on research, prevention, and care and from improved diets and more satisfactory housing —has surely contributed to economic growth by creating a more productive stock of human capital. But an even larger contributor has been education. Properly conceived, education produces a labor force that is more skilled, more adaptable to the needs of a changing economy, and more likely to develop the imaginative ideas, techniques, and products which are critical to the processes of economic expansion and social adaptation to change. By doing so—by contributing to worker productivity—the education process qualifies handsomely as a process of investment in human capital.

The increasing level of formal education among the U.S. labor force has been continuous and sizeable. In 1940, the male labor force aged 18—64 averaged (a median of) 7.7 years of schooling. By 1952 it averaged 10.6 years, and by 1962, 12.1 years, somewhat more than a completed high school education.[3] In Canada, the educational investments embodied in the male labor force have also been rising, more modestly, from 7.6 to 7.8 years between 1941 and 1951,[4] but more rapidly, to around 8.5 years or more, between 1951 and 1961.[5]

The value of education, like the value of all forms of investments in people, is far more than financial. Education is a vital segment of the full life. Still, while we attach great significance to the cultural value of education, public policy toward higher education has apparently emphasized more pragmatic aspects of education, at least in the United States. In an excellent recent monograph, Alice M. Rivlin traces the history of Federal legislation affecting higher education in the United States.[6] She finds that, in case after case, beginning as long ago as 1785, federal legislation ostensibly designed to aid higher education actually had more practical objectives, such as aid to farmers (land grants for establishing agricultural universities) and reduction of unemployment (college-classroom construction in the 1930's). Citizens, or at least legislators, seem to have demanded consistently some evidence that the support of higher education is a profitable investment.

The National Defense Education Act—involving substantial loans, grants, and fellowships—may have signaled the beginning of a new era in which higher education *in general*—not merely those parts which have narrowly practical value—is receiving public attention and support. Yet efforts by economists to determine the financial returns from education in general and the contribution of education to economic growth may be interpreted as attempts to discover whether this new attitude toward higher education is justified on narrow financial grounds. The final verdict is not yet in.

But the growth of expenditures on education continues. Public education expenditures in the U.S. climbed above $24 billion in 1963, from $10 billion only a decade earlier.[7] Since 1900, total expenditures on education in the United States have increased four times as rapidly as total expenditures on physical plant and equipment; in 1900, education expenditures were only 9 percent of investment in plant and equipment, but by 1956, they were 34 percent,[8] and now they are 37 percent.

In analyzing the economic value of education, it is useful to view education as an industry—a user of resources and a producer of outputs. An economy has limited resources and cannot produce all the goods and services we would like to have. Therefore, efforts should be expanded to identify and to measure the values of the education industry's outputs, as well as the costs of all the resources it uses. It is not enough to exhort the virtues of education. While some urge that education merits added support, others press for more resources for health, while still others are urging the expansion of efforts to improve diets or housing, or construct more parks or wider and safer highways.

Unhappily, we must make choices. If they are made without recognition of the full benefits and costs of alternative uses of resources, we are not likely to choose wisely. Within this context, the following sections are devoted to what is known, and to what is not known, about the forms and magnitude of benefits from educational investments in human resources. Private and public benefits will be examined.

By "benefits" of education I mean any of three types of effects: those that increase production possibilities, such as increased labor skills; those that reduce costs and thereby make resources available for more productive uses, such as the reduced crime and law enforcement needs that education may bring by enhancing earnings; and those that increase welfare possibilities directly, such as development of public-spiritedness or social consciousness.

Private Benefits from Education

Direct economic gains to individuals from education are sizeable. Two measures of these gains are the greater incomes and the smaller unemployment rates which added schooling seems to bring. Data for both the United States and Canada (Tables 2 and 3) present similar and impressive pictures of the favorable relationships between an individual's educational attainment, his subsequent income, and the prospects for his unemployment.

But let me digress with some words of caution. With reference to the income-education relationship, it is probably not true that the high school dropout in the United States, for example, could increase his annual income from around $4,800 to $5,400 (Table 2), if only he would complete high school. We frequently forget the selection process by which some young people complete more schooling than others. In general, those students who do not drop out are more able, more ambitious, more anxious to learn, and come from families with better job "connections"—all of which assist in lifting their incomes. We cannot be sure how much of the additional incomes associated with additional education is attributable to these factors, and how much is attributable to the schooling itself. The monetary returns from investment in education are doubtless noteworthy, but they are probably not as large as the data in Tables 2 and 3 suggest.

Caution is also required in interpreting the dramatic data on unemployment rates in Tables 2 and 3. It is not unusual to find young people being advised not to quit school partly on the ground that their chances of being unemployed would be reduced if they remained. This approach is too simple. If, by the wave of a magic wand, the entire U.S. labor force could have been endowed with a college education, would the over-all unemployment rate of 6.0 percent in March 1962 have been reduced to only 1.5 percent (Table 2)—the rate for college graduates? I think not.

TABLE 2

Income and Unemployment by Years of Schooling Completed
in the United States

Years of Schooling Completed	Median Income Males, Age 25 and Over 1959	Unemployment Rate March 1962 (percent)
Elementary:		
8 years	$3,892	7.2
High School:		
1-3 years	4,846	8.3
4 years	5,441	5.1
College:		
1-3 years	5,978	3.7
4 years	7,388	1.5

Sources: *U.S. Census, 1960;* and U.S. Department of Labor.

Education alone does not create jobs. It can, however, help cut unemployment by enhancing the matchability of labor-force skills with employer needs. When the task is attaining and maintaining full employment, education is not an adequate substitute for effective government fiscal and monetary policies and high levels of consumer and business demand. However, it is a valuable complement. Let us not expect too much from education, particularly in the short run. Its economic value lies primarily in its contribution to individuals' productive *potential,* rather than in its contribution to the economy's success in achieving that potential.

Having digressed to point up the dangers of over-stating gross economic benefits from education, let me also note that there are important costs as well as benefits of education to students and their families. Costs include more than cash payments. They also include the earnings and production *foregone* because potentially productive people are in school (or in the hospital or physician's office in the case of investments in health), instead of on the job. In fact, a recent estimate for the United States indicates that the costs of high school and college education in the form of foregone income exceed by more than 50 percent the costs incurred directly by the schools.[9]

TABLE 3

Income and Unemployment by Level of Education in Canada

Level of Educational Attainment	Income Distribution 1959				Unemployment Rate February 1960 (percent)
	Under $3,000	$3,000- 5,000	$5,000- 10,000	$10,000 & over	
Did not finish primary school	43	33	22	2	18.7
Finished primary but not secondary school	24	34	37	5	8.0
Finished secondary school or better	20	23	42	15	2.7

Source: Dominion Bureau of Statistics.

Still, when *all* costs are considered, and when an allowance is made for the non-educational factors affecting schooling, our best available evidence for the United States is that formal education does pay in the direct form of enhanced employment opportunities and, thus, of greater incomes. Education is an investment which produces at least as great a financial return as does investment in corporate enterprise—around 10 percent for college, and even more for high school and elementary school.[10]

But the profitability of education does not rest alone on its productivity-increasing or money-income-increasing effects. Some of the value of education accrues to the individual in other forms. The fruits of literacy—an output of elementary education—include the value of its non-market use. Thus, to cite an illustration which closely touches many of us, if a man prepares his own income tax return, he performs a service made possible by his literacy. Were this service provided through the market, it would be priced and included in national income. Assuming that 50 million of the 60 million personal income tax returns being filed each year in the United States are prepared by the taxpayer himself, at a value of $5 per return, a rough estimate of the annual market value of the tax return services performed by taxpayers for themselves is $250 million. Obviously, this is only one minor form of return from literacy. But it is in addition to the benefits from elementary education which accrue in money form.

Social Benefits from Education

If students were the only beneficiaries of schooling, the broad public support for education would probably wither. But as valuable as education is privately, it is even more valuable publicly. Its benefits take diverse forms which extend well beyond the individuals who receive it.

For one thing, education has an important intergenerational value.[11] When today's students reach adulthood, their children will gain by virtue of the informal education received at home. Much learning takes place at home, where the child's attitude toward school is also largely shaped. Better educated parents are more likely to raise children who recognize the value of education, in terms of job opportunities, as well as in terms of cultural opportunities.

This means that the social value of educating women is not zero, even if they never enter the labor force to utilize the skills developed in school. It is a mistake to say that education has value to society only when additional earnings and *marketable* production result. If we think of an "investment" as involving future as distinguished from current returns, then education has an investment component in the form of these intergeneration benefits.[12]

Another group of beneficaries from education is employers, who have a financial interest in the education and training of their employees. An employer's job would be much more difficult and expensive if he had to work with an illiterate and untrained labor force or had to educate and train his own workers.

Education also affects taxpayers in general, who pay—directly or indirectly—for the consequences of the lack of education. For example, insofar as lack of education leads to employment difficulties and crime, the costs of crime prevention, law enforcement, and social unrest—with the related welfare costs—will tend to be high.

These costs, however, may not fall upon taxpayers in the community or area having responsibility for the child's education. The migration of poorly educated people whose behavior patterns and educational attainments differ greatly from those prevailing in the areas they migrate to may necessitate additional effort and expense to permit the migrants to adjust to the new school conditions,[13] if they are children, or to the new social and economic conditions, if they are adults. Thus, *residents of areas of in-migration have a stake in the education of children in the areas of out-migration.* People in the U.S. North have a stake in education in the South. People in Ontario and British Columbia have a stake in education in the maritime provinces. In general, people who are or may be in the same fiscal unit with an individual have a financial stake in the investment in his human capital.

The nation as a whole reaps a return from education through the process of economic growth. In an important study of *The Sources of Economic Growth in the United States,* Edward Denison estimated that 21 percent of the growth of real national income per person employed between 1929 and 1957 was attributable to the greater education of the labor force, while another 36 percent was attributable to the "advance of knowledge," much of which is associated with educational advance.

Broad social benefits.

We have seen that some of the social benefits from education are enjoyed by individuals and groups that are reasonably identifiable. But some of the benefits are distributed so broadly that the nature of specific beneficiaries is obscure. These general social benefits are not less important by virute of their pervasiveness.

For example, literacy is of value not only to the individual possessing it and to employers, but to the entire society. Without widespread literacy, the significance of books, newspapers, and similar information media would dwindle; and it seems fair to say that the communication of information is of vital importance to the maintenance of competition and, indeed, to the existence of a market economy, as well as to the maintenance of political democracy.

Education is, after all, much more than a means of raising productivity or otherwise bringing financial returns. It is also a means of inculcating children with standards of socially desirable attitudes and behavior and of introducing children to new opportunities and challenges. In a free society, it helps to develop greater awareness of, and ability to participate effectively in, the democratic process.

No statistics can be marshalled to "prove" that education itself brings about a stronger democracy, but the relationships between people's educational attainments and their participation in activities that help make a democracy strong are striking. For one thing, education appears to develop in people a sense of citizen duty. Measuring attitudes toward the importance of voting on a five-level scale,[14] interviewers from the Survey Research Center of the University of Michigan found that only 25 percent of the grade school graduates were classified in the top level, while 50 percent of the high school graduates and 60 percent of the college graduates achieved it. None of the college graduates was in the bottom level, though 2 percent of the high school graduates and 12 percent of the grade school graduates were.[15] Similarly, favorable effects of education have been found in its relationship with the degree of political participation. Moreover, as Table 4 shows, the percentage of persons who actually do vote increases with educational attainment.

TABLE 4

Percentage of the Population Voting for President of the United States in the 1952 and 1956 Elections, by Age, Education, Sex, and Region

	Non-South			South		
Age and Sex	Grade School	High School	College	Grade School	High School	College
Less than 34						
Male	60% (52)	78% (175)	88% (81)	19% (32)	55% (69)	81% (32)
Female	44 (55)	73 (285)	90 (90)	13 (47)	41 (111)	74 (23)
34-54						
Male	80 (156)	87 (222)	96 (103)	55 (87)	80 (54)	88 (33)
Female	71 (170)	85 (312)	91 (85)	22 (97)	56 (86)	82 (38)
55 and over						
Male	87 (179)	93 (96)	100 (31)	63 (72)	71 (21)	82 (11)
Female	71 (173)	91 (126)	93 (30)	31 (75)	58 (33)	86 (22)

Note: Sample sizes are in parentheses.

Source: A. Campbell, W. Miller, P. Converse, and D. Stokes, *The American Voter* (New York: John Wiley, 1960), Table 17-11, p. 495. See also Table 17-2, p. 478.

A positive relationship between voter participation and education was also found in my own analysis.[16] Data on voter participation in the 1952 presidential election for each of the 48 states were correlated with (1) the median years of education of the population 25 years of age and older, for 1950, and (2) the percentage of the state population which was urban. The latter variable was included to isolate the presumably greater difficulty of voting in rural areas. The results indicated that schooling explained 42 percent of the interstate variation in voter participation. And when the percentage of population urbanized was held constant, it was found that 61 percent of the interstate variance not explained by urbanization was explained by schooling.

The brevity of this discussion does an injustice to the important and sometimes subtle ways that education strengthens democratic institutions. No attempt has been made here to be thorough in an area where economists probably have little to contribute. Instead, the objective has been simply to recognize the fact that some—and possibly the most important—forms of social benefits from education may defy monetary valuation.

Recapitulation.

We have found that the social benefits from education take many forms and accrue widely through time and space. Some of the benefits from education—and much of what has been said about education also applies to health and other forms of human investments —are not realized by people in the area which financed the investment. Because the location of gains from some human-resource investments are determined by population movement, the process of migration is a process of spatial shifting of those gains. This produces not only an interstate or interprovincial stake in effective policies of human-resource development, but an international stake as well.

The diversity and complex diffusion of benefits from investments in human capital raise important issues as to how education should be financed and what role government should play generally in the development of human resources.

IV. PUBLIC POLICY FOR EDUCATIONAL INVESTMENT IN HUMAN CAPITAL

The education system produces many forms of benefits. Some interesting issues arise, once we recognize that there are external benefits from education (and better health)—benefits to people other than the immediate recipients. For one principle of financing expenditures is that those who benefit from some expenditure should pay for it. Even a partial use of this taxation principle would call for attempts to identify various groups of dir88ect and indirect beneficiaries from investments in human capital and to assess charges in recognition of the distribution of benefits. I do not mean to suggest that the benefit principle should necessarily prevail in financing investments in human capital. However, since many benefits from education are very broadly dispersed, the application of this principle would, in fact, require broad financial support for education and other such investments.

This paper has underscored the need for social recognition of the process of human-resource investment. The previous pages have developed the views that education and health are not merely consumer-type expenditures, but are investments in human-resource productivity; and that benefits from these investments do not merely accrue just to the persons in whom they are made, but extend to other persons as well. Now it is appropriate to focus attention on the responsibility of government in this area.

To begin with, there would be a significant role for government in the human resource field, even if there were no external benefits —even if all benefits accrued to the individual. One reason is that, with particular respect to education, important decisions are made by young people, who may be poor judges of their long-term interests. Dropping out of high school may seem wise to a youth impatient to increase his earnings, but the wisdom of the decision becomes less obvious with the passage of time.

Of course, additional schooling is of value only to those who have the requisite ability and attitude toward learning. There may be little that society can do about a student's ability, but it may be able to shape his attitude toward schooling. This is the goal of many contemporary programs to prevent high school dropouts, in which well-trained guidance counselors can play an especially vital role. And *government has a responsibility to see that, through counselors and otherwise, people are fully informed about the long-run benefits from education, health, and other forms of investments in people.*

A second reason for public concern about the adequacy of private investment in human resources involves the ability of individuals to finance these investments. In education, a proper student attitude and the necessary intellectual ability are not sufficient; financial ability is also required. The costs of obtaining adequate education and health rations their use among low-income families. With respect to schooling, this would be true even if education, from elementary school through university, were "free." As noted above, much of the real cost of schooling is not the out-of-pocket expense, but the income lost by the student. In a poor family, the immediate pressure upon the youngster to augment family income —foregoing investments in his own human capital, if need be—may be enormous.

To some extent, the financial hurdles to private investments in human capital by low-income persons can be overcome by borrowing. But one should not forget the real obstacles to obtaining a loan for educational purposes through the private market. The capital market conventionally provides loans for the purchases of tangible assets which, if necessary, can be taken over by the lender. Loans for education and for other forms of investment in human capital have a special characteristic. The fruits they produce are intangible —they are embodied in people. Therefore, the asset cannot be

attached by an unsatisfied lender. This fact limits the availability of
private loans for financing education or other human capital investments. *Government can help to overcome limitations in the private
capital market through programs of direct aid, loans, and guarantees
of private loans to facilitate investment in people.*

But government responsibility surpasses the need to improve
capital markets and provide counseling. It must help the nation to
recognize that the benefits to *society as a whole* which result from
investment in human resources exceed the direct benefits to the
individual in whom the investment is made. It must help the nation
to recognize that a society bent on economic growth—on raising
living standards and erasing poverty—is a society committed to
change; and change requires a creative, adaptable, and efficient
labor force capable of creating innovations and adjusting to new,
often unforseen, skill requirements. A rigid labor supply is a formidable obstacle to change.

Education can contribute mightily to economic growth by meeting the needs for flexibility and adaptability. But this implies a
greater emphasis on the teaching of *basic* techniques and concepts
and on the postponement of a student's specialization until late in
the educational process. It also implies that the distinction between
"vocational" and "general" education may in reality be a great deal
more fuzzy than conventional usage suggests. In a world of changing technology and skill requirements, the training that appears to
be "general" today may be extremely and directly useful in the
world of work tomorrow. Similarly, education that appears today to
be of direct vocational value may not only be obsolete later, but its
narrowness may intensify the difficulties of adjusting to future manpower demands.

In recognition of the broad social and economic interest in investment in human capital, particularly through education and
health, *it is appropriate and desirable for government policy to encourage individuals to invest more in themselves than they otherwise
would, and perhaps in somewhat different ways.* For example, a
teen-ager may prefer not to continue in school or take certain
health measures, but the rest of society may prefer that he does,
since, as we have seen, it will suffer in many ways if his education,
training, and health are not satisfactory.

Today, tax laws provide greater incentives for investment in
physical assets than for investments in human capital, because the
former are more generally depreciable as a business expense than
are the latter. *Reconsideration of tax policy so as to redress the imbalance is warranted.* Similarly, the tradition that the cost of a

school building or a hospital is a "capital" cost—which can "appropriately" be financed by borrowing—while the cost of salaries for the teachers or medical personnel in that structure is a non-capital expenditure, leads to an unfortunate emphasis on *con*struction relative to *in*struction in the school and elaborate equipment relative to additional personnel in hospitals. Education and health expenditures other than on buildings and equipment also represent investments—less tangible but no less real than the investments in classrooms. *Government should recognize by its words and deeds the breadth of the investment concept and should help lower-level governments and private decision-makers to recognize it also.*

V. CONCLUSION

Some readers may feel that health and education policies are moral issues that should not be subjected to the cold scrutiny of an economist. But surely one need not choose between an economist's view and a philosopher's view of wise public health and education policies. Both are relevant. Indeed, the discussion above has pointed to a number of important though unquantifiable benefits from investing in people. Returns in the form of enhanced productivity are relevant for wise policy-making. But so are non-economic considerations.

Actions taken by society directly influence the creation and the maintenance of human-capital values. Expenditures for education, training, health, and migration may contribute to the value of our human resources. Expenditures on the detection, treatment, and the prevention of accidents and floods and on the provision of adequate housing and diets—all these preserve and enhance the values of our human resources, just as do maintenance and improvement expenditures on physical capital.

Investments in human resources are not alone sufficient to insure rapid economic growth, let alone an effective democracy or a problem-free society. But it now appears that, as a society, we are paying too little attention to our enormously valuable stock of human capital, while we focus great attention on conventional investment. Health and education programs are primary devices for raising productivity and speeding social progress. Government has a critical role to play in promoting an effective human-resource-development program. The challenge is there to be seized.

NOTES

[1] *Economics of Public Health* (Philadelphia: University of Pennsylvania Press, 1961), p. 84.

[2] *Ibid.,* p. 83.

[3] U.S. Department of Labor, "Educational Attainment of Workers, March 1962," Special Labor Force Report No. 30 (1963), p. A-5.

[4] *Statistical Review of Canadian Education, Census* (1951), p. 69.

[5] Estimated from data in the *1961 Census of Canada, Labour Force,* Bulletin 3.1-13, pp. 19-1, 2.

[6] *The Role of the Federal Government in Financing Higher Education* (Washington: Brookings Institution, 1961).

[7] U.S. Department of Health, Education, and Welfare, *Health, Education, and Welfare Trends, 1963* (Washington: GPO, 1963), p. 60.

[8] T. W. Schultz, "Capital Formation by Education," *Journal of Political Economy,* LXVIII (December 1960), 583.

[9] *Ibid.,* p. 580.

[10] Estimates by G. S. Becker, as reported in T. W. Schultz, "Education and Economic Growth," in *Social Forces Influencing American Education* (Chicago: National Society for the Study of Education, 1961), p. 78. See also G. S. Becker, *Human Capital* (New York: National Bureau of Economic Research, 1964).

[11] W. J. Swift and B. A. Weisbrod, "On the Monetary Value of Education's Intergeneration Benefits," *Journal of Political Economy,* LXXIII (December 1965), 643-49.

[12] Tax implications of the existence of intertemporal education returns have been discussed by R. Goode, "Educational Expenditures and the Income Tax," in S. J. Mushkin, ed., *Economics of Higher Education* (Washington: GPO, 1962).

[13] See, for example, C. F. Schmid, V. A. Miller, and B. Abu-Laban, "Impact of Recent Negro Migration on Seattle Schools," in *International Population Conference Papers* (Vienna: Union International pour l'étude scientifique de la population, 1959), pp. 674-83.

[14] V. O. Key, Jr., *Public Opinion and American Democracy* (New York: Knopf, 1961), pp. 324-25; Angus Campbell, Gerald Gurin, and Warren Miller, *The Voter Decides* (White Plains: Row, Peterson, 1954), pp. 194-99.

[15] Key, *op. cit.,* Table 13.3, p. 325. These data were compiled from Survey Research Center studies in 1952 and 1956. See Campbell *et al., op. cit.,* Table B.2, p. 197; and A. Campbell, W. Miller, P. Converse, and D. Stokes, *The American Voter* (New York: John Wiley, 1960), Table 17-5, p. 480.

[16] *External Benefits of Public Education* (Princeton: Princeton University, Industrial Relations Section, 1964), pp. 96, 98.

SUGGESTIONS FOR FURTHER READING—PART I

Becker, Gary S. "Investment in Human Capital: A Theoretical Analysis." *Journal of Political Economy,* Vol. 70, No. 5, Part 2 (Supplement: October 1962), pp. 9-49.

Colberg, Marshal R. *Human Capital In Southern Development, 1939-1963.* Chapel Hill: University of North Carolina Press, 1965.

Denison, Edward F. *The Sources of Economic Growth in the United States and the Alternatives Before Us.* (Supplementary Paper No. 13). New York: Committee for Economic Development, 1962.

Eckaus, R. S. "Investment in Human Capital." *Journal of Political Economy,* Vol. 71 (October 1963), pp. 501-504.

Mincer, Jacob. " Investment in Human Capital and Personal Income Distribution." *Journal of Political Economy,* Vol. 70, No. 5, Part 2 (Supplement: October 1962), pp. 50-79.

Platt, W. J. "Economic Value of Education." *Journal of Secondary Education,* Vol. 38 (October 1963), pp. 39-46.

Schultz, Theodore W. "Education and Economic Growth." In Nelson B. Henry, ed., *Social Forces Influencing American Education.* Chicago: University of Chicago Press, 1961, pp. 46-88.

Schultz, Theodore W. "Investing in Poor People: An Economist's View." *American Economic Review,* Vol. 55, No. 2 (March 1965), pp. 510-520.

Schultz, Theodore W. "Reflections on Investment in Man." *Journal of Political Economy,* Vol. 70, No. 5, Part 2 (Supplement: October 1962), pp. 1-8.

Weisbrod, Burton A. "Education and Investment in Human Capital." *Journal of Political Economy,* Vol. 70, No. 5, Part 2 (Supplement: October 1962), pp. 106-123.

Part II

Educational Expenditures and Worker Productivity

4

SOCIAL AND ECONOMIC FACTORS IN SPENDING FOR PUBLIC EDUCATION

by Jerry Miner

In his monograph, Miner concentrates on factors that influence expenditures by local public school systems. He strongly recommends a more active role by the Federal government to equalize expenditures between localities and states with vastly different financial capabilities. In addition, he discusses specific policy parameters, including further consolidation of school districts, reforms in property taxes, and changes in state grant-in-aid formulas for local school districts.

This monograph is an economic analysis of factors that influence expenditures by local public school systems from the point of view of both normative and positive economic approaches to individual and organizational behavior. Normative aspects of educational spending constitute the subject matter of the chapter that deals with criteria for economically optimum levels of spending in the context of a consumer directed economy. The positive side was examined in the discussion of empirical studies of the factors associated with public school spending and in the description and

Reprinted from *Social and Economic Factors in Spending for Public Education* by Jerry Miner, pp. 139-152 *(The Economics and Politics of Public Education,* 11). Copyright © 1963 by Syracuse University Press, Syracuse, New York. Reprinted by permission of the publisher.

analysis of expenditures in a nationwide sample of local school systems. The normative analysis produces guidelines for the evaluation of expenditures for public schools, while the positive analysis indicates the extent to which actual spending conforms to normative standards and suggests some of the implications of economic, demographic, and social changes for future outlays for local public schools.

ACTUAL AND OPTIMUM PUBLIC EXPENDITURES FOR EDUCATION

Optimum Expenditures

A most important factor in the determination of optimum levels of educational expenditures is the widespread social and economic benefit from education which makes public rather than private finance of education essential. In addition, proper decisions about educational expenditures require that the total of all benefits be taken into account, and as a consequence, a pattern of solely local public finance will fail to register the global nature of the consequences of education in an interdependent market economy with a geographically mobile population.

Another crucial aspect is that the function of education in promoting social mobility and providing for equality of economic opportunity requires that educational attainment be divorced, substantially, from the individual family's capacity to pay and from its social position. To achieve desired ends with regard to opportunity it is often necessary for public decisions to countervene rather than conform to the preferences of parents in the provision of education. At the same time, in a society in which individual preferences are believed to be of great importance in social and economic decisions, the desires of individuals must be reflected in the amount and character of the educational services provided. There is no contradiction here if individual preferences are manifested through democratic political processes which lead to a solution based on consensus rather than through economic processes where the solution is based on an equilibrium for each participant or every family unit.

The nature of education as an economic good makes it difficult to fulfill the requisites of a social or even of an economic optimum. The indivisible character of the benefits of education, the impossibility of the exclusion of nonstudents from sizable gains from educational expenditures, and the desire to use education to break the cycle of poverty and lack of motivation among certain low-income groups would rule out the achievement of an optimum through the market principle, even if education were to be sold at prices which were adjusted for divergences between social and private elements. Provision and finance of education, thus, falls under the budget principle. However, . . . the inability to ascertain individual preferences by political rather than market arrangements and problems of weighting preferences of different persons even if known, makes it impossible to achieve an economic optimum through the budget principle.

In the practice of public finance, taxation of individuals must be based on broad general principles and not on the basis of an exact determination of benefits received from such services as education. Expenditures have to be determined by political consensus and not by a summation of individual demands at given prices in terms of tax payments. Under these circumstances the crucial requisite for the approximation of the optimum in actual expenditures is a political process through which an accurate evaluation can be made of the claims for resources for education in comparison with the claims for other public services. Taxation can then be based on criteria which roughly estimate benefits received after allowance has been made for income redistribution in accordance with the community's view of distributional justice.

The Organization of Education and the Principles of Optimization

The administration of public elementary and secondary education by local governments is an arrangement intended to combine public finance with the greatest responsiveness to individual preferences. At the same time, state contributions to local school revenues serve to reflect the wide geographic scope of the benefits of education. When state aid regulations lead to equalization of expenditures in terms of costs or ability to pay in local school systems, the additional objective of equality of educational opportunity is furthered. Thus, in the context of the present organization of education in the United States, decisions about expenditures can reflect individual preferences, take account of geographic and individual spillover effects, and equalize educational opportunities.

All school systems, however, do not or cannot make use of arrangements conducive to the achievement of optimum levels of expenditures. Some states have statewide school systems or such narrowly defined standards for local schools that preferences within the community have little effect on the character of local education. In other states local sources of finance predominate, so that there is no provision for geographical spillover benefits. Finally, where state aid to local schools is minuscule, or where states grant aid on the basis of local performance rather than on needs or resources, no equalization occurs. Thus, while the general framework for educational organization in the United States permits the application of certain principles of optimization, these methods are not always utilized.

Even when advantage is taken of the opportunities for approaching an optimum within the arrangements for public education that prevail in the United States, there are no direct provisions to take account of interstate spillovers, inequality of incomes among states, and the need for joint consideration of education and the full range of public needs and resources. Federal policies in noneducational areas may, however, indirectly achieve some of these effects.

Federal participation in the finance of local schools is the obvious remedy to the national spillovers of benefits and the inequality of ability to pay for education among states. Only at the federal level can action be taken to provide funds and to distribute the cost of education so that states with lower incomes can provide educational services of a scope and quality similar to those of wealthier states. Complete equalization may not be desirable or even desired, but whatever the extent of interstate educational equalization, only the federal government can accomplish the task. With regard to spillover effects through migration or market transactions, again it is the federal government which is in a position to register demands from and costs to areas outside the state.

Apart from issues of the separation of church and state, the fundamental problem in federal financial participation in local school affairs is the retention of a role for the preferences of persons in local communities. It is naive to insist that federal funds can be provided without any federal control over their use. Yet the view that federal intrusion into local school affairs means surrender of local prerogatives ignores the extent of local autonomy now retained in such programs as public welfare, urban renewal, and public housing where a common complaint is the lack of federal supervision over its own programs. A well-educated population is now a national responsibility; in the highly interdependent society of the United States in this second half of the twentieth century, low rates of economic growth, an ill-informed and irrational electorate, and a lack of trained manpower to achieve broad social and political goals are no longer local but national problems. The rationale for federal participation in local school finances is clear, and it is time to begin to test a program for federal assistance to local elementary and secondary education that leaves adequate leeway for local discretion. The initial plan should be evaluated periodically and modifications adopted as needed, but surely the skills of those familiar with the practice of a federal form of government can rise to this challenge.

The role of the federal government is only one aspect of the problem of optimum levels of educational outlays in the context of alternative public and private expenditures. An evaluation of relevant alternatives is impossible under governmental arrangements that compartmentalize decisions about expenditures for various public programs. A solution to this aspect of the organization of education requires multifunction governmental units with sufficient geographic extent to encompass the major benefits and costs of the functions they administer. But, various public functions have differential spatial impacts, and, if all projects are to be compared, the role for local decision making is virtually eliminated. The problem of the size, functional duties, and taxing powers for various units of government is an issue in the forefront of the theory and practice of public policy in the United States. The concern among public finance economists and political scientists is that most units of local government are too small, and the proliferation of governments with responsibility for special functions such as education, water, and sewage disposal is not likely to promote rational solutions to pressing problems. The remedy most often proposed is increased state participation in these functions combined with consolidation whenever possible and the creation of interstate compacts for problems which transcend state boundaries.[1] To this must be added a role for the federal government if, as is true for education, the function has broad national implications.

Two major lines for improvement emerge from a consideration of each of the important shortcomings of the existing organization of education in the United States. One is the introduction of the federal government into local school finance. Here the task for administrators is the creation of arrangements that will permit federal grants for local education based on national requirements for an educated and skilled citizenry which do not at the same time excessively hamper local prerogatives. The second is the adoption in all states of education laws that take account of statewide geographic spillover effects and at the same time provide a considerable measure of equalization among school systems.

DETERMINANTS OF EXPENDITURES AND CONDITIONS FOR AN OPTIMUM

Local Preferences

A major purpose of local administration of education in the United States is to give an opportunity for the preferences of residents to influence expenditures for education. Direct measures of preferences for education are not readily available, but characteristics of the population such as years of education, per cent of children in nonpublic schools, per cent non-white, and per cent moved into district in last five years are factors that may be closely associated with preferences.

The results of various analyses show that none of these measures exerts a strong effect on the expenditures of individual school systems. Most of the studies reported . . . do not include elements that reflect preferences, although one study found that in states with higher proportions of non-whites and of pupils attending private schools ratios of expenditures to incomes are lower. Although preferences of residents of local communities may shape the general character of the educational system, and determine the allocation of expenditures within the school system, there is little evidence that under present arrangements total expenditure levels vary in accordance with certain obvious measures of local attitudes toward schooling when other relevant factors are taken into account.

Equalization

A major conclusion from the empirical study reported here is that systems for state aid achieve considerable equalization within states. It is probable that equalization is the opposite side of the coin from the failure to find local preferences important in the explanation of expenditures. Despite arguments to the contrary, it appears that state regulations which foster equalization cannot help but reduce the role of local preferences in the determination of expenditures. Differences in total expenditures within states result largely from variations in the proportions of pupils, in costs, and in the extent of auxiliary services. These factors, for the most part, constitute the basis for state aid grants to equalize local burdens. In the process, the effects of factors that reflect local preferences seem to be virtually obliterated.

Perhaps a more direct approach by means of questionnaire surveys on attitudes toward public education would uncover more of an association between preferences and expenditures. However, if state aid measures that promote equalization inhibit the effectuation of local preferences, more refined measurements will not succeed in demonstrating a relationship that does not exist. The effects of local preferences, under these circumstances, may be noted only by examining, as the dependent variable, the composition of the educational services provided.

One apparent exception to equalization within states is the persistently lower total expenditure of dependent school systems. . . . [The] effect of state aid provisions appears to be a major determinant of these lower levels of spending.

The emphasis on equalization within states fails to bridge the gap between states with widely divergent per capita personal incomes and educational needs and costs. If equalization is to mean provision of an adequate minimum level of real school services regardless of local ability, needs, or costs, many states require financial assistance from outside sources. Federal grants-in-aid are the only means for transfers of the size necessary. On the other hand, if equalization is to mean the provision of equal public services throughout the country for equal tax burdens, then a federal program of educational grants weighted in favor of low-income states runs counter to equalization. There are many facets to the conflict between spatial equity in the sense of equal public services for equal tax payments and equity in the distribution sense. However, at bottom, the resolution of this conflict requires a decision: is public finance to be viewed solely as a substitute mechanism for the market and is it to stimulate, as far as possible, its results, or is public finance a political mechanism responsive to both political and market forces? Equalization among states is acceptable under the latter concept. It violates the market approach, however, and because it is not economically neutral it leads to such adjustments as migration to areas where a given level of public services costs less in taxes. The choice between distributional equity and economic neutrality cannot be resolved on analytic grounds; it is a question of social values.

External Effects

A finding that state action raises total expenditures to a level above that which would prevail if local factors alone determined outlays is evidence that external benefits of local education receive consideration. There is, unfortunately, no way to determine the level of educational spending in the absence of state regulation, but variables that deal with state aid can provide some indication of the effect of state participation in local school finances. According to this study, a larger fraction of public school revenues collected by the state is associated with higher levels of total per capita expenditures and lower levels of local per pupil and per capita outlays. It has little effect on per pupil spending. The variables for equalization and general-purpose aid are intended to gauge the effects of different types of state aid, and so do not indicate whether, in general, state aid has a positive or negative influence on expenditures.

Studies reported . . . show the positive effect of intergovernmental revenue in city and state expenditures and support the conclusion that state participation in local school finance does raise total expenditures. Further, the strong positive effect reported here of statewide personal income on expenditures, in contrast to the weak association of local incomes, may be interpreted as evidence that in the absence of state action total expenditures would be considerably lower. On the other hand, it is also possible to conclude that in the absence of state action the positive effect of local incomes would be considerably greater.

The use of revenues from state sources for local education is strong evidence of a wide dispersal of the costs of local education. Still, it is necessary to compare the geographical and personal incidence of state and local taxation before concluding that geographical and personal spillovers have been taken into account by the tax structure. It can be argued, however, that state taxes generally are not returned dollar for dollar to the areas from which they are collected and usually encompass a wider range of taxpayers than does the property tax. Thus, since state taxation provides a substantial portion of revenues for local schools, there is a tendency for the costs of education to be spread among all the residents of a state and not only among those living within the boundaries of the school system.

Although state grants-in-aid and state taxation take account of certain external effects, there is little doubt that without a mechanism for the reflection of national benefits there is a substantial understatement of the external benefits of education and a consequent failure to reach optimum levels of expenditures for local schools.

THE FUTURE: EVENTS AND POLICY

The use of empirical studies such as those described in this monograph to anticipate future levels of educational expenditures is subject to a number of difficulties. First of all, it is necessary to select key independent factors and to determine their relationship, over time, to current expenditures for local schools. The studies reveal a good deal about these key factors, but cross-section relationships often do not show the effects of temporal changes, and relationships found for one period or at one point cannot be expected to remain unchanged as time passes. Secondly, forecasting requires assumptions about future values of the independent variables, and frequently these values cannot be predicted with accuracy.

In the discussion of future trends it is useful to distinguish those independent variables whose values can be influenced by public policy and those determined by forces outside the realm of choice. This distinction, of course, is not entirely determined by the nature of the variable, but also depends on the problem under study. For example, the age distribution of the population and per capita personal income are not policy or instrument variables for the study of local school spending, but there are situations in which these factors can be treated as capable of manipulation by policy measures. In the following brief discussion of the major factors likely to influence future current educational outlays in the United States, only intergovernmental grants, school system organization, and standards of school services are treated as instrument variables.

AUTONOMOUS OR NONPOLICY VARIABLES

Demographic Factors

The factor with the most clear-cut influence on future total spending for public education is the number of children enrolled in public schools. Public school enrollment is likely to grow at a rate slightly in excess of the rate of growth of the number of school-age children because both the proportion in nonpublic schools and the relative frequency of early school drop-outs show signs of falling. Per capita expenditures will rise if the proportion of school-age children increases, and evidence here indicates that per pupil expenditures will not be reduced. Further positive effects on both per capita and per pupil expenditures can be expected as the proportion of pupils in secondary grades grows. While there is no reason to expect an appreciable rise in the proportion of persons in the 14-18-year-old age group, it is probable that pressures for the completion of high school will increase considerably the proportion of pupils in secondary grades in certain less industrialized states.

Other demographic factors have been found important by some investigators. There is research to suggest that an increase in the proportion of non-whites in the population is accompanied by lower public outlays for education. However, the finding here is that when cost and demand factors are taken into account, it seems unlikely that the modest increase in the proportion of non-whites in the population that may occur in the future will lead to lower per capita or per pupil expenditures. On the contrary, it is quite possible that political factors may lead to a change in relationships so that areas which contain relatively large numbers of Negroes will receive increased grants-in-aid. This will bring larger expenditures for education, as part of a program to combat the high rates of delinquency and unemployment and the low wage levels now characteristic of many such areas.

Over-all density is bound to increase as population grows, but there is little evidence that spending for local public education will change as a consequence. The present study does not give any support to the view that increased density directly influences school outlays.

Two further demographic factors, years of education of adults and the proportion of families who have moved recently, were not found, in this study, to have a systematic influence on per capita or per pupil outlays in local school systems.

Income and Property

Apart from population characteristics, specific autonomous economic factors will shape future outlays for public education. The crucial elements here are the levels and distribution of income, and property valuations. Income and property values can be expected to increase during the next decade, but their rates of growth depend on a series of factors outside the control of local school governments.[2] Target rates of growth of GNP of of 4½ to 5 per cent appear out of reach, and a rate of growth of 3 to 3½ per cent may not even be attained in the next decade.

As is generally true of research findings in other areas of public and private spending, estimates of the effect of income on expenditures for public schools are lower for cross-section studies than for time-series analyses. Previous time-series studies estimate the income elasticity of educational spending at about one for the period from 1900 to 1958, with a somewhat higher figure for the postwar years. Other cross-section studies, and the research here, find the income elasticity of different aspects of educational expenditures generally below one. The results of time-series studies are more directly applicable to projections of future expenditures, but they suffer from a failure to take explicit account of changes in key factors such as state aid arrangements during the period under study. Certain of these changes were intended to increase the responsiveness of educational expenditures to income. To anticipate similar increases in expenditures from subsequent rises in income may lead to overestimates.

Unless there are continued changes in arrangements for grants-in-aid and given present-day pressures for improved services for a wide range of local and state government functions, it is unlikely that the responsiveness of educational expenditures to changes in income will exceed an elasticity of one. If, however, a considerable reduction in federal taxation is enacted as an antirecession or growth stimulation measure, state and local governments may find it possible to capture some of these funds for local school finance. Such a situation would produce a higher response of educational expenditures to future increases in income.

Much of what has been said for income also holds for property valuation. Previous research studies generally show close relationships among assessed valuations, family income, and educational spending. The analysis of those states with equalized property values included in this study shows that, with an occasional exception, this variable has the highest partial correlation with all four categories of expenditures.

The postwar growth in educational expenditures was heavily financed out of the property tax, but there is continued discontent with this form of taxation and resistance in many communities to further increases in property tax rates. Increases in per capita or per pupil expenditures attributable to property valuation probably will come from increases in new construction rather than from increased tax rates or assessments on existing property. Revenue from existing property may increase, but only enough to maintain current levels of per pupil outlays in the face of larger enrollments.

POLICY PARAMETERS

Of the major factors which influence expenditures for local public schools, state aid arrangements, size and autonomy of local school governments, and perhaps the scope and quality of school services are subject to the discretion of public officials.

Scope and Quality of Education

To the extent that the scope and quality of educational services are determined by demand and cost factors they are not subject to manipulation by local officials and are thus not a policy parameter. The initial view in this study was that these elements were determined by expenditures and not vice versa. However, the extremely

high partial correlations found for the number of auxiliary personnel per pupil indicate that this aspect of scope and quality has an
effect separate from conventional demand or cost factors. There is
evidence, therefore, that scope and quality are to some extent ex-
penditure-determining rather than expenditure-determined, and
thus constitute a policy variable.

An historical index of the number of principals, superintendents,
and consultants per 1,000 pupils shows a steady rise throughout the
twentieth century.[3] No doubt other measures of scope and quality
would reveal similar increases. The pressures for stronger public
school curricula probably will mount further in response to the
current emphasis on the importance of human resources for the
achievement of national economic and political goals. It is likely
that the states will raise standards of instruction and curricula either by legal imposition on local school systems or by persuasion
through the offers of matching grants, in accordance with techniques such as those now used by the federal government under
the National Defense Education Act.

Organization of School Districts

Consolidation of local school districts long has been proposed as
a cost-reducing measure. However, the continued failure to find
substantiation for the presence of economies of scale in education
makes it doubtful that future expenditures will be reduced by consolidation. Further, since 1942 the number of operating school systems has been reduced from over 100,000 to about 35,000, and
there are strong barriers to the consolidation of the remaining small
districts. Enlargement of the size of school systems may reduce
costs but at the same time be accompanied by an expansion and
improvement of educational services. The failure to find a negative
association between enrollment and expenditures per pupil is not
an argument against consolidation; it is, however, an indication that
future trends in consolidation are unlikely to lead to a reduction in
current outlays per pupil.

Greater autonomy for local school systems in taxation and expenditures has been a rallying cry for educational administrators who
wish to raise outlays. Simple tabulations have shown that expenditures per pupil tend to be higher in independent school systems
and the findings here assign a negative coefficient of dependent
status in a multivariate analysis. Historically the proportion of pupils
in independent school systems has been rising slightly as a consequence of the movement to the suburbs of families with school-age
children. At the same time, in a few states the taxing powers of

local school districts have been somewhat broadened. It is doubtful that a policy-determined shift in the status of present dependent systems would, in and of itself, raise expenditures. The dependent systems are mostly in large cities which face high levels of needs and costs for the entire range of locally provided public services. A shift in status would not eliminate these conditions, but might change state aid distributions so that school systems located in metropolitan areas would receive more aid, and other systems less.

Property Tax Reforms

There are two policy measures that center on taxation. These could provide a substantial once-and-for-all increase in revenues for local school systems and could, therefore, also increase their outlays. One is the reform of tax assessment procedures so that property valuations for tax purposes are more closely related to market values. For a substantial effect such reform must be accompanied by higher over-all effective property tax rates, but removal of the considerable injustices that now characterize assessment procedures in most states might improve the climate for tax rate increases.

A second important reform would be to redefine school district boundaries so that no industrial enclaves and other business and commercial properties are sheltered from property taxation for local schools by specially drawn boundaries. The present tendency for tax concessions and special school district boundaries as an inducement to location of industry serves not only to widen the extent of such practices but also to prevent reform. At present there appear to be strong political resistances to reform of this sort; instead, state corporate income and other business taxes are used to obtain revenue from locally protected industries. Statewide taxes apply equally to all firms, but those sheltered from the local property tax continue to avoid paying their full share of local tax burdens.

Grants-in-Aid

Intergovernmental transfers are generally thought of as the instrument with the greatest potential for influencing educational policies. The analysis here does not include the amount of state aid as an independent variable, but does find that a higher proportion of revenue from state and federal sources has a positive influence on total per capita outlays and a strong negative effect on local expenditures.

To a considerable extent state aid is a substitute for local educational expenditures, and the receipt of state aid for local schools permits the use of local tax revenues for other public functions, such as police and fire protection, which are generally less strongly supported by state grants-in-aid. Thus, to raise per capita or per pupil educational outlays through state aid may require an increase in grants by as much as five dollars per pupil to raise total spending per pupil by one dollar. The consequences of efforts to raise per pupil spending through such an expansion of state aid might be desirable because of the improvement in other public services which would be the beneficiaries of reduced pressures on local revenues for funds for education.

This indirect approach, however, is not an efficient solution to the general problem of local government finance. Intergovernmental grants should be based on costs, needs, and ability to pay for all local government functions, not only for education. State aid as a policy parameter for education should be viewed in the broad context of the finance of all local government functions and not as a matter of trying to get as much as possible for education without regard for other public functions. Acceptance of this principle implies recognition of the need for extensive revision of existing state aid statutes throughout the nation with a view to the integration of grants-in-aid for education with grants for other local public services.

Consideration of the amount of state aid as a policy or instrument variable is not without objection. . . . [Under] a given set of state aid arrangements, historical changes in levels of state grants-in-aid are very closely tied to changes in state per capita personal income. Thus, unless state aid statutes are substantially revised, changes in levels of income are likely to determine, within fairly narrow limits, future levels of intergovernmental grants. Intergovernmental revenues as a proportion of total revenues for local schools are, on the other hand, more a matter of policy, but apparently this fraction does not influence total per pupil outlays.

There is a paradox that emerges from this investigation of policy variables to influence expenditures for local public schools. Those variables whose effects are known, such as population growth, percentage of pupils in high school, state per capita personal income, and even level of state aid per pupil, are not subject to manipulation through policy decisions. The major instrumental variable, alternative state aid arrangements, however, is the factor about whose effects least is known.

NOTES

[1]For a more optimistic view of the capacity of local government to resolve these problems, see Vincent Ostrom, Charles M. Tiebout, and Robert Warren, "The Organization of Government in Metropolitan Areas," LV *American Political Science Review* (December 1961), 831-42.

[2]A portion of future increases in national income and in the family incomes of residents of local communities can be attributed to present-day educational outlays, but it is certainly not possible to argue that local school officials can determine future levels of educational spending by current educational policies aimed at raising income and wealth in the future.

[3]Werner Z. Hirsch, *Analysis of the Rising Costs of Public Education* (Washington: Joint Economic Committee, 1959), 29.

5

THE CONTRIBUTION OF EDUCATION TO ECONOMIC PRODUCTIVITY

by Charles S. Benson

Professor Benson discusses the practical difficulties involved in converting the theory of investment in human capital into measurable public programs with predictable outcomes. He lists a number of variables relating to changes in productivity over and above simple investment in additional years of education. He concludes that the case for increased and improved education is not susceptible to absolute scientific proof, but is better based on the general assumption that good schools are needed for a strong and viable national economy.

When economic growth comes to be accepted as a major concern of government, the public authority will seek to stimulate investment.[1] In this century, economists have seen investment in physical capital (land, structures, durable equipment, and commodity stocks) as the primary means of obtaining a greater volume of output in a society. The contribution of increased investment in human capital (knowledge, skills, attitudes, and other acquired traits that are important in production) to economic growth has been largely ig-

Reprinted from Charles S. Benson, *The Economics of Public Education.* Boston: Houghton Mifflin Company, 1961, pp. 344-350. A briefer version of this excerpt appears on pp. 44-47 of the second edition of this book (1968).

nored.[2] Several recent contributions to the literature have served to correct the imbalance, but only at a high level of abstraction.[3] Suppose that a country wishes to raise its growth rate from a figure of 3 per cent per year to one of 5 per cent (the figures are hypothetical, but let them refer to rate of change in GNP per capita in real terms). In pursuit of the goal, let the government undertake to raise the level of investment by $10 billion a year. (Either direct or indirect means, e.g., more favorable depreciation allowance on corporate tax, could be used.) Given the present characteristics of the productive system, the economist would argue that there is a certain ideal distribution of the $10 billion between increase in physical and increase in human capital. The ratio would not be fixed for all time, but at any one point of time there presumably is an optimum allocation of growth expenditures. However, what this division may be is simply unknown. Whereas the economist has become willing to say that additions to human capital have important effects in raising productivity and should not be ignored in government planning, he is as yet unable to say what degree of emphasis should be placed on the human, as distinct from the physical, factors.

It is universally agreed that education serves to increase the stock of human capital. To say that we cannot measure precisely the contribution of human capital to economic growth is to say that we cannot relate—except in general terms—expenditures on education to economic productivity. Why is this so?

First, it should now be clear to the reader that the information provided by the construction of a productivity index tells us very little about causal relationships in economic growth. An index provides a measure of the rate of past change; it does not reveal how to obtain a higher rate in the future.

Second, let us recognize in candor that many factors impinge on economic productivity. Some are subject only to qualitative assessment at this time. Moreover, the weights that should be assigned to any of the different factors have not yet been determined. Frederick C. Mills, a leading student of economic growth, lists the following factors as being closely related to change in productivity:

the quantity or quality of capital equipment used

the quality of effort input (This may be a change in intensity or a change in average degree of skill. Such a change in average skill may result from a change in the competence of individuals or groups or from a shift in the composition of the work force.)

the ratio of effort input to productive instruments used or to natural resources used (A change in average productivity resulting from the play of diminishing returns would be included in this category.)

the quality of natural resources or material used

the quantity of materials or intermediate products used to produce a standard unit of final product

the amount of non-human power used or the manner of its use

the organization of productive units

working conditions

the effectiveness of administration.[4]

Education affects, directly or indirectly, all of these factors, except possibly the quality of natural resources (and even here, since the exploitation of natural resources itself makes use of the findings of scientific research, one can postulate a connection). But to establish a given gain in productivity as flowing from a given change in educational expenditure is obviously difficult in view of the multifarious factors that impinge on economic growth and the uncertainties about the ways in which they react one upon another. One can, of course, claim all credit for education, i.e., one can be an "educational determinist," but then one will have to explain why the pace of economic advance has remained almost constant for seventy years, in the face of sharply advancing school expenditures.[5]

It might appear easier to relate an increase in quality of education to the rise in productivity in certain manufacturing industries. Historically, interest in productivity change has centered on the manufacturing sector of the economy. Improvements in manufacturing are based in part on advances in technology. Now, if it is true that all the simple inventions have been invented, and that the present-day inventor must have esoteric kinds of knowledge about his field, then it would seem to follow that the inventor's capacity is closely related to the educational advantages he has had. The economist would warn, however, that invention is only part of the process of technological advance. Unless the inventions are "put to work" in the factories, no economic advance occurs.[6] The process of applying inventions to actual work situations is called "innovation." The foremost student of the process of innovation, Joseph Schumpeter, held that this activity, like invention, is the individual performance of the gifted person. The prime characteristics of an innovator are stated to be single-mindedness, imagination, and courage. Schumpeter's major thesis was that the social climate in a capitalistic society gradually becomes less and less favorable for the potential innovator to perform his role.[7] The schools may be a part of such a development; e.g., if they succeed in helping students to become less self-centered, they may at the same time dampen the drive to do something new at whatever the cost.

Another point of contact between school programs and gains in manufacturing productivity is in the training of the work force. Higher skills mean higher output per man-hour, other things being equal. It is, however, not an easy task to relate with specificity the process of skill development of the work force to secondary school education. The basic reason for the difficulty is that, while high school courses represent the end of formal education for most workers, the main part of instruction in the skills of factory jobs occur during the period of employment and not before it. The question at issue is not whether the entrant to the work force has skills, but whether he is able to learn skills within the time and under the methods of instruction available in the plant. Now, the capacity of a new employee to learn certain skills *may* be appraised initially by a full-time personnel officer, but the major part of the training itself—and the judgment of the rate of progress—will be done by men who have strictly a part-time, and perhaps temporary, interest in instruction. The sequence in which the trainee acquires specific skills is different in each plant; and it may vary over time and from one worker to another at the same time in a given plant. The amount of time which a man is given to learn various techniques will depend in part on the short-term rate of growth of particular industries. Necessarily, the standards and methods of training are so diverse, even within one plant, that one cannot yet look for clear and detailed statements on what the schools are doing—or could do—to raise the capacity of the work force.[8]

We arrive at the conclusion that education must rest its case, not on carefully tested hypotheses with respect to the relation between schooling and economic productivity, but simply on the general assumption that quality programs in the schools represent an element of strength in the economy as it continues to search for gains in efficiency.

Such a conclusion does not destroy our statement at the beginning of this chapter that education occupies a strategic place in productivity advance. It means simply that educators, among others, must defend increases in school expenditures without relying on scientific evidence to relate a given amount of expenditure to a specific rate of productivity gain.

There are compelling reasons in terms of productivity for defending these increases. First, the investment cost of obtaining, say, a 5 per cent growth rate through increase in physical capital may be extremely high. It has been estimated that the ratio of savings to national income might have to be doubled or tripled. Such a tentative conclusion suggests that the country could well look to other possible sources of economic improvement to complement the gains that increase in physical capital may offer.[9]

At the same time, certain other tentative conclusions are strongly in favor in education. We mention two: the position of Professor Harold F. Clark and that of Professor Theodore Schultz. A recent statement of the Clark thesis is as follows:

Although . . . nations very greatly in their natural resources, climate and cultural heritage, the high correlation between literacy and per capita income indicates that education is a dominant factor in the economic well-being of any people.[10]

Professor Schultz, in dealing with that rather significant part of economic advance which cannot be accounted for in terms of increase in quantity of labor or in quantity of conventional types of capital goods available, is inclined to accept the hypothesis that the expenditure of resources on education, i.e., the creation of human capital, accounts for a substantial part of the "unexplained" economic growth.[11]

In the present condition of our economy, then, there is some cause to raise our estimate of the significance of education in the process of economic growth. But—and this is the second reason to support increases in school funds—education is subject on two counts to undervaluation. Because education is not property, it cannot be financed in large degree through the private capital market. In this market it stands in an inferior position as compared to physical capital.

The financing of additions to the stock of human capital usually falls largely to the state and the family. The main reason is that human capital, not being property, cannot be owned jointly by the person in whom it is embodied and others, and cannot serve as collateral for a loan.[12]

Next, education will be undervalued in terms of its contribution to economic growth because a large part of the effects of education are never counted in national product measurement. Education has effect on the performance of the work duties of housewives, but these duties are completely ignored in income measurement. Education has effects on the caliber of voluntary community activities: choral groups, drama clubs, local art shows, etc. Education has effects on other uses of leisure time as well, and, in the most complete sense, national income measurement should take account of the satisfactions that are derived from such use.

In terms of economic growth, the third reason to hope that education will have its staunch advocates has to do, once again, with scientific research. It has been stated that

Additions to knowledge are something that society has only just begun to realize that it can buy directly. In the past they have mainly been a by-product of the transmission of existing knowledge; only the innate and quite uneconomic intellectual curiosity of scholars has led to additions to knowledge, as new discoveries obviously tend to reduce the economic value of existing knowledge.[13]

Now, even if the new knowledge does not immediately pass beyond the stage of invention to innovation, it still represents opportunities that can be exploited when the society sees fit. A society, like an individual, is richer (in a real sense) as it comes to face a large number of attractive alternatives.

For these reasons, at least, the claims for education as an agent of productivity change should be made. On the other hand, Professor Renshaw has recently warned us how easy it is to claim too much for education.

. . . One should resist the temptation to attribute all gains in productivity to knowledge and, indirectly, to the formal education of persons who are innovators in the use of resources. In the main, the task of education below the graduate level is distributional. The efficiency of the educational system in distributing knowledge and information should be measured, therefore, on the basis of how well it performs its given tasks, not on the basis of the value of what it has to distribute to society. To make the point more clear it is quite obvious that one would not want to measure the efficiency of retail-trade establishments on the basis of the dollar volume of products sold, since profit margins may vary, as well as selling and other inputs per dollar of profit margin. The retail store with the highest dollar volume might, in fact, yield the smallest returns for each dollar employed or worker hired. It would likewise be unfair to attribute to teacher productivity the entire value of knowledge and information distributed, since other costs, as well as competing distributors, are involved . . . [14]

Under Renshaw's view the contribution of the schools is reduced to a rock bottom level. Elementary and secondary institutions are seen as being wholly concerned with the distribution of knowledge, not with its increase. Most school personnel probably hold that they help their students to develop the capacity to learn and, thus, that they help their students to develop the capacity to discover new things, eventually. Hence, school personnel could say that they offer an indirect contribution to the creation of knowledge. But it is well to note, as Renshaw does, that the instructional staffs in present employment should not attempt to take credit for the total benefits that knowledge brings us, since much of that knowledge is a heritage of the distant past.

NOTES

[1] "Economic growth" can be defined in various ways. For our purpose, let us think of it as the rate of change in GNP (real terms) per man-hour. Actually, this is a broader definition of growth than one that relates output to the composite of all factors used. GNP per man-hour can show an increase (a) as factors are employed more effectively under an existing technology, (b) as we enjoy gains in technology, (c) as the quality (i.e., level of skills, productiveness of machines) of resources is raised, and (d) as simply the quantity of nonhuman resources (physical capital) is increased.

[2] The definition is that of Richard B. Goode. See his article, "Adding to the Stock of Physical and Human Capital," *American Economic Review,* May, 1959, pp. 147-155.

[3] See *ibid.* and also the following contributions: H. Giersch, "Stages and Spurts of Economic Development," *International Social Science Bulletin,* No. 2, 1954, pp. 198-204; Theodore Schultz, "Investment in Man: An Economist's View," *Social Service Review,* June, 1959, pp. 110 ff.; and Gary S. Becker, "Underinvestment in College Education?" *American Economic Review,* May, 1960, pp. 346-354. The latter author follows what is now a common analytical practice of stating returns to education in terms of differential earnings of persons who have different amounts of education. An early study that used the same approach is J. Walsh, "Capital Concept Applied to Man," *Quarterly Journal of Economics,* February, 1935, pp. 257-285. The scheme is not wholly satisfactory. The market in regulating private earned income may not function to reveal the full value of educated persons to the social good. On the other hand, income differentials may reflect differences in IQ, family background, etc., as well as differences in education. For a further general discussion, see The American Assembly, *Goals for Americans,* Englewood Cliffs, N.J., Prentice-Hall, Inc., 1960, especially Chap. 8.

[4] Frederick C. Mills, *Productivity and Economic Progress,* Occasional Paper 38, New York, National Bureau of Economic Research, 1952, p. 25. The list may not be exhaustive. As Gottfried Haberler has stated, " . . . Economic growth is a very complex subject, which cannot be adequately

judged and explained in purely economic terms. Historical perspective, philosophical insight, understanding of different cultures and civilizations, as well as economic and sociological analyses are required to get a proper view of the conditions of economic growth and progress." *International Social Science Bulletin*, No. 2, 1954, p. 159.

[5]Of course, the country may need increasing educational expenditures to maintain a constant rate of growth. . . . [Certain] economic opportunities (the frontier, simple mass production, etc.) have already been exploited. Further, it is reasonable to say that there is a time lag between an increase in educational expenditure and the resultant effects on productivity. Perhaps future generations will be the beneficiaries of the sharp rise in school support in the post-World War II period. But, even so, the higher skills and new knowledge that education helps to supply require the complementary services of physical capital goods in production. Even should it turn out that education is *the* basic determinant of productivity advance, the problem of determing the proper allocation of investment funds between physical and human capital would remain.

[6]Irving H. Siegel, "The Role of Scientific Research in Stimulating Economic Progress," *American Economic Review*, May, 1960, pp. 343-344.

[7]Joseph Schumpeter, *Business Cycles*, New York, McGraw-Hill Book Company, 1939, pp. 85-86.

[8]See C. S. Benson and P. R. Lohnes, "Public Education and the Development of Work Skills," *Harvard Educational Review*, Spring, 1959.

[9]Arthur Smithies, "Productivity, Real Wages and Economic Growth," *Quarterly Journal of Economics*, May, 1960, pp. 189-205. The technical argument is beyond the scope of this book, but the following conclusion is of interest. "These rough calculations seem to put the burden of proof on those who urge that accelerated growth is an easy matter. They suggest, furthermore, the need to explore all possibilities of increasing the productivity trend. While all of such possibilities are likely to be costly, some of them may be cheap in relation to reliance on net capital accumulation." (P. 205.)

[10]Education Department, Chamber of Commerce of the United States, *Education—An Investment in People*, Washington, The Chamber, 1954, p. 42.

[11]Theodore W. Schultz, "The Emerging Economic Scene and Its Relation to High School Education," in F. S. Chase and H. A. Anderson (eds.), *The High School in a New Era*, Chicago, University of Chicago Press, 1958, p. 106.

[12]Goode, *op. cit.*, p. 152.

[13]Henry H. Villard, "Discussion," *American Economic Review*, May, 1960, p. 376.

[14]Edward F. Renshaw, "Will the American Educational System Ever Be Efficient?" *School Review*, Spring, 1958, p. 72.

6

CAPITAL FORMATION BY EDUCATION

by Theodore W. Schultz

In this provocative article, Professor Schultz calculates the cost of education for high school and college and concludes that the major share of educational costs consists of earnings foregone by students while attending school. This concept of lost opportunity costs was not previously considered by other economists. There are other authorities who challenge this view. (See, for example, Article 7 by John Vaizey.)

I propose to treat education as an investment in man and to treat its consequences as a form of capital. Since education becomes a part of the person receiving it, I shall refer to it as *human capital.* Since it becomes an integral part of a person, it cannot be bought or sold or treated as property under our institutions. Nevertheless, it is a form of capital if it renders a productive service of value to the economy. The principal hypothesis underlying this treatment of education is that some important increases in national income are a consequence of additions to the stock of this form of capital. Although it will be far from easy to put this hypothesis to the test, there are many indications that some, and perhaps a substantial part, of the unexplained increases in national income

Reprinted from Theodore W. Schultz, "Capital Formation by Education," *Journal of Political Economy,* Vol. 68, No. 6 (December 1960), pp. 571-583. Reprinted by permission of the publisher and author.

in the United States are attributable to the formation of this kind of capital.[1]

Education can be pure consumption or pure investment, or it can serve both these purposes. But, whatever it is in these respects, education in the United States requires a large stream of resources. The principal task of this paper is to present a set of estimates of the value of the resources that have been entering into education. These resources consist chiefly of two components—the earnings that students forego while attending school and the resources to provide schools. Our estimates begin with 1900, cover the next five decennial years, and close with 1956. The annual factor costs are given in current prices. A major section is devoted to the earnings that students forego while they attend school, both because of their importance and because these foregone earnings have heretofore been neglected. More than half the total resources that enter into high-school, college, and university education consists of the time and effort of students. The section on costs of the educational services that the schools provide introduces estimates of the value of school property used for education, along with current expenditures for salaries, wages, and materials.

Capital formation by means of education is neither small nor a neat constant in relation to the formation of non-human capital. It is not small even if a substantial part of the total cost of education were strictly for consumption. What our estimates will show is that the stream of resources entering into elementary education has increased less than that entering into either high-school or higher education. But, even so, it has been increasing at a larger rate than has the gross formation of physical capital. In 1900 the total cost of elementary education was equal to about 5 per cent of gross capital formation compared to 9 per cent in 1956. Comparable figures for high-school and higher education combined are 4 per cent in 1900 and almost 25 per cent in 1956.

Two more introductory comments seem necessary, one on the neglect of the study of human capital and the other on the moral issue of treating education as an investment in man. A serious fault in the way capital is treated in economic analysis has been the omission of human capital; this was a major part of the burden of my Teller lecture.[2] Had economists followed the conception of capital laid down by Fisher,[3] instead of that by Marshall,[4] this omission, so it seems to me, would not have occurred.

It is held by many to be degrading to man and morally wrong to look upon his education as a way of creating capital. To those who hold this view the very idea of human capital is repugnant, because for them education is basically cultural and not economic in its purpose, because education serves to develop individuals to become competent and responsible citizens by giving men and women an opportunity to acquire an understanding of the values they hold and an appreciation of what they mean to life. My reply to those who believe thus is that an analysis that treats education as one of the activities that may add to the stock of human capital in no way denies the validity of their position; my approach is not designed to show that these cultural purposes should not be, or are not being served by education. What is implied is that, in addition to achieving these cultural goals, some kinds of education may improve the capabilities of a people as they work and manage their affairs and that these improvements may increase the national income. These cultural and economic effects may thus be joint consequences of education. My treatment of education will in no way detract from, or disparage, the cultural contributions of education. It takes these contributions for granted and proceeds to the task of determining whether there are also some economic benefits from education that may appropriately be treated as capital that can be identified and estimated.

Ideally, we should like to have estimates of the formation of human capital, both gross and net, and of the size of the stock. We should also like to know how much, if any, of the increase in national income is attributable to increases in the stock of human capital and what the "rate of return" on investment in education has been. There will then be the question, How do parents and students and public authorities respond to these investment opportunities?[5] In this paper, however, I take only one small step toward answering these questions.

Let me now present the sources of the estimates that follow, making explicit the underlying assumptions and commenting on the data so that the reader may have a basis for determining the limitations of these estimates. The more important economic implications that emerge from this study will be left until later.

I. EARNINGS THAT STUDENTS FOREGO

It will be convenient to draw an arbitrary line between elementary and secondary schools and to assume that no earnings are foregone on the part of children who attend elementary schools.[6] Beyond the eighth grade, however, these earnings become important. The time and effort of students may usefully be approached as follows: (1) Students study, which is work, and this work, among other things, helps create human capital. Students are not enjoying leisure when they study, nor are they engaged wholly in consumption; they are here viewed as "self-employed" producers of capital. (2) Assume, then, that if they were not in school, they would be employed producing (other) products and services of value to the economy, for which they would be "paid"; there is, then, an opportunity cost in going to school. (3) The average earnings per week of those young men and women of comparable age and sex who are not attending school or of students while they are not in school are a measure of the (alternative) value productivity of the students' time and effort. (4) The cost of living of students and non-students may be put aside because they go on whether young people go to school or enter the labor market and are about the same except for minor items, such as books, extra clothes, and some travel in getting to and from school.

Estimates of the earnings that students have foregone were made in the following manner: High-school students were treated separately from college and university students. The year 1949 was taken as a base year in determining the "earnings" per week of young people, both male and females, for each of four age groups. Students' foregone earnings were calculated on the assumption that, on the average, students forego 40 weeks of such earnings, and then expressed in earning-equivalent weeks of workers in manufacturing in the United States. The results appear in Table 1; they indicate that high-school students forego the equivalent of about 11 weeks and college or university students about 25 weeks of such earnings. These 1949 earnings ratios were applied to particular years between 1900 and 1956; an adjustment was then made for unemployment, as set forth in Table 2.

Two sorts of limitations need to be borne in mind in interpreting and in using these estimates. The first pertains to the *11-week* and *25-week* estimates for the base year 1949; the other is inherent in applying the 1949 relationships to other years.

Many of the young people who did work in 1949 were employed for only a few weeks during the year. It seems plausible that their earnings per week would be below those of workers of equivalent abilities who worked most or all of the year. To this extent, our estimates are too low.[7] Also, it could be that students rate somewhat higher per person in the particular abilities for which earnings are received than do those not in school who are earning income. To the extent that there are such differences, other things being equal, our estimates of earnings foregone are again too low. On the other hand, some students have held jobs while they were attending

TABLE 1°

Estimates of Earnings Foregone by High-School and College or University Students in 1949

Age	Median Income (Dollars) (1)	Weeks Worked (2)	Income Per Week (Dollars) (3)	Annual Earnings Foregone in Attending School (Dollars) (4)	In Weeks Equivalent to Average Earnings of Workers in Manufacturing (5)
14-17:					
Male............................	311	24	13.00	520	....
Female........................	301	20	15.00	600	....
18-19:					
Male............................	721	32	22.50	900	....
Female........................	618	29	21.30	852	....
20-24:					
Male............................	1,669	40	41,70	1,669	....
Female........................	1,276	36	35.40	1,416	....
25-29:					
Male............................	2,538	44	57.70	2,308	....
Female........................	1,334	33	40.40	1,616	....
Per Student:					
High School................	.....	...	.....	583†	11 weeks
College or University..	.....	...	.....	1,369‡	25 weeks

°*Sources and Notes:*

Column 1: *United States Census of Population, 1950, Special Report on Education, 1953*, Table 13, except for figures for age group 20-24, which are from Herman P. Miller, *Income of the American People* (New York: John Wiley & Sons, 1953), Table 29. Virtually all the income in these age groups would appear to be from "earnings" according to Miller's Table 34.

Column 2: *United States Census of Population, 1950, Special Report on Employment and Personal Characteristics, 1953*, Table 14. Of the persons who did work in 1949, the Census shows the per cent who worked 1-13, 14-26, 27-39, 40-49, and 50-52 weeks, and, on the assumption that these classes averaged out to 7, 20, 33, 45, and 51 weeks, respectively, these were used as weights.

Column 3: col. 1 divided by col. 2.

Column 4: Assumes that students forego, on the average, 40 weeks of earnings: col. 3 multiplied by 40.

Column 5: *Economic Report of the President, January, 1957*, Table E-25. The average gross weekly earnings for all manufacturing was $54.92: Col. 4 divided by 54.92.

†Students enrolled in high school were approximately half males and half females; 92.7 per cent were allocated to the age group 14-17, and 7.3 per cent to ages 18-19. In making this allocation, it was assumed that those below the ages of 14 offset those above the age of 19 (*Statistical Abstract of the United States, 1956*, Table 126).

‡College or university students were distributed as follows:

Ages	Males (Per Cent)	Females (Per Cent)
14-17............	3.5	5.0
18-19............	18.2	16.0
20-24............	30.6	11.5
25-29............	14.7	0.5
	67.0	33.0

These percentages were used as weights in calculating the estimate of $1,369 (based on *Statistical Abstract of the United States, 1956*, Table 126).

TABLE 2*

Annual Earnings Foregone by Students, Adjusted and Not Adjusted for Unemployment, 1900-1956, in Current Prices

| Year | Average Weekly Earnings, All Manufacturing (Dollars) (1) | Annual Earnings Foregone per Student While Attending | | | |
| | | High School | | College or University | |
		Unadjusted (Dollars) (2)	Adjusted for Un-employment (Dollars) (3)	Unadjusted (Dollars) (4)	Adjusted for Un-employment (Dollars) (5)
1900.........	8.37	92	84	209	192
1910.........	10.74	118	113	269	259
1920	26.12	287	275	653	626
1930.........	23.25	256	224	581	509
1940.........	25.20	277	236	630	537
1950.........	59.33	653	626	1,483	1,422
1956.........	80.13	881	855	2,003	1,943

*Sources:
  Column 1: *Economic Report of the President, January, 1957*, Table E-25, and U. S. Department of Labor; and *Historical Statistics of the United States, 1789-1945*, a supplement to *Statistical Abstract of the United States, 1949*, Ser. D, pp. 134-44.
  Column 2: For high school students, col. 1 multiplied by 11; based on Table 1.
  Column 4: For college and university students, col. 1 multiplied by 25; based on Table 1.
  Columns 3 and 5: The per cent unemployed is based on Clarence D. Long, *The Labor Force under Changing Income and Employment* (a N.B.E.R. study [Princeton: Princeton University Press, 1958]), Appendix C, Table C-1 and, for 1956, Table C-2. Unemployed adult male equivalents in per cent of the labor force were as follows: 1900, 8.2; 1910, 3.9; 1920, 4.2; 1930, 12.4; 1940, 14.7; 1950, 4.1; and 1956, 3.0.

school; the earnings they have received from such jobs should have been subtracted from our estimates. Then, too, young people are probably burdened with more unemployment relative to the number employed than is the labor force as a whole.[8] Thus, of the four factors just mentioned, two pull in one direction and two in the other. They may be compensating factors.

There is also the question: What would the earnings of school-age workers have been if all of them had entered the labor market? But the question is not relevant because our problem is not one that entails a large shift in the number of human agents. The elasticity of the demand, either in the short or the long run, for such workers over so wide a range is not at issue. Instead, we want to know what earnings a typical student has been foregoing at the margin. Even so, our estimates of earnings foregone are substantially reduced by the effects of the large shift of students into summer employment;[9]

the earning figures that we are using, drawing on the 1950 Census, are heavily weighted by this summer employment. As pointed out above, many who did work for pay worked only a couple of months or so.[10]

The other difficulties stem from applying the 1949 "structural" relationships to other periods, especially to earlier years. The only adjustment that has been introduced is that for movements in unemployment. It is not easy to isolate the changes resulting from legislation. Stigler[11] suggests that "on the whole compulsory school attendance laws have followed more than led the increase in enrollments of children over 14." Child labor laws may have done likewise. In any case, these laws may be viewed as a comprehensive private and public effort to invest in education, the child labor laws having the effect of eliminating some job opportunities.[12]

There is a presumption in favor of the view that high-school students in 1949 were attending school more weeks per year than did high-school students in earlier years. Such evidence as I have been able to uncover, however, suggests that for 1900, 1910, and 1920 most high-school students, including those who were attending secondary preparatory schools, were being instructed so that they could win entrance into a college or university and that these students were attending school about as many weeks per year as high-school students in more recent years. Between the early twenties and the mid-forties, there may have been a small dip in this variable as a consequence of the large increases in high-school enrolment and the fact that high-school instruction was no longer devoted primarily to the preparation of students for college.[13]

The weekly earnings of workers who possess the capabilities of students and who are of that age group may have changed substantially since 1900 relative to the earnings of those employed in manufacturing. But it is not possible even to guess whether their earnings have become more or less favorable relative to the earnings of workers in manufacturing. The age groups that appear in Table 1 represent young people who had had more years of schooling than did the same age groups in 1900. But this would also be true of workers in manufacturing. The fact that the wage ratio between skilled and unskilled workers has narrowed may imply that our estimates of earnings foregone by high-school students during the earlier years are somewhat too high, or more plausible, that the estimates for college and university students are on the low side for those years.[14] It would be exceedingly difficult, however, to isolate the effects of these changes.

II. COSTS OF THE SERVICES PROVIDED BY SCHOOLS

Ideally, we want a measure of the annual flow of the inputs employed for education. This flow consists of the services of teachers, librarians, and school administrators, of the annual factor costs of maintaining and operating the school plant, and of depreciation and interest. It should not include expenditures to operate particular auxiliary enterprises, such as providing room and board for students, operating "organized" athletics or other non-educational activities. School expenditures for scholarships, fellowships, and other financial aids to students should also be excluded, because they are in the nature of transfer payments; the real costs involved in student time are already fully covered by the opportunity-cost estimates.

Tables 3 and 4 give these costs of schools for elementary, secondary, and higher education. Each table is essentially self-contained, with sources and notes.

III. TOTAL COSTS OF EDUCATION

The estimates of the costs of elementary education were complete as set forth in column 11 of Table 3, inasmuch as no earnings were foregone in accordance with our assumption.

Table 5 summarizes the principal components entering into the costs of high-school education. A comparison of columns 3 and 6 shows at once the importance of the earnings that students forego relative to total costs of this education. That such foregone earnings should have been a larger proportion of total costs of high-school education during the earlier years (and a larger proportion of total costs of high-school than of college and university education in all years) comes as a surprise. Earnings foregone while attending high school were well over half the total costs in each of the years; they were 73 per cent in 1900 and 60 per cent in 1956; the two low years were 1930 and 1940, when they fell to 57 and 58 per cent of total costs. During 1950 and 1956 they were 62 and 60 per cent, respectively. Other and more general economic implications of these changes in resource costs of high-school education will be considered later.

Table 6 provides similar estimates for college and university education. Here, too, earnings foregone by students are exceedingly important (see cols. 3 and 6). In 1900 and 1910 these earnings were about half of all costs, rising to 63 per cent in 1920 and then falling to 49 per cent in 1930 and 1940. With inflation and

TABLE 3ᵃ

Annual Resource Costs of Educational Services Rendered by Elementary and Secondary Schools in the United States, 1900-1956, in Current Prices
(Millions of Dollars Except Column 4 in Billions)

| | Public Schools | | | | | | Private Schools | | Public and Private Schools | | |
| | Gross Expenditures | Capital Outlay | Net Expenditures | Value of Property | Implicit Interest and Depreciation | Total Public | Gross Expenditures | Total Private | Total | Secondary | Elementary |
Year	(1)	(2)	(3)	(4)	(5)	(6)	(7)	(8)	(9)	(10)	(11)
1900……	215	35	180	.55	44	224	27	28	252	19	233
1910……	426	70	356	1.1	88	444	54	56	500	50	450
1920……	1,036	154	882	2.4	192	1,074	104	108	1,182	215	967
1930……	2,317	371	1,946	6.2	496	2,442	233	246	2,688	741	1,947
1940……	2,344	258	2,086	7.6	608	2,694	227	261	2,955	1,145	1,810
1950……	5,838	1,014	4,824	11.4	912	5,736	783	769	6,505	2,286	4,219
1956……	10,955	2,387	8,568	23.9	1,912	10,480	1,468	1,404	11,884	4,031	7,853

Sources and Notes:

Column 1: Lines 1-6, from *Statistical Abstract of the United States, 1955*, Table 145; line 7 from *Biennial Survey of Education in the United States, 1954-1956*.

Column 2: Lines 1-6 from *Biennial Survey of Education in the United States, 1948-1950*, chap. 2, Table 1; line 7 from the 1954-56 survey.

Column 3: Obtained by subtracting col. 2 from col. 1.

Column 4: From same sources as col. 2.

Column 5: Obtained by taking 8 per cent of col. 4. The distribution of physical assets is placed at 20 per cent land, 72 per cent buildings, and 8 per cent equipment, following Robert Rude's study, "Assets of Private Nonprofit Institutions in the United States, 1890-1948." (N.B.E.R., April, 1954, not published), Table II-2a. With no depreciation or obsolescence on land, 3 per cent on buildings (more obsolescence than colleges and universities because of changing local and community populations to which high schools must adjust) and 10 per cent on equipment, and with an implicit interest rate of 5.1 per cent, we have an 8 per cent rate per $100 of assets per year.

Column 6: Obtained by adding cols. 3 and 5.

Column 7: From same sources as col. 1, except that line 1 is based on the same ratio as line 2 between cols. 1 and 7; line 3 is based on the same ratio as line 4; and line 7 is based on the same ratio as line 6.

Column 8: Obtained by taking the percentage that col. 7 is of col. 1 and multiplying by col. 6. The gross expenditures of private schools ranged from 9.7 to 13.4 per cent of that of public schools. This procedure assumes that capital outlays, value of physical property, and imputed interest and depreciation bear the same relationship to gross expenditures for private as for public schools.

Column 9: Obtained by adding cols. 6 and 8.

Column 10: Obtained by allocating the total of col. 9 between elementary and secondary schools on the basis that it costs 88 per cent more per student in secondary than in elementary schools. Expenditures for high schools determined by using George J. Stigler's estimates appearing in *Employment and Compensation in Education* ("Occasional Papers," No. 33 [New York: National Bureau of Economic Research, 1950]), Tables 7 and 12, Enrolment in elementary schools is given as 33, and in secondary schools as 21 per teacher (using average for last five years in Stigler's table); and average salary of elementary-school teachers in 1938 was $1,876, and of secondary-school teachers it was $2,249. This is as 100 to 120. Accordingly, per student, we have:

$$\frac{120 \div 21}{100 \div 33} \times 100 = \text{an index of } 188 \text{ for teacher salary per student in}$$

secondary schools compared to 100 for that in elementary schools. A slightly lower ratio appears in the *Biennial Survey of Education in the United States, 1939-40*, chap. 1, Table 42, n. 1, in which secondary-school costs per student are placed 74 per cent higher than that in elementary schools. These are, however, no estimates in the 1939-40 survey which permit one to determine expenditures per student for elementary and secondary schools.

TABLE 4*

Annual Resource Costs of Educational Services Rendered by Colleges and Universities in the United States, 1900-1956, in Current Prices
(Millions of Dollars)

Year	Gross Expenditures (1)	Auxiliary Enterprises (2)	Capital Outlay (3)	Net Expenditures (4)	Value of Physical Property (5)	Implicit Interest and Depreciation (6)	Total (7)
1900........	46	9	17	20	254	20	40
1910........	92	18	30	44	461	37	81
1920........	216	43	48	125	741	59	184
1930........	632	126	125	381	1,925	154	535
1940........	758	152	84	522	2,754	220	742
1950........	2,662	539	417	1,706	5,273	422	2,128
1956........	4,210	736	686	2,788	8,902	712	3,500

	Public	Private
	(in Million Dollars)	
1920..............	116	100
1930..............	289	343
1940..............	391	367
1950..............	1,429	1,233
1956..............	2,375	1,835

Sources and notes:
Column ½: Lines 1-6, from *Statistical Abstract of the United States, 1955,* Table 145; and line 7 from *Biennial Survey of Education in the United States, 1954-56.* These expenditures by public and private institutions were as follows:

Column 2: Lines 5-7, same source as col. 1. For the two sets of institutions these were as follows:

	Public	Private
	(in Million Dollars)	
1940	59	93
1950	255	284
1956	364	372

Lines 1-4 were obtained by letting these auxiliary enterprises equal one-fifth of gross expenditures.

Column 3: Lines 4-7 from *Biennial Survey of Education in the United States, 1954-56*, chap. iv, Sec. II; lines 1-3 obtained by taking 6.5 per cent of col. 5, lines 1-3.

Column 4: Obtained by subtracting the sums of cols. 2 and 3 from col. 1.

Column 5: From *Biennial Survey of Education in the United States, 1948-50*, chap. iv, Sec. II, Table I, and *1954-56*. These estimates check closely with those of Robert Rude, "Assets of Private Nonprofit Institutions in the United States, 1890-1948," (National Bureau of Economic Research, April, 1954, not published).

Column 6: Obtained by taking 8 per cent of col. 5; they assume no depreciation and obsolescence on land, 2 per cent on buildings and improvements, and 10 per cent on equipment. Following Robert Rude's study cited above, Table II-2a, these physical assets were distributed 15 per cent to land, 70 per cent to buildings and improvements, and 15 per cent to equipment. Assuming an interest rate of 5.1 per cent, we have per $100 of assets:

Interest on all assets	$5.10
Depreciation and obsolescence	
On buildings and improvements	1.40
On equipment	1.50
Total	$8.00

Column 7: Is the sum of cols. 4 and 6.

TABLE 5°

Earnings Foregone and Other Resource Costs Represented by High-School Education, in the United States, 1900-1956, in Current Prices

Year	Number of Students (Millions) (1)	Earnings Foregone per Student (Dollars) (2)	Total Earnings Foregone (3)	School Costs (Millions of Dollars) (4)	Additional Expenditures (5)	Total (6)
1900.............	.7	84	59	19	3	81
1910.............	1.1	113	124	50	6	180
1920.............	2.5	275	688	215	34	937
1930.............	4.8	224	1,075	741	54	1,870
1940.............	7.1	236	1,676	1,145	84	2,905
1950.............	6.4	626	4,006	2,286	200	6,492
1956.............	7.7	855	6,584	4,031	329	10,944

° Sources:

Column 1: Statistical Abstract of ˌe United State 1955, Table 145; and the Biennial Survey of Education in the United States; 1954-56, chap. 2, Table 44.

Column 2: From Table 2, col. 3.

Column 3: Col. 1 multiplied by col. 2.

Column 4: From Table 3, col. 10.

Column 5: Expenditures for books, supplies, extra clothes, and travel to and from school estimated at 5 per cent of total earnings forgone; hence, 5 per cent of col. 3.

Column 6: Cols. 3 + 4 + 5.

full employment, they then rose to 60 and 59 per cent in 1950 and 1956.

IV. CONCLUDING OBSERVATIONS

When costs of all levels of education are aggregated, the proportion of total costs attributable to earnings foregone has clearly risen over time. This is due to the much greater importance of secondary and higher education in more recent years, a change that outweighs the decline in the foregone-earnings proportion of high-school education alone. For all levels of education together, earnings foregone were 26 per cent of total costs in 1900 and 43 per cent in 1956. Probably the actual 1900 figure should be somewhat higher than this because of foregone earnings of children in the higher grades of elementary school (ignored here), but such an adjustment would not substantially alter the picture.

Between 1900 and 1956, the total resources committed to education in the United States rose about *three and one-half times* (1) relative to consumer income in dollars and (2) relative to the gross formation of physical capital in dollars. Accordingly, if we look upon all the resources going into education as "consumption" based on consumer behavior, our estimates would not be inconsistent with the hypothesis that the demand for education has had a high income elasticity.[15]

If, however, we treat the resources entering into education as "investments" based on the behavior of people seeking investment opportunities, our estimates then are not inconsistent with the hypothesis that the rates of return to education were relatively attractive; that is, they were enough larger than the rate of return to investments in physical capital to have "induced" the implied larger rate of growth of this form of human capital.[16]

Again, it should be stressed that the underlying private and public motives that induced the people of the United States to increase so much the share of their resources going into education may have been cultural in ways that can hardly be thought of as "consumption," or they may have been policy-determined for purposes that seem remote from "investment." Even if this were true, it would not preclude the possibility that the rates of return on the resources allocated to education were large simply as a favorable by-product of whatever purposes motivated the large increases in resources entering into education. If so, the task becomes merely one of ascertaining these rates of return. If, however, consumer and investment behavior did play a substantial role in these private and

TABLE 6[a]

Earnings Foregone and Other Resource Costs Represented by College and University Education in the United States, 1900-1956, in Current Prices

Year	Number of Students (Thousands)	Earnings Foregone per Student (Dollars)	Total Earnings Foregone	School Costs	Additional Expenditures	Total
	(1)	(2)	(3)	(4)	(5)	(6)
				(Millions of Dollars)		
1900........	238	192	46	40	4	90
1910........	355	259	92	81	9	182
1920........	598	626	374	184	37	595
1930........	1,101	509	560	535	56	1,151
1940........	1,494	537	802	742	80	1,624
1950........	2,659	1,422	3,781	2,128	378	6,287
1956........	2,996	1,943	5,821	3,500	582	9,903

[a]Sources:

Column 1: Statistical Abstract of the United States, 1955, Table 145; and the Biennial Survey of Education in the United States; 1954-56, chap. 2, Table 44.

Column 2: From Table 2, col. 5.

Column 3: Col. 1 multiplied by col. 2.

Column 4: From Table 4, col. 7.

Column 5: Expenditures for books, supplies, extra clothes, and travel to and from school estimated at 10 per cent of earnings foregone (of col. 3).

Column 6: Cols. 3 + 4 + 5.

TABLE 7°

Total Costs of Elementary, High-School, and College and
University Education in the United States, 1900—
1956, in Current Prices

Year	Elementary (1)	High School (2)	College and University (3)	Total (4)
		(Millions of Dollars)		
1900................	230	80	90	400
1910................	450	180	180	810
1920................	970	940	600	2,510
1930................	1,950	1,870	1,150	4,970
1940................	1,810	2,900	1,620	6,330
1950................	4,220	6,490	6,290	17,000
1956................	7,850	10,950	9,900	28,700

°*Sources* (figures have been rounded):
Column 1: From Table 3, col. 11.
Column 2: From Table 5, col. 6.
Column 3: From Table 6, col. 6.
Column 4: Cols. 1 & 2 & 3.

public decisions, then, to this extent, economic theory will also be useful in explaining these two sets of behavior.

Not only have the streams of resources entering into elementary, high-school, and higher education increased markedly, but they have changed relative to one another.

1. Though elementary education by this measure has increased at a slower rate than has either of the other two, it has come close to doubling its position relative to gross physical capital formation; it rose from about 5 to 9 per cent of the latter between 1900 and 1956.[17]

The total costs of elementary education have been strongly affected by changes in enrolment and attendance. Increases in the average number of days that enrolled students have attended school played almost as large a part as did the increase in enrolment; the first of these rose 60 and the second 73 per cent between 1900 and 1956. However, it should be noted that this factor of attendance has nearly spent itself: average daily attendance is now within about 10 per cent of its apparent maximum. Enrolment, on the other hand, will turn upward in response to the growth in population. Meanwhile, the salaries of elementary-school teachers have been declining relative to wages generally.[18] Altogether, however, it seems plausible that investment in elementary education will not continue to rise at the rate that it did during the period covered by our estimates.

As previously noted, some earnings were undoubtedly foregone by elementary pupils, especially by children attending the upper grades. We have come upon bits of data that suggest that these earnings may have been appreciable during the early part of this period. Farm families, particularly, at that time still placed a considerable value on the work that their children could do for them; moreover, fully a third of the population had farm residences in 1900 and 1910. Surely, a poor country endeavoring to establish a comprehensive program of elementary education must reckon the cost entailed in the earnings that older children will have to forego.

2. The annual national cost of high-school education has risen markedly, so much so that in 1956 it was equal in amount to nearly 13 per cent of gross physical capital formation compared to somewhat less than 2 per cent in 1900.[19]

Enrolment in high school advanced from 0.7 to 7.7 million between 1900 and 1956. It had already reached 7.1 million in 1940. The effect of the upsurge in population that began in the early forties had started to make itself felt by 1956, the proportion of young people embarking upon a high-school education being very large—indeed, it was approaching its maximum. The increases in this ratio were striking; for example, in 1900 only about 11 per cent of the fourteen to seventeen age group was enrolled in secondary schools; by 1956 the per cent was about 75.[20]

Let me emphasize once more the fact that earnings foregone have made up well over half the total costs of high-school education. In 1956 they were three-fifths of total costs, which is somewhat less than at the beginning of this period. From this experience one may infer that poor countries, even when they are no less poor than were the people of the United States in 1900, will find that most of the real costs of secondary education are a consequence of the earnings that students forego while attending school.

3. The trend of total cost of higher education has been similar to that of high-school costs. It rose at a slightly smaller rate than did total high-school cost in the early part of the period, and at a larger rate later. Relative to gross physical capital formation, it was about 2 per cent in 1900 and slightly less than 12 per cent in 1956.

Enrollment in higher education increased from 328,000 in 1900 to 2,996,000 in 1956. Of the eighteen to twenty-one age group, 4 per cent were in residence and enrolled as undergraduates in higher education in 1900; by 1956, 32 per cent of this age group were thus enrolled. The numbers in the college age group will increase substantially soon, as the children born with the upsurge in birth rates of the early forties reach these ages. The proportion of this age group that will begin higher education is not readily discernible. The upper limit is not near at hand, as it is for elementary and high-school education; there are many indications that it will continue to increase for some time to come.

Earnings foregone by students attending colleges and universities were also about three-fifths of total costs in 1956. Here, however, we appear to observe an upward trend between 1900 and 1956.

4. Altogether, total costs of education have increased much more rapidly than have the total costs of the resources entering into physical capital. Between 1900 and 1956, the total costs of the three levels of education covered by this study have risen from 9 to 34 per cent of the total entering into the formation of physical capital.

Several more steps must be taken, however, before we can gauge the increases in the stock of capital developed by education and its contribution to economic growth. These steps will entail allocating the costs of education between consumption and investment, determining the size of the stock of human capital formed by education, and ascertaining the rate of return to this education.

NOTES

[1] By "unexplained" I mean here the increases in measured national income that exceed the increases in measured resources, treated as inputs. For approximately the same period covered by this study, Solomon Fabricant, in *Basic Facts on Productivity Changes* ("National Bureau of Economic Research Occasional Papers," No. 63 [New York, 1959]), Table 5, presents estimates that show the output of United States private domestic economy as having increased at an average annual rate of 3.5 per cent between 1889 and 1957, whereas total inputs increased at an annual rate of only 1.7 per cent. For the more recent part of this period,

that is, between 1919 and 1957, these annual rates of increase were 3.1 and 1.0 per cent, respectively.

[2] In "Investment in Man: An Economist's View," *Social Service Review,* Vol. XXXIII (June, 1959).

[3] Irving Fisher, *The Nature of Capital and Income* (New York: Macmillan Co., 1906).

[4] Alfred Marshall, *Principles of Economics* (8th ed.; London: Macmillan & Co., Inc., 1930). In discussing definitions of capital, Marshall commented on Fisher's concept as follows: "The writings of Professor Fisher contain a masterly argument, rich in fertile suggestion, in favour of a comprehensive use of the term. Regarded from the abstract and mathematical point of view, his position is incontestable. But he seems to take too little account of the necessity for keeping realistic discussions in touch with the language of the market-place . . . " (Appendix E).

[5] Surely some individuals and families make decisions to invest in some kinds of education, either in themselves or in their children, with an eye to the earnings that they expect to see forthcoming from such expenditures on education. It should be possible to analyze these decisions and their consequences as one does other private decisions that give rise to physical capital formation throughout the economy.

[6] This assumption is plausible enough in the case of our society at the present time. But back no further than 1900, many of these children were of considerable economic value as workers, and some parents were keeping them from school for that reason.

[7] Of males aged fourteen to seventeen who worked in 1959, 44 per cent worked only about 7 weeks (an average) and 19 per cent worked about 20 weeks (average). Similarly, in the case of females aged fourteen to seventeen who worked, 53 per cent worked only about 7 weeks and 21 per cent about 20 weeks (averages). For ages eighteen to nineteen, these figures are smaller, i.e., for males, 24 per cent worked only 7 weeks and 19 per cent about 20 weeks; and for females aged eighteen to nineteen, the two figures are 29 and 23 per cent, respectively. For ages twenty to twenty-four, they are 10 and 12 per cent for males and 17 and 15 per cent for females.

[8] *The Economic Report of the President, January, 1960,* Table D-18, gives some figures that appear relevant. They show total unemployed equal to 5.2 per cent of the total employed, whereas for the fourteen to nineteen age group it was 11.8 per cent.

[9] In 1955, for example, 1.2 million individuals aged fourteen to nineteen entered the labor force between May and July, in contrast to about 0.4 million in the ages twenty to twenty-four.

[10] One can know something about the relation of the number of individuals in these age groups who are gainfully employed to the number enrolled in school. As one might expect, in the youngest of the three age groups, the number gainfully employed (April, 1950) was a little more than one-third the number enrolled in school (October, 1950), whereas for the age

group twenty to twenty-four there were fully seven times as many in the gainfully employed group as there were enrolled in school. The figures for 1950 are as follows:

Ages	Enrolled in School (October) (Millions)	Gainfully Employed or in Labor Force (April) (Millions)
16-17......................	3.06	1.12
18-19......................	1.19	2.39
20-24......................	0.96	7.09
Total......................	5.21	10.60

[11]George S. Stigler, "Employment and Compensation in Education" ("National Bureau of Economic Research, Occasional Papers," No. 33 [New York, 1950]), p. 8 and Appendix B.

[12]In commenting on child labor laws, Albert Rees has called my attention to the *Census of Manufactures* of 1890, which shows that 121,000 children (males under sixteen and females under fifteen) were employed and that their annual earnings were 31 per cent of those of all manufacturing wage earners. This is a substantially higher ratio than that implied for this age group in Tables 1 and 2. Thus using 11 weeks' earnings foregone for 1900 may understate the investment in high-school education at the beginning of this period.

[13]Unfortunately for our purposes, data for the United States do not separate elementary and high-school attendance. The data are mainly for the five to seventeen age group with two sets of figures: (1) the average number of days that schools were in session and (2) the average number of days attended by each enrolled pupil five to seventeen years of age. These are: 1900, 144 and 99 days, respectively; 1910, 156 and 113 days; 1920, 163 and 121 days; 1930, 173 and 143 days; 1940, 175 and 152 days; 1950, 178 and 158 days; and 1956, 178 and 159 days. Thus there has been a 60 per cent increase in the average number of days that each enrolled student attended schools. This rise, however, has been dominated by changes that have occurred in the attendance of elementary students. In the early years, high-school students were heavily concentrated in states that had already established long school sessions and good attendance records. For example, the average number of days attended by high-school students in a sample of such states was 170 days in 1920; a 1925-26 set of 31 states shows 151 days, and another set of states for 1937-38 shows 168 days, rising to 178 days in 1945-46 and 176 days in 1949-50.

[14]Paul G. Keat, "Changes in Occupational Wage Structure, 1900-1956" (unpublished Ph.D. thesis, University of Chicago, March, 1959), p. 77,

estimates the wage ratio of skilled to unskilled workers to have been 205 in 1900 and 149 in 1949.

[15]A 1 per cent increase in real income was associated with a 3.5 per cent increase in resources spent on education, implying an income elasticity of 3.5, had other things stayed constant. Among other changes, the price of educational services rose relative to other consumer prices, offset perhaps in considerable part by improvements in the "quality" of educational services.

[16]Of course, other relevant factors may not have remained constant. For example, it seems plausible to believe that the grip of capital rationing is much less severe presently than it was during earlier years covered by this study.

[17]Whenever I refer to estimates of gross nonhuman or gross physical capital formation, I shall base them on Simon Kuznets' *Annual Estimates 1869-1953* (New York: National Bureau of Economic Research, 1958), Table T-8, technical tables in supplement to summary volume on *Capital Formation and Financing*, mimeographed, used with his permission. Estimates for 1956, roughly comparable with that of Kuznets' series, is the 67.4 billion appearing in *Economic Report of the President, January, 1960*. Table D-1, raised by 26.4 (the per cent by which Kuznets' estimate for 1950 exceeds commerce estimate of that year). Thus we have the total costs of elementary education increasing from $230 to $7,850 million and gross physical capital costs increasing from $4,300 to $85,200 million.

[18]Keat *(op. cit.,* Table 7, p. 25) presents estimates showing that these teachers in 1903 received 58 per cent more earnings than did the average full-time employee in manufacturing during the year, compared to only 19 per cent more in 1956. Comparable figures for high-school teachers are 188 and 36 per cent; and for professors, 261 and 73 per cent.

[19]Beginning with 1940, the total costs of high-school education exceeded that of elementary education; by 1956 they were almost 40 per cent larger. In 1900 it was the other way around, with elementary education nearly three times as large as that of high school, measured in resources used (see cols. 1 and 3 of Table 7).

[20]However, of this fourteen to seventeen age group, 88 per cent was enrolled either in elementary school, high school, or college.

7

THE RETURNS TO EDUCATION
by John Vaizey

John Vaizey, an English economist, takes issue with Schultz's concept of foregone earnings (see Article 6) on the grounds that acceptance of this concept opens the door for all kinds of similar calculations that raise the total opportunity costs to an astronomical level. He concludes that although there is a clear relationship between more education and higher income, it is difficult to measure this with precise accuracy.

If the analogy of education with other productive investment be admitted, it follows that there must be a return. This return will be over a number of years, it is evident. The problem is: to whom does it accrue, and how can it be measured? The two questions are indissolubly linked, since the return can only be estimated if it shows up in some index, and the choice of the appropriate index to investigate is a difficult one. In this chapter I shall examine a number of contributions to show the sort of approaches that can be made to solve the problem. It will be seen that none of them are satisfactory.

First, I shall examine an approach which relates *total* movements in the economy to changes in the factors of production, especially labour and physical capital, and finds that there is another factor, called by a Norwegian author 'the third factor' in which education plays a crucial part. I shall then consider three other approaches to

Reprinted from John Vaizey, *The Economics of Education.* New York: Free Press of Glencoe, 1962, pp. 40-46, 49-53. Reprinted by permission of the publisher.

the question of measuring returns: a discounting of the additional earnings of the educated over those of the uneducated; cost-benefit ratios; and a calculation of 'human capital'. Of these four methods I am inclined to rate the last two as the most satisfactory. . . .

. . . The connexion between physical capital and output has been assumed to be important because it is more obvious; there is no reason to think the connexion between education and output is any less important; it has not yet been demonstrated.

Perhaps there is another way to trace the connexion. This is associated especially with the work of American writers, Theodore Schultz, Gary Becker and other members (past and present) of the University of Chicago department of economics. Basically the argument runs as follows. The contribution of education to human economic welfare can be measured in two ways—its indirect benefits and its direct benefits. The indirect benefits are analogous to those 'external economies' of which Marshall and Pigou wrote; if I open a public park for profit in the centre of the city I may earn a profit; but the benefits of air and space will also accrue to the owners of adjacent properties; and if I provide the park free the uncovenanted benefit to my neighbours will still accrue to them *and be measurable.* Now, as the great economists had all pointed out, the development of learning and skills would be apparent to all as a very considerable external economy of an education system and (from the point of view of national output) provides its chief justification as a free or unsubsidized public service.

The Chicago economists, following the argument developed by Marshall in his mathematical appendix,[1] point out that in principle the direct returns to education can also be measured by assessing the returns to individuals. A man is able to earn more because he is more highly skilled, as a general rule, and therefore by comparing the earnings of people with different educational backgrounds, discounting for mortality rates, unemployment and so on, a great deal can be done to estimate the returns to education. If £6,000 is invested in a machine its returns can be estimated by perfectly orthodox methods of accountancy; similarly £6,000 invested in a boy in the form of Summerfields, Eton and King's is equally capable of earning a return, which can be estimated and differentiated from £600 spent on a boy at St. Philip and St. James' Church of England (all-age) school, North Oxford, by comparing their respective earnings through life. And if you say that one boy may become a penniless priest and the other a prosperous garage proprietor selling painted-up second-hand cars, the protagonists of this form of argument can legitimately point out that a sufficiently large number of cases will give a reasonable average.

The results are striking. The earnings of people with different educational backgrounds are very different from each other. Little work has been done on this recently in Britain, but the subject has been treated exhaustively in America.[2]

The next problem, after having shown the different patterns of earnings of people with different educational backgrounds, is to estimate this as a return to investment in people.[3] The measurement of expenditure on education has to include expenditures by the pupils, their families, charities, and the state, obviously; and it has to be an estimation of the total relevant expenditure; it is not sufficient to count just the fees actually paid. As indicated elsewhere in this book, the estimation of true costs is an extremely difficult business. The American scholars would make it more complicated by adding a notional 'income forgone', in an attempt to measure 'opportunity cost'. In principle, a true economic cost is the cost of acting in a different manner; of forgoing the opportunity to do X because you have chosen to do Y. Thus if the alternative of doing X is idleness its true cost can be nil; if the alternative to building a school is building a television centre, the true cost of building a school is a television centre.

For a student, the alternative to study is often work; therefore, the 'opportunity cost' of education is not only school buildings, teachers' time and so on (which for the most part could be used in some other way) but the time of the students which could go into remunerative employment.[4] Now, for young pupils there is no alternative; the law forbids them to work for money. For students over the compulsory attendance age, however, the situation is different. The Crowther Report[5] contains an estimate of the earnings which would have been forgone in 1958 by pupils aged 15 to 16 if they had been compulsorily kept at school. It was £ 92 million. In the United States the figures are astronomical; Schultz, for example, gives 55 per cent of the costs of graduate or professional school education as income forgone; and 43 per cent of the costs of four years' high school.

It is doubtful whether this exercise is justified. The inclusion of income forgone opens the gate to a flood of approximations which would take the concept of national income away from its origin as an estimation of the measurable flows of the economy; if income forgone is added to education costs it must also be added to other sectors of the economy (notably housewives, mothers, unpaid sitters-in, voluntary work of all sorts); and it is doubtful whether any more useful purpose is served by a statistical exercise of this kind, than could be achieved merely by observing the numbers of people engaged in education.

Analytically, too, it would be necessary to adjust the costs by some notional estimate of benefits incurred while being educated, and these are usually considerable.

It follows then that the usual figure of education expenditure can more appropriately be related to its returns as measured by people's incomes; though it should be borne in mind that this economic calculus is not a measurement of *total* costs and benefits. Even with this more cautious method of calculation, however, the returns are strikingly high, as calculated by Schultz and others, perhaps even bearing out the point made by Pigou and Cannan that the productivity of education is higher than the productivity of physical capital.

In 1939, urban U.S. males with seven to eight years of school earned $175 to $304 a year more than those who had only five to six years of school.[6] In 1956 males aged 25–44 who completed eight years of school earned over $1,000 a year more than those who had less income than this.

Becker calculated that for white urban males with high school education the return on educational costs, including income-forgone, was 14.3 per cent in 1939; and 19.2 per cent after adjusting the income data for mortality and unemployment. For college education, from 1940 to 1955, adjusted for race, ability, unemployment and mortality, the return was 12.5 per cent before tax.[7]

The figures of lifetime income of U.S. males from 18 to 64 are even more striking.[8] So for additional expenditure of $12,500 it is possible, on this view, to earn over a lifetime over $100,000. This calculation was used as the basis for the slogan—'a college education is worth $100,000'.[9]

This rate of return is high, but not perhaps strikingly so for private investment; on the other hand the capital value which is estimated is probably too high, since it includes income-forgone. In general, however, it is apparent that Pigou and Cannan were not speaking in outrageously exaggerated terms, though it would perhaps have been wiser to say that the productivity of physical and intellectual capital was comparable. An American authority[10] states categorically that 'an investment in schooling pays, on the average, a better return than most other investments'.

At this point, however, a note of caution must be added. How far does all this elaborate statistical work justify the *obiter dicta* of Pigou and Cannan?

Hardly at all.

Individual earnings over a lifetime reflect many things. The distribution of incomes between persons represents the outcome of the workings of the whole economy; they are primarily affected therefore, by the movements of the economy. These are due (as has been seen in the examination of Aukrust's work) to a combination of factors —land (or the natural endowments of an economy), physical capital and organization. It is difficult to assign the part played in the movement of the remuneration of any individual or group by factors other than those specifically attributable to the individual or the group. National income is affected greatly, too, by changes in the terms of trade, which are only in part affected by domestic happenings. It is also clear that the degree of monopoly (or the gap between marginal physical productivity and the marginal rate of monetary reward) is variable and substantial.[11]

The rate of unemployment and the degree of competition in the economy affect individuals and groups differently, and with little necessary relation to their educational background, but with substantial effects on their wages. Above all, the ownership of capital, and its inheritance, is the major cause of wide dispersions of income.

This leads to a point of major importance; there is a multiple correlation between parental wealth, parental income, access to educational opportunity, motivation in education, access to the best jobs and 'success' in later life.[12] Above all, there is sheer native wit and ability which will 'out' despite all educational handicaps. It is dreadfully easy to involve oneself in a chicken-and-egg controversy: 'which came first, the income or the education?'—especially in old and class-ridden societies.

It follows, then, that all the statistics may go to show is that incomes are unequal, and that education is unequally distributed; there may be no necessary causal relationship between education and income.

Certainly this would be the view of those who criticize society from a basically socialist point of view; or those who attempt to analyse the returns to education in a socialist society. For if all incomes were equal it would appear to follow that education as such has no *direct* return, which is absurd; the return would be immeasurable by this method. The fundamental points are two. First, there is no necessary validity of income distribution at present as a system of returns to effort, talent, merit or skill; the wage-system is, in fact, a system of administered prices, not market prices.[13] Therefore, these measurements are measuring the consequences of a process of market imperfections so serious as to invalidate the results if they are used to estimate returns to education.[14]

Secondly, the difference between marginal net *private* product and marginal net *social* product is especially great in education. It is no necessary criticism of the methods employed to say that the national income consists of a bundle of goods and services which includes some benefits which are undervalued, and others which are overvalued (for that is to mistakenly criticize an account on moral grounds); but it is a valid criticism to say that the indirect benefits of education are so great that its direct benefits are not necessarily its most important aspect.

Nevertheless, it is possible to disprove too much. . . . Clearly there is a relation between education and income; it is just that it is difficult to measure it accurately and precisely.

One substantive point does emerge: as the great economists pointed out, education can be a great equalizing force, not only socially but economically too. There is an observable trend towards greater equality in incomes in all industrial societies: the greater the degree of industrialization, the greater the degree of equality: there is a far greater bunching round the median income, and the ends of the distribution curve are drawn nearer together. In part this is due to the fact that the average worker is using more capital, so that differences of natural endowment are *less* important; in part it is due to the greater social and geographical mobility of the labour force, which diminishes imperfections in the labour market; but in part it is due to the reduction in educational differences between different groups.[15]

All in all, this work on personal incomes is based on an analogy: an education brings returns, just as an investment in physical capital does; but an apt and striking analogy should not be humourlessly pushed too far. For it breaks down; and it arouses hostility. It is sacrilege to say that men are paid what they are worth, and it is untrue as well; and nothing is gained by saying so. . . .

One method adopted by Schultz was to use an analogy with additions to the stock of capital in measuring the amount of education available in the population at large.[16] Adding together income forgone by students and the resources used in providing formal education, he reaches a total of annual investment in education from 1900 to 1956, in the United States. The process is subject to qualification, he admits; but the analogy with physical capital is a close one, and is justified by the part that acquired skill plays in economic life—a part possibly comparable with physical capital.

In adding together the costs of education he assigns a major role to income foregone.[17] In order to do this he assumes that children above elementary level (roughly 14 or 15) could work in the state of society at present; earlier on, the age would have been lower. He measures their income by multiplying the average weekly earnings 'of young men and women of comparable age and sex while they are not in school, or of those who are not attending school'. These calculations are subject to severe limitations. Part-time earnings of students at school are below the comparable rate for full-time earnings; the students are, on average, more able than those who are earning full-time, and might be expected to get better jobs; the influx of new workers would reduce the average wage-rates of people of comparable age and status who would compete with the newcomers for jobs. Above all the rate of unemployment might well be higher if more people competed for jobs; as Schultz points out, in January 1960, 5.2 per cent of the U.S. labour force was unemployed, and 11.8 per cent of the 14-19 age-group. After making allowances for these reservations Schultz concludes that earnings forgone in the United States totalled $105 million in 1900, and $12,405 million in 1956.

The direct costs of education he calculates as $300 million in 1900, and $16,400 million in 1956. This last estimate of direct cost is different from that given elsewhere in this book, because he also imputes the cost of the depreciation of the physical 'plant' of the schools and colleges. To do this is an alternative to including in the sum a figure for gross physical investment in schools; *net* physical investment plus an imputed sum for depreciation being the relevant sum for exercises of the sort undertaken elsewhere. Since these sums are difficult to calculate we have usually chosen the easier and less accurate method.

As a 'value' of the addition to educational capital stock, the sum of earnings forgone (assuming that it is a valid concept with relevance in this context) and of total outlays or real resources, has to be depreciated to get a net rate of investment; people die and retire from the labour market, and their skills are lost.

At this stage the analogy becomes a little forced. Capital can be valued in innumerable ways; at initial cost, at replacement cost, by multiplying its output by the rate of interest, or by notional values derived from some other criterion. Clearly, if the initial cost is the relevant concept, then Schultz's sum can be adjusted for the amount of 'education capital' no longer in use (because the people in whom it is embodied are dead or retired). If replacement cost is the concept being applied, then the cost *now* of giving a comparable education to that received in the past by members of the labour fource is the relevant economic quantum.[18]

But what do all these sums tell us? The reason why financial values are given to physical capital is because it is heterogeneous. It is impractical to present estimates which are an inventory of miscellaneous objects: '16 power stations + 12 wheelbarrows + 3 motorways + 200 lorries = 17 oil tankers + 3 docks' is not a possible equation, whereas if monetary values are given to each item they can be added up. Now, the point of adding up the 'educational capital' of mankind is to be able to say—for example—that its production (or its value) has cost society as much, or represents as much effort, as the stock of physical capital. For this purpose an annual comparison of the amount spent on education with the amount spent on physical capital is insufficient, because the working life of an educated person is different from the working life of physical equipment; consequently, the comparison is not necessarily a satisfactory one. (All this is on the assumption, argued above, that the comparison of the two types of investment does not represent too forced an analogy.)

The critical thinker might observe at this point, however, that the analogy between physical capital and intellectual capital is really becoming forced: the series of dubious statistical exercises elaborated above does not really add any precision to the original point —that intellectual capital is important and should be taken into account, as well as physical capital, in estimating the resources put into the productive process. And we must remember, too, that we are in grave danger of forgetting that physical capital is but one part of the real resources used: 'land' is a concept used in economics to include those actual resources like agricultural land, coal reserves, gold reserves and so on, which added to man-made capital form the total relevant stock of *things* used in production. Similarly labour is equivalent to manpower, *plus* its skills, *plus* the huge stock of ideas and potentially productive talent locked up, for instance, in libraries and in the family, which do not directly impinge on the economic process but which have a fundamental importance in determining its limits of action. Adding up education costs as a method of valuing educational capital and comparing these money values with physical capital is not comparing like with like unless some allowance is made for the cultural values of education (which are not directly productive) and for education given to non-producers, in the economic sense.

Clearly, however, because the sum cannot be done in any direct way, the analogy is not necessarily weakened; it *is* an analogy which is to be used, not a direct comparison that is to be made. If this is so, then there is some point in exercises which add up the stock of educational experience of different countries, and then compare them. For example, if the labour force of the U.K. and Germany is the same, and the average length of education of the typical worker is ten years in one and eight years in the other, it is sensible to say that the labour forces weighted by factors of 10 and 8 respectively, represent the educational capital of the country; and the sum can be refined by giving weights for different kinds of education, and so on. The comparisons will be rough, but they are indicative of something very genuine; and they can be used to adjust comparisons of national capital stocks, either between countries, or from decade to decade. Nevertheless, comparisons of this kind are useful because they correct the impressions given by direct comparison based on single years. For example, since 1950, or so, the English probably have given more education to young people than the Scots; yet the stock of education in Scotland is higher than in England because over the last 400 years the Scots have given more—often far more—education to their people than the English have.

A simple method of making these comparisons is to take the Census reports of the educational experience of the occupied population[19] and to weight it by their potential working life. In addition, the 'reserves' of education can be computed by calculating the educational stock of those who are not in employment; and the rates of entry into and withdrawal from the labour market can give an indication of how fast the capital stock is being added to or run down. Nations like the U.S.S.R. and the U.S.A. with very large proportions of young people in their populations, and with rapidly developing educational systems, can add dramatically to their educational stocks; nations like the United Kingdom, whose demographic balance is more normal, have to put proportionately more effort into their educational systems in order to achieve the same rate of accumulation.

Further refinements are possible by making allowances for differences in educational quality; a person with a degree has 16 years of education, compared with a minimum permissible of 10; yet his education may be worth far more than a ratio of 8:5. Similarly, particular *types* of education may be more useful than others.

This, in sum, is the most sensible way of applying the notion of a 'stock of capital' to the output of education.

In this chapter I have been through a number of analyses of the returns to education, and I have shown that within a series of rather severe limits the analogy of education with physical capital is a useful method of looking at the problem of how much should be spent on education. Calculations of the sort suggested might well lead to a series of more rational decisions about the size of the education system than have been taken in the past.

NOTES

[1] It is noteworthy that in other respects a great deal is owed by the Chicago school to Pigou, who treats of education with great force. Lord Dalton, in his useful book on *The Inequality of Incomes* (1st edition, 1920) deals with this subject most comprehensively, and especially with the works of other economists. The student will find Lord Dalton's book a salutary corrective to the more enthusiastic writings of the *laissez-faire* school.

[2] It forms, of course, a major part of the work of Lord Dalton. His purpose was to criticize inequality; theirs, to explain it.

[3] A. C. Pigou, *Wealth and Welfare*, London, 1912, argued that the marginal net product of resources wisely invested in persons is higher than that of resources wisely invested in material capital; a given sum wisely expended on the health and education of the people, and especially of the young, will increase production by a greater amount than the same sum wisely expended by private persons on the creation of new capital (pp. 355-6 and 163-4, quoted by Lord Dalton, London, *The Inequality of Incomes*, 1920, pp. 148-9.) Cannan, as Lord Dalton points out, makes the same point. (*Wealth*, London, 1914.)

[4] Economists of the sort who make these calculations always ignore students' wilful desires to do good to others for nothing.

[5] *15-18*, Report of the Central Advisory Council for Education (England), Vol. I, H.M.S.O., 1959, p. 57.

[6] Schultz, quoting Morton Zeman, *A Quantitative Analysis of White-Non-white Income Differentials in the United States,* unpublished Ph.D. thesis, University of Chicago, 1955.

[7] Gary S. Becker 'Underinvestment in College Education,' *Proceedings, American Economic Review,* May 1960, and quoted by Schultz from a paper by Becker.

[8] 'In 1958, the average elementary school graduate could expect a lifetime income of about $182,000 as compared with about $258,000 for the average high school graduate . . . a college graduate could expect to receive about $435,000.' This is about $40,000 per year of schooling. (Herman Miller 'Income in Relation to Education,' *American Economic Review,* December 1960, p. 982.)

[9] Herman P. Miller, *Annual and Lifetime Income in Relation to Education, 1939-1959.* U.S. Bureau of Census, 1959 (unpublished), table 15, cited in his 'Income in Relation to Education,' *American Economic Review,* December 1960.

[10] Miller, *American Economic Review,* December 1960, p. 963.

[11] M. Kalecki, *Theory of Economic Dynamics,* London, 1954.

[12] The works on educational opportunity and social mobility quoted in the

Bibliography all deal with this point in great detail. Suffice it to say here that good breeding earns more in most societies than a good education.

[13] Barbara Wootton (Baroness Wootton of Abinger), *The Social Foundations of Wage Policy*, London, 1956.

[14] See John Vaizey and Michael Debeauvais, *Some Economic Aspects of Educational Development in Europe*, Paris, 1961.

[15] Some of this evidence is reviewed in Charles Benson, *The Economics of Public Education*, New York 1961.

[16] T. W. Schultz, 'Capital Formation by Education,' *Journal of Political Economy*, December, 1960.

[17] See above for the more profound objections to this procedure.

[18] Since the rates of depreciation differ, annual sums of outlays on capital are really not very significant for comparative purposes. Schultz's figures are annual rates.

[19] See Clarence D. Long, *The Labor Force Under Changing Income and Employment*, Princeton, 1958; using Long's data Schultz calculates that 'equivalent school years' rose from 116 million to 740 million in the American labour force between 1900 and 1957.

148

SUGGESTIONS FOR FURTHER READING—PART II

Becker, Gary S. "Underinvestment in College Education?" *American Economic Review,* Vol. 50, No. 2 (Papers and Proceedings: May 1960), pp. 346-354.

Becker, Gary S. and B. R. Chiswick. "Education and the Distribution of Earnings." *American Economic Review,* Vol. 56, No. 2 (Papers and Proceedings: May 1966), pp. 358-369.

Chance, W.A. "Long Term Labor Requirements and Output of the Educational System." *Southern Economic Journal,* Vol. 32 (April 1966), pp. 417-428.

Committee for Economic Development. *Raising Low Incomes Through Improved Education* (A Statement on National Policy). New York: Committee for Economic Development, 1965.

Eckaus, R. S. "Economic Criteria for Education and Training." *The Review of Economics and Statistics,* Vol. 46, No. 2 (May 1964), pp. 181-190.

Fleischer, Belton M. "The Effect of Income on Delinquency." *American Economic Review,* Vol. 56, No. 1 (March 1966), pp. 118-137.

Fogel, Walter. "The Effects of Low Educational Attainment on Incomes." *Journal of Human Resources,* Vol. 1, No. 2 (Fall 1966), pp. 22-40.

Hansen, W. Lee, Burton A. Weisbrod, and William J. Scanlon. "Determinants of Earnings: Does Schooling Really Count?" Madison, Wisconsin: University of Wisconsin, The Institute for Research on Poverty (mimeographed), August 1968.

Houthakker, H. S. "Education and Income." *Review of Economics and Statistics,* Vol. 41, No. 2 (February 1959), pp. 24-28.

Miller, Herman P. "Annual and Lifetime Income in Relation to Education, 1939-1959." *American Economic Review,* Vol. 50, No. 5 (December 1960), pp. 962-986.

Miller, Herman P. "Lifetime Income and Economic Growth." *American Economic Review,* Vol. 55, No. 2 (May 1965), pp. 521-529.

Miller, Herman P. *Rich Man, Poor Man.* New York: Thomas Y. Crowell Company, 1964.

Morgan, James and M. David. "Education and Income." *Quarterly Journal of Economics,* Vol. 77 (August 1963), pp. 423-437.

Morgan, James and Charles Lininger. "Education and Income: Comment." *Quarterly Journal of Economics,* Vol. 78, No. 2 (May 1964), pp. 346-347.

Sexton, Patricia Cayo. *Education and Income.* New York: Viking Press, 1961.

Tobin, James. "On Improving the Economic Status of the Negro." *Daedalus,* Vol. 94, No. 4 (Fall 1965), pp. 878-898.

U.S. Bureau of the Census. "Occupation by Earnings and Education." *U.S. Census of Population: 1960.* PC(2)-7B. Washington: Government Printing Office, 1963.

Part III

Benefits and Costs of Education

8

THE NATURE OF EDUCATION BENEFITS AND THEIR SPILL-OVERS

by Burton A. Weisbrod

Burton Weisbrod directs attention to the social benefits of education that accrue over and above economic returns, including benefits to the individual's family, his children, neighbors, employers, and society. The author admits, however, that measurement of these intangible benefits is extremely difficult.

Before we can analyze the spill-over benefits of public education we must grasp the nature of the total benefits; only then can we decide which benefits spill over, and in what ways. Thus, the present chapter is in two principal parts. The first, and longer, part discusses the forms of social benefits from education; it includes a discussion of benefits realized by the student and by family members, although our primary concern is with the benefits as seen by persons outside the family. It is not concerned explicitly with the community, and, in fact, it attempts to look at benefits from education far more broadly than is required for the subsequent analysis of geographic external benefits. The second part of the chapter discusses some of the means by which intercommunity spill-overs of

Reprinted from Burton A. Weisbrod, *External Benefits of Public Education.* Princeton, New Jersey: Princeton University Industrial Relations Section, Department of Economics, 1964. Pp. 15-39. Copyright, 1964, Industrial Relations Section, Princeton University. Reprinted by permission of the publisher.

benefits occur. Both parts deal with their subjects broadly; they leave the intensive analyses to following chapters. We deal with public elementary and secondary education, but many of the findings will be applicable to all levels of schooling, and to private as well as public education.

I

Most economic analysis of returns from education has focused on the contribution of education to earning capacity (and, presumably, to production capacity). While this has been valuable, it is only part of the picture, and perhaps not even a large part. Even aside from those market imperfections which create inequalities between wages and marginal productivity, earnings are an incomplete measure of the productivity of education to the extent that production occurs outside the market.

In addition, emphasis on incremental earnings attributable to education disregards external effects. Schooling benefits many persons other than the student and his present family. It benefits the student's future children, who will receive informal education in the home; and it benefits neighbors, who may be affected favorably by the social values developed in children by the schools, and even by the quietness of the neighborhood while the schools are in session. Schooling benefits employers seeking a trained labor force; and it benefits the society at large by developing the basis for an informed electorate. Compulsory school attendance and public (rather than private) support for education in the United States both suggest that external economies from either the production or consumption of education are believed to be important.[1]

From the vantage point of one interested in optimal resource allocation, it is essential to consider all benefits from some action (as well as all costs). Whether the benefits (or costs) involve explicit financial payments, or whether they are internal to, or external from, a particular decision-maker is irrelevant.

In the private sector of the economy, private benefits from goods and services are reflected in consumer demand; assuming economic rationality, competition, and the absence of external effects, private producers will meet the demand in a socially optimal manner. But when goods and services have significant external effects the private market is inadequate. If the public sector attempts to provide the service, and if consumer sovereignty is to reign, the extent of consumer demand must be judged. It is worth emphasizing that analyzing benefits (or costs) does not preclude specifying which people reap the returns (or incur the costs). In fact, we shall attempt to identify the benefits of education by recognizing the beneficiaries of the education process.

In the discussion which follows, a "benefit" (that is a real benefit) will refer to anything that pushes outward the utility possibility function for the society. Included would be (1) anything which increases production possibilities, such as increased labor productivity; (2) anything which reduces the need to incur costs such as for law enforcement, thereby releasing resources for alternative uses; and (3) anything which increases welfare possibilities directly, such as development of public-spiritedness or social consciousness of one's neighbor. Anything which merely alters relative prices without affecting total utility opportunities for the group under consideration will not be deemed a social benefit (or loss). For example, if expanded education reduces the number of household servants, so that the wage rates of those remaining rise, this rise would not constitute either a benefit or loss from education, but rather a financial transfer between servants and employers. Without making interpersonal utility comparisons we cannot say more. Of course, the increased productivity of those with the additional education is a benefit of type 1.

We turn, now, to the forms of real benefits of education. We begin with an examination of benefits which are realized directly by the student, and then move on to benefits realized by others. One form of benefit to the student is the "financial return" accompanying additional education. A second form is the "financial option" return. Previously unconsidered, this benefit involves the value of the opportunity to obtain still further education. Third are the non-monetary "opportunity options," involving the broadened individual employment choices which education permits; fourth are the opportunities for "hedging" against the vicissitudes of technological change. And fifth are the non-market benefits.

Direct Financial Return

Census Bureau data relating level of income to level of educational attainment show an unmistakable positive correlation. A number of investigators have estimated returns from investment in education by attributing these observed income differentials to education.[2] Some have recognized the presence of factors other than education which affect income and which are positively correlated with level of education. These factors include intelligence, ambition, informal education in the home, number of hours worked, social mobility, and family wealth; they lead to the presumption that, in general, persons who have obtained more education would have greater incomes than persons with less education, even without the additional schooling.[3] At the same time, at least one study has attempted to isolate some of the non-education variables affecting incomes; it found that median salaries rose with additional amounts of post-high-school education, even after adjustments were made for (1) level of high school class rank, (2) intelligence-test scores, and (3) father's occupation.[4] Apparently at least part of the additional incomes of the more educated population are the results of their education.

Although income or earnings differentials attributable to education may be of considerable significance to the recipients, the social significance depends upon the relationship between earnings differentials and (marginal) productivity differentials. We know that market imperfections may make earnings a poor measure of one's contribution to output, and that in a growing economy cross-section age-earnings data will understate future earnings. One writer has suggested that older workers may receive more than their marginal productivity because status and seniority rules maintain wages while productivity is falling.[5] But even assuming that earnings equal current marginal productivity, estimation of lifetime productivity from cross-section earnings data tends to understate future productivity of today's young workers; this is true because in a growing society each new cohort of people into the labor force comes with better education and knowledge. These two examples suggest that the observed current earnings of men are less than fully satisfactory as reflections of future marginal productivity. Much work remains before we can feel confident of our ability to measure adequately the influence of education on productivity. Perhaps more serious, because apparently it has not been recognized, is a methodological limitation to previous estimates of the financial return to education. We turn to this now.

Financial Option Return

Given our interest in resource allocation, we should like to know what financial return from additional education a person can expect. It was suggested above that income differentials associated with education-attainment differentials would have to be adjusted for differences in ability, ambition, and other variables before we could isolate the education effects; and that an adjustment for systematic differences between earnings and productivity would also be required. Let us assume that these adjustments have been made and that we have computed the present values of expected future earnings of an average person with j and k years of education, *ceteris paribus;* it is our contention that this would be an erroneously low estimate of the gross return which may be expected from the additional education.

The value of additional education may be thought of as having two components: (a) the additional earnings resulting from completion of a given level of education (properly discounted to the present, of course), and (b) the value of the "option" to obtain still further education and the rewards accompanying it. Thus, for example, a decision to obtain a high-school education involves not only the likelihood of obtaining the additional earnings typically realized by a high-school graduate but also involves the value of the opportunity to pursue a college education.[6] The value of the option to obtain additional education will tend to be greater the more elementary the education. For the "highest" level of formal education, the value of the option is clearly zero, except insofar as the education provides the option to pursue independent work.

The option-value approach attributes to investment in one level of schooling a portion of the additional return over cost which can be obtained from further education—specifically, that portion which is in excess of the opportunity cost rate of return.[7] Although part of the return from college education is indeed attributed to high-school education, there is no double-counting involved. In fact, the procedure is the same as that involved in the valuation of any asset, where the decision to retain or discard it may be made at various times in the life of the asset. Consider the following case: a machine is offered for sale. The seller, anxious to make the sale, offers an inducement to the buyer in the form of a discount on the purchase of a replacement machine when the present one wears out. Analyzing the prospective buyer's current decision, we see that he is being offered a combination of (1) a machine now, and (2) a discount (or option) "ticket" for possible future use. Both may have value, and both should be considered by the prospective buyer.

Let us assume that the machine has been purchased and used, and the owner is now deciding whether he should buy a replacement. Needless to say, the rate of return expected from the prospective machine will be a function of its cost net of the discount. The profit-maximizing buyer will compute the rate of return on the net cost and compare it with the opportunity cost of capital. Thus, in a real sense, the discount ticket has entered into two decisions: to buy the original machine and to buy the replacement. But this is not equivalent to any erroneous double-counting.

The machine discount-ticket analogy also makes clear the point that the value of the option (or discount) cannot be negative. If a greater rate of return is available elsewhere, the value of the option merely becomes zero, as long as it need not be used. Thus, as long as a high-school graduate need not go on to college the value of the option to go cannot be negative. It is formally conceivable, however, that a positive option value of elementary-school education could consist of a negative value for the high-school component and a larger, positive value for the college component.

The value of the option to pursue additional schooling depends upon (1) the probability of its being exercised and (2) the expected value if exercised. In the absence of further information, factor 1 may be estimated by the proportion of persons completing a particular level of education who go on to a higher level. The expected value of the option if exercised, factor 2, is any excess of the return on that increment of education over the return obtainable on the best comparable alternative investment.

If the option value of education has been overlooked by parents, as it has been by economists, there would be a tendency toward underinvestment in education. If time horizons are short so that, for example, a prospective high-school student and his parents sometimes fail to consider that a few years later the child may wish he could be going on to college, there will be a systematic downward bias to the valuation of education by individuals.

The words "option" and "opportunity" have appeared repeatedly in the discussion above. Indeed, it seems that in many respects the value of education is a function of the additional options which became available to a person having it—job options, income-leisure-security options, additional-schooling options, on-the-job learning options, way-of-life options.

Recognizing the existence of such options suggests a possible means of estimating the monetary equivalent value of non-monetary returns from certain education. Thus, the college graduate who chooses to go to graduate school and then enter academic life may be assumed to obtain a total (not merely monetary) return on his graduate education costs at least equal to what he could have obtained from a comparable alternative investment. In general, added education widens the variety of job opportunities, and to some extent people with more education may choose employment which provides additional non-monetary rewards, such as greater security, perhaps even at the expense of an actual reduction in monetary rewards. To the extent that this is so, and that knowledge of alternatives exists, previous estimates of the individual returns to education, utilizing incremental income or earnings figures for people with two different levels of education, have had a downward bias. If monetary returns from, say, graduate education turn out to be less than comparable alternative returns, the difference would be a minimum measure of non-monetary returns, though not necessarily of the employment-associated return alone. This assumes that such differences are the results of different opportunities or preferences, not of different abilities unconnected with education.

"Hedging" Option

There is another respect in which education provides a person with options: the increased ability to adjust to changing job opportunities. With a rapid pace of technological change, adaptability (which may be a noteworthy output of additional education) becomes important. Education may be viewed as a type of private (and social) hedge against technological displacement of skills. New technology often requires new skills and knowledge; and those persons having more education are likely to be in a position to adjust more easily than those with less education, and to reap the returns from education which the new technology has made possible. This line of reasoning suggests that a more general academic curriculum is desirable since it permits greater flexibility than a curriculum which requires earlier specialization.

Insofar as the return resulting from greater flexibility is realized in the form of earnings, it will be reflected directly in the estimated monetary value of education. The hedging option has additional value, however, to the extent that people have a preference for greater security and stability of earnings.

The hypothesis that added schooling develops added labor-force flexibility and thereby facilitates adjustments to changing skill requirements suggests the following implication: the higher the level of an individual's formal education attainment, the more he can benefit from additional on-the-job training, and, therefore, the more on-the-job training he will obtain. Jacob Mincer's data support this view;[8] through time, investment in learning on the job is increasingly being concentrated on persons with education beyond elementary school. He estimates that in all three years, 1939, 1949, and 1958, on-the-job training costs per person were positively correlated with the level of education. Moreover, a trend is observable—in 1939, on-the-job training costs per person with elementary education were 38 percent of costs per college-educated person; in 1949 they were 30 percent; and by 1958, 28 percent. Over the twenty-year period, training costs per capita for elementary-educated persons actually declined (in constant dollars), while they climbed 13 percent for college-trained persons.

Non-Market Returns

So far we have discussed the return to education which is realized by the individual in terms of his employment conditions. But some of the value of education to the individual accrues in other forms. For example, the fruits of literacy—an output of elementary education—include, in addition to consumption aspects, the implicit value of its non-market use. To illustrate: when a person prepares his own income tax return he performs a service made possible by his literacy. Were this service provided through the market, it would be priced and included in national income.[9]

Assume that roughly fifty million of the sixty million personal income tax returns filed per year are prepared by the taxpayer himself. At a value of $5.00 per return, a low estimate of an average charged by an accountant for preparing a not-too-complex return, we arrive at an annual market value of the tax return services performed by taxpayers for themselves of $250 million. Relative to T. W. Schultz's estimate of total elementary school costs of $7.8 billion in 1956,[10] this suggests a current year return of 3.2 percent of the current investment in literacy. And this is only one, obviously minor, form of return from literacy which the individual enjoys.

This attempt to place a value on a particular use of literacy is subject to at least the following criticism: were it not for the widespread literacy in this country we would probably not have the present type of income tax system operating, and, therefore, we would adjust to illiteracy in a less costly way than having others (say, accountants) prepare tens of millions of returns. The adjustment might involve government tax assessments or a resort to another type of tax such as one on expenditures. Therefore, the literacy value estimate presented above is on the high side, in terms of the alternative tax collection cost in the absence of literacy.

A very rough estimate has been attempted of the cost of collecting an alternative form of tax—a sales tax—which would not require such a literate population, in order to compare it with the collection cost of the income tax. In doing this we do not imply that the two taxes are equally "good" in terms of their distributional or allocative effects. The assumption is that a principal reason for the relative tax collection efficiency of the income tax is the work performed by the taxpayer in preparing his own return. For the year 1940, the all-states average cost of collecting state personal income taxes was $1.50 per $100 collected, while the comparable figure for the states' general sales taxes was $2.00 per $100 collected. In the same year, collection costs per $100 of federal personal income tax were estimated at $1.68,[11] while there was no federal sales tax.

In the absence of a superior alternative we have assumed that a federal sales tax would cost one-third more to collect than the federal personal income tax, the same relationship as held for the states' sales and income taxes. Assuming the 1960 Internal Revenue Service estimate of collection costs, approximately forty cents per $100, to apply to the personal income tax, then a one-third increase in the cost of collecting $50 billion (1959 individual income tax receipts) would involve an additional $66 million—approximately 0.8 percent of elementary school costs.[12]

We may now turn to the benefits of education which are external to the student. If all benefits of education accrued to the student, then, assuming utility-maximizing behavior and access to capital markets, there would be little reason for public concern about the adequacy of education expenditures—unless publicly supported education were an efficient way of altering the personal distribution of income in a desired way.

Income redistribution effects aside, it seems clear that access to the capital market is imperfect and also that a child, even at high school or college age, is in a poor position to make sensible long-run decisions regarding the amount or type of education, though advice from teachers, counselors, and parents may improve the decision. But these imperfections hardly appear to explain the massive public expenditures in support of education—more than $19 billion in 1960, including capital outlays.[13] We are led to the position that to understand why education is of public concern as well as to project demand for education and to determine whether expanded education is warranted on allocative-efficiency grounds alone, we should pay more attention to identifying and quantifying external benefits of education.[14] This section of the chapter suggests a framework for analyzing these benefits and considers opportunities for measurement.

As economists, our interest in external benefits is typically related to the question of whether all benefits (as well as costs) of some action are taken into account by the decision-maker. The issue is whether the benefits are or are not captured by the decision-maker, since the assumption of utility or profit maximization is ordinarily interpreted to imply that benefits will be recognized by the decision-maker if, but only if, he is able to obtain them. Insofar as parents and children make joint decisions on purchases of education, with none of them being a very expert, experienced buyer, those benefits which are less apparent and indirect are likely to be overlooked. Parents thinking of their children may even neglect the less direct benefits to themselves, discussed below. Moreover, benefits to nonfamily members are probably not considered at all.

In principle, the recipients of external benefits from some activity (for example, education) should be willing to subsidize the activity and, indeed, should seek to subsidize it. The voting mechanism and taxation provide the means for subsidization. Analysis of voting behavior may shed some light on the question of whether external benefits are recognized and have an effect on decisions. But regardless of whether or not subsidies are actually paid by "outsiders," we need to identify and measure the magnitudes of external benefits to determine the returns on resources devoted to education.

Persons receiving external benefits from a student's education may be divided into three broad groups, though the same people may be in more than one: (1) residence-related beneficiaries—those who benefit by virtue of some relationship between their place of residence and that of the subject; (2) employment-related beneficiaries—those who benefit by virtue of some employment relationship with the subject; (3) society in general.

Residence-Related Beneficiaries

Current family of the subject.

While the purpose of schooling is obviously education, the manner in which it is provided may result in incidental, even accidental, but nevertheless valuable, by-products; in the case of elementary education, such a by-product is child care. Schools make it possible for mothers who would otherwise be supervising their youngsters to do other things. For those mothers who choose to work, we have an estimate of the productivity of the child-care services—their earnings. This rests on the assumption that the mothers would not work if a sitter had to be hired but do work when the child is in school. If mothers would make other child-care arrangements in the absence of schools, then a better measure of value than earnings-obtained would be the cost of hiring a baby sitter or making some alternative custodial arrangement.

In March 1956, there were 3.5 million working mothers in the United States with children six to eleven years of age.[15] Assuming that as few as one million of these mothers would not work except for the schools (the others being willing to let their children stay with hired persons or other members of the family or friends, or simply to care for themselves), and assuming $2,000 as the earnings of each mother during the school year, the value of the child-care services of elementary school may be estimated as roughly $2 billion per year.[16] Estimating total resource costs (excluding capital outlays but including implicit interest and depreciation) of public and private elementary schools in 1956 at $7.8 billion,[17] we reach the startling conclusion that elementary school support provided a return of 25 percent of cost in the by-product form of child-care services, alone.[18] This disregards the value of these services to mothers who do not choose to work; since the value is certainly greater than zero, the total value of the child care is even more than 25 percent of cost.

The increased production from working mothers tends to offset the foregone production from students in school. Various writers have emphasized students' foregone earnings as a cost of education, and have debated its magnitude, but have not considered the fact that some mothers' earnings are made possible by the fact that children forego earnings to remain in school. Of course, while these benefits of education are external to the student, they are internal to the current family unit.

Future family of the subject.

When the student reaches adulthood and becomes a parent, the children will benefit from his or her education by virtue of the informal education which the children receive in the home. The presence and relevance of such education is recognized, but no attempts to estimate its value have been made. If scores on achievement tests could be related to educational attainments of parents, adjusting for variation in students' ability, we might obtain some information about the extent of education in the home. This might be translated into equivalent years in school, to which a value, perhaps average cost, could be attributed.

If we think of the investment-consumption distinction as involving whether or not benefits accrue in the "present" (consumption) or in the "future" (investment), then education has an investment component in the form of these intergeneration benefits.[19] If we generalize the conception of investment to include not only inter-temporal benefits,[20] but also interpersonal benefits, then the child-care role of schools, discussed above, represents an investment in the productivity of mothers. Similarly, other interpersonal benefits examined below will constitute investment aspects of educational expenditures.

Neighbors.

As we consider more extended groups, beginning with the individual receiving the education and then his family (present and future), we come to his neighbors. Education affects them at least in the following ways: by inculcating acceptable social values and behavior norms in the community children and by providing children with alternatives to unsupervised activities which may have antisocial consequences. The second is essentially of short-period significance—during the time the child is of school age. The first effect is clearly of long-period consequence, following the student as he grows, and as he moves. As the student achieves adulthood, and as he migrates, the social values developed in part through his education continue to affect his "neighbors."[21]

The hypothesis that education does affect neighbors might be tested by studying voting behavior on school issues among nonparents. We might hypothesize that their voting would be influenced by the extent to which students emigrate after completion of school, so that any potential external benefits (or costs) to neighbors would be realized by persons in other communities. Perhaps some notion of the magnitude of external, neighborhood benefits—at least to the extent they are recognized—could be obtained in this manner.

Taxpayers.

Related to the effects of education on neighbors are the effects on those who pay (directly or indirectly) for the consequences of the lack of education. For example, insofar as lack of education leads to employment difficulties and crime, law enforcement costs will tend to be high. Thus may education provide social benefits by reducing the need for incurring these "avoidance costs," to the advantage of taxpayers.

Education also benefits taxpayers in other communities. The migration of poorly educated persons having behavioral patterns and educational attainments differing from those prevailing in the new areas may necessitate additional effort and expense to permit the in-migrant children to adjust to the new school conditions.[22] Thus, people in areas of in-migration have a stake in the education of children in the areas of out-migration. People who are or may be in the same fiscal unit with an individual have a financial stake in his education.

Employment-Related Beneficiaries

The education of one worker may have favorable external effects on the productiviy of others. Where production involves the cooperative effort of workers, flexibility and adaptability of one worker will work to the advantage of others. Productivity of each member of the group influences the productivity of each other member. In such a case, each worker has a financial interest in the education of his fellow workers. The relevance of this interdependence for the present context rests on the assumption that education develops the properties of flexibility and adaptability. Further study is required to determine the extent to which the assumption is valid, and if it is, to estimate its significance.

Employers may also have a financial interest in the schooling and training of their employees. Much of education improves the quality of the labor force and thereby bestows some benefits to employers of the workers insofar as market imperfections or the "specific"[23] nature of the education result in failure of the employer to pay the worker his full (marginal revenue) productivity. Under perfectly competitive conditions, short-run advantages to employers would become benefits to consumers or resource owners in the long run.

Society in General

We have seen that some of the benefits from education are enjoyed by individuals and groups that are reasonably identifiable. But some of the benefits are distributed broadly either spatially or temporally, so that the nature of individual beneficiaries is obscure. These shall be considered under the heading "Society in General," which thus becomes somewhat of a residual category of benefits. Literacy has social value beyond its value to the individual possessing it and to employers. Without widespread literacy the significance of books, newspapers, and similar media for the transmission of information would dwindle; and it seems fair to say that the communication of information is of vital importance to the maintenance of competition and, indeed, to the existence of a market economy, as well as the maintenance of political democracy. The American voting process would be seriously impaired by widespread illiteracy.

Along the same lines it should be noted that the substantial role played by checking deposits in our economy requires, among other things, generalized literacy and competence with arithmetic operations. It is not necessary to argue the issue of cause versus effect, but only to recognize the essentiality of literacy—a principal output of elementary education—to the present state of our economic development. Nor does saying this deny the possibility that other factors were also indispensable to growth.

Equality of opportunity seems to be a frequently expressed social goal. Education plays a prominent role in discussions of this goal, since the financial and other obstacles to education confronted by some people are important barriers to its achievement. If equality of opportunity is a social goal, then education pays social returns over and above the private returns to the recipients of the education, although there may be some private costs to previous holders of privileged positions.

Although the long-term effect of education on future earnings is surely the most powerful income distribution consequence of education,[24] there are also some short-term effects. These occur through the provision by schools of things traditionally considered to be private consumer goods and services—including subsidized lunch programs, musical instrument lessons, and driver-training courses.

Training of persons in particular kinds of skills may result in important external benefits if there are bottlnecks to economic development. In the context of underdeveloped economies, one writer, while particularly noting the political significance of primary and higher education, and the prestige significance of the latter, argues: "Secondary education is essential to the training of 'medium' personnel (elementary teachers, monitors, officials, middle classes). The shortage of such people is today a real obstacle to economic development."[25] But without perfect capital markets and appropriate subsidization programs, these socially valuable people may be unable to capture for themselves the full value of their contribution. Therefore, their earnings would understate the full social benefits of their education. On the other hand, there are surely cases in which education brings differentials in income which exceed the differentials in social marginal product.

We might summarize our findings. Some of the benefits of education are realized at the time the education is being received (that is, in the "short" run); others, after the formal education has been completed (that is, in the "long" run). Benefits to mothers, in terms of the child-care role of schools, and benefits to neighbors, in keeping children "off the streets" are realized while the education is being obtained. Any benefits associated with subsequent employment of the student as well as benefits to the student's future children are realized later.

We have found, further, that benefits from education occur not only at various times but also in various places. The benefits of education do not necessarily accrue to people in the area or in the school district which financed the child's education. In particular, some of the benefits depend upon the individual's place of residence, which may change. Location of many residence-related benefits as well as employment-related benefits will be determined partly by population migration, though this is not generally true of benefits to family members and to society as a whole. While it is not necessarily true that total benefits will depend upon one's location, the point is that the particular beneficiaries will be a function of the location of the individual. Thus, the process of migration is a process of spatial shifting of some of the external effects of education.

Some interesting questions are raised simply by the recognition that external benefits of education exist, and that they are not all in broad, amorphous form; that is, that to some extent these benefits accrue to particular, rather well-defined, groups. Thus, to the extent that the education system at the elementary level is producing child-care services as an output, benefit-principle taxation would suggest that families of the children might pay for these benefits.[26] In general, a desire to use this taxation principle would imply attempts to identify various groups of beneficiaries to assess taxes in recognition of the functional and geographical distribution of benefits. In pointing this out, there is no attempt to argue that the benefit principle, in contrast to the ability-to-pay or some other principle, should prevail.

It seems that there is a legitimate question concerning the justice of requiring broad, public support for education insofar as the benefits are narrow and private, except as an income-redistributive device. For example, to the extent that there is really no educational sacrifice involved in having children attend split-shift classes, so that the real motive for the abolition of split-shifts is to make life more comfortable for mothers who have all of their children in school at the same time, then a question of equity arises: should non-parents be expected to share the costs associated with the provision of these child-care services for parents? The answer may not be an unequivocal "no," but the question deserves further consideration. Except for lack of information, or a total disavowal of benefit-principle taxation, there is little rationale for failure of our education-tax system to recognize the existence of particular groups of beneficiaries.

There is another strong reason for identifying benefits and beneficiaries. To the extent that the distribution of tax burdens for the support of education differs substantially from the distribution of education benefits, it is likely that education will be either un-dersupported or oversupported from an allocative-efficiency stand-point, given the existing preference structure and distribution of income and wealth. At the same time, one objective of education policy may be to change the distribution of income.

Both with respect to equity and allocative efficiency in educa-tion, the phenomenon of migration needs to be recognized. Insofar as some of the benefits of education depend upon the location of the individual and insofar as this location is a variable over his lifetime, some of the benefits from education accrue to people who have played no part at all in the financing of this particular person's education. This would seem to be especially pertinent with respect to areas of substantial net in- or out-migration. On benefit-principle grounds, areas experiencing net in-migration might be expected to subsidize educational activities in areas of net out-migration, par-ticularly if highly productive people were involved, and even if their productivity would have been lower in the origin area. Sub-sidy in the opposite direction might be justified insofar as the inmi-grants to an area are relatively unproductive compared to its out-migrants. Needless to say, there are good and powerful argu-ments in favor of financing education at a local level. However, a thorough analysis of the issue would seem to require recognition of the points raised here.

The analytic approach to benefit identification employed in this section is one of many alternatives; it does appear to have the advantage of focusing on the time and location dimensions of edu-cation benefits, and these are relevant to the study both of effi-ciency in the allocation of resources between education and other ends, and of equity in the financing of education.

It is clear that even with much additional effort we shall be unable to measure all the relevant benefits of education. At the same time the following three points are worth noting, and they summarize the views expressed in this section: (1) identification of benefits is the logical step prior to measurement and, therefore, recognizing the forms of benefits represents some progress; (2) determination of what it is we are trying to measure will make it easier to develop useful quantification methods; (3) some reasonable measures of some education benefits are possible.

II

Aside from the effects of school tax shifting, are there any economic reasons why the quantity and quality of education provided by some community should be of interest to "outsiders"? Such interest would exist if, among other possibilities, (1) outsiders' productivity or employment prospects were affected by the level of productivity of persons educated elsewhere; or (2) outsiders' tax burdens were affected by the level of welfare payments to persons educated elsewhere. This division is between "real," or technological, effects and "pecuniary," or transfer, effects. As one example of the latter, consider this case: community A provides high quality education, and as a result unemployment rates among its former students are low. Community B, in the same state, may benefit insofar as unemployment in the state is lower than it would otherwise be (that is, insofar as some unemployment is "structural"), and thus smaller unemployment compensation taxes and relief payments are needed. These reductions in unemployment and welfare payments are not additional "real" gains to society as a whole; they are reductions in transfer payments from B to A. But to the outsiders, B, they are benefits from A's expenditures on education.

Transfer benefits are not limited to persons in the same state. Migration brings into a common fiscal unit people educated in various parts of the country; in this way, too, the adequacy of schooling provided in one area may subsequently affect persons who had been "outsiders." Thus, under existing fiscal structures many outsiders share in the financial burdens resulting from inadequate education—that is, share the financial benefits of adequate education. And so they have a stake in the educational activities of other communities—on behalf of people they may never meet. . . .

Many of the spatial spill-overs we discuss occur through migration. Educational capital is embodied in people; thus the returns from this investment occur as the individuals use the capital, wherever they may be located. If the community regards its aggregate income as something to be maximized, and if education has contributed to that income, then loss of income accompanying out-migration of persons educated locally is a loss of one of the benefits from public education. . . . The severity of the loss cannot be specified, however, without knowledge of the community welfare function.

Even if a community does not regard out-migration as the cause of loss of the *entire* incremental earnings stream generated by education, it may be concerned with the loss of the tax revenue portion of those earnings. . . . Relatively few communities have explicit taxes on income,[27] but most if not all do tax real or personal wealth, and greater income is likely to lead to greater wealth.

In addition to the spill-overs of monetary benefits, there may be spill-overs of non-monetary, non-market, benefits of education. For example, people with more education are likely to make larger contributions of their own labor to civic and charitable causes,[28] and to be community leaders. We do not want to value the productivity of these services at zero simply because they may be unremunerated. If the education caused the increased willingness or ability to undertake these non-market activities then the out-migration of such public spirited persons from the community in which they were educated is a spill-out, or export, of education benefits.[29] The origin area produced benefits realized by the destination area.

NOTES

[1]Similarly, but perhaps more clearly, compulsory smallpox vaccination together with public provision of vaccine reflects external economies of "consumption" of the vaccine.

[2]On the relation between educational attainment and earnings see G. Becker, "Underinvestment in College Education?" *American Economic Review, Proceedings,* L, (May 1960), pp. 346-54; H. S. Houthakker, "Education and Income," *Review of Economics and Statistics,* XLI (February 1959), pp. 24-28; H. P. Miller, "Annual and Lifetime Income in Relation to Education," *American Economic Review,* L (December 1960), pp. 962-86; E. F. Renshaw, "Estimating the Returns to Education," *Review of Economics and Statistics,* XLII (August 1960), pp. 318-24; W. L. Hansen, "Total and Private Rates of Return on Investment in Schooling," *Journal of Political Economy,* LXXI (April 1963), pp. 128-40.

[3]See D. S. Bridgman, "Problems in Estimating the Monetary Value of College Education," *Review of Economics and Statistics, Supplement,* XLII (August 1960), p. 181.

[4]Dael Wolfle, "Economics and Educational Values," *Review of Economics and Statistics, Supplement,* XLII (August 1960), pp. 178-79. See also his *America's Resources of Specialized Talent* (New York: Harper & Bros., 1954); and Wolfle and Joseph G. Smith, "The Occupational Value of Education for Superior High School Graduates," *Journal of Higher Education,* 27 (1956), pp. 201-13.

[5]Mary Jean Bowman, "Human Capital: Concepts and Measures," in Selma J. Mushkin (ed.), *Economics of Higher Education* (hereinafter cited as "Higher Education") (Washington: U.S. Government Printing Office, 1962), p. 86.

[6]Research by Jacob Mincer suggests that additional schooling also provides opportunities to obtain additional on-the-job training (see his "On-the-

job Training: Costs, Returns, and Some Implications," *Journal of Political Economy, Supplement,* LXX (October 1962), pp. 50-79, especially Table 1. The value of this opportunity should be included in the financial option approach developed here.

[7]For an algebraic presentation of the method for computing the option value of various incremental levels of schooling, see Appendix C.

[8]*Op.cit.,* Tables 1 and 2. But E. F. Renshaw predicts that the principal educational requirements of the 1960s, with respect to the labor force, will be directed toward trade schools and apprenticeship programs ("Investment in Human Capital" [unpublished manuscript, 1960], p. 13).

[9]It could be argued that the service (like many others in national income and product) is not a final output, but a cost item (cost of tax collection), and thus should not be included in estimates of production; but since it is often difficult to distinguish clearly outputs from inputs in our national accounts, and since our national income and product accounts principally measure effort expended, it would be interesting to make some estimate of the market-value equivalent of the services performed by a person in preparing his own income tax return.

Inclusion of the value of this non-market production as an educational benefit presupposes that this represents a net increase in the value of the individual's total non-market activities and that the opportunity cost of performing additional non-market production is essentially zero.

Richard Goode has suggested in correspondence that, although the failure to consider non-market production leads to understatement of the return to education, "nevertheless, there seems to be little danger that this omission will lead to an undervaluation of educational benefits in comparing time periods, countries, and population groups with different amounts of formal education." He presents "the hypothesis that the greater the amount of formal education the greater the proportion of goods and services acquired through the market. If this is true, estimates based on money earnings or national income statistics may exaggerate the contribution of education to real income differentials or growth."

[10]Education and Economic Growth," *Social Forces Influencing American Education* (hereinafter cited as "Economic Growth") (Chicago: National Society for the Study of Education, 1961), p. 64, Table 5.

[11]James W. Martain, "Costs of Tax Administration: Statistics of Public Expenses," *Bulletin of the National Tax Association,* 29 (February 1944), pp. 132-47, as cited in Charles A. Benson, *The Economics of Public Education* (Boston: Houghton Mifflin Co., 1961), p. 145.

Estimation of collection costs is subject to the common difficulty of the allocation of joint costs; furthermore, we really know little about scale economies in tax collection, or about the difference in degree of enforcement of state and federal taxes, so that it is dangerous to apply state cost figures to the federal level.

[12]Actually we should note that a number of years of education is required to develop "literate" people but also that, once developed, they presum-

ably retain the knowledge. Were we to take into account the number of tax returns an average person may be expected to file during his lifetime, a higher rate of return would appear.

[13]U.S. Department of Health, Education, and Welfare, *Health, Education, and Welfare Trends, 1961* (Washington: U.S. Government Printing Office, 1961), pp. 52, 53.

[14]It is true, however, that economies of scale (with respect to the number of students) would also be a sufficient explanation for the public interest in education.

[15]U.S. Bureau of the Census, *Marital and Family Status of Workers: 1956,* Series P.-50, No. 73 (Washington: U.S. Government Printing Office, April 1957), Table 3, p. 11.

[16]For those mothers who would be willing to hire baby sitters, obtainable for, perhaps, $1,000 per year, the value of the school-child-care services is this alternative cost of $1,000, instead of $2,000. Of the 3.5 million working mothers with children six to eleven years old, approximately 1.5 million also had children twelve to seventeen. Some of the older children could conceivably care for the younger ones; but even considering the remaining 2 million, the assumption that one-half would not work except for the care provided by schools seems plausible and even conservative.

[17]Schultz, "Economic Growth," p. 85.

[18]If working mothers employ housekeepers as substitutes and if they incur other additional costs in working (for example, transportation and additional clothes), these added costs should be deducted from the gross returns.

[19]Schultz has also recognized this point: "The education of women . . . reduces the subsequent effective costs of education because of the critical role that mothers play in motivating their children to obtain an education and to perform well while they are attending school. Thus, if we could get at the factors underlying the perpetuation of education, it is likely that we would discover that the education of many persons not in the labor force contributes heavily to the effective perpetuation of the stock of education. To the extent that this is true, some part of the education not in the labor force contributes to this investment process." ("Economic Growth," *op.cit.,* pp. 74-75.)

[20]Tax implications of the existence of intertemporal education returns have been discussed by R. Goode, "Educational Expenditures and Income Tax," in Mushkin (ed.), *Higher Education,* pp. 281-304.

[21]One writer points out: "Education has effects on the caliber of voluntary community activities: choral groups, drama clubs, local art shows, etc." (Benson, *op.cit.,* p. 349.)

[22]See, for example, C. F. Schmid, V. A. Miller, and B. Abulaban, "Impact of Recent Negro Migration on Seattle Schools," *International Population Conference Papers* (Vienna: Union International pour l'Étude Scientifique de la Population, 1959), pp. 674-83.

[23]As the term is used by Gary S. Becker "specific" training is that which raises the marginal productivity of the worker in one firm more than it raises his productivity in other firms. By contrast, "general" training raises marginal productivity equally in many firms. Since, under competitive conditions, wage rates are determined by workers' marginal productivities in other firms, a worker with "specific" training would be expected to receive a wage less than his actual marginal revenue productivity but more than his alternative productivity. Becker, "Investment in Human Capital: A Theoretical Analysis," *Journal of Political Economy, Supplement,* LXX (October 1962), pp. 9-49.

[24]The relation between education and income distribution has been studied by J. Mincer, "Investment in Human Capital and Personal Income Distribution," *Journal of Political Economy,* LXVI (August 1958), pp. 281-302 and L. Soltow, "The Distribution of Income Related to Changes in the Distributions of Education, Age and Occupation," *Review of Economics and Statistics,* XLII (November 1960), pp. 450-53.

[25]Michel Debeauvais, "Economic Problems of Education in the Underdeveloped Countries," in International Association of Universities, *Some Aspects of Educational Development in Europe* (Paris: International Universities Bureau, 1961), pp. 116-17.

[26]This point came out in a discussion with Julius Margolis.

[27]Actually, as of July 1, 1960, municipal income taxes were levied in only five states—Kentucky, Ohio, Pennsylvania, Missouri and Alabama. In each of the latter two, only one community had such a tax—St. Louis and Gadsden. In Kentucky, ten communities levied income taxes; in Ohio, the number was sixty-one, of which fifty-one had populations under 50,-000. Municipal income taxation was most widely used in Pennsylvania, where it originated; income taxes were imposed by thirty cities; 240 boroughs, 40 townships, and 800 school districts. (Advisory Commission on Intergovernmental Relations, *Local Nonproperty Taxes and the Coordinating Role of the State* (Washington: U.S. Government Printing Office, 1961), Table 19, p. 38.

[28]See footnote 21.

[29]It is possible that the people who go to school longer would be more public spirited even if they had not obtained the additional education. If so, the education would not cause the observed non-market contributions by better-educated people.

9

EDUCATION AND POVERTY

by Thomas I. Ribich

*Thomas I. Ribich discusses in considerable detail the rela-
tionship between educational investments and the War on
Poverty. In reviewing the theoretical underpinnings of
cost-benefit analysis, he concludes that the rate of return
for persons who complete their education cannot easily be
applied to school dropouts. Many school dropouts lack the
capability of students who go on to graduation. Ribich,
like other authors in the field, raises cautionary admoni-
tions regarding the broad applicability of cost-benefit
analysis as an instrument for public policy. He suggests
that the strongest case for increased educational expenditures for the poor may lie in non-economic arguments.*

A major presumption of the war on poverty is that education and
training are especially effective ways to bring people out of poverty. How well founded is this presumption? Which types of education are most productive? This study develops techniques that may
help to answer such questions and it suggests the direction such
answers may take.

The basic analytical technique used in this study is benefit-cost
analysis, an approach that represents economics in one of its most
venturesome moods. To many noneconomists, however, the technique suggests the replacement of wisdom with a limited mechani-

Reprinted from Thomas I. Ribich, *Education and Poverty.* Washington, D.C.: The
Brookings Institution, 1968, pp. 1-15, 101-109, 113-125. © 1968 by The Brookings
Institution, 1775 Massachusetts Avenue, N.W., Washington, D.C. 20036.

cal procedure. To many economists it appears to rest too much on the unsteady foundation of theoretical welfare economics.

But with public policy already committed to a war on poverty, many of the standard objections to benefit-cost procedures have reduced force. The first aim of the war, after all, can be viewed as essentially an economic one of raising the incomes of the poor. This makes the task of benefit-cost analysis a great deal easier. For while such computations can never hope to give an accurate weighing to all advantages and disadvantages, they can measure reasonably well the economic impact on the directly affected individuals.

A related advantage of working within the context of a war on poverty is that the poverty program gives the economists some guide to income distribution preferences. The implicit consensus of a publicly sponsored antipoverty campaign is that one group, the individuals in poverty, have greater "need" for additional income than do other people. Thus the usual agnosticism of the theoretical welfare economist on redistribution questions seems inappropriate in this instance. A dollar gain for the poor at the cost of less than a dollar for the average taxpayer apparently brings a net gain for society. Dollar amounts thus become an unusually good proxy for the underlying notion of overall economic welfare, and the comparison of dollar benefits with dollar costs becomes directly relevant for policy questions.

Before specific computations can be undertaken in a benefit-cost framework, several conceptual and methodological issues must be resolved. To set the stage, some straightforward applications of the economics of education are reviewed.

THE SIMPLE CASE FOR EDUCATION

In the history of economic thought, education has consistently been a favored means of social improvement, especially for the poor. Economists' enthusiasm for education has at times brought together strange bedfellows. Adam Smith and Karl Marx both emphasized the critical need for improved education in developing general aptitudes among working men as well as in countering the erosion of public responsibility brought on by the division of labor. Malthus and Ricardo, though frequently at odds, agreed that more education was required to improve the moral fiber of the lower classes.[1]

Many of the arguments for the public support of education are based on the observation that education is of great benefit to society in general and not just to the specific individuals who are educated. But this does not help in answering the question of whether an additional expenditure on education at this point in time is an efficient way of raising the incomes of the poor.[2] What is needed instead is a reason why individuals undertake less educational investment in themselves than is warranted by the personal rate of payoff to education.

Human Capital Investment

The most general reason that can be provided relies on the idea of an inherent capital market imperfection that holds back *all* forms of human investment, not only education. Milton Friedman argues:

> If a fixed money loan is made to finance investment in physical capital, the lender can get some security for his loan in the form of a mortgage or residual claim to the physical asset itself, and he can count on realizing at least part of his investment in case of necessity by selling the physical asset. If he makes a comparable loan to increase the earning power of a human being, he clearly cannot get any comparable security; in a non-slave state, the individual embodying the investment cannot be bought and sold.[3]

Thus, among equally expensive things a poor person might wish to purchase with borrowed funds, a tangible and resalable item is most attractive to the lender. The prospective financier is more apt to be interested if the contemplated investment is a building or a machine rather than an equally costly course of study. The upshot is apparent: in terms of benefits to individuals, there is a tendency for less than an optimal amount to be invested in human capital.

With borrowing made difficult, the individual himself can, of course, postpone investment until his savings accumulate. Unfortunately, the peculiarities of human capital make such postponement unusually expensive; for if a man in pursuit of education withdraws from the labor force, his loss in wages can be quite heavy.[4] But a perhaps more pervasive problem is the reduction in total lifetime return on his investment. The absence of resale value for human capital means that the investment is income-yielding only so long as the original investor lives. The contrast with investments in physical capital is readily apparent. Once a factory, for instance, is constructed and turned into a profitable venture, the capitalized value of the future earnings stream can be sold and the original entrepreneur can depart, taking with him a large share of an income stream that continues to be generated despite his absence. For education there is no parallel option.

In short, when human capital is the contemplated investment, the individual with little cash finds himself in a dilemma. If he tries to plunge ahead immediately, he encounters a hostile capital market and very high interest rates (should he be fortunate enough to find a creditor). If he delays, rising opportunity costs and a shortened stream of returns begin to close in. Thus, allowing the possibility of postponement seems only to heighten the difference between physical and human capital. For the individual the pressures still play against educational investment.

But analyzing the behavior of a single individual trying to make an investment choice—human versus physical—understates the difference between the two forms of investment.

The trouble with the example of the lone unaffluent young person is the temptation to conclude that the only thing that separates human and physical investment is the *ease* of postponement. This indeed is the suggestion of Gary Becker's argument that an eighteen-year-old who tries to invest in physical capital, rather than advanced education, would have nearly the same borrowing difficulties. Becker points out that the "collateral provided by his equipment would probably be very imperfect"; and the young man's only consolation is that he "might, without too much cost, postpone the investment for a number of years until his reputation and equity were sufficient to provide the 'personal' collateral required to borrow funds."[5] But is there any real cost at all? The young man of course loses something by being rebuffed in his early borrowing attempt, but this is inadequate proof that the investment itself will be postponed and that a net loss *for society* occurs.

Indeed, there is very good reason to suspect that society does *not* suffer on balance. The youth who cannot exploit a particular physical investment is likely to find that the investment opportunity does not wait for him. If the contemplated investment (for example, a new factory) is truly profitable, chances are a well-established man will take advantage of it, and the implied increase in productivity will be realized with little delay. Thus the problems of youth and poverty need not imply any lag at all in the rate of physical investment; and the rate of return on such investment should, therefore, remain reasonably close to the interest rate at which the most trustworthy in the community can borrow. In human investment, however, the young man who could profit greatly from his investment in education is also a vital part of the investment opportunity. If he delays (or fails altogether to acquire) his education, the delayed (or missed) opportunity cannot be exploited by another, more seasoned investor. For the productivity gain to be realized, the young man must personally engage in an act of investment.

This difference can be brought into clearer focus by considering Marshall's observation that business ability is positively related to the ownership of physical capital, and skilled entrepreneurs will therefore control great amounts of such capital.[6] Becker applies this to suggest a parallel between human and physical investment: namely, that relatively bright people tend to invest relatively more in themselves.[7] But there would seem to be a very sharp divergence in this parallel. For physical capital, it is apparent that a relatively small group of specialized individuals can exploit a vast proportion of the available opportunities in an economy—there is hardly a limit on the number of good business sites that an able businessman can purchase and use. On the other hand, an able investor in human capital has, so to speak, only one business site at his disposal: his own talent. Only a limited amount of capital can be "erected" on this "site." This means that, in the case of education, the exploitation of all good "sites" requires investment activities by multitudes of people, many of whom have weak collateral and poor market knowledge.[8]

This is not to say that the prospective eighteen-year-old businessman in Becker's example is no worry at all. When financiers fail to trust youthful businessmen, it can be inferred that the supply of entrepreneurial talent is restricted, tending to drive up the price of entrepreneurial services and thereby to curtail the total number of physical investments undertaken. But given the fact that a single experienced businessman can successfully initiate a large number of projects, there is doubt that this is a serious concern.[9] Moreover, there is reason to think that the supply of skilled businessmen is largely a problem of *human* capital. Perhaps the eighteen-year-old would do well to get a degree in industrial management rather than thrashing around in the business world until his "personal" collateral builds up.

The various aspects of the embodiment problem in human capital can thus be understood best as a deductive chain: (1) for a given individual, human capital is exceptionally poor collateral to offer a prospective creditor; (2) an effort to avoid borrowing, by waiting until savings accumulate, turns out to be an expensive proposition and can deter human capital investments once the early opportunity is missed; (3) in contrast, postponement by an individual of an investment in physical capital does not usually mean that the investment itself is neglected or that the rate of return is substantially influenced; and (4) there is no market tendency for human investment decisions to become effectively specialized and centralized. The implication is essentially the same as before: natural mar-

ket forces tend to keep the rate of return on human capital well
above that on other investments, creating the presumption that
education is an especially efficient way of intervening to help the
poor.

It may well be that the embodiment problem (and its logical
consequences) is only a minor factor influencing educational attainment and educational expenditures. For instance, the "subculture of poverty" may be the most important factor in explaining
and predicting individual educational decisions among the poor[10]
and in determining whether added educational investments are
appropriate. The poor may have biases against the classroom that
lead them to systematically underrate the power of education,
thus implying that society should counter this "irrationality" by
greatly increasing its efforts on the education front. But it may be
that the poor will not respond effectively to education unless poverty itself is first ameliorated. Though research on the social and
psychological attributes of the poor is illuminating,[11] there is little
agreement on whether (on balance) the existence of a subculture
of poverty weakens or strengthens the case for education.

Another, more obvious facet of the educational investment
problem is the heavy social support of education already in existence. This force surely operates to raise the total investment in
education above what it would otherwise be. The issue can be
simply reduced to the question of whether or not the present
level of subsidization is sufficient to overcome the "natural" ten-
dencies toward underinvestment in education. The answer to this
question is not apparent. If there is a tendency for the public
sector to receive less than an optimal allotment of resources, the
counterbalancing force of subsidization is likely to be insufficient.
Moreover, the poor, being a politically weak minority group, may
receive less than a "fair share" of expenditures in the public sector. On the other hand, since education is publicly valued for
many reasons other than the private income gained by those educated, education may already receive fiscal support far in excess
of what could be justified in terms of financial profitability. The
current level of support may be more than is necessary to coun-
teract the capital market barriers to private educational investment. If this is true, the rate of return to education may already
be very low and the attempt to raise private incomes via added
education may even entail costs in excess of the resulting pure
financial gain. In that case, further expansion of education would
be an expensive way to bring people out of poverty.

The net effect of these opposing forces cannot be reckoned by

casual observation and inference. Actual measurement of gains
and costs is required. Several studies have attempted to do this.

The Payoff Rate From Continued Education

For the most part, the empirical studies testing the hypothesis of
underinvestment in education have concentrated on estimating the
payoff for continuing formal education through an additional block
of years. The aim is to measure how profitable it is for an average
student to attend an additional two (or perhaps four) years in the
regular educational sequence, and to judge whether this payoff rate
is high enough to justify the encouragement of heavier flows of
students through these levels of schooling.[12] Thus far, indications
are that the payoff is sufficiently high. Those who attempt to make
an empirical case for giving education a large role in the battle
against poverty generally rely upon this evidence.[13] The payoff
rates calculated in the school continuation studies are sometimes in
the form of discounted benefits as a ratio of costs, but more often
they are expressed as internal rates of return specifying the rate of
discount necessary to equate returns with costs. Both "private" and
"social"[14] rates of return have been computed. The former equate
estimated after-tax lifetime income gain with personal costs borne
by the individual who continues his education. The latter equate
before-tax gains with the total resource costs of the extra years of
education, regardless of who pays what part of the bill. Though
many differences can be found in computational technique and in
final tallies, practically all of the studies arrive at the conclusion that
the payoff rate for continued education at all levels is remarkably
high—something in excess of 10 percent for college education and
perhaps as high as 50 percent for increments at lower levels.[15] On
both a private and a social basis, the empirical consensus suggests
that increasing the flow of students at any level is an investment
whose costs are easily covered by the anticipated financial benefits.

Although this result is widely accepted and frequently cited, a
number of critics have suggested that the conceptual difficulties
involved in estimating the returns to education are serious enough
to undermine a pro-education conclusion.[16] Some critics question
how much more a person really earns because of the *independent*
influence of extra education. The trained individual does not, like
a business investment, generate a directly observable profit. As a
proxy for actual returns, we can compare the lifetime income
stream of a person who manages to complete a given number of
school years with that of a person who terminated sooner. The
difference between the two streams is the proxy. Unfortunately,

those who depart at an earlier point in the educational sequence are not precise counterparts of the people who continue, and in fact are typically less able as students and, presumably, as workers. Consequently, they are likely destined for relatively lower incomes in any event. Therefore, the observed and unadjusted income differentials are probably inflated estimates.

As long as returns estimates are based on income differentials between individuals who continue schooling and those who do not, there will never be a completely adequate answer to this criticism. It can always be asserted that students who opt for continuation are blessed with character traits that might elude even the most skillfully designed objective tests. Nevertheless, considerable progress has been made during the last few years in controlling for at least the tangible differences—in aptitudes and in social and personal characteristics—between individuals who terminate schooling at different levels.

The most notable work along these lines has been performed by Becker.[17] He estimates that the unadjusted private rate of return for going to college, calculated at 13 percent, is reduced to something greater than 11 percent after making all the adjustments permitted by the available information. The more sketchy data relating to lower levels of educational attainment deter his attempts at similar formal adjustments for these levels. He does note, however, that the available clues point to a slightly greater adjustment factor for these levels; but since unadjusted payoff rates are much higher, he concludes that the adjustments would still leave these rates at enticingly high levels. More refined empirical work remains to be done on this question. Still, the small effect of the readily measurable characteristics has shifted (at least to some degree) the burden of proof to those who claim that controlling for "all" interfering variables would plunge the rate of payoff to education to unfavorable levels.[18]

A second popular attack concedes the differential ability issue, but questions whether the higher incomes of the better educated represent a net gain for the community. Graduating from high school or college may mean much higher lifetime incomes even for the sort of people who usually terminate earlier; but—so the critique runs—that merely implies that employers have a preference for degree holders that, in turn, may be founded largely on a belief that graduates have demonstrated desirable ambition and persistence by the successful completion of a long course of study. If the graduates had not been available, nongraduates might have been hired at roughly the same rate of pay and have performed on the job at roughly the same level of efficiency. Thus, while the individual may find a diploma useful in the scramble for high paying jobs, his gain may entail a commensurate loss for someone else. And, as a corollary, it could be argued that the individual who escapes poverty by an education route may, in the process, "bump" a fellow worker into the poverty category.

But those who drop out in the middle of high school or college succeed in earning appreciably more than those who never started, thus implying that something more than the magic of the diploma attracts employers.[19] It could, of course, be argued that employers are impressed even by an unsuccessful effort to obtain a diploma. Conversely, however, they might be repelled by the apparent tendency of the prospective employee to start a project and then not finish it.

Moreover, there is a positive relationship between the measured amount learned by individuals completing the *same* level of schooling and their income during their working years.[20] This suggests that the absorption of learning is economically rewarding in and of itself. Though it might be argued that employers are dazzled by high grades when selecting employees, it is interesting to note that the observed income differential between low scoring and high scoring students was recorded several years after (and in most cases over a decade after) the termination of schooling. It would seem more reasonable to believe that demonstrated competence on the job rather than a lingering reputation as a good student with good grades led to this differential.

Finally, there is a large gap between actual economic growth of the American economy and the growth that can be explained by the measured increases in physical capital and in the size of the labor force. If it is insisted that education does little in improving the actual efficiency of workers, one is hard pressed to account for the size of this gap.[21] One would have to assign an implausibly large amount of credit to technological change.

Though none of these arguments is absolutely clinching, together they succeed in strengthening the link between education and productivity; and with this link more secure, it becomes harder to claim that the income gain experienced by an educated individual simply comes at the expense of someone else. This does not mean that the entire income gain observed is a net social gain, but it does imply a large part of it probably is.

To sum up, the present state of empirical knowledge suggests that the forces tending to produce underinvestment in education are stronger than the countervailing force of current government subsidization. While it is true that the payoff rate evidence noted here does not relate specifically to the people in poverty, it would nevertheless seem to apply a fortiori to this group. It is the poor, after all, who are likely to have the most difficulty in getting around capital market imperfections and the other problems associated with the fact that education is an embodied investment. Moreover, the existence of exceptionally high rates of payoff for lower levels of schooling also suggests that underinvestment in education is a problem closely associated with poverty: it is the children of the poor who most often leave school early, and it is the earliest school leavers who have the highest odds for earning poverty level incomes.

It should again be noted that the above line of argument does not take account of the social benefits of education or the nonfinancial returns to the individual. . . . However, given the focus of the present study on the relation between poverty and education, our primary concern will continue to be with the personal income impact of education.

CURRENT FEDERAL POLICY

A disquieting feature of the evidence on the rate of return to education is its oblique, and thus uncertain, relationship to contemporary policy. Current federal education programs attempt to help the poor to continue their formal schooling, but the primary emphasis nevertheless lies in two other directions. One direction is the establishment of special types of training outside the regular school system: preschool classes in the form of Operation Headstart, and vocationally oriented training through programs like Job Corps and Neighborhood Youth Corps. The second major approach, the aim of Title I of the Elementary and Secondary Education Act of 1965, involves increasing the quality of formal education for poor children at both primary and high school levels.[22]

This is not to say that the continuation of formal schooling is not anticipated as a result of these programs. Indeed, one of the stated motives of the Neighborhood Youth Corps is the encouragement of school continuation. It works toward this end by providing part-time subsidized work for students who feel financial pressures to quit school and by counseling and training dropouts (and potential dropouts) in the hope that they will perceive more clearly the connection between learning and future income, thus inducing them to return to (or remain in) high school. Similarly, the preschool programs and the improved quality of education in the regular school years should, to some extent, induce a higher proportion of pupils to stay in school longer. But, despite these aims and expectations, there is little question that the current antipoverty efforts are founded on a belief that simple prolongation of schooling, of present quality, is of secondary importance.

Good reasons can be given for this belief. On an optimistic note, one might argue that, while encouraging youths to continue school has a respectable payoff rate, the current education programs should result in even larger economic gains for the poor per dollar spent. In defense of preschool training, one might cite the recently accumulated evidence that critical habits of learning are acquired in the preschool years, implying that additional schooling time at the beginning may be the most efficacious way to lengthen the duration of education.[23] Job-oriented training too is a form of extra schooling, and since it is geared specifically to the development of marketable skills, it could be argued that it should have at least as much economic effectiveness as a commensurate amount of general education. Finally, increasing the quality of schooling and (presumably) increasing the amount learned in the same period of time have the economic appeal of entailing no extra costs in the form of foregone income.

Another, less cheerful, point of view begins with the presumption that schools servicing a decidedly underprivileged clientele are, for various reasons, seriously ineffective in their current mode of operation.[24] Thus, while encouraging an "ordinary" potential dropout to continue formal schooling might be a good idea, the slum school dropout may be missing out on very little by his early departure. Moreover, even if continuation would be conomically advantageous to the slum school youth, it might be argued that the school has typically performed such a poor job of winning the trust of the pupil that a large and expensive effort is required to persuade him of this advantage. If slum schools appear deficient enough to raise these sorts of speculations, one might well turn to educational programs outside the regular school system and attempt simultaneously to do as much as possible about reforming and improving the quality of instruction in public schools.

Regardless of the reasoning behind the current legislation—and there will be no attempt here to judge which points of view are most prominent and most persuasive—the fact remains that the impact of the educational changes recently put into effect is not the kind of impact or change measured by the payoff-rate evidence discussed in the immediately preceding section. New measurements are needed that have a more direct bearing on current policy. . . .

INTERGENERATIONAL EFFECTS

It is frequently argued that improving the education of the present generation of poor people will have large positive effects on future generations as educational values pass from parent to child. From this it is sometimes speculated that educational expenditures have the unique characteristic of solving the poverty problem once and for all: a successful educational experience for one generation means that future progeny will take naturally to education and very few will end up with skills so meager as to earn only poverty level incomes. It seems clear, however, that such hopes for future generations depend upon a substantial educational gain by the current generation of the poor. Unfortunately, this first step, the large initial thrust upward, is not necessarily easy to induce. According to the computations of the preceding chapters, most special educational efforts—of the kind and scope examined—in behalf of the poor can be expected to yield only modest gains. The available evidence thus does not allow a confident and cheerful prediction that a dose of extra educational effort will immunize all future generations against poverty.

Still, small as well as large gains in learning and income are likely to be transmitted, and to that extent the poverty problems of future generations will be less serious as a result of present education efforts. Quantifying this future-generation gain and adding it to the gain of the initially educated generation would, therefore, seem to be an important refinement in our estimate of benefits. The following calculation attempts to gauge the relative importance of the intergenerational effect of education.

In estimating intergenerational benefits, it would be convenient to relate the education of the parents directly to the economic success of offspring. Unfortunately, available data do not permit such one-step procedures. The only reasonable alternative is to relate parents' educational attainment with children's, and then infer income gain from the latter.

A recent study of American families by the University of Michigan's Survey Research Center is the best source for making this intergenerational education link.[25] Information is in the form of years of education completed. Specifically, it indicates how much longer a child is likely to stay in school in the event that the family head experiences more years of education . . . . [The] educational advance from high school dropout to high school graduate seems to be of greatest relevance. For educational gains in this range, the Michigan study suggests that family heads who graduate (rather than drop out) raise children who end up going to school 1.1 years

longer on the average.[26] In other words, two years of extra education in the first generation seem to result in more than one year of
extra schooling in the next generation.

One shortcoming of this estimate is that it fails to reckon adequately with the educational attainment of the family head's wife.
In the large majority of cases, the family head is a married male
whose wife presumably has had at least as much contact with the
children as he has. Since males with relatively more education are
usually married to relatively better educated wives, the apparent
second-generation effect of the family head's education is in part a
result of the wife's higher educational attainment. The Michigan
study indicates that this is generally the case, but because the statistical analysis treats mother's and father's educations asymmetri-
cally, it is not possible to tell if her role is more or less important
than the father's.[27] In the absence of this information the fairest
assumption would seem to be that both father's and mother's educations must be increased by 2 years in order for the full 1.1 years
to be gained by the next generation.

Settling on this assumption is, however, only a small part of the
problem. If we are to arrive at even a rough estimate of the pecuniary implications of second generation effects, several more assumptions and several numerical manipulations are required. For
purposes of this illustrative calculation, the assumptions are simplis-
tic and approximate. They consist of the following:

1. Each person in the first generation marries, and each family
has (on the average) 2.5 children who are born when the married
couple is 25 years of age.[28]

2. The educational improvements experienced by both the first
and second generations affect males and females to the same degree. That is to say, the initial educational improvement leads to a
2 year gain by each male and female experiencing the improvement, and a 1.1 year gain by both sexes in the next generation.
Males and females are also assumed to be of equal number in both
generations.

3. For the second generation, the income gain associated with a
given yearly gain in education is represented by cross-section earn-
ings-by-education data from the 1960 census. As with our earlier
computations, the figures are mean lifetime earnings differences
between dropouts and graduates weighted by race.[29]

4. The only education gain experienced by the second generation is in the form of longer schooling (of 1.1 years); therefore,
added costs of this extra schooling must be deducted from gains. As
with the measure of returns, second generation costs are based on

1959 figures. These are estimated at $580 per year for income foregone[30] and $515 per year for the direct costs of high school education.[31]

To proceed from here, it is helpful to restate two of the assumptions in terms of individuals. Since every couple receiving better education results in 2.5 better educated children, each individual implies 1.25 better educated children. With this restatement, financial benefits for the second generation can be related to 2 years extra education for a "typical" member of the first generation. This will amount to the financial implication of 1.1 years education for 1.25 individuals.

Combining all the above assumptions and discounting (by 5 percent) all returns and costs back to the time when the first generation receives its improved education results in the dollar balances in the middle column of Table 1. Two different starting points were used for the discounting, one assuming that the first generation's gain of 2 years begins in nursery school (age 4), and the other that it begins at age 15. The resulting amounts seem respectably large, but it must be remembered that the assumed initial gain by the first generation was also substantial. The present value of the added income experienced by the first generation, as a result of 2 years added education, appears in the last column of Table 1. The first generation's gains far outweigh the second generation's, the latter being approximately 14 percent of the former for both starting points of the discounting process.

To reinterpret these findings in light of the analysis in earlier chapters, it must first be recalled that the short-run educational gains observed were typically in the form of yearly equivalent gains in achievement rather than lengthened educational careers. In Chapters 3, 4, and 5 the income effect of these yearly equivalent gains was treated as if they constituted actual continuance of schooling. If we wish to "generalize" intergenerational effects, a parallel and no less plausible assumption can be employed: that gains in yearly equivalent academic achievement experienced by the first generation have the same impact on the second generation as do longer educational careers experienced by the first generation. Thus, we might say that a two year gain in academic achievement on the part of the first generation—even though no elongation of schooling is involved—yields the same benefits for the second generation as that calculated in Table 1. And, to generalize still further, it can be argued that income gains computed in the earlier chapters on a one generation basis should all be adjusted upward by 14 percent in order to take account of the financial gains to the

TABLE 1

First and Second Generation Income Benefits from
First Generation's Improved Education

Improved Education Begins	Second Generation Income[a]	First Generation Income[b]
Age 15	$909	$6,349
Age 4	$531	$3,798

[a]Net of extra costs for a 2-year education gain by first generation.
[b]For 2-year education gain.

next generation. This new revised figure could then be compared
to initial costs to yield a benefit-cost estimate adjusted for second
generation effects.

It goes without saying that the above calculation is extremely
tenuous. It depends upon many of the assumptions used in Chapters 3, 4, and 5, plus a few more. The nub of the problem is attempting to predict, on the basis of current relationships, what will
happen a good many years from now. This difficulty is present in
all the earlier calculations, and it is unavoidably compounded in the
estimation of second generation benefits. And, as in many of the
earlier calculations, there is no sure way to establish whether the
estimate based on current relationships is overoptimistic or over-
pessimistic.[32]

In addition to the technical problems of estimation, it is no less
important to keep in mind that transfers or other forms of direct
help may also have favorable repercussions on academic and economic careers of children in the families directly benefited. Several
observers have argued this position forcefully, and the only systematic research available supports this view.[33] To put the matter
another way, it is probably possible to "break the cycle of poverty"
at many points. An important implication of this is that the calculated second generation benefits attributed to education may not
constitute a clear net advantage as compared to direct help. If
education does have a net advantage along these lines, it likely is
not as great as our calculations suggest.

SUPRAMARGINAL CHANGE

One of the implicit assumptions underlying all the previous calculations is that a program of antipoverty education results in only a "marginal" change in the educational composition of the labor force. That is, the increased flow of better educated workers, due to antipoverty programs, is assumed to be only a small increase over the regular flow and a relatively insignificant addition to the total supply of all such workers. Similarly, the reduction in supply of all poorly educated workers is assumed to be insignificant as compared to the total supply. Without this assumption of marginal change it is difficult to justify the use of earnings differentials in the recent past as a basis for estimating returns from current programs. The presumption that contemplated educational changes do not greatly alter the composition of the work force, and that relative earnings will therefore not be perceptibly influenced by such changes, is a common characteristic of practically all recent work in calculating the returns to education. And it would seem a fair presumption in this study as well, as long as one thinks in terms of the relatively small size of current antipoverty efforts. But when one speaks of eliminating all poverty and plans to accomplish this mainly through educational improvements, it becomes apparent that shifting wage relationships must be reckoned with.

Several economists have pondered the possibility of shifts in earning relationships brought on by a large dose of increased education for the poor. Their judgment by and large has been that such shifts reinforce the case for education. The point emphasized is that even the poor people who do *not* receive improved education experience benefit, due to the shrinking supplies of poorly educated workers.[34] The smaller supplies mean higher earnings for the poor and poorly educated; this, it is argued, should surely count as progress toward the goal of complete poverty elimination.

Those who have made this argument have not developed it much beyond the stage of saying that higher earnings among the neglected poor is a desirable secondary effect of antipoverty education. Despite its apparent simplicity, the contention is extremely difficult to integrate into a benefit-cost framework.

Let us suppose that the analysis, based on the assumption of a marginal change in better educated workers, yields a benefit-cost ratio less than unity. This supposition is supported by much of the illustrative analysis presented above and, in any event, seems the only circumstance worth considering in that what we really want to know is whether recognition of a "supramarginal" effect might incline us to use education when we might not otherwise. If we employ the perspective of the representative citizen as developed in Chapter 2, the problem might be simply phrased as follows: While educating a group of poorly educated individuals entails higher costs than necessary to bring about a given income improvement for the newly educated group, the remaining educationally neglected individuals will require a smaller amount of transfers per individual in order to arrive at a respectable level of income. Of course, workers who are already better educated will experience some decline in incomes, but perhaps this decline still leaves them with earnings above the poverty range. . . .

PSYCHIC RETURNS

As stated in Chapter 1, the improved education of the poor can potentially give rise to many sorts of benefits. Our attention has been fixed on the enhanced material well-being of those in poverty. Though there were good reasons for this narrow focus, there is nevertheless an obligation to suggest how the other benefits of education might be evaluated and perhaps quantified. Much has been written by economists on this valuation problem, but little in the context of an antipoverty effort. The comments in this and the following sections are aimed at the special considerations present in this context.

Probably the most frequently mentioned role of education is the development of character and intellect as ends in themselves, independent of the financial gain these may bring. Economists usually label such benefits "psychic returns" or the "consumption element" of education. Among nonmonetary benefits subsumed under this heading are the satisfaction of working in an interesting and pleasant job and the immediate pleasures of experiencing a good education. Although many have urged that psychic returns be given a monetary weight, no serious empirical research has been attempted along these lines, and few specific research suggestions have been submitted. There is little reason to think that such an estimate can be accomplished with any more ease in the context of poverty.

One possible way to derive a monetary value for individual psychic returns is to canvass the persons experiencing the education, or perhaps their parents. The student or parent might be asked: How much would you pay for a better education if you anticipated that this education brought about *no* change in lifetime money income? A perfectly foresightful individual could conceivably discount the joys and pains he expects to flow from his (or his child's) educational experience, and a reply could be phrased in terms of a single dollar-and-cents figure. While actually conducting a survey along these lines is probably out of the question, it can be argued that this valuation procedure should be imagined by the people charged with making final decisions. By keeping in mind what is known about the preferences of those in poverty, one might thus avoid a paternalistic judgment about psychic returns.

On the other hand, it could be argued that reshaping the preferences of the poor is an important and unavoidable element of an antipoverty education program. Instilling the "right" sort of attitudes about work and ambition is frequently considered a way in which better education reduces poverty. And if we are willing to bring about these taste changes, there is little reason for squeamishness in making the judgment that poor people should be taught to appreciate educational values more than they do or in reasoning that the poor will have a higher regard for such values after the education is experienced. But even if the decision is to be frankly paternalistic, this does not dispense with the need to determine the degree to which specific educational improvements for the poor do result in differences in outlook, style of life, etc. And on that, I have encountered no compelling evidence that indicates even the general magnitude of such changes.

If we wish eventually to say more about this question, interdisciplinary studies are required. Envisioning the shape of this research is difficult, and considerable subjectivity will probably have to be employed in interpreting the findings. Unfortunately, the only alternative to such research is introspection and the chance anecdote.

REDUCING DEPENDENCY

Another appealing aspect of an education solution to poverty is avoidance of a "handout" connotation. There is little point in reviewing the plentiful and well known rhetoric on this point. It would seem useful, however, to discuss the main facets of thought behind this sentiment.

On the general theme of dependency there are at least three related variations suggesting that education is a form of action superior to transfers and most other types of direct help. The first of these was mentioned earlier: that direct redistribution, even in the form of a negative income tax, is bound to produce some disincentive to work, implying in turn that the transfer bill may be higher than initially anticipated. Though there appear to be no convincing estimates of the magnitude of work disincentive under various transfer schemes, such measurements are within the realm of possibility, and an "adjusted" cost for a transfer program might be derived that could, without great difficulty, be integrated into an evaluative framework similar to that developed in Chapter 2.[35]

Two other points cannot be assessed so directly. The first is the argument that anyone who fails to work as much or as hard as he might—because of the disincentive of transfer payments—is in essence "voluntarily" poor and thus "undeserving" of an income supplement. A related argument is that even if transfers do not discourage a maximum work effort, the recipients are nevertheless partially dependent upon the state, and this might be harmful for self-esteem or at least not as dignified as earning one's way out of poverty.[36] On the basis of these two judgments, some observers seem to feel that education is a preferable antipoverty instrument even if it requires exceedingly high costs to achieve the same antipoverty goal. Nevertheless, it is likely that most people "have their price" on this issue, and at some very low payoff rate for education, there are few who would continue to insist on an education approach.

This does not mean an easy consensus is attainable. Many will continue to view all transfers as odious devices of last resort, and others will consider transfers a relatively harmless extension of progressive taxation. On balance, the public image of direct redistribution seems to be unfavorable. Attitudes toward public employment and subsidized housing are not much better. Education, in comparison, is relatively free of the handout stigma. Thus, for this reason alone, a financial benefit-cost ratio for education of less than unity might be tolerated for antipoverty purposes.

It must be remembered, however, that a set of programs designed to eliminate poverty *must* include at least some transfer elements. Some poverty afflicted members of the community are beyond working age or incapacitated in various ways. For these, education may do no material good at all. And this raises the question of what to do for those whom education can help only a very little. The gradation of the benefits from education, from those cases where little is gained up to those who can be helped a great deal, needs to be specified; and the sentiment in favor of education must be given quantitative content in order to specify when education or a transfer type program is more appropriate. Reaching a public consensus on this issue that has quantitative content is of course very difficult, but there is no reason to think it is any more difficult than the decision on where to establish poverty lines.

EQUALITY OF OPPORTUNITY

Much of what was said in the two preceding sections applies to the goal of equal opportunity. Once more the issue boils down to making a subjective judgment about the importance of the goal and deciding upon the degree to which this inclines us to use an education approach to poverty.

It is especially important, however, to remember that equality in expenditures per pupil is no guarantee that academic outcomes will be the same for children of low and high socioeconomic status. Indeed, evidence from the Project Talent survey indicates that the achievement levels of low status pupils in the *highest* expenditure school districts are still much lower than those of high status pupils in the *lowest* expenditure districts.[37] This raises the question of how equality of opportunity is to be defined. Should the definition be in terms of the quality and magnitude of the resources devoted to the education of low and high status pupils, or should it be in terms of academic accomplishment and (or) the degree of actual social and economic mobility? Expenditures per pupil and achievement test scores are only proxies for these two standards, but they make clear that the difference between the two standards is very great.[38]

There is no question that equal attainment is a much more ambitious goal than equal educational quality (or quantity). It may even be—given the fact that formal education is only part of the total learning experience and is not the sole contributor to the child's growth and development—that, under existing arrangements, the goal is unattainable. Since socioeconomic background still makes a great difference in the degree to which individuals can profit from education, formal equality in educational expenditures is a milestone of dubious significance.

The immediate reason for raising this definitional matter is to emphasize that meaningful equality of opportunity is not around a nearby corner easily reached by an education approach to poverty. The choice of weapons in the war on poverty, at least on the present scale, can only make a small contribution toward complete realization of the equality of opportunity goal as stated in its more ambitious and probably more meaningful form. The contribution should not, of course, be ignored. But it is worth noting once more that direct help to poor families should have some positive effect on the academic performance of children, and thus also make a contribution to the goal of equal opportunity. In summary, the goal of equal opportunity can be viewed as a valid, though hardly an overriding, reason why we might be inclined to emphasize education in an antipoverty campaign.

EXTERNALITIES

As in the case of psychic returns, many diverse elements are summed up by the term "externalities." As argued in Chapter 2, the removal of poverty can itself be described and analyzed as an externality. This analysis depended upon empathic concern for those with low incomes. The more typical case of an external benefit involves more selfish motivation; and many of these external benefits may justifiably affect our choice of antipoverty weapons.

Other studies have devoted ample discussion to the numerous externalities that might flow from improved education.[39] Possible externalities range from the social benefit of having a better informed electorate to the chance that an extra dose of education will spark a latent genius into becoming a great benefactor of mankind. While many of these are very speculative and assessable only in a highly subjective way, some categories of external benefits are at least partially amenable to direct dollar measurement. Of special interest here are various forms of antisocial behavior—for example, juvenile delinquency—whose suppression requires large public expenditures. Improved education for underprivileged youths could very likely lower the frequency of such behavior and thus the costs of policing, incarceration, and treatment. Cost savings can be used as an approximation of the magnitude of benefit.

While cost savings of this nature are often mentioned, information on the determinants of antisocial behavior has not been sufficiently complete to encourage a quantitative estimate of what this element might add to the benefits of improved education. However, a recent study by Fleisher on the determinants of juvenile delinquency permits a rough calculation of possible cost savings.[40]

Fleisher does not study directly the association between education and delinquency, but he manages to calculate a convincing estimate of the relation between family income and delinquency. This he does by a cross-section multiple regression analysis of lower income groups in 101 large cities. He concludes that "in extremely delinquent areas, . . . a 10 percent rise in income may be expected to reduce delinquency rates by between 15 and 20 percent when the income change occurs in highly delinquent areas and is of the type that will reduce the number of broken families as well." In Fleisher's words, "it appears that the effect of income on delinquency is not a small one."[41] But here we must be cautious. "Not small" is a relative thing. And for our purposes, it is necessary to put Fleisher's results in terms of absolute dollar amounts before we can hope to get a clear picture of how it compares to the sorts of magnitudes we have calculated so far.

First, it can be estimated that a 10 percent income gain means about a $300 increase in yearly family income for those residing in "high delinquency areas."[42] Number of arrests per year per 1,000 males younger than 25 is Fleisher's unit of account on the delinquency side of the equation. A 15 to 20 percent drop of this index amounts to roughly five fewer arrests per 1,000 young males.[43] Now it might be asked, what is the *total* income gain for a given community required to reduce arrests by five? For purposes of a rough estimate, it seems fair to assume (a) that families have an average size of four individuals, and (b) that one out of every four individuals is a male under 25 years of age. With these assumptions, it follows that 1,000 families are necessary in order to have 1,000 young males present. Thus, if each family gains $300, the total income gain required to have five fewer arrests amounts to $300,000.

As a final step we might estimate how much a community saves in police costs when a reduction in delinquency results in five fewer arrests per year. In 1960 (the base year in our earlier calculations and in Fleisher's) arrests in cities totaled approximately 5 million, and police costs about $1.3 billion.[44] Dividing the latter figure by the former suggests that arrests cost $260 apiece. That is to say, if five fewer arrests are needed, and police costs decline proportionately, a savings of $1,300 can be anticipated. And even this is a liberal estimate since the marginal costs are undoubtedly below the average.

Thus, a total income gain of $300,000 in high delinquency areas can be said to bring about a $1,300 reduction in the needed costs of public safety. This cost reduction amounts to less than 0.5 percent of the direct income gain. Of course, there can—and should— be added to this cost reduction a variety of other savings and benefits: for example, the costs of the judicial process, of damage caused by delinquency, of the "life of crime" that the first delinquency may lead to, etc. It is, however, hard to imagine that these would substantially alter the order of magnitude of the result.

If it is assumed that education results in a reduced inclination toward crime solely through the effect of higher earned incomes, then the above estimates would seem directly applicable. But if improved education, in and of itself, results in a higher degree of socialization and restraint in its recipient, then the above figure would be an underestimate. This is because education and income are not perfectly correlated. Hence, two communities that differ by exactly $300 in family income will not generally have average educational attainments such that we would have predicted this $300 difference. Rather, the differential educational attainments will be somewhat smaller. Therefore, it might be reasoned that if the increase in a community's educational level is sufficient to raise the average family income by $300, the reduction in juvenile delinquency would be greater than is indicated by the straight cross-section comparison of "lower-income" groups with different levels of income.

To derive a more accurate estimate we need to separate the effects of increases in earned income, income transfers, and educational attainments. Fleisher was not able to do so, and his summary of related research indicates that no one else has been able to.[45] But despite the obvious shortcomings of the above calculation and the numbers on which it is based, the order of magnitude is nevertheless intriguing. Moreover, it is doubtful whether a more careful analysis would greatly change the general conclusion that savings in the public safety costs of juvenile delinquency are a very small fraction of the direct income gains experienced because of education. In addition, it must be remembered that other forms of antipoverty action, including direct transfers, should also be expected to have positive effects on the rate of antisocial acts.

Thus, at least for the time being, it is difficult to argue that consideration of the tangible savings in social costs should very much alter the direction or magnitude of our antipoverty efforts.

ECONOMIC GROWTH

Much of the scholarly interest in the economics of education, especially in the early 1960's, stemmed from the belief that increased education would contribute to accelerated economic growth. Of late, the goal of growth has faded somewhat from the spotlight in domestic policy debates. Nevertheless, a few brief comments seem called for on how this goal relates to the preceding analysis.

One of the reasons for thinking that increased education might encourage growth is the earlier observation that the American economy has experienced historical growth in national income far in excess of what would be anticipated on the basis of historical increases in men and machines. A substantial part of this unexplained gap may be due to various externalities in production generated by an increasingly better educated labor force. Exactly how much can be attributed to increased education, and how much to other economic developments, is still very much an open question. It is, therefore, not clear whether the growth-inducing externalities of education justify special emphasis on expanding this particular sector of the economy as opposed to other sectors. Moreover, it is worth noting that technological breakthroughs are what most economists seem to have in mind when they cite growth externalities as a by-product of education. This suggests that the very advanced levels of education are chiefly responsible for this variety of externality. When talking about the provision of respectable elementary and secondary education for underprivileged children, this consideration might justifiably be neglected.

Another and more palpable way in which antipoverty education might contribute to the goal of growth is the earnings gains directly experienced by the poor. If increases in money national income per se are considered socially laudable, it could be argued that the increased earnings of the poor should, in some fashion, be "double counted"—once for their contribution to poverty reduction and again for their contribution to economic growth.

It should not be forgotten, however, that there are other ways of stimulating economic growth. Tax incentives to corporate investment is one of these ways. The before-tax rate of return to corporate capital has been estimated to be about 12 percent[46]—well above the implied rate of return for the changes in general education considered in Chapters 3, 4, and 5. This implies that increasing corporate incentives would yield considerably more growth per dollar of present consumption sacrificed than would antipoverty education—at least of the kind and size examined. If growth is what we are after, the education of the poor would be only one of many ways—and not necessarily one of the better ways—to that end.

Still, the use of education now rather than of transfers in the future does imply that total savings and investment are increased. This in turn should reduce the felt need to stimulate investment in physical capital. It might be argued that investment in education would permit a reduction, say, of the investment tax credit since part of the growth goal is being achieved via education. The consequent amount of revenue savings could then be added to the benefits perceived by the typical citizen. A calculation of this sort is not as simple as it might first appear. Clear specification of growth targets is required. The effectiveness of tax incentives in increasing investment must also be known. And one must take into account the fact that less stimulus to physical investment will likely have some detrimental effect on the future incomes of the presently poor.

SUMMARY OF ADDITIONAL BENEFITS

The analysis of this chapter does not add a great deal to the "case for education" as it applies to the goal of poverty reduction. Intergenerational benefits turn out to be a small fraction of first generation benefits. And the implication of supramarginal change can, at present, be expressed in only a qualitative fashion: the extension of education may be justified somewhat beyond the point where simple benefit-cost ratios have a value of unity.

The other anticipated advantages of education are another matter. If one feels strongly enough about the psychic benefits of education, the corrupting influence of transfer payments, the goal of equal opportunity, or the need for economic growth, education might be a preferred course of action even if its measurable contribution to poverty reduction is small per dollar of cost. For most of these goals, additional measurements can be of assistance, but they cannot dictate what the trade off should be between reducing poverty and furthering other social aims.

An earlier caution deserves repeating: alternatives to education may do nearly as much (and in some cases, more) to achieve some of the "side" benefits frequently anticipated from education. It is not enough to say that improved education has a second generation effect, promotes more equal opportunity, and reduces antisocial behavior. Simple income transfers should, to some extent, do the same. And more specific forms of direct help (for example, improved housing) may give rise to secondary effects every bit as great as those accruing from an equal dollar amount of improved education. Future measurements and policy judgments should not ignore this possibility.

Finally, it should be noted that the considerations raised in this chapter could also alter our preferences for different types of educational change. In particular, vocational education may not be clearly preferable to general education as was suggested by the benefit-cost calculations. General education probably results in bigger second generation effects, greater psychic returns, and more externalities than does vocational education.

NOTES

[1]For a survey of eighteenth and nineteenth century economic comments on education, see John Vaizey, *The Economics of Education* (Free Press, 1962), pp. 15-25.

[2]Social benefits—or, to use the technical term, "external" benefits—do, of course, have relevance when it comes to making final decisions about the appropriate magnitude and types of education. Thus, even though the focus of this study is on the limited question of the efficiency of education in raising the income of the poor, externalities are examined in detail in Chap. 6.

[3]Milton Friedman, "The Role of Government in Education," in Robert A. Solo (ed.), *Economics and the Public Interest* (Rutgers University Press, 1955), p. 137. The first clear statement of the idea appears to be A. C. Pigou, *The Economics of Welfare* (4th ed.; Macmillan, 1932), pp. 746-47.

[4]See J. R. Walsh, "Capital Concept Applied to Man," *Quarterly Journal of Economics,* Vol. 49 (1935), pp. 255-85. Increasing family responsibilities also make any temporary belt-tightening more painful.

[5]Gary S. Becker, *Human Capital* (National Bureau of Economic Research, 1964). p. 58.

[6]Alfred Marshall, *Principles of Economics* (9th ed.; Macmillan, 1961), Vol. 1, p. 312.

[7]Becker, *Human Capital,* p. 63.

[8]A number of early discussions come close to this argument. Marshall himself notes that "the action of competition, and the survival in the struggle for existence . . . tend in the long run to put the building of factories and steam engines in the hands of those who will be ready and able to incur every expense which will add more than it costs to their value as productive agents. But the investment of capital in the rearing and early training of the workers of England is limited by the resources of parents in the various grades of society. . . . " (Marshall, *Principles of Economics,* p. 561.) See also Wesley C. Mitchell, "The Backward Art of Spending Money," *American Economic Review,* Vol. 2 (1912), pp. 269-81; and Pigou, *The Economics of Welfare,* p. 274. Our argument differs mainly in its explicit connection with the general problem of "embodied" investment.

[9]Marshall, despite his somber worries about underinvestment in education, is quite sanguine about the supply of entrepreneurial services. "[There are] many routes . . . by which a man of great natural business ability can work his way up high in some private firm or public company, [and] we may conclude that wherever there is work on a large scale to be done in such a country as England, the ability and the capital required for it are pretty sure to be speedily forthcoming." (*Principles of Economics,* p. 312.)

[10]For discussion of this subject see Frank Riessman, *The Culturally Deprived Child* (Harper & Row, 1962), and Kenneth Clark, *Dark Ghetto* (Harper & Row, 1965), Chap. 5.

[11] Much of the research is designed to give teachers and school administrators the necessary empathy to reach children with poor backgrounds; for a review of the literature see Benjamin S. Bloom, Allison Davis, and Robert Hess, *Compensatory Education for Cultural Deprivation* (Holt, Rinehard & Winston, 1965).

[12] See Theodore W. Schultz, "Education and Economic Growth," in Nelson B. Henry (ed.), *Social Forces Influencing American Education* (University of Chicago Press, 1961); Becker, *Human Capital;* W. Lee Hansen, "Total and Private Rates of Return to Investment in Schooling," *Journal of Political Economy,* Vo. 71, No. 2 (April 1963), pp. 128-40; and Giora Hanoch, "Rates of Return, 1960," University of Chicago, Office of Agricultural Research, Paper No. 6428, Nov. 12, 1964 (unpublished).

[13] See Committee for Economic Development (CED), *Raising Low Incomes Through Improved Education* (CED, 1965), pp. 16, 17; Theodore W. Schultz, "Investing in Poor People: An Economist's View," *American Economic Review,* Vol. 55, No. 2 (May 1965), pp. 515-16; and Michael S. March, "Poverty: How Much Will the War Cost?" *Social Service Review,* Vol. 39 (June 1965), pp. 141-56.

[14] The "social" rate of return referred to here is *not* an estimate of all social benefits produced by education, but the lifetime personal income differentials produced by various amounts of education.

[15] Hanoch, using 1960 census data, derives rates well above 50 percent for some educational increments below the high school level ("Rate of Return, 1960," Table 1, pp. 14-15). Burton A. Weisbrod ("Education and Investment in Human Capital," *Journal of Political Economy,* Vol. 70, No. 5, Supplement [October 1962], pp. 111-12) argues that the 35 percent rate computed by Schultz *(Social Forces Influencing American Education)* for primary school education should be raised to 54 percent because of the "option value" associated with being able to attend higher levels of schooling as a result of successfully completing a lower level. For the rationale behind the "option value" estimate and a critique of it, see App. C.

[16] See Edward F. Renshaw, "Estimating the Returns to Education," *Review of Economics and Statistics,* Vol. 42, No. 3 (August 1960), pp. 318-24; Harry Shaffer, "Investment in Human Capitol: Comment," *American Economic Review,* Vol. 51, No. 5 (December 1961), pp. 1026-35; and R. S. Eckaus, "Economic Criteria for Education and Training," *Review of Economics and Statistics,* Vol. 46, No. 2 (May 1964), pp. 181-90.

[17] *Human Capital,* especially pp. 79-90, 125-26.

[18] James Morgan and Martin David ("Education and Income," *Quarterly Journal of Economics,* Vol. 77, No. 3 [August 1963], pp. 423-37) demonstrate that if one adopts sufficiently harsh assumptions, returns can be pushed close to zero for some educational increments. Their assumptions and controls, however, are overly severe. In multiple regressions performed on their sample survey of workers, at least two of the variables controlled for—supervisory responsibility and attitude of the respondent

to achievement—very likely picked up some effects of education that are natural concomitants of greater productivity and income. But even more influential than "overcontrol" is their use of differences in full-time earnings associated with different educational attainments as the basis for estimating returns, rather than the more orthodox procedure of using yearly earnings unadjusted for employment. The studies cited in note 12 all considered the reduction of time unemployed, and the consequent increase in lifetime earnings, as part of the benefit from education. Morgan and David do not, though they concede that "some unemployment might be directly attributable to the lack of flexibility and foresight associated with less formal education" *(ibid.,* p. 436). The handling of differential unemployment rates is discussed in Chap. 3, pp. 42-49.

[19]In the studies cited in note 12, p. 8, the rate of return for completing only two years of high school was found to be nearly as high as that for completing high school, the rate for completing only "some" college below 10 percent though above 5 percent, and the rate on four years of college in the neighborhood of 12 percent. This difference may be attributed to the prestige of the degree, but it may just as easily be explained as an indivisibility phenomenon: the learning acquired at the beginning of college may be rendered much more useful if complemented by more specialized courses in the later years.

[20]See in particular Dael Wolfle and J. Smith, "The Occupational Value of Education for Superior High School Graduates," *Journal of Higher Education* (April 1956), pp. 201-13; and Donald S. Bridgman, "Success in College and Business," *Personnel Journal,* Vol. 9 (June 1930), pp. 1-18. Both focus on the relationship between class standing and later income. Preliminary results of a study relating the scores of servicemen on the Armed Forces Qualifying Test, years of school completed, and income as recorded in Social Security records indicate a stronger partial correlation between test scores and later-life income than between school years and later-life income. See Phillips Cutright, " A Pilot Study of Factors in Economic Success and Failure Based on Selective Service and Social Security Records," Social Security Administration, 1964 (mimeo).

[21]For a recent discussion, see Edward F. Denison, "Measuring the Contribution of Education (and the Residual) to Economic Growth," plus comments and rejoinder, in *The Residual Factor and Economic Growth* (Paris: Organization for Economic Cooperation and Development, 1964), pp. 13-100.

[22]For a concise description of the federal education efforts relating to poverty, see *Economic Report of the President, January 1966, Together with the Annual Report of the Council of Economic Advisers,* pp. 94-100.

[23]Benjamin S. Bloom, *Stability and Change in Human Characteristics* (Wiley, 1964), has been especially influential in directing attention to the preschool years.

[24]Two well-documented accounts with this point of view are HARYOU

(Harlem Youth Opportunities Unlimited), *Youth in the Ghetto* (HAR-YOU, 1964); and James B. Conant, *Slums and Suburbs* (McGraw-Hill, 1961).

[25]James N. Morgan and others, *Income and Welfare in the United States* (McGraw-Hill, 1962).

[26] *Ibid.*, p. 273.

[27]On wife's educational attainment, the Michigan study controls only for the *difference* in attainment between husband and wife (*ibid.*, p. 274). If their attainments are the same no further adjustment is made. Thus, if both have high school educations, they are compared directly with couples both with less than high school educations. Similarly, a high school graduate husband whose wife dropped out of high school is compared with a high school dropout husband with a grade school educated wife (etc.). If, then, the absolute level of wife's education is important to the educational attainment of children, it is clear that controlling for only husband-wife differences gives too much credit to the husband's attainment. A later calculation in the Michigan study seems to show that wife's attainment has a substantial independent influence on offspring; but it does not allow a judgment as to whose education is more influential.

It should also be noted that the relationship of 2 years of educational attainment in the first generation to 1.1 years in the second was derived after controlling for twelve factors besides attainment differences (*ibid.*, pp. 272-74). Among the most important were occupation of the family head and his highest income. Interestingly enough, the observed intergenerational transmission of education was *increased* at some attainment levels after adjustment; for instance, at the dropout to high school graduation level the unadjusted figures show only a 0.8 year gain for the second generation associated with high school graduation on the part of the first generation. An explanation for this is not readily available. In any event, the 2 year to 1.1 year relationship was meant (at least in theory) to be a gauge of the influence of parents' educational attainment independent of "all other" factors.

[28]The estimate of 2.5 children per family is based on 1960 census data: for all families with own children of any age, 2.3 children is the average; for all nonwhite families, 2.9 (U.S. Department of Commerce, Bureau of the Census, *U.S. Census of Population: 1960*, "Families," PC[2]-4A, Table 4). The assumption that all children are born when parents are exactly 25 years of age is borrowed from Burton A. Weisbrod and William J. Swift, "On the Monetary Value of Education's Intergeneration Effects," *Journal of Political Economy*, Vol. 73, No. 6 (December 1965), pp. 643-49. Although they deal with the same problem we are in the midst of, there are substantial differences in approach. Most important is their use of the "option value" formula to derive an internal rate of return figure for the second generation. Skepticism about the use of this formula was noted earlier. For a critical

discussion of the option value procedures see App. C.

[29]See notes in Table 5.

[30]See notes in Table 4.

[31]Direct costs are estimated by building on the current cost figure of $341 per high school pupil for urban districts (from U.S. Department of Health, Education, and Welfare, Office of Education, *Current Expenditures Per Pupil in Public School Systems: Urban School Systems, 1957-58* [1959], Table 6c). It is adjusted upward for: (1) non-instructional overhead prorated to the high school level (an 18 percent adjustment based on the ratio of operation, maintenance, and student service overheads to instructional costs for the entire school system [*ibid.,* Table 3]), yielding a cost of $402; (2) implicit interest and depreciation (22 percent of current costs, according to the Rude-Schultz estimate in Theodore Schultz, "Education and Economic Growth," in Nelson B. Henry (ed.), *Social Forces Influencing American Education* [University of Chicago Press, 1961], p. 85), raising cost to $490; and (3) yearly increases in per student expenditures for all levels during the late 1950's (a 5 percent adjustment to put the figures on a 1959 basis; see U. S. Department of Commerce, Bureau of the Census, *Statistical Abstract of the United States, 1962,* p. 121), resulting in the $515 cost. That figure is lower than Schultz's estimate—$568—of high school costs in 1956 ("Education and Economic Growth," pp. 65, 85) as well as his figure adjusted to a 1959 base of well over $600. Schultz adds in "additional expenses" to the student (books, supplies, extra clothes, and travel) which he assumes to be 5 percent of income foregone, but provides no evidence that these costs are any greater for a student than for a typical worker. Moreover, he derives instructional costs for high school indirectly by splitting costs for all levels of public schooling according to a 1938 study of salaries and pupil-teacher ratios that indicates costs in secondary schools are nearly twice as high as in elementary schools. Recent data (see note 10, p. 94) suggest that secondary school costs are less than 50 percent higher than elementary.

[32]On the cost side, the assumptions have been more charitable than those used by other researchers (see note 41, p. 59 and note 7, p. 104). The great uncertainty, though, is with the nature of earnings differentials connected with education several decades from now. Our earlier discussion suggested that an "ability" adjustment should more than cancel out the growth in differentials (pp. 57-59). But for decades hence, this is a much more dubious proposition.

[33]S. Michael Miller and Martin Rein make the point in the following fashion: "Would increasing the income of a poor family do as much to increase the children's interest in further advance as would specific training programs? We are not confident that the results of a study of these alternative ways of spending poverty funds would support a training program, separate from improving the economic conditions of families and neighborhoods. True, *some* youth would escape from poverty

more easily than before, but would the greater number of youth? Economic and social change may have to precede the call for individual responsibility and adjustment." ("The War on Poverty: Perspectives and Prospects," in Ben B. Seligman [ed.], *Poverty as a Public Issue* [Free Press, 1965], p. 289). Harry G. Johnson notes the "strong possibility that the preoccupation of parents with the earning of money—especially in broken homes—is an important factor in the perpetuation of poverty among the children of the poor" (in "The Economics of Poverty," *American Economic Review,* Vol. 55, No. 2 [May 1965], pp. 543-44). The best and most relevant empirical work available appears to be Robert A. Dentler and Mary Ellen Warshauer, *Big City Dropouts* (New York: Center for Urban Education, 1965). Based on a multiple correlation (crosssection) analysis of 131 large cities, this study concludes that a fair amount of the variance among cities in dropout rates and in adult functional illiteracy is statistically explained by rates of Aid to Families with Dependent Children payments, and by spending rates on (noneducational) public projects such as hospitals and parks (*ibid.,* pp. 28-31, 46-54).

[34]This line of argument can be found in A. C. Pigou, *The Economics of Welfare* (4th ed.; Macmillan, 1932), p. 753; Committee for Economic Development (CED), *Raising Low Incomes Through Improved Education* (CED, September 1965), pp. 18-19; Thomas N. Carver, "A Conservative's Ideas on Economic Reform," *Quarterly Journal of Economics,* Vol. 74, No. 4 (November 1960), pp. 536-42; and James Tobin, "On Improving the Economic Status of the Negro," *Daedalus,* Vol. 94, No. 4 (Fall 1965), pp. 888-89.

[35]A review of available research bearing on the disincentive effect of transfers can be found in Christopher Green, *Negative Taxes and the Poverty Problem* (Brookings Institution, 1967).

[36]*Economic Report of the President, January 1964, Together with the Annual Report of the Council of Economic Advisers* states that "Americans want to *earn* the American standard of living by their own efforts and contributions. It will be far better, even if more difficult, to equip and to permit the poor of the Nation to produce and to earn the additional $11 billion, and more" (p. 77). A similar view is expressed by the Committee for Economic Development: " . . . as among ways of helping the least fortunate it is surely better, in most cases, to help them to improve their earning capacity than simply to transfer income to them from others— better in terms of the burden on others as well as in terms of the dignity of those assisted" (*Raising Low Incomes Through Improved Education,* p. 21).

[37]The table below contrasts test score performance for pupils in the bottom socioeconomic quintile with that of pupils in the next-to-highest quintile. The figures refer to the North and West subsample of Project Talent; all pupils took the tests near the end of twelfth grade; and test scores are averages of the academic and nonacademic test composites. All defini-

tions are the same as those in Table 7.

School District Expenditures per Pupil	Mean Test Score for Low Status Pupils, in Yearly Equivalents	Mean Test Score for High Status Pupils, in Yearly Equivalents
Less than $200	9.82	11.92
$200-$300	10.25	12.82
$300-$400	10.32	13.17
$400-$500	10.53	13.06
More than $500	10.43	13.88

Scores above 12.0 should *not* be interpreted as equivalent to the performance of college freshmen; they are simple linear extrapolations based on the difference in mean test scores between high school grade levels. (Information from Project Talent Data Bank.)

[38]Most recent commentary argues that social justice does demand something more than equal amounts of resources (of apparently equal quality) devoted to the public schools attended by the poor and by the affluent. Indeed, it is very difficult to find a contemporary essay that argues that equality in resources has any special interest at all. There is also general skepticism that equal educational services can even be defined. The typical teacher, having "middle class" predilections, is frequently thought to be so hostile and out of touch with lower class children that he (she) in essence becomes a very different sort of person when confronting a classroom of slum children as compared to a classroom of children from the suburbs. (See Kenneth Clark, *Dark Ghetto* [Harper & Row, 1965], Chap. 5.)

[39]See especially Burton A. Weisbrod, *External Benefits of Public Education: An Economic Analysis* (Princeton University, Department of Economics, Industrial Relations Section, 1964); Weisbrod, "Education and Investment in Human Capital," *Journal of Political Economy,* Vol. 70, No. 5, Supplement (October 1962), pp. 106-23.

[40]Belton M. Fleisher, "The Effect of Income on Delinquency," *American Economic Review,* Vol. 56, No. 1 (March 1966), pp. 118-37.

[41]*Ibid.,* pp. 134-35.

[42]This presumes that the income gain occurs among low income groups only. Fleisher worked with mean family incomes in the second and fourth quartiles of income. Technical problems prevented him from dealing with the lowest income quartile, but he argues that the relationship between second quartile incomes and delinquency is a good proxy for the effect of gains in the lowest quartile (*ibid.,* pp. 132, 134). A 10 percent gain in income in the second quartile amounts to about $470 gain in family income for high delinquency areas (*ibid.,* p. 126). For the present calculation it is assumed that a $300 income gain among the very

lowest income groups has the same delinquency prevention effect as does a $470 gain for slightly better off families.

43 *Ibid.*, pp. 134-35. "High delinquency" areas have an arrest rate of 24 per 1,000. The figure of 5 fewer arrests entails the assumption that no income gains occur in the upper ranges of income simultaneously with the gains in the lower ranges. If gains did occur simultaneously in the upper ranges, the calculated reduction in arrests (according to Fleisher's estimates) would not be as great (*ibid.*, pp. 132-34).

44The figure on arrests is calculated from data in U.S. Department of Commerce, Bureau of the Census, *Statistical Abstract of the United States, 1962*, p. 153. The published figure applies to cities that include 73 percent of all individuals living in cities. This total was multiplied by 1.4 to estimate arrests in all cities and thus make the arrest figure comparable with the police expenditure information. The latter was taken from U.S. Department of Commerce, *Compendium of City Government Finances in 1960*, C-CF60-No. 2 (1961), Table I, p. 8.

45The Effect of Income on Delinquency," pp. 133-34 (footnote).

46Gary S. Becker, *Human Capital* (National Bureau of Economic Research, 1964), p. 120.

10

COST-BENEFIT ANALYSIS IN EDUCATION

by Jack Wiseman

Professor Wiseman discusses some of the problems in eva-
luating costs and benefits in education and suggests that
one difficulty in measuring the returns to the individual
and to society is that the yardsticks used are subject to
personal value judgments. He stresses the particular diffi-
culty of developing adequate qualitative indices to distin-
guish between the impact of like expenditures for
schooling in different systems, areas, and groups.

A conference of this kind is properly concerned with the improvement of decisions about public policy. I have consequently taken as
my problem the relation between studies of "investment" in education and the rationale of policy decisions. This is not to suggest that
I would wish such studies to be judged, or to be judged solely, by
their ability to illuminate policy questions: I agree with Professor
Schultz[1] that research cannot expect to begin by "asking the right
questions," since the discovery of those questions may itself be an
end-consequence of the research. At the same time, many of those
concerned with "human resource" studies do believe their work to
be relevant to public policy: Professor Schultz says also that such
studies are " . . . laying the foundations for an economic growth
policy which assigns a major role to schooling. . . . "

Reprinted from Jack Wiseman, "Cost-Benefit Analysis In Education," *The Southern
Economic Journal,* Vol. 32, Part 2 (July 1965), pp. 1-12. Reprinted by permission of
the publisher.

In these circumstances, it might be thought not unreasonable to expect that "human investment" studies would reduce the importance of policy disagreements about education, or at the least permit the more precise specification of the nature of such disagreements and hence facilitate their resolution. But superficial observation suggests that the growth of analytical understanding and empirical information has been accompanied by continuing (increasing?) disagreement among economists, and between economists and others, about such fundamental matters of education policy as the "right" size and character of public finance of education provision.

In asking why this should be so, and suggesting how the areas of disagreement might be reduced, I shall try from time to time to suggest how my argument relates to the special problems of the South. But I pretend to no expertise in this domestic problem, and in any case, my concern is rather with the identification of some of the questions to which we need answers than with the provision of answers (policy prescriptions) that I could believe to be universally and unambiguously acceptable. At least some of the issues to be considered incorporate choices between, and/or the weighting of, policy ends: and I do not pretend that I know how to provide technical solutions to problems of this kind.

It is also not my intention simply to be critical of existing "human resource" studies. In my view, recent developments and interest in the study of human resources, associated particularly with the pioneering studies of Professor Schultz and now the concern of an increasing number of specialists, have already resulted in tremendous analytical illumination and in much ingenious and fruitful empirical research. Indeed, I would regard the evolving integration of "human resource" studies with the existing corpus of economic analysis as one of the major breakthroughs of the last few decades. Further, few of the individual problems to which I shall draw attention are unfamiliar. But they are not commonly brought together in a policy context, and I believe that the attempt to do so may be illuminating both about the nature and interpretation of cost-benefit studies themselves and about the general difficulties of policy decisions concerned with the use and development of human resources.

SOME PROBLEMS OF BENEFIT-COST STUDIES

This section is not concerned with any particular study, but assumes a general acquaintance with the relevant literature and a general understanding of the procedures used in benefit-cost studies of human resource problems. Nor is it intended as an exhaustive critique: the sole purpose is to direct attention to some of my own problems and confusions concerning the use of benefit-cost studies to guide public policy.[2]

Economic and other "Values"

It is widely recognized that education serves ends (variously designated as "cultural," "spiritual," etc.) not normally thought of as economic. This is not generally regarded as destructive of the utility of economic studies (and, presumably, their policy relevance): it is in the nature of theory to abstract from some attributes of a problem, and to do so is not inconsistent with these attributes being thought important. Equally, the fact that these attributes exist does not in a logical sense destroy the relevance of studies of the chosen problem. Thus, Balogh and Streeten, e.g., in a paper generally critical of "human investment" studies, argue that it is mistaken to object to the economist's "sordidly mercenary" approach because it involves a "perversion of values": at the least, we might learn something about what the pursuit of these "other values" is costing us.[3]

However, while I would agree that there is no *necessary* conflict between the study of the economic implications of education provision and any particular view of its other attributes, I would argue that the way we *in fact* study education as an investment perforce involves us in confusions between the two. Further, these confusions are of particular importance in a policy context. The point is of sufficient importance to merit elucidation in another form. Essentially the (implicit or explicit) justification for distinguishing the economic implications of education from its other attributes is on grounds of division of labor: we can leave the consideration of other aspects to those qualified to deal with them, and these independent functions can then be "integrated" or "co-ordinated" at the policy level into a common "education policy" framework. After all, this is the rationale of division of labor elsewhere: the efficiency of the specialization of functions depends upon the possibility of coordinating the results. But while this may be what economists like to think they are doing, it is questionable whether it is what they are in fact doing. Rather, we study one aspect of a common process, admit the "indivisibility" of that process (i.e., that economics is not distinct from culture but an aspect of it), but shift on to others the responsibility of discovering how the piece that we have elected to study and quantify fits into the organic whole. Lee R. Martin provides us with a useful illustration (though there are numerous others): "The writer pleads guilty," he says, "to having—however unintentionally—implied a technological elite and the superior utility of technical knowledge, but it is difficult to over-estimate the importance of humanistic or social values in an advanced civilisation. Although the writer senses intuitively [*sic*] the overwhelming importance of these factors, he leaves their discussion to better qualified scholars."[4] These same superior creatures would presumably also be left to spell out the (logical and empirical) relationships between these "overwhelmingly important" factors and the economic magnitudes that the author believes economists should study. This attitude is not only too modest: it is also unreasonable, and in the event impossible of fulfillment.

Of course, the reason for the difficulty has not gone unrecognized: the same education which changes the economic attributes of an individual simultaneously changes his "extra-economic" characteristics. Also, that change is inseparable from the person undergoing it. A person who makes an "educational investment" in himself can sell the fruits of that investment, but cannot market the asset itself: in Mrs. Robinson's phrase, the present capital value of future personal earnings has a metaphysical but not an actual financial meaning.[5] Similarly, the "non-economic" consequences of education are in effect changes in the human personality. These also clearly inhere in the person educated, though of course they may *affect* others.

In fact, as the following sections argue, the consequence of these difficulties has been that studies of human investment have not been (and perhaps cannot be) free of implicit or explicit propositions about other values: it is for this reason that they have produced less policy accord than might have been expected.

We shall consider first the problems of assessing the returns from education to individuals, then turn to social benefits and costs: both throw up questions of the kind described.

The Returns to Individuals from Education

(a) *Benefits:* It is conceptually possible to discover the "gain" that an individual obtains from some specified type of education by comparing the changes in his income-stream that result from the education with the costs that he must incur in order to obtain it.

Ideally, the economist's interest is in measuring "real" rather than monetary returns. On the benefit side, this means that "psychic" returns as well as monetary ones must be considered, or, to use an alternative terminology, that we treat education as a form of consumption as well as a form of investment for the individual.

No-one has suggested any direct method of evaluating "psychic" returns" (which accrue to other kinds of resource-use as well as "human investment" uses), and the indirect methods are not very satisfactory. A possible procedure is to use the relative growth of human and physical capital to make inferences about the "real returns" to education, and then to use the difference between this and the money returns to assess the relative "psychic returns" to education and to physical capital. But even long-run information about growth of capital of various types is capable of a wide variety of possible explanations (changes in risk attitudes, in actual rates of return to different kinds of capital, and so on) about which we have very little information as yet. Further, the results so far would seem in any case to be statistically inconclusive, in that the evidence could be compatible with either lower or higher psychic returns to education than to physical capital. Finally, the evidence throws no light on the "spread" of psychic returns between individuals: and it will shortly be appreciated that for our present purposes this is not a trivial omission.

While "psychic returns" associated with any kind of resource-use are difficult to evaluate, there are special problems in the case of education (and other "human investments") that complicate the question further. In the first place, there is a fundamental fashion in which the two types of psychic return differ in character. A man may obtain a "psychic" (consumption) return from "running his own business," or from owning land. In such cases, we can distinguish the source of the return, and identify the time-period over which it accrues (the period of control of the business or ownership of the land). In the case of education, it has already been pointed out that the education process is indivisible and also that the "asset" cannot be separated from the consumer of its services.

In the second place, "consumption" of education has at least two forms. It may consist in the enjoyment obtained from the "education process" during that period of becoming educated (i.e., using the facilities of an educational institution) which simultaneously improves the individual's expectations of future earnings, and it may consist in the "psychic returns," obtained from having been educated, but enjoyed during the rest of the individual's life. Most writers believe both types of return to be relevant, and it is frequently suggested that they can be distinguished by considering the first as a form of current consumption and the second as consumption of the services of a durable consumption good (the earlier education). However, the analogy is a dubious one: apart from the difficulty of distinguishing the capital from the return to it, the character and "value" of the long-run "psychic returns" to individuals from education are unusual, to say the least.

It is the essence of the education process that it changes attitudes, expectations and preference patterns: it takes Beatlemaniacs and turns them into Bach lovers. In the nature of things, the *ex ante* process of valuation of the "consumption" return to education by individuals is usually going to be different from the valuation that these individuals would make *ex post:* there are indeed arguments that it is a central purpose of the educational process to produce such a change. Be that as it may, there is clearly an awkward question to be answered. For our graduated student now gets psychic returns from having been educated to appreciate Bach. But he can no longer tolerate the Beatles. Should we not deduct the (notional) "loss" of consumption that this latter change implies? Or should we abandon the attempt to measure psychic returns as fruitless? Or should we treat only the *ex post* valuation (at what point?) as relevant, despite the fact that it has been created by the education itself?

It might appear that the position could be recovered by recourse to the old philosophical conundrum: How does a pig know whether it is better to be a pig than a philosopher? And how does a philosopher know? J. S. Mill would have answered this by arguing, essentially, that the philosopher was in a better position to choose than the pig, because he better understood the alternatives placed before him. Essentially similar "choice-widening" propositions have begun to appear in the literature of the new welfare economics. However, in my view they fit the character of education but poorly: the process is one of *changing* tastes rather than (or as well as) of widening the range of choices. An education cannot be kept like a row of (subjective) suits in a closet, so that a man can retain the (Beatle) suit he began with, add others to it in the process of education, but remain free to return to the original clothing whenever he so chooses.

One popular way to deal with the intractability to measurement of education "consumption" is to assert that the education of a person's tastes must have an unambiguously positive continuing value to him.[6] (The illiterate native is always "happier" for being introduced to the education system of an industrial society.) If we assign some positive value to consumption, then we can treat the other returns to education as "investment" returns. Apart from its arbitrariness, such a procedure leaves some important questions unanswered. Is the assertion that "consumption" returns are positive a logical proposition, or a personal value judgment? Is there no relation between the precise form of education, the methods by which it is provided, and the "psychic" returns to it?[7]

A similar point has been made by Shaffer, who draws attention to the fact that some school attendance in the U.S.A. is compulsory, and hence outside the area of private decision-making.[8] Schultz dismissed this as irrelevant to problems of measurement: the "investment" rate of return to those educated, he says, is unaffected by the way they obtained access to (educational) resources, in the same way that the value of a physical investment is unaffected by its being publicly or privately financed.[9] But while this rejoinder is not without any substance, it is nevertheless seriously misleading. The problem of assessing the "consumption" value of publicly-provided goods not rationed by prices is a central one in public finance, and the present problem is in part an extension of this one. Further, whatever may be the position concerning "investment" return, it is clear that the "consumption" value of education must be related to the opportunity-cost situation of the individuals being educated. That situation is determined by the available alternatives, and compulsory schooling clearly affects these, e.g., by ruling out (or increasing the costs of) such alternatives to school as going fishing. This argument in turn leads naturally to one that is perhaps more fundamental for present purposes: whose valuations are or should we be measuring? If there is compulsion to attend school, this would suggest that the community does not accept the valuations placed upon education by children and/or parents. It is clear that the valuation of their education by children will be different from its valuation by others and may well be negative for many of them at some ages. If they were free to choose, they would "consume" different amounts and types of education from those that their parents would choose, and these latter in turn would differ from the "valuations" of society as decided by the government.[10] Whose valuations are we to count?

There is a clear sense in which a decision whether and how to make education compulsory is a decision about whose valuations are relevant to policy. When we measure the "returns" to education, that is, we measure the results of a given method or provision. Thus to assert that the method chosen (incorporating e.g. some type of compulsion) is irrelevant to the measured magnitudes is not only to assert that the same situation could have been produced by other means (e.g., without compulsion), but also that the "consumption" value of the education itself is unaffected by the division of rights and obligations for education between children, parents, and governments.[11] Insofar as this assertion is unacceptable, it follows that the difficulties of distinguishing "consumption" and "investment" returns to education are not simply technical, but are related also to existing policies and to some system of "social" values.

It should now be apparent that we are concerned with something more than a philosophical quibble. *The measured "returns" to educational spending are intimately connected with the nature of access to educational resources, and this in turn is intimately related to the value of education to individuals, families, and society. If we are to translate statistics into policy, we must be prepared to show what difference we think would be made to our data if educational policies were changed in character (as well as if existing policies were extended or contracted), and/or to specify those social values (such as the rights and obligations of families), that we believe to be ineluctable.*

(b) *Costs:* The interesting problems from our present point of view concern the "costs" of earnings foregone in obtaining education. Up to a point, the disagreement about whether or not such earnings are a "real" cost is a sham fight, in that the "right" solution must depend upon the actual and postulated alternative conditions being considered. There are, however, two ways in which problems of policy become entangled with those of valuation: both can be treated briefly since the argument follows the same line as that of the previous section.

The first problem has already been indicated. The calculation of foregone earnings involves an answer to the question "What would have happened if the students being educated had been less or differently educated?" This must depend upon the alternative situation postulated, so that to answer the question precisely *implies* the elucidation of the alternative (education and other) policies that would pertain in the new situation. A common means of escape from this problem is to assume (implicitly or explicitly) that the adjustment would be "marginal," in the sense that methods of education provision are considered unchanged, and the numbers of persons "moving" in and out of education are treated as too small to affect relative earnings in different occupations, etc. This "solution," however, fits badly with the aggregative methods of computation used: it also makes the results of dubious value for policy if the changes being considered are global in character (such as the general introduction of equal educational opportunity for non-whites in the South), and/or affect *methods* as well as volume of education provision.

The second problem concerns the treatment of leisure. One way to "pay" for education may be to take less leisure than "would" have been taken had the individual taken a job not involving education. Thus, the "opportunity-cost" of obtaining education is not just foregone earnings, but the sum of this and foregone leisure, somehow valued in money. Up to a point, this is a technical rather than a conceptual matter. The difficulties of including leisure in calculations of income or output are well-known, and those concerned with "human investment" estimates are scarcely to be blamed for not resolving this difficulty within their chosen field. But there are some additional considerations. One aspect of the "taste-changing" consequences of education is likely to be a change in leisure-preference, so that changes in the distribution of time between education, work for income, and leisure may reflect not just the "constant" opportunity-cost situation of the individual but also the influence of increasing "consumption" of education upon him.[12] Again, the character of the opportunity-cost of leisure is clearly related to the general nature of access to educational resources: a comparison of Britain (where the student once admitted to a university is generally provided with a living allowance) and the U.S.A. is a sufficient illustration of this.

In sum, computations of the "costs" of education to individuals unavoidably contain more or less implicit assumptions about *methods* as well as volume of education provision, and the implications of these need to be spelled out in detail if statistical information about rates of return is to be given a policy construction.

Social Returns from Education

The costs of, and benefits from, education provision to society differ from the returns to individuals. The nature of these "social" gains and losses has been usefully classified e.g. by Weisbrod.[13] Also, while it is generally agreed that the social effects of education are difficult to quantify, it has been argued that upper and lower limits can be set—e.g., by using before-tax differentials to measure the lower limit, and the "residual factor" in growth studies such as Denison's to measure the upper one.[14] Existing studies suggest that the difference between the two is uncomfortably large. But what concerns us more in the present context is that the procedure ignores important qualitative problems of the education process.[15]

For present purposes, it is pointful to adopt a classification of social costs and benefits that is less detailed and differently specified than those just referred to. The most useful distinction for us is between those benefits and costs that can (conceptually at least) be attributed to economic units (individuals, households, etc.), in the sense that those units would be willing to pay rather than forego the relevant benefit, and those "social" gains from education that do not have this characteristic. The first group comprises all those benefits (costs) that the individual being educated does not capture, but which clearly accrue to others. There are two broad (polar) types of such benefits (costs). One is the type that accrues to specific and identifiable economic units (e.g., the income of A is raised as a result of the education of B). The other is generalized: it is the "public good" economic benefit that the community at large obtains from B having been educated, the benefit being "consumed" by the community at large and not directly imputable to individuals. While both these types of indirect consequence of education are difficult to assess, the problems are technical rather than philosophical: we are fairly clear about what we want to measure but at a loss as to how to do it. But failing agreed means of measurement, it must remain doubtful what light recognition of the existence of social costs and benefits (externalities) of these types can throw upon the problems of education policy. Coase, Buchanan, and others[16] have demonstrated, conclusively in my view, that the existence of externalities provides no *a priori* reason to believe that resource-allocation will be affected in any particular way, or e.g. that such allocation would be improved (and economic growth encouraged?) were the gainers and losers in fact penalized and compensated. Further, it has to be recognized that the way benefits and costs are allocated between persons is determined by the institutional arrangements through which access to education is provided: we therefore cannot hope to relate these kinds of externalities to policy decisions save by their incorporation in a model (analytical framework) that embraces those institutional arrangements.

The other broad group of social "benefits" is even more indirect, but there is ample evidence that economists interested in "human investment" attach great importance to it. It consists in the "gains to society" that education confers by encouraging "cultural advance," improving the "character" of the community, the "quality" of leadership and of economic and social decisions, and so on. The essential matter here is that it is fundamentally open to question whether these are "values" at all in the economist's sense, and whether they are even conceptually measurable.[17] Thus, Musgrave for example argues for the reservation of education policy decisions to the educated, on grounds that they understand the "value" of education better than others.[18] If we accept this, our benefit-cost study presumably would include the "valuations" only of the "informed." But what should we put in as a measure of the "costs" (e.g., by restriction of choice) imposed on others? Another version emphasizes the social value of an informed society and electorate. But informed about what? All Russian schoolchildren learn about communism, and an interpretation of capitalism that stigmatizes it as evil. American children seem to learn the opposite. Which electorate is being the better "informed" through education? Who is competent to "value" these social "benefits"? These are problems that have defied political philosophers for generations. I am not so foolish as to criticize economists for not providing agreed answers to them. But neither am I happy to see them swept into a dust-bag labelled "other social benefits." Our statistical observations about the returns to education as an investment are built upon the actual answers that have been and are being given to questions like these: we should recognize this rather than try to deal with the difficulty by a taxonomic evasion.

The affinity of these arguments with the ones put forward in earlier sections is clear, as is the conclusion. Unless it can be clearly demonstrated that there are "social costs" that are "economic" (and quantifiable) in a sense distinguishable from "social values" of other kinds, the results of "human investment" studies must be difficult to translate into policy recommendations.

This is the more true since it must now be clear that there is no unique (or simple) relation between "social" and "private" returns to education. For example, a given volume of public expenditure for educational purposes must be expected to affect private "investment" and "returns" differentially according to the manner in which it is spent.[19]

Failing agreed solutions to such problems, our only recourse is to acknowledge that "social benefits" if broadly defined, are (at least in part) not an "economic" category at all in the ordinary sense, to recognize that there is a relation between the (notionally) measurable aspects of education as a social investment and the broader social context and institutional environment within which the education is provided, and to avoid allowing personal value judgments to masquerade as objective propositions or potentially quantifiable magnitudes.

CONCLUSIONS AND SUGGESTIONS

It is one thing to parade one's own difficulties and confusions, quite another to make positive suggestions for future progress, and to relate the argument to a specific issue such as education policy in the South. But the discussion does suggest some kinds of future development that would be fruitful, and also throws some light upon our specific policy problem. The proposals divide conveniently into two groups, concerned respectively with the further development and policy-orientation of benefit-cost studies, and with the need for more comparative and other studies adopting alternative approaches to education provision.

The Bearing of Benefit-cost Studies on Policy-making

I have already made clear that I do not wish to suggest that the study of "human investment" through such things as education has or can have no value. On the contrary, I believe the conception to be fruitful of understanding: to take an example of direct interest to myself, I would expect these developments to produce radical changes in our approach to public finance. But it is consistent with this to be concerned about the bearing of actual studies upon public policy. I have argued that there are serious interpretative problems awaiting answers, and I would suggest that many economists are themselves ambivalent in their interpretation of the results of "human investment" studies.

The basic need might be put in the form that the parameters of benefit-cost studies in this field are insufficiently specified for their policy scope and relevance to be assessed, particularly by non-economists. But this formulation perhaps gives the problem too technical a flavor: the parameters in question incorporate e.g. distinctions between *ends* and *means* of a particularly difficult kind (is public provision of education an end in itself or a means to other ends, and if the latter, precisely what other ends?), and/or the attachment of "values" to attributes of education that lie outside any direct economic nexus. The economist cannot be expected to provide impeccable answers to such questions: but this does not justify his pushing the problems aside, and I have argued that in any case he is unable to do so. It is sensible to distinguish conceptually between value judgments, *a priori* propositions, and "scientific" (empirically tested) statements. But it is futile to pretend that benefit-cost studies can be so organized that they incorporate statements only of the last type, leaving the others to be made by whoever cares to make use of the economist's "scientific" information. If this neat distinction is not possible, then it will be both intellectually more satisfactory and practically more rewarding to accept the situation, and to devote time and thought to spelling out the nature of the "social," etc., characteristics of empirical studies that we believe to influence the observed magnitudes.

In fact, I do not think it can be denied that economists not infrequently have particular but implicit "social ends" in mind when interpreting "human investment" studies. For example, if it is "reasonable" to divide the costs of education into a "consumption" and an "investment" component, it would seem reasonable also to make the same distinction in deciding public policies concerned to meet these costs. But such an inference is not usually made or pursued: methods of finance are either ignored or policy concerning them is debated on quite different "social" grounds. Similar questions arise in the interpretation of statistics of the returns to education of whites and non-whites. Thus, Shaffer has pointed out that if education is treated as an investment for purposes of policy decision, then a higher rate of return to whites than to non-whites would seem to provide an argument for shifting (education) resources from the latter group to the former.[20] Criticism of this position has been concerned less to deny the validity of the inference *qua* inference than to argue about the statistics.[21] But let us suppose Shaffer's data to be accurate, for purposes of argument. How many economists would accept his policy inference? If we do not, and we wish to be listened to, then do we not have an obligation to set out *in advance* the other policy objectives (such as non-discrimination, in some sense, in access to education) that we intend to treat as constraints?[22] Further refinement of statistics is no substitute for such explicit value judgments. Rather, it is likely to invite the unkind and generally unjustified comment that we start from our conclusions and pursue our statistics simply to the point at which "the correlation is good enough."

Of course, we can take the position that we are concerned only to present the evidence: it is for others to use it. But it has been the tenor of my argument that empirical studies are not easily to be separated from the general social and educational environment concerned: such a detached attitude will become plausible only if we can reach a point at which it is possible unambiguously to solve the valuation problems I have described, and to predict the economic consequences of changes in the *environment* as well as of changes in the *volume* of education provision. (In the case for example of the education of non-whites is it not clear that the economist's contribution to policy-making is concerned at least as much with the consequences of methods of provision as with those of the size of educational spending?) Given the difficulties to which I have drawn attention (and particularly the relation between the things we treat as "values" and existing social arrangements), I would expect such a day to be long in coming. In the meantime, it is pointful to try to improve the methods by which we assess returns to "investment in education," but I would suggest that it is also important, given the difficulties, to put some of our capital into other baskets. These complementary approaches are the concern of the next (and final) section.

The Education "Market"

Interest in benefit-cost studies of education is clearly not un-related to the way education is commonly provided, and particularly to the degree of absence or inhibition of market arrangements. While many of those interested in "human investment" would accept the relevance of (market) institutional arrangements to their studies, the argument is sometimes made that to examine such arrangements for economic policy purposes is not particularly pointful because "education is not a commodity like soap." If this means that there may be social values involved in decisions about the production and distribution of education that are not involved in the production and distribution of soap, it is of course true enough. But, equally, there is an important sense in which education *is* a commodity (economic good) like any other: those who object to its being so considered not uncommonly also seize on evidence of high (economic) rates of return to argue for increased educational spending. In my view (and I do not suggest that it would not be shared by many others), there is point in studying education provision in particular environments as a resource-allocation process. Indeed (as other writers have recognized), such studies are probably a necessary complement to benefiit-cost analyses, and may prove to be the most fruitful approach that we have available to us to qualitative problems concerned with such matters for example as the relation between *methods* of education provision (which determine the character of the "market") and the value of education as an investment and as a stimulus to economic growth.

Essentially, "market-oriented" studies have to be concerned with the behavior of individuals, families, governments and other social groups as producers or consumers of education: they examine the behavior of the "knowledge industry" in which the educated are the consumers, and schools and other relevant enterprises the "producers." Studies adopting this general approach already exist, and can be described in four broad (but overlapping) groups.

(a) Studies concerned with actual methods of provision. These need to be descriptive, institutional and quantitative, and to distinguish relevant types of education rather than treat it as a global magnitude, as would an applied study of the steel industry. But they also need to be analytic, in the sense that they are concerned to relate the results to the structure of the market (and e.g. to assess the consequences of changes in that structure), to defined criteria of "efficiency," and to such extra-economic "values" (ends) as seem relevant. I would regard Machlup's study of U.S. arrangements as a pioneering effort in this field.

(b) Normative studies such as those of Friedman,[23] Peacock and Wiseman,[24] and Johnson[25] concerned to set out the relations between particular (market, etc.) systems of education provision and postulated economic and social goals. While such studies may have some limited empirical content, their contribution lies rather in the stimulus they provide for the clearer specification of ends and means in the making of education policy. The need for this clearer specification has already been argued to be a significant problem in the policy interpretation of benefit-cost studies.

(c) Broader, but still "market-oriented" studies. I have in mind here studies related to a wider and different social context, which nevertheless throw incidental light upon the implications of particular methods of education provision. There are two studies of this kind that are of topical interest: Becker's study of the economics of discrimination,[26] and Hutt's[27] recently published study of the economics of the color bar in South Africa. This latter sets out to argue that the economic inferiority of the non-whites has been perpetuated and reinforced by institutional arrangements affecting (inhibiting) the operation of markets. While little is provided by way of quantification, Hutt nevertheless argues a convincing case, in my view, for the nature of the ends-means relations that have produced the results he describes. Certainly, he illuminates the character of public policy in the relevant area, and demands refutation. This is not to argue that more statistical data would have detracted from the study, but rather to reinforce the argument that such studies and quantitative research into "human investment" are powerfully complementary rather than substitutable activities.

We should also include in this section studies of voting systems after the pattern of Buchanan and Tullock.[28] If education has important "social" characteristics, then we must expect education decisions to be made at least partly through the political process. Consequently, we need to learn more not only about the individual (private) "consumption" and "investment" demand for education, but also about the relation (e.g.) between voting systems and the (public) demand for it.

(d) While (international and inter-regional) comparisons of returns to "human investment" are already under way, less interest has yet been evinced in the comparative study of institutional arrangements. This is an obvious necessity internationally, if we are not simply to produce "education tables" capable of as wide a variety of policy interpretations as are the present "growth tables." It is also relevant to the problems of the South: the spelling out of the precise nature of the different barriers to educational opportunity facing whites and non-whites, and attempts to assess (even if only qualitatively) the likely results of their removal, is an obvious and valuable way of supplementing more aggregative studies.

If further argument for such comparative-market-institutional studies is needed, it may be worth pondering upon the lack of success which has so far attended attempts to relate educational policies and historical growth rates. Might not greater understanding of differences in methods of education provision help to resolve this problem?

In conclusion, let me repeat that I do not believe these alternative approaches to contain a panacea. Rather, I am very uncertain as to how useful a policy tool benefit-cost studies *alone* can ever become, and suggest therefore (on the same grounds that others have argued for a liberal rather than a narrow technical education system because of uncertainty about future demands for labor) that we should not neglect these complementary approaches.

NOTES

[1]Theodore W. Schultz, *The Economic Value of an Education* (New York: Columbia University Press, 1963).

[2]An exhaustive list of relevant studies, as well as a very valuable survey of the literature, is provided by T. W. Schultz (see note 1). I have also been fortunate enough to be able to read Gary S. Becker's study *Investment in Education,* now awaiting publication by N.B.E.R.

[3]T. Balogh and P.P. Streeten, "The Coefficient of Ignorance," *Bulletin of the Oxford University Institute of Economics and Statistics,* May 1963, p. 104.

[4]Lee R. Martin, "Research Needed on the Contribution of Human, Social and Community Capital to Economic Growth," *Journal of Farm Economics,* February 1963, p. 82, n. 10.

[5]Joan Robinson, *The Accumulation of Capital* (London: Macmillan, 1965), pp. 11-12.

[6]See e.g. Schultz, *op. cit.,* p. 51 n.

[7]The reader will perhaps recognize the close resemblance between the special case here being argued and the general approach to the relation between economic and other values that permeates the work of Frank H. Knight. I believe the work of Professor Knight to be sufficiently germane to merit quotation at length:

"To state the fundamental issue briefly at the outset, are the motives with which economics has to do—which is to say human motives in general—'wants,' 'desires' of a character which can adequately be treated as *facts* in the scientific sense, or are they 'value,' or 'oughts,' of an essentially different character not amenable to scientific description or logical manipulation? For if it is the intrinsic nature of a thing to grow and change, it cannot serve as a scientific datum. A science must have a 'static' subject-matter; it must talk about things which will 'stay put'; otherwise its statements will not remain true after they are made and there will be no point to making them. Economics has always treated desires or motives as facts, of a character susceptible to statement in propositions, and sufficiently stable during the period of the activity which they prompt to be treated as causes of that activity in a scientific sense. It has thus viewed life as a process of satisfying desires. If this is true then life is a matter of economics; only if it is untrue, or a very inadequate view of the truth, only if the 'creation of value' is distinctly more than the satisfaction of desire, is there room for ethics in a sense logically separable from economics." *The Ethics of Competition* (New York & London: Harper & Brothers, 1935), p. 21.

"The facts, as emphasized, are altogether against accepting any balance-sheet view of life; they point rather toward an evaluation of a far subtler sort than the addition and subtraction of homogeneous items, toward an ethics along the line of aesthetic criticism, whose canons are of another sort than scientific laws and are not quite intellectually satisfying. We cannot accept want-satisfaction as a final criterion of value because we do not in fact regard our wants as final; instead of resting in the view that there is no disputing about tastes, we dispute about them more than anything else; our most difficult problem in valuation is the evaluation of our wants themselves and our most troublesome want is the desire for wants of the 'right' kind." *Ibid.,* pp. 41-2.

"But man is also a problem-solving entity at the higher level of critical deliberation about ends, or free choice of ends on the basis of thinking, illustrated by the pursuit of truth. That is, he is a being who seeks, and in a real sense creates, values. The essential significance of this is the fact that man is interested in changing himself, even to changing the ultimate core of his being. This is the meaning of being active. It makes a categorical distinction between men and all other objects of knowledge. We cannot be sure that other objects are not conscious, or even that they are devoid of will; but if they have any conscious, will-attitude toward themselves it is limited, as far as we can tell, to the *perserverare in esse suo.* They do not strive to change their own nature or character—or, indeed to 'convert' fellow-members of their species; and in so far as scientific categories apply, they do not undergo change at all, in their ultimate nature. In contrast with natural objects—even with the higher animals—man is unique in that he is dissatisfied with himself; he is the discontented animal, the romantic, argumentative, aspiring animal. Consequently, his behaviour can only in part be described by scientific principles or laws." *Freedom and Reform* (New York & London: Harper & Brothers, 1947), pp. 236-7.

[8]Harry G. Shaffer, "Investment in Human Capital: Comment," *American Economic Review,* December 1961.

[9]Theodore W. Schultz, "Investment in Human Capital: Reply," *American Economic Review,* December 1961.

[10]I.e., the community's "valuation" of the consumption of education by individuals. We are not at this point concerned with indirect ("social") returns.

[11]Would it be entirely unfair to suggest that such a view is most likely to appeal to the better educated, who have more than one reason to overvalue education—and to point out that it is this better-educated group that is primarily concerned in the policy debate?

[12]Machlup has drawn attention to the positive correlation between amount of education and hours of work in the U.S.A. See *The Production and Distribution of Knowledge in the United States* (Princeton, N.J.: Princeton University Press, 1962), p. 112.

[13]Burton A. Weisbrod, *External Benefits of Public Education* (Princeton University: Industrial Relations Section Research Reports, no. 105, 1964).

[14]Edward F. Denison, *The Sources of Economic Growth in the United States and the Alternatives Before Us* (New York: Committee for Economic Development, 1962).

[15]I have discussed these matters further in a joint paper with Alan T. Peacock, "Economic Growth and the Principles of Educational Finance in Developed Countries," Paper for O.E.C.D. Conference on the Finance of Education, September 1964. See also Harold W. Groves, *Education and Economic Growth* (Washington, D.C.: National Education Association, 1961).

[16]The recent literature is summarized in R. Turvey, "On Divergences between Social Cost and Private Cost," *Economica,* August 1963.

[17]Were the social "values" of pre-nineteenth century Germany enhanced by subsequent emphasis on education?

[18]R.A. Musgrave, *Theory of Public Finance* (New York: McGraw-Hill, 1959), pp. 13-15.

[19]For examples, see Schultz, *The Economic Value of an Education,* and Balogh and Streeten, *op. cit.*

[20]Shaffer, *op.cit.*

[21]Schultz, "Investment in Human Capital: A Reply," *loc.cit.*

[22]Of course, this argument is not confined to education policy but is general in scope: economists are perhaps less ready to give it explicit recognition than they might be. For example, monopoly policy involves not only views about the relation between monopoly power, resource allocation, technical progress, and so on; but also an attitude to the preservation of freedom of choice as an end in itself. But it properly diminishes the influence of economists' arguments if they invoke their judgments of value on this last issue only after all other ("technical") arguments have been used.

[23]M. Friedman, "The Role of the Government in Education," in *Economics and the Public Interest,* Robert A. Solo, ed. (New Brunswick, N.J.: Rutgers University Press, 1955).

[24]Alan T. Peacock and J. Wiseman, *Education for Democrats* (London: Institute of Economic Affairs, 1964).

[25]Harry G. Johnson, "The Social Policy of an Opulent Society," in *Money, Trade and Economic Growth* (Cambridge, Mass.: Harvard University Press, 1962).

[26]Gary S. Becker, *The Economics of Discrimination* (Chicago, Ill.: University of Chicago Press, 1957).

[27]W.H. Hutt, *The Economics of the Colour Bar* (London: Institute of Economic Affairs, 1964).

[28]J.M. Buchanan and G. Tullock, *The Calculus of Consent* (Ann Arbor, Mich.: University of Michigan Press, 1962).

SUGGESTIONS FOR FURTHER READING—PART III

Benson, Charles S., ed. *Perspectives on the Economics of Education.* Boston: Houghton Mifflin, 1963.

Bowen, William G. *Economic Aspects of Education.* Princeton, New Jersey: Princeton University Press, 1965.

Bowman, Mary Jean. "Social Returns to Education." *International Social Science Journal,* Vol. 14 (Winter 1962), pp. 647-659.

Clark, Harold F. "Education and Poverty." In *The Disadvantaged Poor: Education and Employment.* Third Report of the Task Force on Economic Growth and Opportunity. Washington, D.C.: U.S. Chamber of Commerce, 1966, pp. 153-172.

Clark, Kenneth B. "Education of the Minority Poor—The Key to the War on Poverty." In *The Disadvantaged Poor: Education and Employment.* Third Report of the Task Force on Economic Growth and Opportunity. Washington, D.C.: U.S. Chamber of Commerce, 1966, pp. 173-188.

Hanoch, Giora. "An Economic Analysis of Earnings and Schooling." *Journal of Human Resources,* Vol. 2, No. 3 (Summer 1967), pp. 310-329.

Hansen, W. Lee. "Total and Private Rates of Return to Investment in Schooling." *Journal of Political Economy,* Vol. 71, No. 2 (April 1963), pp. 128-140.

Schultz, Theodore W. *The Economic Value of Education.* New York: Columbia University Press, 1963.

Schultz, Theodore W. "The Rate of Return in Allocating Investment Resources to Education." *Journal of Human Resources,* Vol. 2, No. 3 (Summer 1967), pp. 293-309.

Part IV

PPBS

11

THE POLITICAL ECONOMY OF EFFICIENCY: COST-BENEFIT ANALYSIS, SYSTEMS ANALYSIS AND PROGRAM BUDGETING

by Aaron Wildavsky

PPBS is an analytical technique that is having increasing impact on all branches of government. It will be noted in Article 14 (Hirsch) that PPBS is beginning to be applied to public education programs. Professor Wildavsky was a major contributor to the two symposia on PPBS published by the Public Administration Review *in 1966 and 1969. As a leading authority on the federal budgeting process, he examines the concept of economic efficiency, which underlies cost-benefit analysis. He indicates the difficulty of developing unchallengeable cost-benefit techniques in a society in which different interest groups may gain or lose from different types of expenditures. He is particularly skeptical about the sweeping claims made for PPBS techniques in the Department of Defense under Secretary Robert McNamara.*

There was a day when the meaning of economic efficiency was reasonably clear.

Reprinted from Aaron Wildavsky, "The Political Economy of Efficiency: Cost-Benefit Analysis, Systems Analysis and Program Budgeting," *Public Administration Review,* Vol. XXVI, No. 4 (December 1966), pp. 292-310. Reprinted by permission of the publisher.

An objective met up with a technician. Efficiency consisted in meeting the objective at the lowest cost or in obtaining the maximum amount of the objective for a specified amount of resources. Let us call this "pure efficiency." The desirability of trying to achieve certain objectives may depend on the cost of achieving them. In this case the analyst (he was graduated from being a mere technician) alters the objective to suit available resources. Let us call this "mixed efficiency." Both pure and mixed efficiency are limited in the sense that they take for granted the existing structure of the political system and work within its boundaries. Yet the economizer, he who values efficiency most dearly, may discover that the most efficient means for accomplishing his ends cannot be secured without altering the machinery for making decisions. He not only alters means and ends (resources and objectives) simultaneously but makes them dependent on changes in political relationships. While he claims no special interest in or expertise concerning the decision apparatus outside of the market place, the economizer pursues efficiency to the heart of the political system. Let us call this "total efficiency." In this vocabulary, then, concepts of efficiency may be pure or mixed, limited or total.

A major purpose of this paper is to take the newest and recently most popular modes of achieving efficiency—cost-benefit analysis, systems analysis, and program budgeting—and show how much more is involved than mere economizing. *Even at the most modest level of cost-benefit analysis, I will try to show that it becomes difficult to maintain pure notions of efficiency. At a higher level, systems analysis is based on a mixed notion of efficiency. And program budgeting at the highest levels leaves pure efficiency far behind its overreaching grasp into the structure of the political system. Program budgeting, it turns out, is a form of systems analysis, that is, political systems analysis.*

These modes of analysis are neither good for nothing nor good for everything, and one cannot speak of them as wholly good or bad. It is much more useful to try to specify some conditions under which they would or would not be helpful for various purposes. While such a list could not be exhaustive at this stage, nor permanent at any stage (because of advances in the art), it provides a basis for thinking about what these techniques can and cannot do. Another major purpose of this paper, therefore, is to describe cost-benefit and systems analysis and program budgeting as techniques for decision-making. I shall place particular stress upon what seems to me the most characteristic feature of all three modes of analysis: the aids to calculation designed to get around the vast areas of uncertainty where quantitative analysis leaves off and judgment begins.

COST-BENEFIT ANALYSIS

. . . One can view cost-benefit analysis as anything from an infallible means of reaching the new Utopia to a waste of resources in attempting to measure the unmeasurable.[1]

The purpose of cost-benefit analysis is to secure an efficient allocation of resources produced by the governmental system in its interaction with the private economy. The nature of efficiency depends on the objectives set up for government. In the field of water resources, where most of the work on cost-benefit analysis has been done, the governmental objective is usually postulated to be an increase in national income. In a crude sense, this means that the costs to whomever may incur them should be less than the benefits to whomever may receive them. The time streams of consumption gained and foregone by a project are its benefits and costs.

The aim of cost-benefit analysis is to maximize "the present value of all benefits less that of all costs, subject to specified restraints."[2] A long view is taken in that costs are estimated not only for the immediate future but also for the life of the project. A wide view is taken in that indirect consequences for others—variously called externalities, side-effects, spillovers, and repercussion effects—are considered. Ideally, all costs and benefits are evaluated. The usual procedure is to estimate the installation costs of the project and spread them over time, thus making them into something like annual costs. To these costs are added an estimate of annual operating costs. The next step involves estimating the average value of the output by considering the likely number of units produced each year and their probable value in the market place of the future. Intangible, "secondary," benefits may then be considered. These time streams of costs and benefits are discounted so as to obtain the present value of costs and benefits. Projects whose benefits are greater than costs may then be approved, or the cost-benefit ratios may, with allowance for relative size, be used to rank projects in order of desirability.

Underlying Economic and Political Assumptions

A straightforward description of cost-benefit analysis cannot do justice to the powerful assumptions that underlie it or to the many conditions limiting its usefulness. The assumptions involve value judgments that are not always recognized and, when recognized, are not easily handled in practice. The limiting conditions arise partly out of the assumptions and partly out of severe computational difficulties in estimating costs, and especially benefits. Here I can only indicate some major problems.

Cost-benefit analysis is based on superiority in the market place,[3] under competitive conditions and full employment, as the measure of value in society. Any imperfection in the market works against the validity of the results. Unless the same degree of monopoly were found throughout the economy, for example, a governmental body that enjoys monopolistic control of prices or outputs would not necessarily make the same investment decisions as under free competition. A similar difficulty occurs where the size of a project is large in comparison to the economy, as in some developing nations. The project itself then affects the constellation of relative prices and production against which its efficiency is measured. The assumption based on the classical full employment model is also important because it gives prices special significance. Where manpower is not being utilized, projects may be justified in part as putting this unused resource to work.

The economic model on which cost-benefit analysis depends for its validity is based on a political theory. The idea is that in a free society the economy is to serve the individual's consistent preferences revealed and rationally pursued in the market place. Governments are not supposed to dictate preferences nor make decisions.

This individualist theory assumes as valid the current distribution of income. Preferences are valued in the market place where votes are based on disposable income. Governmental action to achieve efficiency, therefore, inevitably carries with it consequences for the distribution of income. Projects of different size and location and compostion will transfer income in different amounts to different people. While economists might estimate the redistributive consequences of various projects, they cannot, on efficiency grounds, specify one or another as preferable. How is this serious problem to be handled?

Benefit-cost analysis is a way of trying to promote economic welfare. But whose welfare? No one knows how to deal with interpersonal comparisons of utility. It cannot be assumed that the desirability of rent supplements versus a highway or dam can be measured on a single utility scale. There is no scientific way to compare losses and gains among different people or to say that the marginal loss of a dollar to one man is somehow equal to the gain of a dollar by another. The question of whose utility function is to prevail (the analyst verus the people involved, the upstream gainers versus the downstream losers, the direct beneficiaries versus the taxpayers, the entire nation or a particular region, and so on) is of prime importance in making public policy.

The literature on welfare economics is notably unable to specify an objective welfare function.[4] Ideally, actions would benefit everyone and harm no one. As an approximation, the welfare economist views as optimal an action that leaves some people better off and none worse off. If this criterion were applied in political life, it would result in a situation like that of the Polish Diet in which anyone who was damaged could veto legislation. To provide a way out of this impasse, Hicks and Kaldor proposed approval of decisions if the total gain in welfare is such that the winners could compensate the losers. But formal machinery for compensation does not ordinarily exist and most modern economists are highly critical of the major political mechanism for attempting to compensate, namely, log-rolling in Congress on public works projects.[5] It is a very imperfect mechanism for assuring that losers in one instance become winners in another.

Another way of dealing with income distribution is to accept a criterion laid down by a political body and maximize present benefits less costs subject to this constraint. Or the cost-benefit analyst can present a series of alternatives differing according to the individuals who pay and prices charged. The analyst must not only compute the new inputs and outputs, but also the costs and benefits for each group with whom the public authorities are especially concerned. No wonder this is not often done! Prest and Turvey are uncertain whether such a procedure is actually helpful in practice.[6]

Income redistribution in its most extreme form would result in a complete leveling or equality of incomes. Clearly, this is not what is meant. A more practical meaning might be distributing income to the point where specific groups achieve a certain minimum. It is also possible that the operational meaning of income redistribution may simply be the transfer of some income from some haves to some have nots. Even in the last and most minimal sense of the term it is by no means clear that projects that are inefficient by the usual economic criteria serve to redistribute income in the desired direction. It is possible that some inefficient projects may transfer income from poorer to richer people. Before the claim that certain projects are justified by the effect of distributing income in a specified way can be accepted, an analysis to show that this is what actually happens must be at hand.

Since the distribution of income is at stake, it is not surprising that beneficiaries tend to dominate investment decisions in the

political arena and steadfastly refuse to pay for what they receive
from government tax revenues. They uniformly resist user charges
based on benefits received. Fox and Herfindahl estimate that of a
total initial investment of three billion for the Corps of Engineers
in 1962, taxpayers in general would pay close to two-thirds of the
costs.[7] Here, greater use of the facilities by a larger number of
beneficiaries getting something for nothing inflates the estimated
benefits which justify the project in the first place. There may be
a political rationale for these decisions, but it has not been developed.

In addition to redistributing income, public works projects have
a multitude of objectives and consequences. Projects may generate
economic growth, alleviate poverty among some people, provide
aesthetic enjoyment and opportunities for recreation, improve public health, reduce the risks of natural disaster, alter travel patterns,
affect church attendance, change educational opportunities, and
more. No single welfare criterion can encompass these diverse objectives. How many of them should be considered? Which are susceptible of quantification? The further one pursues this analysis, the
more impassable the thicket.

Limitations in the Utility of Cost-Benefit Analysis

One possible conclusion is that at present certain types of cost-
benefit analysis are not meaningful. In reviewing the literature on
the calculus of costs and benefits in research and development, for
example, Prest and Turvey comment on "the uncertainty and un-
reliability of cost estimates . . . and . . . the extraordinarily complex
nature of the benefits. . . . "[8]

Another conclusion is that one should be cautious in distinguishing the degree to which projects are amenable to cost-benefit analysis.

. . . When there are many diverse types of benefits from a project and/or
many different beneficiaries it is difficult to list them all and to avoid
double counting. This is one reason why it is so much easier to apply
cost-benefit analysis to a limited purpose development, say, than it is to the
research and development aspects of some multi-purpose discovery, such
as a new type of plastic material. . . . It is no good expecting those fields
in which benefits are widely diffused, and in which there are manifest
divergences between accounting and economic costs of benefits, to be as
cultivable as others. Nor is it realistic to expect that comparisons between
projects in entirely different branches of economic activity are likely to be
as meaningful or fruitful as those between projects in the same branch. The
technique is more useful in the public-utility area than in the social-ser-
vices area of government.[9]

If the analysis is to be useful at all, calculations must be simplified.[10] The multiple ramifications of interesting activities can be taken into account only at the cost of introducing fantastic complexities. Prest and Turvey remark of one such attempt, that "This system . . . requires knowledge of all the demand and supply equations in the economy, so is scarcely capable of application by road engineers."[11] They suggest omitting consideration where (1) side effects are judged not terribly large or where (2) concern for these effects belongs to another governmental jurisdiction.[12]

If certain costs or benefits are deemed important but cannot be quantified, it is always possible to guess. The increasing use of recreation and aesthetic facilities to justify public works projects in the United States is disapproved by most economists because there can be a vast, but hidden, inflation of these benefits. For example, to attribute the same value to a recreation day on a reservoir located in a desert miles from any substitute source of water as to a day on an artificial lake in the heart of natural lake country is patently wrong. Economists would prefer to see recreation facilities listed in an appendix so that they can be taken into account in some sense, or, alternatively, that the project be presented with and without the recreation facilities, so that a judgment can be made as to whether the additional services are worth the cost.[13]

Economists distinguish between risk, where the precise outcome cannot be predicted but a probability distribution can be specified, and uncertainty, where one does not even know the parameters of the outcomes. The cost-benefit analyst must learn to live with uncertainty, for he can never know whether all relevant objectives have been included and what changes may occur in policy and in technology.

It is easy enough to cut the life of the project below its expected economic life. The interest rate can be raised. Assumptions can be made that costs will be higher and benefits lower than expected. All these methods, essentially conservative, are also highly arbitrary. They can be made somewhat more systematic, however, by sensitivity analysis in which length of life, for instance, is varied over a series of runs so that its impact on the project can be appraised.

Lessening uncertainty by hiking the interest or discount rate leads to greater difficulties, for the dominance of "higher" criteria over economic analysis is apparent in the frustrating problem of choosing the correct interest rate at which to discount the time streams of costs and benefits essential to the enterprise. Only an interest rate can establish the relationship between values at different periods of time. Yet people differ in preferences for the present versus the intermediate or long-run value. Moreover, the interest rate should also measure the opportunity cost of private capital that could be used to produce wealth elsewhere in the economy if it had not been used up in the form of tax income spent on the project under consideration. Is the appropriate rate the very low cost the government charges, the cost of a government corporation like TVA that must pay a somewhat higher rate, the going rate of interest for private firms, or an even higher rate to hedge against an uncertain future? As Otto Eckstein has observed," . . . the choice of interest rates must remain a value judgment."[14]

If the efficiency of a project is insensitive to interest costs, then these costs can vary widely without mattering much. But Fox and Herfindahl discovered that if Corps of Engineer projects raised their interest (or discount) rate from 2⅝ to 4, 6, or 8 per cent, then 9, 64, and 80 per cent of their projects, respectively, would have had a benefit-cost ratio of less than unity.[15] This single value choice among many has such large consequences that it alone may be decisive.

The Mixed Results of Cost-Benefit Analysis

Although cost-benefit analysis presumably results in efficiency by adding the most to national income, it it shot through with political and social value choices and surrounded by uncertainties and difficulties of computation. Whether the many noneconomic assumptions and consequences actually result in bascially changing the nature of a project remains moot. Clearly, we have come a long way from pure efficiency, to verge upon mixed efficiency.

Economic analysts usually agree that all relevant factors (especially nonmarket factors) cannot be squeezed into a single formula. They therefore suggest that the policy maker, in being given the market costs and benefits of alternatives, is, in effect, presented with the market value he is placing on nonmarket factors. The contribution of the analyst is only one input into the decision, but the analyst may find this limited conception of his role unacceptable to others. Policy makers may not want this kind of input; they may want *the* answer, or at least an answer that they can defend on the basis of the analyst's legitimized expertise.

The dependence of cost-benefit analysis on a prior political framework does not mean that it is a useless or trivial exercise. Decisions must be made. If quantifiable economic costs and benefits are not everything, neither would a decision-maker wish to ignore them entirely. The great advantage of cost-benefit analysis, when pursued with integrity, is that some implicit judgments are made explicit and subject to analysis. Yet, for many, the omission of explicit consideration of political factors is a serious deficiency.

The experience of the Soil Conservation Service in lowering certain political costs may prove illuminating. For many years the Service struggled along with eleven major watershed projects involving big dams, great headaches, and little progress. Because the watersheds were confined to a single region, it was exceedingly difficult to generate support in Congress, particularly at appropriations time. The upstream-downstream controversies generated by these projects resulted in less than universal local approval. The SCS found itself in the direct line of fire for determining priorities in use of insufficient funds.

Compare this situation with the breakthrough which occurred when SCS developed the small watershed program. Since each facility is relatively inexpensive, large numbers can be placed throughout the country, markedly increasing political support. Agreement on the local level is facilitated because much less land is flooded and side payments are easier to arrange. A judicious use of cost-benefit analysis, together with ingenious relationships with State governors, places the choice of priorities with the States and yet maintains a reasonable level of consistency by virtue of adherence to national criteria. Errors are easier to correct because the burden of calculation has been drastically reduced and experience may be more easily accumulated with a larger number of small projects.

Consider the situation in which an agency finds it desirable to achieve a geographical spread of projects in order to establish a wider base of support. Assume (with good reason) that cost-benefit criteria will not permit projects to be established in some states because the value of the land or water is too low. One can say that this is just too bad and observe the agency seeking ways around the restriction by playing up benefits, playing down costs, or attacking the whole benefit-cost concept as inapplicable. Another approach would be to recognize that federalism—meaning, realistically, the distribution of indulgences to State units—represents a political value worth promoting to some extent and that gaining nation-wide support is important. From this perspective, a compromise solution would be to except one or two projects in each State or region from meeting the full requirement of the formula, though the projects with the highest benefit-cost ratio would have to be chosen. In return for sacrificing full adherence to the formula in a few instances, one would get enhanced support for it in many others.

Everyone knows, of course, that cost-benefit analysis is not the messiah come to save water resources projects from contamination by the rival forces of ignorance and political corruption. Whenever agencies and their associated interests discover that they cannot do what they want, they may twist prevailing criteria out of shape: Two projects may be joined so that both qualify when one, standing alone, would not. Costs and benefits may be manipulated, or the categories may be so extended that almost any project qualifies. On the other hand, cost-benefit analysis has some "good" political uses that might be stressed more than they have been. The technique gives the responsible official a good reason for turning down projects, with a public-interest explanation the Congressman can use with his constituents and the interest-group leader with his members.

This is not to say that cost-benefit analysis has little utility. Assuming that the method will continue to be improved, and that one accepts the market as the measure of economic value, it can certainly tell decision makers something about what they will be giving up if they follow alternative policies. The use of two analyses, one based on regional and the other on national factors, might result in an appraisal of the economic costs of federalism.

The burden of calculation may be reduced by following cost-benefit analysis for many projects and introducing other values only for a few. To expect, however, that the method itself (which distributes indulgences to some and deprivations to others) would not be subject to manipulation in the political process is to say that we shall be governed by formula and not by men.

Because the cost-benefit formula does not always jibe with political realities—that is, it omits political costs and benefits—we can expect it to be twisted out of shape from time to time. Yet cost-benefit analysis may still be important in getting rid of the worst projects. Avoiding the worst where one can't get the best is no small accomplishment.

SYSTEMS ANALYSIS

The good systems analyst is a "chochem," a Yiddish word meaning "wise man", with overtones of "wise guy." His forte is creativity. Although he sometimes relates means to ends and fits ends to match means, he ordinarily eschews such pat processes, preferring instead to relate elements imaginatively into new systems that create their own means and ends. He plays new objectives continuously against cost elements until a creative synthesis has been achieved. He looks down upon those who say that they take objectives as given, knowing full well that the apparent solidity of the objective will dissipate during analysis and that, in any case, most people do not know what they want because they do not know what they can get.

Since no one knows how to teach creativity, daring, and nerve, it is not surprising that no one can define what systems analysis is or how it should be practiced. E.S. Quade, who compiled the RAND Corporation lectures on systems analysis, says it "is still largely a form of art" in which it is not possible to lay down "fixed rules which need only be followed with exactness."[16] He examined systems studies to determine ideas and principles common to the good ones, but discovered that "no universally accepted set of ideas existed. It was even difficult to decide which studies should be called good."[17]

Systems analysis is derived from operations research, which came into use during World War II when some scientists discovered that they could use simple quantitative analysis to get the most out of existing military equipment. A reasonably clear objective was given, and ways to cut the cost of achieving it could be developed, using essentially statistical models. Operations research today is largely identified with specific techniques: linear programming; Monte Carlo (randomizing) methods; gaming and game theory. While there is no hard and fast division between operations research and systems analysis, a rough separation may perhaps be made. The less that is known about objectives, the more they conflict, the larger the number of elements to be considered, the more uncertain the environment, the more likely it is that the work will be called a systems analysis. In systems analysis there is more judgment and intuition and less reliance on quantitative methods than in operations research.

Systems analysis builds models that abstract from reality but represent the crucial relationships. The systems analyst first decides what questions are relevant to his inquiry, selects certain quantifiable factors, cuts down the list of factors to be dealt with by aggregation and by eliminating the (hopefully) less important ones, and then gives them quantitative relationships with one another within the system he has chosen for analysis. But crucial variables may not be quantifiable. If they can be reduced to numbers, there may be no mathematical function that can express the desired relationship. More important, there may be no single criterion for judging results among conflicting objectives. Most important, the original objectives, if any, may not make sense.

It cannot be emphasized too strongly that a (if not the) distinguishing characteristic of systems analysis is that the objectives are either not known or are subject to change. Systems analysis, Quade tells us, "is associated with that class of problems where the difficulties lie in deciding what ought to be done—not simply how to do it—and honors go to people who . . . find out what the problem is"[18] Charles Hitch, the former Comptroller of the Defense Department, insists that:

. . . learning about objectives is one of the chief objects of this kind of analysis. We must learn to look at objectives as critically and as professionally as we look at our models and our other inputs. We may, of course, begin with tentative objectives, but we must expect to modify or replace them as we learn about the systems we are studying—and related systems. The feedback on objectives may in some cases be the most important result of our study. We have never undertaken a major system study at RAND in which we are able to define satisfactory objectives at the beginning of the study.[19]

Systems analysts recognize many good reasons for their difficulties in defining problems or objectives. Quade reaches the core: "Objectives are not, in fact, agreed upon. The choice, while ostensibly between alternatives, is really between objectives or ends and non-analytic methods must be used for a final reconciliation of views."[20] It may be comforting to believe that objectives come to the analyst from on high and can be taken as given, but this easy assumption is all wrong. "For all sorts of good reasons that are not about to change," says Hitch, "official statements of national objectives (or company objectives) tend to be nonexistent or so vague and literary as to be non-operational."[21] Objectives are not only likely to be "thin and rarified," according to Wohlstetter, but the relevant authorities "are likely to conflict. Among others there will be national differences within an alliance and within the nation, interagency, interservice, and intraservice differences. . . . "[22]

Moreover, even shared objectives often conflict with one another. Deterrence of atomic attack might be best served by letting an enemy know that we would respond with an all-out, indiscriminate attack on his population. Defense of our population against death and destruction might not be well served by this strategy,[23] as the Secretary of Defense recognized when he recommended a city-avoidance strategy that might give an enemy some incentive to spare our cities as well. Not only are objectives large in number and in conflict with one another, they are likely to engender serious repercussion effects. Many objectives, like morale and the stability of alliances, are resistant to quantification. What is worth doing depends on whether it can be done at all, how well, and at what cost. Hence, objectives really cannot be taken as given; they must be made up by the analyst. "In fact," Wohlstetter declares, "we are always in the process of choosing and modifying both means and ends."[24]

Future systems analysts are explicitly warned not to let clients determine objectives. A suggestive analogy is drawn with the doctor who would not ignore a patient's "description of his symptoms, but . . . cannot allow the patient's self diagnosis to override his own professional judgment."[25] Quade argues that since systems analysis has often resulted in changing the original objectives of the policymaker, it would be "self-defeating to accept without inquiry" his "view of what the problem is."[26]

I have stressed the point that the systems analyst is advised to insist on his own formulation of the problem because it shows so closely that we are dealing with a mixed concept of efficiency.

Adjusting objectives to resources in the present or near future is difficult enough without considering future states of affairs which hold tremendous uncertainty. Constants become variables; little can be taken for granted. The rate of technological progress, an opponent's estimate of your reaction to his latest series of moves based on his reaction to yours, whether or not atomic war will occur, what it will be like, whether we shall have warning, whether the system we are working on will cost anything close to current estimates and whether it will be ready within five years of the due date—on most of these matters, there are no objective probabilities to be calculated.

An effective dealing with uncertainty must be a major goal of systems analysis. Systems analysis is characterized by the aids to calculation it uses, not to conquer, but to circumvent and mitigate some of the pervasive effects of uncertainty. Before a seemingly important factor may be omitted, for example, a sensitivity analysis may be run to determine whether its variation significantly affects the outcome. If there is no good basis for calculating the value of the factor, arbitrary values may be assigned to test for extreme possibilities. Contingency analysis is used to determine how the relative ranking of alternatives holds up under major changes in the environment, say, a new alliance between France and Russia, or alterations in the criteria for judging the alternatives, such as a requirement that a system work well against attacks from space as well as earth. Contingency analysis places a premium on versatility as the analyst seeks a system that will hold up well under various eventualities even though it might be quite as good for any single contingency as an alternative system. Adversary procedures may be used to combat uncertainty. Bending over backwards to provide advantages for low ranking systems and handicaps for high ranking systems is called a fortiori analysis. Changing crucial assumptions in order to make the leading alternatives even, so that one can judge whether the assumptions are overly optimistic or pessimistic, is called break-even analysis.[27] Since all these methods add greatly to the burden of calculation, they must be used with some discretion.

A variety of insurance schemes may also be used to deal with uncertainty. In appraising what an opponent can do, for instance, one can assume the worst, the best, and sheer inertia. In regard to the development of weapons, insurance requires not one flexible weapon but a variety of alternatives pursued with vigor. As development goes on, uncertainty is reduced. Consequently, basic strategic choice involves determining how worthwhile paying for the additional information is by developing rival weapons systems to the next stage. The greater the uncertainty of the world, the greater the desirability of having the widest selection of alternative weapons to choose from to meet unexpected threats and opportunities. Alchian and Kessel are so wedded to the principle of diversified investment that they "strongly recommend this theorem as a basic part of systems analysis."[28]

As a form of calculation, systems analysis represents a merger of quantitative methods and rules of thumb. First, the analyst attempts to solve the problem before he knows a great deal about it. Then he continuously alters his initial solution to get closer to what he intuitively feels ought to be wanted. Means and ends are continuously played off against one another. New objectives are defined, new assumptions made, new models constructed, until a creative amalgam appears that hopefully defines a second best solution, one that is better than others even if not optimal in any sense. In the famous study of the location of military bases conducted by Albert Wohlstetter and his associates at the RAND Corporation, widely acknowledged as a classic example of systems analysis, Wohlstetter writes:

The base study . . . proceeded by a method of successive approximations. It compared forces for their efficiency in carrying a payload between the bases and targets without opposition either by enemy interceptors or enemy bombers. Then, it introduced obstacles successively: first, enemy defenses; then enemy bombardment of our bombers and other elements needed to retaliate. In essence, then, the alternative systems were tested for their first-strike capability and then they were compared for their second-strike capacity. And the programmed system performed in a drastically different way, depending on the order in which the opposing side struck. In the course of analyzing counter-measures and counter-counter-measures, the enemy bombardment turned out to be a dominant problem. This was true even for a very much improved overseas operating base system. The refueling base system was very much less sensitive to strike order. It is only the fact that strike order made such a difference among systems contemplated that gave the first-strike, second-strike distinction an interest. And it was not known in advance of the analysis that few of the programmed bombers would have survived to encounter the problem of penetrating enemy defenses which had previously been taken as the main obstacle. The analysis, then, not only was affected by the objectives considered, it affected them.[29]

The advantage of a good systems study is that by running the analysis through in theory on paper certain disadvantages of learning from experience may be avoided.

If the complexity of the problems encountered proved difficult in cost-benefit analysis, the burdens of calculation are ordinarily much greater in systems analysis. Many aspects of a problem simply must be put aside. Only a few variables can be considered simultaneously. "Otherwise," Roland McKean tells us, "the models would become impossibly cumbersome, and . . . the number of calculations to consider would mount in the thousands."[30] Formulas that include everything may appear more satisfactory but those that cannot be reduced "to a single expression are likely to convey no meaning at all. . . . "[31] Summing up their experience, Hitch and McKean assert that:

. . . analyses must be piecemeal, since it is impossible for a single analysis to cover all problems of choice simultaneously in a large organization. Thus comparisons of alternative courses of action always pertain to a part of the government's (or corporation's) problem. Other parts of the over-all problem are temporarily put aside, possible decisions about some matters being ignored, specific decisions about others being taken for granted. The resulting analyses are intended to provide assistance in finding optimal, or at least good, solutions to sub-problems: in the jargon of systems and operations research, they are sub-optimizations.[32]

Although admitting that much bad work is carried on and that inordinate love of numbers and machines often get in the way of creative work,[33] practitioners of systems analysis believe in their art. "All of them point out how the use of analysis can provide some of the knowledge needed, how it may sometime serve as a substitute for experience, and, most importantly, how it can work to sharpen intuition."[34] Systems analysis can increase explicitness about the assumptions made and about exclusions from the analysis. The claim is that systems analysis can be perfected; sheer intuition or unaided judgment can never be perfect.

Yet there is also wide agreement that systems analysts "do philosophy,"[35] that they are advocates of particular policy alternatives. What Schelling calls "the pure role of expert advisor" is not available for the analyst who "must usually formulate the questions themselves for his clients."[36] Beyond that, Wohlstetter argues that systems analysts can perform the function of integrating diverse values. New systems can sometimes be found that meet diverse objectives.[37] The politician who gains his objectives by inventing policies that also satisfy others, or the leader of a coalition who searches out areas of maximum agreement, performs a kind of informal systems analysis.

All these men, however, work within the existing political structure. While cost-benefit analysis may contain within it implicit changes in existing governmental policies, it poses no direct challenge to the general decision-making machinery of the political system. Program budgeting is a form of systems analysis that attempts to break out of these confines.

PROGRAM BUDGETING

It is always important, and perhaps especially so in economics, to avoid being swept off one's feet by the fashions of the moment.[38]

So this new system will identify our national goals with precision. . . . [39]

On August 25, 1965, President Johnson announced that he was asking the heads of all Federal agencies to introduce "a very new and revolutionary system" of program budgeting. Staffs of experts set up in each agency would define goals using "modern methods of program analysis." Then the "most effective and the least costly" way to accomplish these goals would be found.[40]

Program budgeting has no standard definition. The general idea is that budgetary decisions should be made by focusing on output categories like governmental goals, objectives, end products or programs instead of inputs like personnel, equipment, and maintenance. As in cost-benefit analysis, to which it owes a great deal, program budgeting lays stress on estimating the total financial cost of accomplishing objectives. What is variously called cost-effectiveness or cost-utility analysis is employed in order to select "alternative approaches to the achievement of a benefit already determined to be worth achieving."[41]

Not everyone would go along with the most far-reaching implications of program budgeting, but the RAND Corporation version, presumably exported from the Defense Department, definitely does include "institutional reorganization to bring relevant administrative functions under the jurisdiction of the authority making the final program decisions." In any event, there would be "information reporting systems and shifts in the power structure to the extent necessary to secure compliance with program decisions by the agencies responsible for their execution."[42] Sometimes it appears that comprehensiveness—simultaneous and complete examination of all programs and all alternatives to programs every year—is being advocated. Actually, comprehensiveness has been dropped (though not without regret) because "it may be too costly in time, effort, uncertainty, and confusion."[43] There exists considerable ambivalence as to whether decisions are implicit in the program categories or merely provide information to improve the judgment of governmental officials.

Programs are not made in heaven. There is nothing out there that is just waiting to be found. Programs are not natural to the world; they must be imposed on it by men. No one can give instructions for making up programs. There are as many ways to conceive of programs as there are of organizing activity,[44] as the comments of the following writers eloquently testify:

It is by no means obvious . . . whether a good program structure should be based on components of specific end objectives (e.g., the accomplishment of certain land reclamation targets), on the principle of cost separation (identifying as a program any activity the costs of which can be readily segregated), on the separation of means and ends (Is education a means or an end in a situation such as skill-retraining courses for workers displaced by automation?), or on some artificially designed pattern that draws from all these and other classification criteria.[45]

Just what categories constitute the most useful programs and program elements is far from obvious . . . If one puts all educational activities into a broad package of educational programs, he cannot simultaneously include school lunch programs or physical education activities in a Health Program, or include defense educational activities (such as the military academies) in the Defense Program. . . . In short, precisely how to achieve a rational and useful structure for a program budget is not yet evident.[46]

In much current discussion it seems to be taken for granted that transportation is a natural program category. But that conclusion is by no means obvious.[47]

A first question one might ask is whether, given their nature, health activities merit a separate, independent status in a program budget. The question arises because these activities often are constituents of, or inputs into, other activities whose purpose or goal orientation is the dominating one. Outlays by the Department of Defense for hospital care, for example, though they assist in maintaining the health of one segment of the population, are undertaken on behalf of national defense, and the latter is their justification.[48]

The difficulties with the program concept are illustrated in the space program. A first glance suggests that space projects are ideally suited for program budgeting because they appear as physical systems designed to accomplish different missions. Actually, there is a remarkable degree of interdependence between different missions and objectives—pride, scientific research, space exploration, military uses, etc.—so that it is impossible to apportion costs on a proper basis. Consider the problem of a rocket developed for one mission and useful for others. To apportion costs to each new mission is purely arbitrary. To allocate the cost to the first mission and regard the rocket as a free good for all subsequent missions is ludicrous. The only remotely reasonable alternative—making a separate program out of the rocket itself—does violence to the concept of programs as end products. The difficulty is compounded because the facilities that have multiple uses like boosters and tracking networks tend to be very expensive compared to the items that are specific to a particular mission.[49] Simple concepts of programs evaporate upon inspection.

Political realities lie behind the failure to devise principles for defining programs. As Melvin Anshen puts it, "The central issue is, of course, nothing less than the definition of the ultimate objectives of the Federal government as they are realized through operational decisions." The arrangement of the programs inevitably affects the specific actions taken to implement them. "Set in this framework," Anshen continues, "the designation of a schedule of programs may be described as building a bridge between a matter of political philosophy (what is government for?) and . . . assigning scarce resources among alternative governmental objectives."[50]

Because program budgeting is a form of systems analysis (and uses a form of cost-benefit analysis), the conditions that hinder or facilitate its use have largely been covered in the previous sections. The simpler the problem, the fewer the interdependencies, the greater the ability to measure the consequences of alternatives on a common scale, the more costs and benefits that are valued in the market place, the better the chances of making effective use of programs. Let us take transportation to illustrate some of the conditions in a specific case.

Investments in transportation are highly interdependent with one another (planes versus cars versus trains versus barges, etc.) and with decisions regarding the regional location of industry and the movements of population. In view of the powerful effects of transportation investment on regional employment, income, and competition with other modes of transport, it becomes necessary to take these factors into account. The partial equilibrium model of efficiency in the narrow sense becomes inappropriate and a general equilibrium model of the economy must be used. The combination of aggregative models at the economy-wide level and inter-region and inter-industry models that this approach requires is staggering. It is precisely the limited and partial character of cost-effectiveness analyses, taking so much for granted and eliminating many variables, that make them easy to work with for empirical purposes. Furthermore, designing a large-scale transportation system involves so close a mixture of political and economic considerations that it is not possible to disentangle them. The Interstate Highway Program, for example, involved complex bargaining among Federal, State, and local governments and reconciliation of many conflicting interests. The development of certain "backward" regions, facilitating the movement of defense supplies, redistribution of income, creating countervailing power against certain monopolies, not to mention the political needs of public officials, were all involved. While cost-utility exercises might help with small segments of the problem, J. R. Meyer concludes that, "Given the complexity of the political and economic decisions involved, and the emphasis on designing a geographically consistent system, it probably would be difficult to improve on the congressional process as a means of developing such a program in an orderly and systematic way."[51]

On one condition for effective use—reorganization of the Federal government to centralize authority for wide-ranging programs—proponents of program budgeting are markedly ambivalent. The problem is that responsibility for programs is now scattered throughout the whole Federal establishment and decentralized to State and local authorities as well. In the field of health, for example, expenditures are distributed among at least twelve agencies and six departments outside of Health, Education, and Welfare. A far greater number of organizations are concerned with American activities abroad, with natural resources and with education. The multiple jurisdictions and overlapping responsibilities do violence to the concept of comprehensive and consistent programs. It "causes one to doubt," Marvin Frankel writes, "whether there can exist in the administrative echelons the kind of overall perspective that would seem indispensible if Federal health resources are to be rationally allocated."[52] To G. A. Steiner it is evident that "The present 'chest of drawers' type of organization cannot for long be compatible with program budgeting."[53] W. Z. Hirsch declares that "if we are to have effective program budgeting of natural resources activities, we shall have to provide for new institutional arrangements."[54] Yet the inevitable resistance to wholesale reorganization would be so great that, if it were deemed essential, it might well doom the enterprise. Hence, the hope is expressed that translation grids or crossover networks could be used to convert program budget decisions back into the usual budget categories in the usual agencies. That is what is done in Defense, but that Department has the advantage of having most of the activities it is concerned with under the Secretary's jurisdiction. Some program analysts believe that this solution will not do.

Recognizing that a conversion scheme is technically feasible, Anshen is aware that there are "deeply frustating" issues to be resolved. "The heart of the problem is the fact that the program budget in operation should not be a mere statistical game. Great strategic importance will attach to both the definition of program structure and content and the establishment of specific program objectives (including magnitude, timing, and cost)."[55] The implications of program budgeting, however, go far beyond specific policies.

It will be useful to distinguish between policy politics (which policy will be adopted?), partisan politics (which political party will win office?), and system politics (how will decision structures be set up?). Program budgeting is manifestly concerned with policy politics, and not much with partisan politics, although it could have important consequences for issues that divide the nation's parties. *My contention is that the thrust of program budgeting makes it an integral part of system politics.*

As presently conceived, program budgeting contains an extreme centralizing bias. Power is to be centralized in the Presidency (through the Budget Bureau) at the national level, in superdepartments rather than bureaus within the executive branch, and in the Federal government as a whole instead of State or local governments. Note how W. Z. Hirsch assumes the desirability of national dominance when he writes: "These methods of analysis can guide Federal officials in the responsibility of bringing local education decisions into closer harmony with national objectives."[56] G. A.

Steiner observes that comprehensiveness may be affected by unrestricted Federal grants-in-aid to the states because "such a plan would remove a substantial part of Federal expenditures from a program budgeting system of the Federal government."[57] Should there be reluctance on the part of State and local officials to employ the new tools, Anshen states "that the Federal government may employ familiar incentives to accelerate this progress."[58] Summing it up, Hirsch says that "It appears doubtful that a natural resources program budget would have much impact without a good deal of centralization."[59]

Within the great Federal organizations designed to encompass the widest ramifications of basic objectives, there would have to be strong executives. Cutting across the sub-units of the organization, as is the case in the Department of Defense, the program budget could only be put together by the top executive. A more useful tool for increasing his power to control decisions vis-a-vis his subordinates would be hard to find.[60]

Would large-scale program budgeting benefit the Chief Executive? President Johnson's support of program budgeting could in part stem from his desire to appear frugal and also be directed at increasing his control of the executive branch by centralizing decisions in the Bureau of the Budget. In the case of foreign affairs, it is not at all clear whether it would be preferable to emphasize country teams, with the budget made by the State Department to encompass activities of the other Federal agencies abroad, or to let Commerce, Agriculture, Defense, and other agencies include their foreign activities in their own budgets. Program budgeting will unleash great struggles of this kind in Washington. An especially intriguing possibility is that the Bureau of the Budget might prefer to let the various agencies compete, with the Bureau coordinating (that is, controlling) these activities through a comprehensive foreign affairs program devised only at the Presidential level.

Yet is it not entirely clear that Presidents would welcome all the implications of program budgeting. It is well and good to talk about long-range planning; it is another thing to tie a President's hands by committing him in advance for five years of expenditures. Looking ahead is fine but not if it means that a President cannot negate the most extensive planning efforts on grounds that seem sufficient to him.[61] He may wish to trade some program budgeting for some political support.

In any event, that all decisions ought to be made by the most central person in the most centralized body capable of grabbing hold of them is difficult to justify on scientific grounds. We see what has happened. First pure efficiency was converted to mixed efficiency. Then limited efficiency became unlimited. Yet the qualifications of efficiency experts for political systems analysis are not evident.[62]

We would be in a much stronger position to predict the consequences of program budgeting if we knew (a) how far toward a genuine program budget the Defense Department has gone and (b) whether the program budget has fulfilled its promise. To the best of my knowledge, not a single study of this important experiment was undertaken (or at least published) before the decision was made to spread it around the land. On the surface, only two of the nine program categories used in the Defense Department appear to be genuine programs in the sense of pointing to end purposes or objectives. Although strategic retaliation and continental defense appear to be distinct programs, it is difficult to separate them conceptually; my guess is that they are, in fact, considered together. The third category—general purpose forces—is presumably designed to deal with (hopefully) limited war anywhere in the world. According to Arthur Smithies, "The threat is not clearly defined and neither are the requirements for meeting it. Clearly this program is of a very different character from the other two and does not lend itself as readily to analysis in terms either of its components or of its specific contribution to defense objectives."[63]

What about the program called airlift and sealift? These activities support the general purpose forces. Research and development is carried on presumably to serve other defense objectives, and the same is true for the reserve forces.

No doubt the elements that make up the programs comprise the real action focus of the budget, but these may look less elegant when spread into thousands of elements than they do in nine neat rows. When one hears that hundreds of program elements are up for decision at one time,[64] he is entitled to some skepticism about how much genuine analysis can go into all of them. Part of the argument for program budgeting was that by thinking ahead and working all year around it would be possible to consider changes as they came up and avoid the usual last minute funk. Both Hitch[65] and Novick[66] (the RAND Corporation expert on defense budgeting) report, however, that this has not worked out. The services hesitate to submit changes piecemeal, and the Secretary wants to see what he is getting into before he acts. The vaunted five year plans are still in force but their efficacy in determining yearly decisions remains to be established.

One good operational test would be to know whether the Department's systems analysts actually use the figures from the five year plans in their work or whether they go to the services for the real stuff. Another test would be whether or not the later years of the five year projections turn out to have any future significance, or whether the battle is really over the next year that is to be scooped out as part of the budget. From a distance, it appears that the services have to work much harder to justify what they are doing. Since McNamara's office must approve changes in defense programs, and he can insist on documentation, he is in a strong position to improve thinking at the lower levels. The intensity of conflict within the Defense Department may not have changed, but it may be that the disputants are or will in the future be likely to shout at a much more sophisticated level. How much this is due to McNamara himself, to his insistence on quantitative estimates, or to the analytic advantages of a program budget cannot be determined now. It is clear that a program budget, of which he alone is master, has helped impose his will on the Defense Department.

It should also be said that there are many notable differences between decision-making in defense and domestic policy that would render suspect the transmission of procedures from one realm to the other. The greater organizational unity of Defense, the immensely large amounts of money at stake, the extraordinarily greater risks involved, the inability to share more than minimal values with opponents, the vastly different array of interests and perceptions of the proper roles of the participants, are but a few of the factors involved.

The Armed Services and Appropriations Committees in the defense area, for example, are normally most reluctant to substitute their judgment on defense for that of the President and the Secretary of the Department. They do not conceive it to be their role to make day to day defense policy, and they are apparently unwilling to take on the burden of decision. They therefore accept a budget presentation based on cavernous program categories even though these are so arranged that it is impossible to make a decision on the basis of them. If they were to ask for and to receive the discussion of alternative actions contained in the much smaller program elements on which McNamara bases his decisions, they would be in a position to take the Department of Defense away from its Secretary.

There is no reason whatsoever to believe that a similar restraint would be shown by committees that deal with domestic policies. It is at least possible that the peculiar planning, programming, and budgeting system adopted in Defense could not be repeated elsewhere in the Federal establishment.

POLITICAL RATIONALITY

Political rationality is the fundamental kind of reason, because it deals with the preservation and improvement of decision structures, and decision structures are the source of all decisions. Unless a decision structure exists, no reasoning and no decisions are possible. . . . There can be no conflict between political rationality and . . . technical, legal, social, or economic rationality, because the solution of political problems makes possible an attack on any other problem, while a serious political deficiency can prevent or undo all other problem solving. . . . Non-political decisions are reached by considering a problem in its own terms, and by evaluating proposals according to how well they solve the problem. The best available proposal should be accepted regardless of who makes it or who opposes it, and a faulty proposal should be rejected or improved no matter who makes it. Compromise is always irrational; the rational procedure is to determine which proposal is the best, and to accept it. In a political decision, on the other hand, action never is based on the merits of a proposal but always on who makes it and who opposes it. Action should be designed to avoid complete identification with any proposal and any point of view, no matter how good or how popular it might be. The best available proposal should never be accepted just because it is best; it should be deferred, objected to, discussed, until major opposition disappears. Compromise is always a rational procedure, even when the compromise is between a good and bad proposal.[67]

We are witnessing the beginning of significant advances in the art and science of economizing. Having given up the norm of comprehensiveness, economizers are able to join quantitative analysis with aids to calculation of the kind described by Lindblom in his strategy of disjointed incrementalism.[68]

Various devices are employed to simplify calculations. Important values are omitted entirely; others are left to different authorities to whose care they have been entrusted. Here, sensitivity analysis represents an advance because it provides an empirical basis to justify neglect of some values. Means and ends are hopelessly intertwined.

The real choice is between rival policies that encapsulate somewhat different mixes of means and ends. Analysis proceeds incrementally by successive limited approximations. It is serial and remedial as successive attacks are made on problems. Rather than waiting upon experience in the real world, the analyst tries various moves in his model and runs them through to see if they work. When all else fails, the analyst may try an integrative solution reconciling a variety of values to some degree, though meeting none of them completely. He is always ready to settle for the second or third best, provided only that it is better than the going policy. Constrained by diverse limiting assumptions, weakened by deficiencies in technique, rarely able to provide unambiguous measures, the systems, cost-benefit, and program analysis is nonetheless getting better at calculating in the realm of efficiency: Alas, he is an imperialist at heart.

In the literature discussed above there appears several times the proposition that "the program budget is a neutral tool. It has no politics."[69] In truth, the program budget is suffused with policy politics, makes up a small part of President Johnson's partisan politics, and tends towards system politics. How could men account for so foolish a statement? It must be that they who make it identify program budgeting with something good and beautiful, and politics with another thing bad and ugly. McKean and Anshen speak of politics in terms of "pressure and expedient adjustments," "haphazard acts . . . unresponsive to a planned analysis of the needs of efficient decision design." From the political structure they expect only "resistance and opposition, corresponding to the familiar human disposition to protect established seats of power and procedures made honorable by the mere facts of existence and custom."[70] In other places we hear of "vested interests," "wasteful duplication," "special interest groups," and the "Parkinson syndrome."[71]

Not so long ago less sophisticated advocates of reform ignored the political realm. Now they denigrate it. And, since there must be a structure for decision, it is smuggled in as a mere adjunct of achieving efficiency. Who is to blame if the economic tail wags the political dog? It seems unfair to blame the evangelical economizer for spreading the gospel of efficiency. If economic efficiency turns out to be the one true religion, maybe it is because its prophets could so easily conquer.

It is hard to find men who take up the cause of political rationality, who plead the case for political man, and who are primarily concerned with the laws that enable the political machinery to keep working. One is driven to a philosopher like Paul Diesing to find the case for the political:

. . . the political problem is always basic and prior to the others. . . . This means that any suggested course of action must be evaluated first by its effects on the political structure. A course of action which corrects economic or social deficiencies but increases political difficulties must be rejected, while an action which contributes to political improvement is desirable even if it is not entirely sound from an economic or social standpoint.[72]

There is hardly a political scientist who would claim half as much. The desire to invent decision structures to facilitate the achievement of economic efficiency does not suggest a full appreciation of their proper role by students of politics.

A major task of the political system is to specify goals or objectives. It is impermissible to treat goals as if they were known in advance. "Goals" may well be the product of interaction among key participants rather than some "deus ex machina" or (to use Bentley's term) some "spook" which posits values in advance of our knowledge of them. Certainly, the operational objectives of the Corps of Engineers in the Water Resources field could hardly be described in terms of developing rivers and harbors.

Once the political process becomes a focus of attention, it is evident that the principal participants may not be clear about their goals. What we call goals or objectives may, in large part, be operationally determined by the policies we can agree upon. The mixtures of values found in complex policies may have to be taken in packages, so that policies may determine goals as least as much as general objectives determine policies. In a political situation, then, the need for support assumes central importance. Not simply the economic, but the *political* costs and benefits turn out to be crucial.

A first attempt to specify what is meant by political costs may bring closer an understanding of the range of requirements for political rationality.[73] Exchange costs are incurred by a political leader when he needs the support of other people to get a policy adopted. He has to pay for this assistance by using up resources in the form of favors (patronage, logrolling) or coercive moves (threats or acts to veto or remove from office). By supporting a policy and influencing others to do the same, a politician antagonizes some people and may suffer their retaliation. If these hostility costs mount, they may turn into reelection costs—actions that decrease his chances (or those of his friends) of being elected or reelected to office. Election costs, in turn, may become policy costs through inability to command the necessary formal powers to accomplish the desired policy objectives.

In the manner of Neustadt, we may also talk about reputation costs, i.e. not only loss of popularity with segments of the electorate, but also loss of esteem and effectiveness with other participants in the political system and loss of ability to secure policies other than the one immediately under consideration. Those who continually urge a President to go all out—that is, use all his resources on a wide range of issues—rarely stop to consider that the price of success in one area of policy may be defeat in another. If he loses popularity with the electorate, as President Truman did, Congress may destroy almost the whole of his domestic program. If he cracks down on the steel industry, as President Kennedy did, he may find himself constrained to lean over backwards in the future to avoid unremitting hostility from the business community.

A major consequence of incurring exchange and hostility costs may be undesirable power-redistribution effects. The process of getting a policy adopted or implemented may increase the power of various individuals, organizations and social groups, which later will be used against the political leader. The power of some participants may be weakened so that the political leader is unable to enjoy their protection.

The legitimacy of the political system may be threatened by costs that involve the weakening of customary political restraints. Politicians who try to suppress opposition, or who practice election frauds, may find similar tactics being used against them. The choice of a highly controversial policy may raise the costs of civic discord. Although the people involved may not hate the political leader, the fact that they hate each other may lead to consequences contrary to his desires.

The literature of economics usually treats organizations and institutions as if they were costless entities. The standard procedure is to consider rival alternatives (in consideration of price policy or other criteria), calculate the differences in cost and achievement among them, and show that one is more or less efficient than another. This typical way of thinking is sometimes misspecified. If the costs of pursuing a policy are strictly economic and can be calculated directly in the market place, then the procedure should work well. But if the costs include getting one or another organization to change its policies or procedures, then these costs must also be taken into account.[74] Perhaps there are legal, psychological, or other impediments that make it either impossible or difficult for the required changes to be made. Or the changes may require great effort and result in incurring a variety of other costs. In considering a range of alternatives, one is measuring not only efficiency but also the cost of change.

Studies based on efficiency criteria are much needed and increasingly useful. My quarrel is not with them as such, at all. I have been concerned that a single value, however important, could triumph over other values without explicit consideration being given these others. I would feel much better if political rationality were being pursued with the same vigor and capability as is economic efficiency. In that case I would have fewer qualms about extending efficiency studies into the decision-making apparatus.

My purpose has not been to accuse economizers of doing what comes naturally. Rather, I have sought to emphasize that economic rationality, however laudible in its own sphere, ought not to swallow up political rationality—but will do so, if political rationality continues to lack trained and adept defenders.

NOTES

[1] A. R. Prest and R. Turvey, "Cost-Benefit Analysis: A Survey," *The Economic Journal,* Vol. LXXV, December, 1965, pp. 683-735. I am much indebted to this valuable and discerning survey. I have also relied upon: Otto Eckstein, "A Survey of the Theory of Public Expenditure Criteria," in *Public Finances: Needs, Sources, and Utilization,* National Bureau of Economic Research (New York, Princeton University Press, 1961), pp. 439-504; Irving K. Fox and Orris C. Herfindahl, "Attainment of Efficiency in Satisfying Demands for Water Resources," *American Economic Review,* May, 1964, pp. 198-206; Charles J. Hitch, *On the Choice of Objectives in Systems Studies* (Santa Monica, The RAND Corporation, 1960); John V. Krutilla, "Is Public Intervention in Water Resources Development Conducive to Economic Efficiency," *Natural Resources Journal,* January, 1966, pp. 60-75; John V. Krutilla and Otto Eckstein, *Multiple Purpose River Development* (Baltimore, Johns Hopkins Press, 1958); and Roland N. McKean, *Efficiency in Government Through Systems Analysis with Emphasis on Water Resources Development,* (New York, 1958).

[2] Prest and Turvey, *ibid.,* p. 686.

[3] In many important areas of policy such as national defense it is not possible to value the product directly in the market place. Since benefits cannot be valued in the same way as costs, it is necessary to resort to a somewhat different type of analysis. Instead of cost-benefit analysis, therefore, the work is usually called cost-effectiveness or cost-utility analysis.

[4] A. Bergson, "A Reformulation of Certain Aspects of Welfare Economics," *Quarterly Journal of Economics,* February, 1938; N. Kaldor, "Welfare Propositions and Interpersonal Comparisons of Utility," *Economic Journal,* 1939, pp. 549-52; J. R. Hicks, "The Valuation of Social Income," *Economica,* 1940, pp. 105-24; I. M. D. Little, *A Critique of Welfare Economics,* (Oxford, 1950); W. J. Baumol, *Welfare Economics and the Theory of the State* (Cambridge, 1952); T. Scitovsky, "A Note on Welfare Propositions in Economics," *Review of Economic Studies,* 1942, pp. 98-110; J. E. Meade, *The Theory of International Economic Policy,* Vol. II: *Trade and Welfare* (New York, 1954).

[5] For a different view, see James M. Buchanan and Gordon Tullock, *The Calculus of Consent: Logical Foundations of Constitutional Democracy* (Ann Arbor, University of Michigan Press, 1962).

[6] Prest and Turvey, *op. cit.,* p. 702. For a contrary view, see Arthur Maas,

"Benefit-Cost Analysis: Its Relevance to Public Investment Decisions," Vol. LXXXX *The Quarterly Journal of Economics,* May, 1966, pp. 208-226.

[7]Irving K. Fox and Orris C. Herfindahl, "Attainment of Efficiency in Satisfying Demands for Water Resources," *American Economic Review,* May, 1964, p. 200.

[8]Prest and Turvey, *op. cit.,* p. 727.

[9]*Ibid.,* pp. 729, 731.

[10]David Braybrooke and Charles Lindblom, *A Strategy for Decision* (New York, 1963).

[11]Prest and Turvey, *op. cit.,* p. 714.

[12]*Ibid.,* p. 705.

[13]See Jack L. Knetch, "Economics of Including Recreation as a Purpose of Water Resource Projects," *Journal of Farm Economics,* December, 1964, p. 1155. No one living in Berkeley, where "a view" is part of the cost of housing, could believe that aesthetic values are forever going to remain beyond the ingenuity of the quantifier.

[14]Otto Eckstein, *op. cit.,* p. 460.

[15]Fox and Herfindahl, *op. cit.,* p. 202.

[16]E. S. Quade, *Analysis for Military Decisions* (Chicago, 1964), p. 153.

[17]*Ibid.,* p. 149.

[18]*Ibid.,* p. 7.

[18]Charles J. Hitch, *op. cit.,* p. 19.

[20]E. S. Quade, *op. cit.,* p. 176.

[21]Charles J. Hitch, *op. cit.,* pp. 4-5.

[22]Albert Wohlstetter, "Analysis and Design of Conflict Systems," in E.S. Quade, *op. cit.,* p. 121.

[23]See Glenn H. Snyder, *Deterrence and Defense* (Princeton, 1961).

[24]Wohlstetter in Quade, *op. cit.,* p. 122.

[25]E. S. Quade, *op. cit.,* p. 157. Quade attempts to soften the blow by saying that businessmen and military officers know more about their business than any one else. But the import of the analogy is clear enough.

[26]*Ibid.,* pp. 156-57.

[27]Herman Kahn and Irwin Mann., *Techniques of Systems Analysis* (Santa Monica, The RAND Corporation, 1957), believe that *"More than any single thing,* the skilled use of a fortiori and break-even analyses separate the professionals from the amateurs." They think that convincing others that you have a good solution is as important as coming up with one.

[28]Armen A. Alchian and Reuben A. Kessel, *A Proper Role of Systems Analysis* (Santa Monica, RAND Corporation, 1954), p. 9.

[29]Albert Wohlstetter in E. S. Quade, *op. cit.,* pp. 125-26.

[30]R. N. McKean, "Criteria," in E. S. Quade, *op. cit.,* p. 83.

[31] E. S. Quade, *op. cit.,* p. 310.

[32] Charles J. Hitch and Roland N. McKean, *The Economics of Defense in the Nuclear Age* (Cambridge, Harvard University Press, 1961), p. 161.

[33] See Hitch on "Mechanitis—putting . . . machines to work as a substitute for hard thinking." Charles Hitch, "Economics and Operations Research: A Symposium. II," *Review of Economics and Statistics,* August, 1958, p. 209.

[34] E. S. Quade, *op. cit.,* p. 12.

[35] *Ibid.,* p. 5.

[36] T. C. Schelling, "Economics and Operations Research: A Symposium. V. Comment," *Review of Economics and Statistics,* August, 1958, p. 222.

[37] Albert Wohlstetter in E. S. Quade, *op. cit.,* p. 122.

[38] Prest and Turvey, *op. cit.,* p. 684.

[39] David Novick, Editor, *Program Budgeting* (Cambridge, Harvard University Press, 1965), p. vi.

[40] *Ibid.,* pp. v-vi.

[41] Alan Dean, quoted in D. Novick, *ibid.,* p. 311.

[42] R. N. McKean and N. Anshen in D. Novick, *ibid.,* pp. 286-87. The authors say that this aspect of program budgeting is part of the general view adopted in the book as a whole.

[43] Arthur Smithies in *ibid.,* p. 45.

[44] A look at the classic work by Luther Gulick and Lyndall Urwick, *Papers on the Science of Administration* (New York, Columbia University Press, 1937), reveals considerable similarity between their suggested bases of organization and ways of conceptualizing programs.

[45] N. Anshen in D. Novick, *op. cit.,* pp. 19-20.

[46] G. A. Steiner in *ibid.,* p. 356.

[47] A. Smithies in *ibid.,* p. 41.

[48] Marvin Frankel in *ibid.,* pp. 219-220. I have forborne citing the author who promises exciting discussion of the objectives of American education and ends up with fascinating program categories like primary, secondary, and tertiary education.

[49] See the excellent chapter by M. A. Margolis and S. M. Barro, *ibid.,* pp. 120-145.

[50] *Ibid.,* p. 18.

[51] J. R. Meyer in *ibid.,* p. 170. This paragraph is based on my interpretation of his work.

[52] M. Frankel, *ibid.,* p. 237.

[53] *Ibid.,* p. 348.

[54] *Ibid.,* p. 280.

[55] *Ibid.,* pp. 358-59.

[56] *Ibid.,* p. 206.

[57] *Ibid.,* p. 347.

[58] *Ibid.,* p. 365.

[59] *Ibid.,* p. 280.

[60]See my comments on this effect in *The Politics of the Budgetary Process* (Boston, 1964), p. 140. For discussion of some political consequences of program budgeting, see pp. 135-142.

[61]See William H. Brown and Charles E. Gilbert, *Planning Municipal Investment: A Case Study of Philadelphia* (Philadelphia, University of Pennsylvania Press, 1961), for an excellent discussion of the desire of elected officials to remain free to shift their commitments.

[62]It may be said that I have failed to distinguish sufficiently between planning, programming, and budgeting. Planning is an orientation that looks ahead by extending costs and benefits or units of effectiveness a number of years into the future. Programming is a general procedure of systems analysis employing cost-effectiveness studies. In this view program budgeting is a mere mechanical translation of the results of high level systems studies into convenient storage in the budgetary format. No doubt systems studies could be done without converting the results into the form of a program budget. This approach may have a lot to be said for it and it appears that it is the one that is generally followed in the Department of Defense in its presentations to Congress. But if the systems studies guide decisions as to the allocation of resources, and the studies are maintained according to particular program categories and are further legitimatized by being given status in the budget, it seems most unlikely that programming will be separated from budgeting. One is never sure whether too much or too little is being claimed for program budgeting. If all that program budgeting amounts to is a simple translation of previous systems studies into some convenient form of accounting, it hardly seems that this phenomenon is worth so much fuss. If the program categories in the budget system are meaningful, then they must be much more than a mere translation of previously arrived at decisions. In this case, I think that it is not my task to enlighten the proponents of program budgeting, but it is their task to make themselves clear to others.

[63]A. Smithies in Novick, *op. cit.,* p. 37.

[64]See U.S. House Appropriations Committee Subcommittee on Department of Defense Appropriations for Fiscal 1965, 88th Congress, 2nd Session, IV, p. 133. McNamara asserted that some 652 "subject issues" had been submitted to him for the fiscal 1965 budget.

[65]Charles Hitch, *Decision Making for Defense* (Berkeley, University of California Press, 1965).

[66]Novick, *op. cit.,* p. 100.

[67]Paul Diesing, *Reason in Society* (Urbana, 1962), pp. 198, 203-4, 231-32.

[68]Braybrooke and Lindblom, *op. cit.* See also Lindblom, *The Intelligence of Democracy* (New York, 1965).

[69]M. Anshen in D. Novick, *op. cit.,* p. 370.

[70]*Ibid.,* p. 289.

[71]*Ibid.,* p. 359.

[72]Paul Diesing, *op. cit.,* p. 228.

[73]I am indebted to John Harsanyi for suggestions about political rationality.

[74]In the field of defense policy, political factors are taken into account to the extent that the studies concentrate on the design of feasible alternatives. In the choice of overseas basing, for example, the question of feasibility in relation to treaties and friendly or unfriendly relationships with other countries is considered. Thus it seems permissible to take into account political considerations originating outside of the country, where differences of opinions and preferences among nations are to some extent accepted as legitimate, but apparently not differences internal to the American policy.

12

YARDSTICKS FOR GOVERNMENT: THE ROLE OF PPBS

by Melvin R. Levin

*Professor Levin concentrates on the use of PPBS in govern-
ment operations and concludes that its principal use may
be to serve as a management tool to assist capable administrators to gain control over their departments. He suggests
that the use of PPBS as an instrument in choosing between
alternative policies may be limited, particularly in controversial areas and unless and until the technique is made
sufficiently simplified to be used effectively by persons of
modest competence.*

NEW TOOLS: PPBS

The technique of introducing an energetic new broom to clean
out old stables is as old as history. Faced with a complex, ectoplas-
mic mess, the traditional approach is to locate a strong-willed, effective administrator and to turn him loose. What PPBS offers is a
possible means of economizing on virtuosos. It offers a new way of
systematizing program management.

Reprinted from Melvin R. Levin, *Community and Regional Planning: Issues in
Public Policy.* Praeger Special Studies in U.S. Economic and Social Development.
New York: Frederick A. Praeger, Publishers, 1969, pp. 42-63. Reprinted by permis-
sion of the publisher.

PPBS is a method for analyzing programs in terms of outputs as related to expenditures.[1] Properly designed, it can be an important tool in the selection of alternatives because it can help to evaluate relative results from different kinds of public investments. The design of an effective system is predicated on two very critical assumptions. The first is that a substantial, reliable flow of timely information, probably through a computerized system, will be available to program administrators. The second and even more basic prerequisite is the existence of a program design that organizes information in a meaningful framework for decisions because it is of little consequence to have access to a vast amount of marginally relevant material that cannot be put to use in answering critical questions. One can be sympathetic to those who suggest that the problem is not generating more information because administrators are already swamped with more data than they can profitably absorb and that, anyway, most important decisions are political and judgmental.[2] However, while there is obviously far too much statistical trivia on hand and the computers will generate a lot more, there remains a clear need for reliable *relevant* information on program impacts. Further, there is insufficient accurate followup information on programs in which the payoff is necessarily delayed as, for example, in education and health. Just as important, there is inadequate data that can be used to weight various programs designed to achieve similar objectives, as, for example, alternative manpower training programs. A critical distinction must, therefore, be made between masses of marginal data and the important information, much of which is not currently available and must either be forcibly excavated from a reluctant bureaucracy or generated through new research. As one observer suggests, we generate much data, but, at least in the vital field of education, it doesn't tell us what we want to know.

When we survey the voluminous, yet unsuitable, data now available for assessing the products of education, we must conclude that practically none of it measures the output of our educational system in terms that really matter (that is, in terms of what students have learned). Amazement at the revelation of the tremendous lack of suitable indicators is almost overshadowed by the incredible fact that the nation has, year after year, been spending billions of state and local tax dollars on an enterprise without knowing how effective the expenditures are, or even if they are being directed to stated goals.[3]

One prerequisite of PPBS is that program objectives must be clearly defined, and the questions to be answered and the measures of performance must be part of a plan extending over a period of several years in the future. While there should be no suggestion that dubious programs be permitted to run on and on in the hope of long-term results or even worse, of doubling expenditures for unproductive programs on the ground that results will then surely follow, PPBS does not eliminate the need for a strong common-sense judgment on what constitutes a reasonable input of time, funds, and effort. Given this vital prerequisite—good sense—PPBS offers a way to evaluate systematically the relationship between ends and means. Properly used, it offers the possibility of escaping some of the biases injected when information is filtered through the prisms of existing agencies and current programs. For the administrator, PPBS can be an almost unprecedented method of clearing away, conceptually at least, the dense accumulation of underbrush that often obscures the paths between present programs and possible goals.

Despite these obvious advantages, there is an important caveat. If it can be said that the navy is a machine "designed by geniuses to be run by idiots," PPBS is still very much at the genius stage. The technique is not yet routinized to the point where it can be managed by persons of modest competence; in its present, pioneering stage, PPBS calls for remarkable qualities of objectivity, thorough grounding in operations, and a creative intellect. It is clear that the federal government will have to set the pace simply because there are more intelligent executives in Washington than in most of the state and local agencies. In time, a diluted, vulgarized, simplified version of PPBS will filter out through the federal establishment and down to state and local government.

Up to this point, our discussion has largely focused on the potential benefits of PPBS. If we are honest, we must squarely face some of the inherent limitations of the technique, the dangers in its use, and the difficulties in converting it into a form suitable for wide consumption. The interesting and, on the whole, melancholy history of the abortive attempts to inject cost-benefit techniques developed for water-resource projects into such other government operations as urban renewal may be remembered. Other extremely attractive innovations have foundered on the rocks of inherent but not fully recognized rocks and shoals.

THE TEMPORAL TEMPTATION: PLANNING FOR THE MILLENIUM?

While it is impossible to identify all of the problems likely to be encountered in applying PPBS techniques at the various governmental levels, we can begin to delineate a few of the more outstanding obstacles. Experience suggests that many future problems cannot be anticipated, but even a brief analysis suggests that the PPBS approach will encounter a full quota of obstacles as it wends its painful way through the government agencies.

One of the specific reasons for the increasing enthusiasm to stretch public agencies on the PPBS rack is the difference of attitude toward the passage of time between most political leaders and many bureaucrats. The pat distinction—between statesmen (good) who allegedly plan for the next generation and politicians (bad) who are concerned exclusively with winning the next election—loses some of its meaning when it is recognized that, like the politician, the statesman's career is a painstaking, step-by-step affair in which immediate problems must be overcome if one is to be permitted to work on grand designs with long-term impacts. It may be recalled that Abraham Lincoln numbered among his many gifts a remarkable ability to manipulate postmasterships and popular generals to win elections. The inherent incompatibility between long-term, comprehensive plans and the pragmatic "project" orientation of the politician has been discussed at some length by Alan A. Altshuler and Edward C. Banfield, among others.[4] PPBS does have the benefit of isolating program elements for inspection, and hence escapes some of the odium (and futility) attendant on large-scale, slow moving, closely interwoven, comprehensive plans that tend to be pretty much ignored.

This preamble is by way of suggesting that one of the chief problems in arriving at reasonable goals and translating them into reality with the help of PPBS relates to different time scales. PPBS is supposed to have required four years from design to fruitful results in the DOD and may take even longer in other agencies. The politician and his upper-echelon appointed executives must think in terms of efforts that yield perceptible, publicly demonstrable progress within a year or two. This is not to say that they are opposed to programs aimed at achieving medium- and long-term objectives, but they are confronted with an unending series of crises calling for immediate action. As a rule, an elected official has relatively little time or attention to devote to those who plan vast operations that may or may not bear fruit in his successor's administrations but that obviously have only a marginal relevance to his current problems—not the least of which is his re-election.

This sense of political urgency is usually shared by the appointed executive at the highest level to almost the same degree as the elected official. At one conference, for example, a senior administrator remarked that a junior planner, disillusioned by the futility of long-range planning, had remarked that henceforth the planning profession should concentrate on short-range efforts. The young man subsequently explained that by "short range" he meant five years. The senior official suggested that this time span, while an improvement on some previous programs that moved at glacial pace, was still far too extended for political utility. He argued, that from the viewpoints of the voting public, the President and Congress and appointed supergrade executives like himself who are charged with implementing legislation, five years is a political lifetime; half a decade may embrace a change in control of the Senate, two Congressional elections, and a turnover in the Presidency. If there were no substantive payoff within two years, the planning operation was not likely to secure much support, he observed.

The matter of timing is crucial to any number of government programs ranging from the Supreme Court's variously interpreted "deliberate speed" for racial integration of school systems to the surfeit of hastily drawn program requirements and preposterous deadlines that have confounded the local poverty program administrator. Determining the point at which a digestion problem arises in assimilating new legislation, at which a transient political opportunity for reform must be exploited despite the risks of overloading a frail administrative structure, and the point at which cautious delay may fade into indefinite postponement calls for delicate exercises in judgment. Critics of the politicians' and reformers' penchant for haste may be reminded that passion more often than prudence makes the political world go round. Waiting for plans to be perfected is usually an exercise in theological patience rather than practical politics. Successful politics and administration are largely matters of seizing fleeting opportunities. PPBS will have to adjust to this built-in urgency if it is to have much significant impact on policy. This means that with or without PPBS, program planners and administrators must be prepared to offer judgments and recommendations on the basis of incomplete information, half-finished matrices, and subjective hunches because events refuse to wait until the last word in research and program evaluation has been spoken.

If it can be assumed, as a general rule, that more progress may be achieved by launching a leaky administrative vessel than by waiting for the waters to recede, PPBS does offer a method of testing for hidden holes below the waterline, both prior to and after embarkation. There would seem to be no reason why a preliminary PPBS (like cost-benefit) analysis should not be required as a prerequisite to justify proposed new endeavors as well as to test existing programs. The danger would seem to be in the misuse of half-baked PPBS as another handy method of formulating plausible rationalizations for shoddy programs. A false aura of scientific objectivity can be enlisted to sell more than patent medicines.

HOW MUCH COMMITMENT?

If there is one central problem in implementing reform legislation and injecting controversial new techniques, it is the combination of underlying resistance to change by vested interests and the minimal support at the crucial moment vouchsafed by those who had previously been lavish with friendly rhetoric. It takes a lot of pushing to penetrate the layers of inertia and hostility, and unless there is genuine and real muscle to back up the speeches, the result is frustration and disillusionment.

The phrase "lip service" is used to denote verbal commitment to an objective unaccompanied by any real efforts to achieve it. Accusations that those in power are freer with promises than with action are of ancient vintage, and doubtless, cave drawings will someday be discovered attacking the probity of some clan chieftain who solemnly promised happier hunting but failed to deliver on his pledged word. This gulf between words and deeds was perhaps a major key to the domestic credibility gap of 1967-68. It has been charged, for example, that at the 1967-68 level of expenditures, the war on poverty was no more than a series of skirmishes, and that the bold promises of clean rivers, pure air, and slumless cities would not be redeemed by minimal budgetary allocations. In neither instance was the administration's budgetary request nor the subsequent dehydrated Congressional appropriation consonant with either the stirring rhetoric of the legislative preambles or the eloquent Presidential messages.

It should by no means be suggested that skimping on money is the only way of slowing progress on a program like PPBS that promises to upset many bureaucratic applecarts. Belief in good intentions may be severely tested. The administrative saboteur who wishes to give the appearance of cooperation and open-mindedness or indeed the politician who is not committed to his platform beyond election day or is simply short of budgetary funds has a wide choice of weapons. The PPBS movement may be slowed to a walk by solemn and protracted bickering on details and concentration on tangential or irrelevant issues. Defensive bureaucracies and powerful client groups can agree on selecting policy and implementing committees that offer a combination of incompatible views, clashing temperaments, and feeble administrative sense. One step beyond, artistic undercutting can be managed by relegating the program to unsympathetic, weak, and/or captive administrators certain to decelerate forward movement.

Even progress designed to achieve ostensibly noncontroversial goals are susceptible to blockage at the operating level. For example, community development programs aimed at the presumably consensual objective of improving the local economy are so much the rule that the city which openly opts for the economic status quo is a rarity. Yet, although all communities affirm their verbal adherence to efforts aimed at stimulating new economic growth, for various corporate or personal reasons, leaders in some communities have been fertile in devising techniques that halt every concrete step in this direction. When adherence to a common goal is barely skin deep, a cynic might suggest that opponents can think of a problem for every solution.

While it is not difficult to discover any number of instances in which practice is not consonant with ideals in the city hall or the state house, skepticism can be exaggerated to the point of paranoia. PPBS can play a significant role even in its early stages by examining, clarifying goals because goals possess a force of their own, even if long unachieved. The exposure of hypocrisy is often an effective method of squaring current reality with accepted objectives. As Gunnar Myrdal correctly predicted with respect to America's treatment of the Negro, a moral commitment to a goal, even if long unfulfilled, can in time be a powerful weapon in securing passage of corrective measures.[5] By linking program achievement to goals, PPBS can be a significant lever for social change. It can document, in detail, our modest progress in moving toward accepted goals. PPBS may, as one of its by-products, provide copious ammunition for basic reforms.

Conflicting Goals and Priorities

At bottom, PPBS assumes that meaningful goals exist against which programs can be tested and evaluated. This is quite an assumption. Certainly there is no shortage of goals and objectives, but there is considerable difficulty in assigning priorities between them.

The financial limitations placed on Great Society programs in fiscal 1967-68 point up two most serious problems. The first and most obvious involved finances. Escalation of the American involvement in Vietnam, a conflict that has been assigned priority over domestic programs, had absorbed the financial reserves for the projected expansion of Great Society programs. Appropriations for the war on poverty, model cities, aid to education, and antipollution measures reflect this budgetary malnutrition. The rhetoric remained unchanged, but the money was not there, nor was it likely to be forthcoming within the next fiscal year. Widespread racial rioting during the summer of 1967 did not elevate priorities for the city slum population to the damn-the-deficit level that has historically been accorded only to overseas conflicts.

Were the lavish resources that are being expended in Vietnam available for civilian use—perhaps $30 billion in 1967—the situation might be far different. To place this figure in perspective, it has been estimated that perhaps a $12 billion annual subsidy would raise all of the nation's poor above the poverty line. As things are, a series of difficult choices were forced on the administration and the Congress in 1967. The primary reaction to stringency was to fund fully only politically popular programs while small poultices were applied to social inflammations. In the first category, the Appalachian Regional Commission received virtually all it requested, and the poverty program and aid for elementary and secondary education were funded at roughly the level of the previous year. In the second category, only $75 million was allocated for summer jobs in a spectacularly unsuccessful attempt to head off disturbances in the Negro slums; the model cities program was drastically truncated in the House of Representatives, and the House laughed to death the famous rat control bill before reversing its stand after the 1967 summer riots.

Should military expenditures continue to claim a similar or growing share of the gross national product, more strains on civilian programs can be anticipated. The revolution of rising expectations may, in fact, result in an intensification of internecine struggles by warring interest groups, all of whom can reasonably claim that a budget reduction would jeopardize an important national goal. Such battles might pit rural and urban areas against each other and could stimulate conflicts between programs designed to aid the aged as against efforts to help dependent children and lead to demands that funds be allocated to public transportation against pleas for more highways. The struggle could easily spread to include civil wars among urban, ethnic, and racial groups as well as choices between equally valid national and international goals. Perhaps the bitter struggles for poverty funds among neighborhoods of some cities are ominous omens of coming disturbances. Paradoxically, limitations on funds may force the pace of moves to introduce PPBS and other program soul searching by the federal agencies. It will not be the first time an ill wind has blown a little good.

For Motherhood or Flag?

It would be an error to suggest that goal setting for PPBS can be translated into a simple matter of financial priorities. Were this in fact the case, a cutback in overseas commitments and subsequent release of a major share of the federal surplus would eliminate problems of choosing between alternate goals and priorities by permitting a massive advance on a broad program front; virtually all significant budget requests could be honored. But there is obviously much more involved in achieving goals than a doubling or redoubling of appropriations. There are implicit conflicts between various goals. To cite a specific example, massive intown highway construction to provide easy access for a dispersed population to their work places and other destinations (as perhaps desired by a voting majority) is in conflict with other urban goals such as neighborhood stability and efficient urban development patterns. An across-the-board green light that includes heavy allocations for more urban expressways is therefore likely to diminish the possibility of achieving other, equally accepted objectives.

There is a more significant problem: Experience has proved that higher appropriations in themselves may not yield the desired results. In fact, it has been charged that appropriations may have precisely the opposite effect for which they were intended. To cite one example, Scott Greer has charged that the net result of an expenditure of $3 billion in urban renewal funds was a net reduction in the number of housing units available to low-income families.[6] Others have pointed out that funds allocated to regulatory agencies may end up as a kind of supplemental budget for the industries supposedly being regulated. Furthermore, there is often a matter of outright wastefulness of various types, including some programs that have outlived their usefulness, others that make no visible impact on their clients, and still others that leap from one costly, abortive experiment to another. It is hardly necessary to point out that a weak or stubbornly foolish bureaucracy wedded to obsolete ideas and practices can dissipate very large sums without commensurate product.[7] The Middle Eastern sheikdoms are not the sole instances where funds have been squandered with little resulting public benefit. There are instances in which additional funds may make a bad situation worse. Allocating new money to the old men may perpetuate and reinforce rather than remove the problems that the input of funds was supposed to solve. On the other hand, a prime argument for PPBS is that very often much can be achieved with little in the way of new allocations. Within urban areas, for example, training and recruitment programs for the police, better selection and promotion policies for the schools, and more effective housing-code enforcement may be undramatic, but a realistic PPBS may discover that modest improvements like these —aimed at doing better with what we have—may be of more lasting benefit than some massive, costly programs.

The idea that progress is purchasable, that military victory and social progress can be achieved by more lavish spending, is not purely American, but it would be fair to say that Americans seem to be especially prone to suggestions that in larger budgetary allocations can be found the answers to intricate domestic and foreign problems. One reason for the surge of interest in PPBS is that faith in this simple-minded approach may be waning; at least a limited awareness that less money and more hard thinking may provide part of the answer is slowly creeping through the federal establishment. Success in this endeavor may compensate for temporary, less than hoped for funding of domestic programs.

It is clear that one of the basic problems with the selection of goal and program priorities which must provide the basis for effective PPBS is that the nation seems firmly committed to just about everything good—slum-free communities with healthful, attractive environment, and moral uplift, high-paying jobs for the employable, and livable incomes for welfare recipients. It is entirely possible that within a generation or two, when the gross national product doubles and trebles, it will be feasible to provide the trillions of dollars needed to achieve these goals. Meanwhile, as has been suggested, choices must be made not only between the clearly vital programs and the obvious marginalia but between a number of efforts that are normally accorded high-priority status. If this were not sufficient complication, there is evidence that some goals may be in direct conflict with other, equally cherished objectives.

It may be useful to cite a case that caused much concern in the mid-1960's, the improvement of housing conditions for Negro slum dwellers. Each avenue selected or recommended to achieve this highly desirable goal seems to be in actual or potential conflict with other goals and values:

1. Fair housing programs to provide access to relatively affluent suburan communities for Negroes able to afford such housing seriously deplete the thin leadership stratum in the ghetto. Open hous-

ing of this type may defeat the objective of strengthening stable Negro community leadership.

2. Programs aimed at large-scale dispersal of the ghetto to white areas through rent supplements, creating pockets of public housing or other means, may lead to early, violent conflict in previously orderly white working-class and lower-middle-class communities.[8] These strata of the population seem to be afflicted with disproportionate amounts of insecurity and bigotry that often take overt physical expression. Similar although less explosive opposition may be encountered in moving large numbers of low-income Negroes into close proximity to middle- and upper-income groups. There may also be some resistance to the dispersal concept from advocates of black power who view the ghetto as a political base and see its dilution as reducing Negroes to a permanent political minority status among Caucasian majorities.

3. Improving housing within the ghetto through construction of public housing and/or large-scale renovation and rehabilitation will tend to perpetuate housing and school segregation and the economic and social divisions that breed mutual fear and hostility. On the other hand, requiring public-housing projects (or other housing under direct government control) to be fully integrated may alleviate the pervading pattern of segregation to only a limited extent because the net result is likely to be the creation of socially unstable oases in the midst of all-Negro areas.

4. Permanent improvement in housing conditions for slum residents will require a fundamental change in living habits of many disadvantaged families. There is no hard data on the proportion of low-income Negroes in the ghetto who differ from the white and Negro middle class only in their lack of money, sharing similar values and aspirations. Many Negroes are moving each year into the middle class and it is apparent that more would do so if the path could be made easier. In contrast, a substantial, although undetermined proportion of Negroes and Caucasians apparently do not share middle class and/or (even) working-class values, as, for example, a moderate respect for property and cleanliness. A minority of building residents who are not yet housebroken can reduce a new public housing structure or a private apartment building to a shambles in short order. Effecting a significant large-scale improvement in slum housing may therefore require isolating and possibly retraining hard core vandals under close supervision and/or selecting and segregating slum residents who can be relied on not to wreck the building in which they live. However, this

kind of supervision can easily be labeled a bigoted, callous move to create racial or low-income concentration camps.

This example may suggest some of the limitations of PPBS. The technique can indicate progress and program impact, but it cannot reconcile the irreconciliable. Perhaps it is wisest to agree with the conclusion that its principal usefulness is educational: It will force agencies to do some unaccustomed, rigorous, systematic thinking about their programs.[9]

This is not to suggest that PPBS will revolutionize the ways in which goals are formulated and implemented. The United States (and perhaps most nations) seems to develop goals through some mysterious organic process. A climate of opinion is gradually established in the press, in the articulate portion of the community, among business leaders and among a few bellwether reformers in the Congress. Gradually, as this process of subliminal educational exposure percolates into the lairs of the Philistines, it becomes transformed into legislation and thence settles firmly into the political landscape.

A classic example of the osmotic process of goal formation is discernible in the field of public higher education. In the late 1950's and early 1960's, a decision seems to have been taken in a number of states to provide every qualified high school graduate with an opportunity for a low-cost college education at a public institution located within commuting distance of his home. This frightening outline, is now an accepted, unchallenged feature of the political environment. The same is discernible with respect to a variety of programs that have undergone the same process.

DESIGN FOR GENIUSES?

Perhaps none of the problems that surround the injection of PPBS into the governmental bloodstream is more crucial than the supply of trained, or trainable, technically capable manpower. The belated realization that shortages of qualified manpower rather than shortages in funds are crucial obstacles to program implementation has already been reflected in evaluation programs, funded by the Office of Economic Opportunity, the Department of Housing and Urban Development (HUD), and Health, Education, and Welfare (HEW), among others. It is also reflected in legislation introduced by the U.S. Civil Service Commission (the Intergovernmental Personnel Act of 1967), by Senator Edmund S. Muskie, and by HUD and HEW to expand the supply of trained professionals. In addition, some federal agencies have begun to tap outside manpower to conduct critiques of major programs, a form of independent evaluation that was almost unthinkable only a few years before.

Whatever corrective measures are under way or in prospect, the current situation is far from promising. The Joint Economic Committee looking into federal human resource programs found, for example, that although its queries did not call for "the extensive analytical effort, special studies, detailed program examinations, and financial tabulations" that are required by the Bureau of the Budget, the questions bearing on economic impact "referred to types of information which apparently were unfamiliar to some of the Government personnel who were called upon by their agency heads to prepare the replies."[10] Only a few agencies were able to prepare an effective response (that is, the Social Security Administration, the Office of Manpower Policy, Evaluation, and Research, and "several" units of the DOD). But the committee expressed its hopeful belief that such difficulties will "gradually be overcome by the disciplines of the formal PPBS which carries its own internal sanctions" but it "anticipated a transitional period of incomplete analyses and shallow analyses of costs and benefits." The Joint Economic Committee concluded on a grim but realistic note, calling attention to the immensity of the task:

Either there is a scarcity of penetrating analysis in many program operating units or the assignment to prepare responses was often given to persons who were not familiar with program analyses . . . Much work needs to be done in the clarification of objectives and concepts, the formulation of analytical techniques, the explanation of procedures to individuals called upon to produce the necessary studies, and the definition of criteria for the interpretation and evaluation of findings. This will require a continuous process of examination and instruction throughout the executive branch.[11]

It is possible that the committee was somewhat naive in its initial expectations. Douglass Cater has quoted a Brookings Institution study to the effect that the Congress has done little to strengthen the top-level civil service. The top 3,000 or more career executives who head the various bureaus and divisions were found to be "predominantly inbred. . . . Many had started in government service at a lower level, had risen through the ranks by concentrating on specialties and are frequently indifferent to the larger problems of government."[12]

As noted previously, staffing problems encountered at the federal level are multiplied exponentially in most state and local governments. One can agree with George C. S. Benson that "in some states the personnel is superior to federal personnel,"[13] and still hold with Charles R. Adrian that, of the three levels of government, "The states have been slowest of all to professionalize and this has crippled the administrator at that level in his attempts to share in the decision-making process."[14]

Assuming that competent staff can somehow be located to operate PPBS in government agencies, questions arise as to the orientation and direction of this staff. PPBS is not a neutral, value-free process. The measurement techniques selected can have a powerful influence on goals and priorities. PPBS cannot itself define benefits, nor can it determine what kind of weights should be given to alternative results affecting different income groups and different, conflicting objectives.

It must be understood that while PPBS can be useful in re-examining old prejudices, it is no guarantee against new forms of snobbery. To cite a specific example, critical problems may arise because the program-design assignment is virtually certain to be relegated to holders of college degrees whose middle-class outlook will undoubtedly be reflected overtly or subtly in the performance standards and targets. In effect, technicians whose orientation reflects the status and aspirations of a particular social class are called on to set standards for programs affecting lower-income people with different living patterns and often with different aspirations. This is not a new situation. It may be recalled that standard intelligence tests have aroused considerable opposition on the ground that they are formulated in a middle-class framework, and hence the test scores discriminate against working-class children. In the mid-1960's, one of the basic questions was whether the poor or the redevelopment areas were or should be evaluated on the basis of their progress in effecting a transition into the national, middle-class mainstream.

Obviously some amount of class bias is inevitable in any program because a substantial amount of conformity to middle-class standards is usually a prerequisite for admission to the ranks of the goal setters and program designers. However, it is vital to recognize that either by calculation or simply because certain values are assumed as "givens" by the planners, unless great care is taken, PPBS, or indeed any system of performance evaluation, reflects and measures a relatively narrow spectrum of activities closely linked to the background of the designers. This may suggest that impartial, independent opinion should be brought into the design phase. More than likely, in time there may be demands for "maximum, feasible participation of the poor" in designing goals and performance measures for welfare, education, housing, and other programs. This may entail equipping the various client groups with the technical assistance advocates needed to protect their interests in program design and performance measurement. From the viewpoint of dissenting client groups, whenever controversial matters are involved, no panel of savants and/or corporation presidents is likely to produce a satisfactory consensus in assigning program priorities or in deciding exactly what it is that should be measured.

This brings us, of course, to the inevitable question: Should programs be geared to the tastes, abilities, and aspirations of the majority; or should goal setters and administrators continue to assume a paternal responsibility for remolding the masses in a middle-class image?

Much can be and has been said on both sides of this issue of mass and class. In recent years, there has been considerable attention to the need for redressing the traditional, quasi-elitest thrust of government operations by according greater weight to the opinions and values of the public as a whole or of major and minor elements of the population. The evils of government-by-expert and government programs designed by small groups of relatively affluent and articulate persons imposing their standards on the inarticulate majority, on the unorganized, the politically inarticulate, the currently unpopular, and the minority groups have been given wide currency.

Unfortunately, because government rests on a foundation of successful communication and manipulation of expertise and money, there is no easy solution to this dilemma. One obvious response is to ensure that every group has its capable spokesmen to give its interests adequate representation not only in the political arena but also in technical disputes. This would entail that some planners, economists, and sociologists join the legal professions in preparing partisan briefs for clients, a development which in any event seems to be well on its way in some new fields, particularly city planning.[15] But it would be a mistake to limit attention to the organized or potentially organizable.

Provision must also be made to guarantee adequate protection for submerged segments of the population. The question is how to achieve this objective for groups (like children on welfare) who cannot communicate easily or perhaps at all. There is also the problem of securing representation for groups who are obviously able to make themselves heard but who cannot or will not devote sufficient attention to complex operations in the face of competing issues that demand their attention. It is often difficult to secure meaningful responses from interests like downtown businesses—organizations which one would believe wholly capable of participating fully in the process of setting goals and performance standards. Even the goals established for a discrete and manageable area like the Minneapolis Central Business District evoked little comment from the downtown businessmen whose interests were presumably most directly involved. In fact, the detailed planning subsequently undertaken to implement goals evoked little reaction in Minneapolis until the plans were subsequently simplified in highly specific terms that clearly indicated the potential impact on traffic, or parking patterns, or on individual business establishments.[16] If PPBS design is to avoid charges of backroom manipulation and dictatorship-by-technician, it will obviously be necessary to translate a highly technical process into bread-and-butter terms meaningful to potential clients.

The experience in Minneapolis suggests that preparation of generalized goals is a task congenial to politicians, civic and business leaders, but involving them in a continuing dialogue with professionals is likely to be frustrating. Few nonprofessionals can devote the time and effort necessary to master a technical subject, and most groups are unable to employ a capable protagonist, nor are they willing to empower a technician to commit the organization to significant planning proposals. Because few interests are in a position to employ qualified lobbyist representatives, the result is that it usually falls to the technician to seek out meaningful responses from many of his client groups, particularly those without the technical knowledge or funds to employ professionally trained spokesmen. This, of course, does not place an unusual amount of responsibility on the professional but rather recognizes a situation that has always existed.

As John Dyckman observes, "most social planners have at least a modified caretaker orientation."[17] Leonard J. Duhl sees the planner-forecaster as an agent of social change acting as a kind of ombudsman, "returning the franchise" to the people partly by serving as a communications link with the "invisible colleges" of intellectuals and partly through conscious efforts as a political manipulator.[18] It is incumbent on the technician involved in PPBS design to develop a concept of short-run and long-run client interests. If he is to engage in this perilous activity, he cannot attend the luxury of technically neutral detachment. As Dyckman suggests, he will not be handed a ready-made packet of goals in the form of a set of well-ordered preference functions, and the task of discerning "latent" goals will take great patience and much interpretation.

It should be made clear that the relatively restricted technically supportive role suggested for the PPBS staff is at variance with other views on the function of the program-planner in government. A more exalted pivotal role is identified by John Friedmann, who underscores the potential of the researcher-planner as an agent in effecting social change, and implicitly, in assuming a major responsibility in selection of goals and programs. In his articles on "innovative planning"[19] Friedmann differentiates between the cautious creatures engaged in sanctioned, gradualist planning with its emphasis on effective allocation of resources within a system of incremental change, and the innovative planner. The latter seems to be a cross between a swashbuckler and an *eminence grise* who has deliberately chosen to become an engineer of rapid change in performing a planning, advisory, and manipulative role, working closely with top-level executives.

The innovator seeks to legitimize new social objectives by concentrating on main points of leverage and, like a bold staff Saul Alinsky, he seeks to "organize dissatisfied creative minorities to translate general value propositions into new institutional arrangements." Concentrating his efforts on making maximum use of all available resources by focusing on areas likely to produce the greatest changes, he eschews comprehensive planning in favor of strategic actions based on what he interprets as demonstrable results. Because innovative planning is associated with periods of crisis and change (like the present), Friedmann feels that it is currently more prevalent than the conservative, allocative variety.

While it may be argued that in playing this free-wheeling semi-conspiratorial role, the planner arrogates responsibilities which are, or should be, in the province of the elected official, it can be countered that he functions as the chosen instrument of the politician. If he operates under a loose rein, it may be presumed that either he possesses the full confidence of his boss and has the sense to check sensitive decisions with his elected superiors or that his tenure will be short lived. Further, it may be assumed that this *modus operandi* has considerable attractions for the results-oriented politician, provided the planner stays out of too much hot water. Under varying job descriptions, most incumbents number practicing bureaucrat-planners-researchers among their trusted subordinates. These are people who can be relied on to get a job done without bothering their superiors and without making too many waves. They are usually prepared to serve as loyal expendables; if things go wrong, they deflect the blame from the man who appointed them whether or not the trouble arose from bad luck or faithful adherence to orders. In fact, because a considerable amount of

friction from change-resisters is inevitable, the turnover among innovators may be substantial. For this reason a quick, thrusting, hit-
and-run strategy is clearly in order rather than the incremental
type of planning associated with planners who have hopes of retir-
ing on the job.

Whether this description is accurate or indeed whether it is a
role that planners and administrators should deliberately choose is
open to question. Clearly, some have found this a congenial role,
working as a trusted lieutenant to an imaginative executive. In any
case, the innovator seems to be more suitable for the executive's
personal staff rather than to the staff of technicians committed to
long-term service with a permanent agency. Furthermore, he must
recognize that his enlistment may be drastically curtailed unless he
possesses remarkable personal gifts and a great deal of good luck.
The planner who attempts to manipulate the facts, control the
news, and engage in behind-the-scenes social engineering is likely
to end up in a pot of hot water, particularly if he discusses his role
openly with friendly reporters. It can probably be taken for granted
that social planning will be an uneasy, hybrid mixture of open plans
openly arrived at and the kind of high-minded conspiracies described by Friedmann.

Whatever the particular mix in a particular time and place, there
are areas in which wholly objective tests can be developed as for
example, such indisputable yardsticks for health programs as the
infant mortality rate or family income patterns, the occupational
distribution of minority groups, and the proportion of college
graduates in various communities and population groups. But there
remains a wide latitude for bitter disputes on the type of performance standards to be employed in measuring progress on such basic
issues as the status of the Negro in America or the quality of life in
our cities. The fact is that such performance measures as exist in
these and other areas are traditionally established in societies by a
small group of cultural pacesetters. This returns us to the original
dilemma: Do we set standards that satisfy the current tastes of the
electorate or are there overriding professional standards? If purely
mass standards were to serve as the criterion, the outlook for a host
of subsidized activities ranging from parks and universities to op-
eras and educational television would be bleak indeed. It would
appear to the author, at any rate, that adoption of Philistinism in
the guise of a modern-day slogan of *vox populi, vox Dei,* represents
an abdication of responsibility rather than, as some argue, a
progressive step in the direction of democratic freedom.

The danger of bowing uncritically to popular sentiment shows up

most clearly in relation to racial and religious issues. If local refe-
renda were to be the guide, anti-Negro prejudice would be certain
to bar progress on civil rights in many areas, North as well as South.
While it is perfectly true that it is all too easy for middle- and
upper-class residents (or PPBS designers for that matter) to pre-
scribe racial balance for working-class areas because *their* neighborhoods escape most of the potential hazards to life, schools, and
property,[20] even if it is admitted that there is some rationale for
white backlash, abject surrender to popular bigotry is hardly the
answer.

To a degree this mass-class argument is, in every sense of the
word, academic. Whatever the technique in vogue for measuring
the popular will—elections, polling, or revolution—in the end, most
decisions are made by elites. Decisions may be modified or influenced by systems that accord greater weight to wider strata of
public opinion, but the number of persons actually involved in decision-making is almost always very small. Nor is there any indication
that mass education and mass communication have fundamentally
enlarged the proportion of the population which has a significant
influence on decisions. The civil rights movement, like the earlier
successful efforts aimed at securing legal and political equality for
labor unions and women, has enlarged the spectrum of clienteles
who must be taken into account in formulating and administering
public policy. As government and society grow more complex, the
distance between technician, administrator, and politician can be
bridged only in part by mass media, opinion polls, periodic elections, sporadic disorders, technical interpreters, advocates, and om-
budsmen. Demonstrations are a method of calling attention to a
cause, not a consistent approach to influencing day-to-day program
operations. For this reason, the burden of representation of much of
the public will continue to fall in great measure to program designers and administrators. There must be an awareness of this extremely important responsibility.

The person at the upper echelons in government also has broader
responsibilities. He must not be contented with programs and
efforts good enough to satisfy his clients but short of what he knows
is desirable and possible. Moreover, he is, or should be, an educator
rather than either a bureaucratic calculating machine or a pliable
professional survivor. He has a duty to the spirit and substance of
his program rather than solely to generate laudatory comments in
the legislature and the press. PPBS, if he uses it properly, can serve
him as an effective teaching aid. On the other hand, if he misuses
it or promises too much from its use, the result is likely to be grow-

ing cynicism and suspicion on the part of client groups convinced that a new black art has been developed to justify unpopular decisions.

WHO KILLED COCK ROBIN?

Like military combat, the challenges entailed in mounting a genuine PPBS operation cannot be fully appreciated until one has actually been in the field. From its inception through its inescapable revision, the designer is called upon to render a series of judgments involving interpretations of legislative intent, community values, and professional standards.

One of the thorniest problems in measuring impacts is disentangling programs from their environmental context. It is necessary to identify the role of each layer of government, of each relevant program, and of other societal factors that may have an equally important influence on events. Moreover, since the sum is often greater than the total of the individual parts, the combined impact of various programs must also be examined.

In attempting to isolate the effects of any single government program in the field of health or employment, for example, it is extremely difficult to determine, with certainty: (1) which changes occurred as a direct result of a particular program, (2) which changes can best be classified as indirect or corollary impacts, and (3) which changes are attributable to exogenous factors. A manpower-training operation, for instance, can exhibit a combination of all these: A group of trainees may be hired as a result of a good literacy campaign, because of an unanticipated increase in the gross national product, success in a local area development effort, or a modification of union rules or company policy. The inherent merits of program design and execution may have little relation to success in locating good jobs for the trainees.

Tracing the indirect impact of a program or its effects in combination with other programs is often a tricky affair. One example may be cited: the relationship between poverty programs, singly and in combination, and the violent disorders that erupted in the Negro ghettos during the summer of 1967. In the spring of 1966, officials in poverty agencies claimed that the constellation of programs financed and administered by the Office of Economic Opportunity (OEO) had been instrumental in taking the steam out of riots by providing hope, tangible accomplishments, and employment for potential agitators. During the summer outbreaks, critics subsequently suggested, with somewhat tenuous logic, that, on the contrary, racial disorders occurred in some measure because poverty programs had titillated but not satisfied the aspirations of the poor. In partial agreement with this stand, Sargent Shriver later pointed out that poverty funds represented only a fraction of the amounts requested by the riot cities, indicating that larger allocations might be more effective in muffling violent protests. From a slightly different perspective other observers suggested that the modest improvements introduced by the poverty programs and related efforts by the mid-1960's had accentuated social disequilibrium by breaking through the thick crust of despairing passivity that had kept the slums passive under worse conditions (such as the 1930's Depression).

Obviously identifying cause and effect is far from an easy task under these conditions. Programs do not operate in a vacuum, and it is not always possible to state with certainty that effect B was caused in part or in whole by program A.

There is a further problem in creating defensible yardsticks for evaluating programs: Assessing highway beautification, open space, historic preservation, the impact of placing utility lines in urban areas underground, of cultural development, and other programs in purely monetary terms is ridiculous. How is the quality of life to be measured, and who is to do the measuring? How can emotions like pain, grief, humiliation, anger, and happiness be converted into comparable dollar units? Costs and emotions are often related, but it is hard to enter them on the same balance sheet even after the linkage has become obvious. The decades of humiliation and despair that exploded in the 1967 racial disorders have had measurable consequences running into hundreds of millions in property damage. However, the anger and hatred that led to the arson and robbery are *not* quantifiable.

There is also an obvious temptation to expend many years and much money in assessing the probable, possible, and conceivable, and the immediate, middle-range, and long-term relationship between programs and consequences both in the so-called pure and applied categories. An affluent nation can pursue all kinds of research avenues that might be of value and it is feasible to feed the entire pack rather than run the risk of starving one of the hounds that might have caught the quarry. The difficulty is that much time and effort may be expended in belaboring the obvious. The ancient gibe that a sociologist is a man who spends $100,000 to locate a brothel has more than a glimmer of truth in it. On a more sophisticated level, there is the danger of overconcentration on one or a few enticing aspects of a problem to the exclusion of other, possibly more promising, research areas. The results may make a good deal of sense but they may divert attention if the study suffers from tunnel vision that fails to take account of the major dramas on the periphery. In short, while research is needed to identify the relationship between specific programs and their impact, it is just as hard to formulate useful research studies as it is to design effective programs.

In formulating program design for PPBS, it must be recognized that the information received in the form of impressive print-outs and charts may, nevertheless, be superficial and misleading. Any number of key items may be missing, as, for example, confidential information on program impact in slum areas or sensitive data pointing to administrative lapses. There is also the question of how far to rely on self-justifying statistics furnished by separate agencies with similar or identical missions. Substantial knowledge is necessary to reach behind the budget and performance data when attempting to measure the relative effectiveness of different but overlapping programs such as the OEO's Neighborhood Youth Corps, which is six times more expensive per trainee but is also relatively six times more productive. On the other hand, there may be corollary, nonmonetary benefits (such as a fresh perspective for trainees) that compensate for the higher costs.

To summarize, PPBS offers a number of extremely attractive prospects. It may shed new light on tired programs and demonstrate just how much we do not know about government and the society in which we live. On the other hand, overselling or overrelying on PPBS would be tempting fate. Quite probably the by-products of the intellectualization of government represented by PPBS will be a species of technical warfare between warring advocates, each of whom can point out the fallacies in assumptions, values, and techniques of his opponents, their programs and their recommendations. In brief, PPBS may become a new arena for informed but nonetheless deadly conflict.

At the risk of appearing tiresome, it must be noted that one critical shortcoming appears glaringly obvious when we consider introducing new and intricate programs. PPBS calls for outstanding intelligence in the design and evaluation phase and solid competence in its operation. It cannot conceivably be made a foolproof, self-adjusting mechanism. Surely the technique is beyond the current capacities of many government agencies, particularly in state and local government. Ideally, the process should be delayed until there is assurance of adequate staffing, but government does not work in a simple, logical progression. Realistically, the best that one can probably hope for is that parallel, strenuous efforts will be made to enlarge the supply of trained staff as PPBS is diffused through the governmental structure. After much preliminary floundering, people competent to handle the mechanics of the system will be available, and we can proceed to the next plateau. On these Plains of Abraham to be scaled in the 1970's will be waged interesting technical battles involving ideological and value issues that reach into the heart of government.

NOTES

[1]For an excellent, very short, but authoritative description of PPBS, see statement of Charles L. Schultze, Director, Bureau of the Budget, *Hearing* Before the Subcommittee on Intergovernmental Relations, "Creative Federalism," 90th Cong., 1st Sess., Pt. I, pp. 388-419.

[2]See the comments of Professor Charles A. Reich, Hearings Before a Subcommittee of the Committee of Government Operations, House of Representatives, *The Computer and Invasion of Privacy* (Washington, D.C.: U.S. Government Printing Office, 1966), pp. 22-42.

[3]Wilbur J. Cohen, "Education and Learning," *The Annals,* issue entitled *Social Goals and Indicators,* Vol. 373 (September, 1967), pp. 87-88.

[4]See Alan A. Altshuler, *The City Planning Process, A Political Analysis* (Ithaca, N.Y.: Cornell University Press, 1965), chaps. 4-6. Also Edward C. Banfield, *Political Influence* (Glencoe, Ill.: The Free Press, 1961), chaps. 8, 9, and 12.

[5]For opposing views on this critical matter, see C. Wright Mills, *The Power Elite* (New York: Oxford University Press, 1956); Floyd Hunter, *Community Power Structure* (Chapel Hill, N.C.: University of North Carolina Press, 1953); and Edward M. Banfield, *Political Influence* (Glencoe, Ill.: The Free Press, 1961). Also Gunnar Myrdal, *An American Dilemma, The Negro Problem and American Democracy* (New York: Harper and Bros., 1946).

[6]Scott Greer, *Urban Renewal and American Cities: The Dilemma of Democratic Intervention* (Indianapolis: Bobbs-Merrill, 1965), p. 3.

[7]See Senator Edmund S. Muskie, "Manpower: The Achilles Heel of Creative Federalism," *Public Administration Review,* June, 1967.

[8]See Herbert Gans, *The Levittowners* (New York: Pantheon Books, 1967), especially pp. 427-28.

[9]See William Gorham, "Notes of a Practitioner," *The Public Interest,* issue entitled *PPBS, Its Scope and Limits* (Summer, 1967), 408.

[10]U.S., Joint Economic Committee, Subcommittee on Economic Progress, *Federal Programs for the Development of Human Resources,* I (Washington, D.C.: U.S. Government Printing Office, December, 1966), 31.

[11]*Ibid.,* p. 31, p. 92.

[12]Douglass Cater, "The Fourth Branch," *Power in Washington* (New York: Vintage Books, 1964).

[13]George C. S. Benson, "Trends in Intergovernmental Relations," *The Annals*, issue entitled *Intergovernmental Relations in the United States*, Vol. 359, May, 1965, 5.

[14]Charles R. Adrian, "State and Local Government Participation in the Design and Administration of Intergovernmental Programs," *The Annals, ibid.*, pp. 36-37.

[15]Paul Davidoff, "Advocacy and Pluralism in Planning," *Journal of the American Institute of Planners*, XXXI (November, 1965).

[16]Altshuler, *op. cit.*, pp. 235-90.

[17]John Dyckman, "Social Planning, Social Planners, and Planned Societies," *Journal of the American Institute of Planners*, XXXII (March, 1966), 70-71.

[18]Leonard J. Duhl, "Planning and Predicting: Or What to Do When You Don't Know the Names of the Variables," in *Daedalus*, issue entitled *Toward the Year 2,000: Work in Progress* (Summer, 1967), pp. 779-88.

[19]John Friedmann, "Planning as Innovation: The Chilean Case." *Journal of the American Institute of Planners*, XXXII (July, 1966).

[20]William Lee Miller, *The Fifteenth Ward and the Great Society* (New York: Harper and Row, 1966), chap. 6, pp. 99-111.

13

RESCUING POLICY ANALYSIS
FROM PPBS

by Aaron Wildavsky

In his second major contribution to the Public Administration Review *symposia, Professor Wildavsky argues that
his earlier forecasts of problems in applying PPBS to government programs were fully justified. In a real world beset
by political problems, he comes to a startling conclusion:
"No one knows how to do program budgeting." He suggests an alternative—selective policy analyses on critical
issues for executive and congressional use.*

Everyone knows that the nation needs better policy analysis. Each
area one investigates shows how little is known compared to what
is necessary in order to devise adequate policies. In some organizations there are no ways at all of determining the effectiveness of
existing programs; organizational survival must be the sole criterion
of merit. It is often not possible to determine whether the simplest
objectives have been met. If there is a demand for information the
cry goes out that what the organization does cannot be measured.
Should anyone attempt to tie the organization down to any measure
of productivity, the claim is made that there is no truth in numbers.
Oftentimes this is another way of saying, "Mind your own business." Sometimes the line taken is that the work is so subtle that it

Reprinted from Aaron Wildavsky, "Rescuing Policy Analysis from PPBS," in *Public Administration Review: PPBS Re-examined,* Vol. XXIX, No. 2 (March/April
1969), pp. 189-202. Reprinted by permission of the publisher.

resists any tests. On other occasions the point is made that only those learned in esoteric arts can properly understand what the organization does, and they can barely communicate to the uninitiated. There are men so convinced of the ultimate righteousness of their cause that they cannot imagine why anyone would wish to know how well they are doing in handling our common difficulties. Their activities are literally priceless; vulgar notions of cost and benefit do not apply to them.

Anyone who has weathered this routine comes to value policy analysis. The very idea that there should be some identifiable objectives and that attention should be paid to whether these are achieved seems a great step forward. Devising alternative ways of handling problems and considering the future costs of each solution appear creative in comparison to more haphazard approaches. Yet policy analysis with its emphasis upon originality, imagination, and foresight, cannot be simply described. It is equivalent to what Robert N. Anthony has called strategic planning: " . . . the process of deciding on objectives of the organization, on changes in these objectives, on the resources used to attain these objectives. . . . It connotes big plans, important plans, plans with major consequences."[1] While policy analysis is similar to a broadly conceived version of systems analysis,[2] Yehezkel Dror has pointed up the boundaries that separate a narrow study from one with larger policy concerns. In policy analysis,

1. Much attention would be paid to the political aspects of public decision-making and public policy-making (instead of ignoring or condescendingly regarding political aspects). . . .
2. A broad conception of decision-making and policy-making would be involved (instead of viewing all decision-making as mainly a resources allocation). . . .
3. A main emphasis would be on creativity and search for new policy alternatives, with explicit attention to encouragement of innovative thinking. . . .
4. There would be extensive reliance on . . . qualitative methods. . . .
5. There would be much more emphasis on futuristic thinking. . . .
6. The approach would be looser and less rigid, but nevertheless systematic, one which would recognize the complexity of means-ends interdependence, the multiplicity of relevant criteria of decision, and the partial and tentative nature of every analysis. . . . [3]

Policy analysis aims at providing information that contributes to making an agency politically and socially relevant. Policies are goals, objectives, and missions that guide the agency. Analysis evaluates and sifts alternative means and ends in the elusive pursuit of policy recommendations. By getting out of the fire-house environment of day-to-day administration, policy analysis seeks knowledge and opportunities for coping with an uncertain future. Because policy analysis is not concerned with projecting the *status quo*, but with tracing out the consequences of innovative ideas, it is a variant of planning. Complementing the agency's decision process, policy analysis is a tool of social change.

In view of its concern with creativity, it is not surprising that policy analysis is still largely an art form; there are no precise rules about how to do it. The policy analyst seeks to reduce obscurantism by being explicit about problems and solutions, resources and results. The purpose of policy analysis is not to eliminate advocacy but to raise the level of argument among contending interests. If poor people want greater benefits from the government, the answer to their problems may not lie initially in policy analysis but in political organization. Once they have organized themselves, they may want to undertake policy analysis in order to crystallize their own objectives or merely to compete with the analyses put forth by others. The end result, hopefully, would be a higher quality debate and perhaps eventually public choice among better known alternatives.

A belief in the desirability of policy analysis—the sustained application of intelligence and knowledge to social problems—is not enough to insure its success, no more than to want to do good is sufficient to accomplish noble purposes. If grandiose claims are made, if heavy burdens are placed on officials without adequate compensation, if the needs of agency heads are given scant consideration, they will not desire policy analysis. It is clear that those who introduced the PPB system into the federal government in one fell swoop did not undertake a policy analysis on how to introduce policy analysis into the federal government.

In a paper called "The Political Economy of Efficiency,"[4] written just as PPBS was begun in national government, I argued that it would run up against serious difficulties. There is still no reason to change a single word of what I said then. Indeed, its difficulties have been so overwhelming that there is grave danger that policy analysis will be rejected along with its particular manifestation in PPBS. In this essay I shall assess the damage that the planning-programming-budgeting system has done to the prospects of encouraging policy analysis in American national government. Then I would like to suggest some ways of enabling policy analysis to thrive and prosper.

WHY DEFENSE WAS A BAD MODEL

A quick way of seeing what went wrong with PPBS is to examine the preconditions for the use of this approach in the Defense Department, from which it was exported throughout the federal government. The immediate origins of PPBS are to be found in The RAND Corporation,[5] where, after the Second World War, a talented group of analysts devoted years of effort to understanding problems of defense policy. It took five years to come up with the first useful ideas. Thus the first requisite of program budgeting in Defense was a small group of talented people who had spent years developing insights into the special problems of defense strategy and logistics. The second requisite was a common terminology, an ad hoc collection of analytical approaches, and the beginnings of theoretical statements to guide policy analysis. When Secretary of Defense Robert McNamara came into office, he did not have to search for men of talent nor did he have to wait for a body of knowledge to be created. These requisites already existed in some degree. What was further necessary was his ability to understand and to use analytical studies. Thus the third requisite of program budgeting is top leadership that understands policy analysis and is determined to get it and make use of it.

The fourth requisite was the existence of planning and planners. Planning was well accepted at the various levels of the Defense Department with the variety of joint service plans, long-range requirement plans, logistical plans, and more. Military and civilians believed in planning, in coping with uncertainty and in specifying some consequences of policy decisions. The problem as the originators of PPBS saw it was to introduce cost considerations into planning; they wanted to stop blue-sky planning and to integrate planning and budgeting. They wanted to use the program budget to bridge the gap between military planners, who cared about requirements but not about resources, and budget people, who were narrowly concerned with financial costs but not necessarily with effective policies.

Policy analysis is expensive in terms of time, talent, and money. It requires a high degree of creativity in order to imagine new policies and to test them out without requiring actual experience. Policy analysis calls for the creation of systems in which elements are linked to one another and to operational indicators so that costs and effectiveness of alternatives may be systematically compared. There is no way of knowing in advance whether the analysis will prove intellectually satisfying and politically feasible. Policy analysis is facilitated when: (a) goals are easily specified, (b) a large margin of error is allowable, and (c) the cost of the contemplated policy makes large expenditures on analysis worthwhile. That part of defense policy dealing with choices among alternative weapons systems was ideally suited for policy analysis. Since the cost of intercontinental missiles or other weapons systems ran into the billions of dollars, it was easy to justify spending millions on analysis.[6] The potential effectiveness of weapons like intercontinental missiles could be contemplated so long as one was willing to accept large margins of error. It is not unusual for analysts to assume extreme cases of damage and vulnerability in a context in which the desire for reducing risk is very great. Hence a goal like assuring sufficient destructive power such that no enemy strike could prevent devastation of one's country may be fuzzy without being unusable. If one accepts a procedure of imagining that possible enemies were to throw three times as much megatonage as intelligence estimates suggest they have, he need not be overly troubled by doubts about the underlying theory. If one is willing to pay the cost of compensating against the worst, lack of knowledge will not matter so much. The point is not that this is an undesirable analytic procedure, quite the contrary, but the extreme cases were allowed to determine the outcomes.

Inertia

The introduction of new procedures that result in new policies is not easy. Inertia is always a problem. Members of the organization and its clientele groups have vested interests in the policies of the past. Efforts at persuasion must be huge and persistent. But there are conditions that facilitate change. One of these is a rising level of appropriations. If change means that things must be taken away from people in the organization without giving them anything in return, greater resistance may be expected. The ability to replace old rewards with larger new ones helps reduce resistance to change. The fact that defense appropriations were increasing at a fast rate made life much easier for Mr. McNamara. The expected objections of clientele groups, for example, were muted by the fact that defense contractors had lots of work, even if it was not exactly what they expected. Rapid organizational growth may also improve the possibilities for change. The sheer increase in organizational size means that many new people can be hired who are not tied to the old ways. And speedy promotion may help convince members that the recommended changes are desirable.

The deeper change goes into the bowels of the organization, the more difficult it is to achieve. The more change can be limited to central management, the greater the possibility for carrying it out. The changes introduced in the Defense Department did not, for the most part, require acceptance at the lower levels. Consider a proposed change in the organization of fighting units that would drastically reduce the traditional heavy support facilities for ground forces. Such a change is not easily manipulated from Washington. But the choice of one weapons system over another is much more amenable to central control. The kinds of problems for which program budgeting was most useful also turned out to be problems that could be dealt with largely at the top of the organization. The program budget group that McNamara established had to fight with generals in Washington but not with master sergeants in supply. Anyone who knows the Army knows what battle they would rather be engaged in fighting.

The ability of an organization to secure rapid change depends, of course, on the degree of its autonomy from the environment. I have argued elsewhere[7] that the President of the United States has much more control over America's foreign policy than over its domestic policy. In almost any area of domestic policy there is a well-entrenched structure of interests. In foreign and defense policy, excluding such essentially internal concerns as the National Guard, the territory within the American political system is not nearly so well defended; there are far fewer political fortifications, mines, and boobytraps.

Personnel

Experienced personnel may be a barrier to change. They know something about the consequences of what they are doing. They may have tried a variety of alternatives and can point to reasons why each one will not work. If I may recall my low-level Army experience (I entered as a private first class and was never once demoted), the usual reply to a question about the efficacy of present practice was, "Have you ever been in combat, son?" But the most dramatic changes introduced in the Pentagon had to do with questions of avoiding or limiting nuclear war, in which no one had a claim to experience and in which the basic purpose of analysis is to make certain that we do not have to learn from experience. If the system fails, the game is over. And since McNamara's men possessed a body of doctrines on defense policy, they had an enormous advantage over regular military who were for a long time unable to defend themselves properly in the new field.[8]

The new policy analysts did not accept the currency of military experience. In their view, naked judgment was not a satisfactory answer to why a policy should be adopted. The Army might know the fire-power of an infantry division, but fire-power was not "effectiveness." Competition among the services for appropriations, however, was favorable to PPBS. There was a defense budget that covered virtually all of the Department's subject matter. There were defense missions in which trade-offs could be made between the services. Resources could actually be diverted if the analysis "proved" a particular service was right. Programs could easily be developed because of the facile identification of program with weapons systems and force units. Once the military learned the jargon, they were willing to play the game for an extra division or carrier. So long as dollar losses in one program were more than made up by gains in another, the pain of policy analysis was considerably eased.

The favorable conditions for the limited use of program budgeting in the Department of Defense do not exist in most domestic agencies. There are no large groups of talented policy analysts expert in agency problems outside of the federal government. These nonexistent men cannot, therefore, be made available to the agencies. (The time has passed when eighth-rate systems engineers in aerospace industries are expected to solve basic social problems overnight.) Most agencies had few planners and even less experience in planning. There is no body of knowledge waiting to be applied to policy areas such as welfare and crime. A basic reason for wanting more policy analysis is to help create knowledge where little now exists. There are only a few agencies in which top managers want systematic policy analysis and are able to understand quantitative studies. Goals are not easily specified for most domestic agencies. Nor do they usually have handy equivalents for programs like expensive weapons stystems. What Thomas Schelling has so pungently observed about the Department of State—it does not control a large part of the budget devoted to foreign policy— is true for the domestic departments and their lack of coverage as well.[9]

Except for a few individual programs like the proposals for income supplements or assessing the desirability of a supersonic transport, the cost of most domestic policies does not rise into the billions of dollars. Congress and interested publics are not disposed to allow large margins of error. Instead of increasing, the availability of federal funds began declining soon after the introduction of program budgeting. A higher level of conflict was inevitable, especially since the acceptance of proposed changes required the acquiescence of all sorts of people and institutions in the far-flung reaches of the agencies. Social workers, city officials, police chiefs, welfare mothers, field officers, and numerous others were involved in the policies. Program budgeting on the domestic side takes place in a context in which there is both less autonomy from the environment and a great deal more first-hand experience by subordinates. On these grounds alone no one should have been surprised that program budgeting in the domestic agencies did not proceed as rapidly or with as much ostensible success as in the Defense Department.[10]

NO ONE CAN DO PPBS

In past writings I argued that program budgeting would run up against severe political difficulties. While most of these arguments have been conceded, I have been told that in a better world, without the vulgar intrusion of political factors (such as the consent of the governed), PPBS would perform its wonders as advertised. Now it is clear that for the narrow purpose of predicting why program budgeting would not work there was no need to mention political problems at all. It would have been sufficient to say that the wholesale introduction of PPBS presented insuperable difficulties of calculation. All the obstacles previously mentioned, such as lack of talent, theory, and data, may be summed up in a single statement: *no one knows how to do program budgeting.* Another way of putting it would be to say that many know what program budgeting should be like in general, but no one knows what it should be in any particular case. Program budgeting cannot be stated in operational terms. There is no agreement on what the words mean, let alone an ability to show another person what should be done. The reason for the difficulty is that telling an agency to adopt program budgeting means telling it to find better policies and there is no formula for doing that. One can (and should) talk about measuring effectiveness, estimating costs, and comparing alternatives, but that is a far cry from being able to take the creative leap of formulating a better policy.

Pattern of Events

On the basis of numerous discussions with would-be practitioners of program budgeting at the federal level, I think I can describe the usual pattern of events. The instructions come down from the Bureau of the Budget. You must have a program budget. Agency personnel hit the panic button. They just do not know how to do what they have been asked to do. They turn, if they can, to the pitifully small band of refugees from the Pentagon who have come to light the way. But these defense intellectuals do not know much about the policy area in which they are working. That takes time. Yet something must quickly come out of all this. So they produce a vast amount of inchoate information characterized by premature quantification of irrelevant items. Neither the agency head nor the examiners in the Bureau of the Budget can comprehend the material submitted to them. Its very bulk inhibits understanding. It is useless to the Director of the Budget in making his decisions. In an effort to be helpful, the program analysis unit at the Budget Bureau says something like, "Nice try, fellows; we appreciate all that effort. But you have not quite got the idea of program budgeting yet. Remember, you must clarify goals, define objectives, relate these to quantitative indicators, project costs into the future. Please send a new submission based on this understanding."

Another furious effort takes place. They do it in Defense, so it must be possible. Incredible amounts of overtime are put in. Ultimately, under severe time pressure, even more data is accumulated. No one will be able to say that agency personnel did not try hard. The new presentation makes a little more sense to some people and a little less to others. It just does not hang together as a presentation of agency policies. There are more encouraging words from the Budget Bureau and another sermon about specifying alternative ways of meeting agency objectives, though not, of course, taking the old objectives for granted. By this time agency personnel are desperate. "We would love to do it," they say, "but we cannot figure out the right way. You experts in the Budget Bureau should show us how to do it." Silence. The word from on high is that the Bureau of the Budget does not interfere with agency operations; it is the agency's task to set up its own budget. After a while, cynicism reigns supreme.

PPBS must be tremendously inefficient. It resembles nothing so much as a Rube Goldberg apparatus in which the operations performed bear little relation to the output achieved. The data inputs into PPBS are huge and its policy output is tiny. All over the federal government the story is the same: if you ask what good has PPBS done, those who have something favorable to say invariably cite the same one or two policy analyses. At one time I began to wonder if the oil shale study[11] in the Interior Department and the maternal and child health care program[12] in Health, Education, and Welfare were all that had ever come out of the programming effort.

The orders to expand PPBS did not say, "Let us do more policy

analysis than we have in the past." What it said was, "Let us make
believe we can do policy analysis on everything." Instead of focusing attention on areas of policy amenable to study, the PPBS apparatus requires information on *all* agency policies.

Program Structure

The fixation on program structure is the most pernicious aspect
of PPBS. Once PPBS is adopted, it becomes necessary to have a
program structure that provides a complete list of organization objectives and supplies information on the attainment of each one. In
the absence of analytic studies for all or even a large part of an
agency's operations, the structure turns out to be a sham that piles
up meaningless data under vague categories.[13] It hides rather than
clarifies. It suggests comparisons among categories for which there
is no factual or analytical basis. Examination of a department's program structure convinces everyone acquainted with it that policy
analysis is just another bad way of masquerading behind old confusions. A mere recitation of some program categories from the Department of Agriculture—Communities of Tomorrow, Science in
the Service of Man, Expanding Dimensions for Living—makes the
point better than any comment.

Even if the agency head does understand a data-reduction-sum-
marization of the program budget, he still cannot use the structure
to make decisions, because it is too hard to adjust the elaborate
apparatus. Although the system dredges up information under numerous headings, it says next to nothing about the impact of one
program on another. There is data but no causal analysis. Hence the
agency head is at once oversupplied with masses of numbers and
undersupplied with propositions about the impact of any action he
might undertake. He cannot tell, because no one knows, what the
marginal change he is considering would mean for the rest of his
operation. Incremental changes at the Bureau of the Budget at the
agency level are made in terms of the old budget categories. Since
the program structure is meant to be part of the budget, however,
it must be taken as a statement of current policy and it necessarily
emerges as a product of organizational compromise. The program
structure, therefore, does not embody a focus on central policy
concerns. More likely, it is a haphazard arrangement that reflects
the desire to manipulate external support and to pursue internal
power aspirations. Being neither program nor budget, program
structure is useless. It is the Potemkin Village of modern administration. The fact that generating bits of random data for the program structure takes valuable time away from more constructive

concerns also harms policy analysis. The whole point of policy analysis is to show that what had been done intuitively in the past may be done better through sustained application of intelligence. The adoption of meaningless program structures, and their perversion into slogans for supporting existing policies, does not—to say the least—advance the cause of policy analysis.

Gorham Testimony

I do not mean to suggest that the introduction of PPBS has not led to some accomplishments. Before we consider the significance of these accomplishments, however, it is essential that we understand what PPBS has manifestly *not* done. One could hardly have a better witness on this subject than William Gorham, formerly Assistant Secretary (Program Coordination), Department of Health, Education, and Welfare, and now head of the Urban Institute, who is widely acknowledged to be an outstanding practitioner of program budgeting.

At the highest level of generality, it is clear that PPBS does not help in making choices between vast national goals such as health and defense, nor is PPBS useful in making tradeoffs between more closely related areas of policy such as health, education, and welfare. In his testimony before the Joint Economic Committee, Gorham put the matter bluntly:

Let me hasten to point out that we have not attempted any grandiose cost-benefit analysis designed to reveal whether the total benefits from an additional million dollars spent on health programs would be higher or lower than that from an additional million spent on education or welfare. If I was ever naïve enough to think this sort of analysis possible, I no longer am. The benefits of health, education, and welfare programs are diverse and often intangible. They affect different age groups and different regions of the population—over different periods of time. No amount of analysis is going to tell us whether the Nation benefits more from sending a slum child to pre-school, providing medical care to an old man or enabling a disabled housewife to resume her normal activities. The "grand decisions" —how much health, how much education, how much welfare, and which groups in the population shall benefit—are questions of value judgments and politics. The analyst cannot make much contribution to their resolution.[14]

It turns out that it is extremely difficult to get consensus on goals within a single area of policy. As a result, the policy analysts attempt to find objectives that are more clearly operational and more widely acceptable. Gorham speaks with the voice of experience when he says:

Let me give you an example. Education. What we want our kids to be as a result of going to school is the level of objective which is the proper and the broadest one. But we want our children to be different sorts of people. We want them to be capable of different sorts of things. We have, in other words, a plurality of opinions about what we want our schools to turn out. So you drop down a level and you talk about objectives in terms of educational attainment—years of school completed and certain objective measures of quality. Here you move in education from sort of fuzzy objectives, but very important, about what it is that you want the schools to be doing, to the more concrete, less controversial, more easily to get agreed upon objectives having to do with such things as educational attainment, percentage of children going to college, etc.

I think the same thing is true in health and in social services, that at the very highest level objective, where in theory you would really like to say something, the difficulty of getting and finding a national consensus is so great that you drop down to something which is more easily and readily accepted as objectives.[15]

What can actually be done, according to Gorham, are analytic studies of narrowly defined areas of policy. "The less grand decisions," Gorham testified, "those among alternative programs with the same or similar objectives within health—can be substantially illuminated by good analysis. It is this type of analysis which we have undertaken at the Department of Health, Education, and Welfare."[16] Gorham gives as examples disease control programs and improvements in the health of children. If this type of project analysis is what can be done under PPBS, a serious question is raised: Why go through all the rigamarole in order to accomplish a few discrete studies of important problems?

A five-year budget conceived in the hodge-podge terms of the program structure serves no purpose.[17] Since actual budget decisions are made in terms of the old categories and policy analysis may take place outside of the program structure, there is no need to institutionalize empty labels. If a policy analysis has been completed, there is no reason why it cannot be submitted as part of the justification of estimates to the Bureau of the Budget and to Congress. For the few program memoranda that an agency might submit, changes could be detailed in terms of traditional budget categories. Problems of program structure would be turned over to the agency's policy analysts who would experiment with different ways of lending intellectual coherence to the agency's programs. There would be no need to foist the latest failure on a skeptical world. Nor would there be battles over the costs of altering a program structure that has achieved, if not a common framework, at least the virtue of familiarity. The difference is that stability of categories in the traditional budget has real value for control[18] while the embodiment of contradictions in the program structure violates its essential purpose.

INCENTIVES FOR POLICY ANALYSIS

PPBS discredits policy analysis. To collect vast amounts of random data is hardly a serious analysis of public policy. The conclusion is obvious. The shotgun marriage between policy analysis and budgeting should be annulled. Attempts to describe the total agency program in program memoranda should be abandoned. It is hard enough to do a good job of policy analysis, as most agency people now realize, without having to meet arbitrary and fixed deadlines imposed by the budget process.[19] There is no way of telling whether an analysis will be successful. There is, therefore, no point in insisting that half-baked analyses be submitted every year because of a misguided desire to cover the entire agency program. The Budget Bureau itself has recently recognized the difficulty by requiring agencies to present extensive memoranda only when major policy issues have been identified. It is easier and more honest just to take the program structure out of the budget.

The thrust of the argument thus far, however, forces us to confront a major difficulty. Policy analysis and budgeting were presumably connected in order to see that high quality analysis did not languish in limbo but was translated into action through the critical budget process. Removing policy analysis from the annual budget cycle might increase its intellectual content at the expense of its practical impact. While formal program structures should go —PPBS actually inhibits the prospects for obtaining good analysis that is worth translating into public policy—they should be replaced with a strong incentive to make policy analysis count in yearly budgetary decisions. I am therefore proposing a substitute for PPBS that maintains whatever incentive it provided for introducing the results of policy analysis into the real world without encouraging the debilitating effects.

The submission of program memoranda supported by policy analysis should be made a requirement for major dollar changes in an agency's budget. The Bureau of the Budget should insist that this requirement be met by every agency. Agency heads, therefore, would have to require it of subunits. The sequence could operate as follows:

1. Secretary of agency and top policy analysts review major

issues and legislation and set up a study menu for several years. Additions and deletions are made periodically.

2. Policy analysts set up studies which take anywhere from six to 24 months.

3. As a study is completed for a major issue area, it is submitted to the Secretary of the agency for review and approval.

4. If approved, the implications of the study's recommendations are translated into budgetary terms for submission as a program memorandum in support of the agency's fiscal year budget.

No one imagines that a mechanical requirement would in and of itself compel serious consideration of policy matters. No procedure should be reified as if it had a life of its own apart from the people who must implement it. This conclusion is as true for my suggestion as for PPBS. We must therefore consider ways and means of increasing the demand for and supply of policy analysis.

Increasing Demand and Supply

The first requirement of effective policy analysis is that top management want it. No matter how trite this criterion sounds, it has often been violated, as Frederick C. Mosher's splendid study of program budgeting in foreign affairs reveals.[20] The inevitable difficulties of shaking loose information and breaking up old habits will prove to be insuperable obstacles without steady support from high agency officials. If they do not want it, the best thing to do is concentrate efforts in another agency. Placing the best people in a few agencies also makes it more likely that a critical mass of talent will be able to achieve a creative response to emerging policy problems.

Policy analysis should be geared to the direct requirements of top management. This means that analysis should be limited to a few major issues. Since there will only be a few studies every year, the Secretary should have time to consider and understand each one. The analytical staff should be flexible enough to work on his priority interests. Consequently, one of the arguments by which program budgeting has been oversold has to be abandoned. Policy analysis will not normally identify programs of low priority. Top management is not interested in them. They would receive no benefit from getting supporters of these programs angry at them. Instead, agency heads want to know how to deal with emergent problems. Practitioners of policy analysis understand these considerations quite well. Harry Shooshan, Deputy Undersecretary for Programs, Department of the Interior, presents a perceptive analysis:

... We have tried to more heavily relate our PPB work and our analytical work to the new program thrusts, and major issues, not because it is easier to talk about new programs, but rather, there is a good question of judgment, on how much time one should spend on ongoing programs that are pretty well set. So you restate its mission and you put it in PPB wrapping and what have you really accomplished?

There are going to be new program proposals, new thrusts of doing something in certain areas. Let's relate our analyses to that and get the alternatives documented as well as we can for the decision-makers. So it is a combination of on the one hand it being difficult to identify low priorities in a manner that really means something and on the other hand, it is the fact of what have we really accomplished by simply putting old programs in new wrappings when new programs really should get the emphasis right now in terms of what are the decisions now before, in my case, the Secretary of the Interior, in terms of what should he know before he makes decisions relative to where he is attempting to go. If I can relate PPB to the decision on his desk today and the near future, I can sell him and in turn, our own Department on the contribution that we can make.[21]

The implications of Shooshan's point go beyond making policy analysis more desirable by having it meet the needs of top management. The subjects for policy analysis ought to be chosen precisely for their critical-fluid-emergent character. These are the places where society is hurting. These are the areas in which there are opportunities for marginal gains. Indeed, a major role for top management is scanning the political horizon for targets of opportunity. Yet the characteristics of these new problems run counter to the criteria for selection that PPBS currently enforces, since they are identified by ambiguity concerning goals, lack of data upon which to project accurate estimates of costs and consequences, and pervasive uncertainty concerning the range of possible changes in program.

There would be a much larger demand for policy analysis if it were supplied in ways that would meet the needs of high level officials. Let us consider the example of the President of the United States. He can certainly use policy analysis to help make better decisions. Substantial policy studies would give him and his staff leverage against the bureaucracy. Knowledge is power. Indeed, command of a particular field would enable Presidents to exert greater control over the agenda for public decision and would give them advantages in competition with all sorts of rivals. Presidents could use perhaps a dozen major policy studies per year of their most immediate concerns. If even a few of these turn out well, the President may be motivated to make use of them. Contrast this with the present inundation of the Executive Office by endless

streams of program "books," summaries, and memoranda that no-
body ever looks at.

What is true of the President is also true for important executives
in the agencies. Policy-oriented executives will want to get better
analysis. Executives wishing to increase their resource base will be
interested in independent sources of information and advice. Those
who would exert power need objectives to fight for. It is neither
fashionable nor efficient to appear to seek power for its own sake.
In polite society the drive is masked and given a noble face when
it can be attached to grand policy concerns that bring benefits to
others as well as to power seekers. The way to gain the attention
of leaders is not to flood them with trivia but to provide examples
of the best kind of work that can be done. The last years of the
Johnson Administration witnessed a proliferation of secret commis-
sions to recommend new policies. The department secretary often
became just another special pleader. If they have any interest in
curbing this development, secretaries may find that producing their
own policy analyses allow them to say that outside intervention is
not the only or the best way to generate new policies.

Congressional Demand

If strategically located Congressmen demanded more policy analysis, there is little doubt that we would get it. What can be done
to make them want more of it? The answer does not lie in surrounding them with large staffs so that they lose their manifestly political
functions and become more like bureaucrats. Nor does the answer
lie in telling Congressmen to keep away from small administrative
questions in favor of larger policy concerns. For many Congressmen
get into the larger questions only by feeling their way through the
smaller details.[22] A threat to deprive Congressmen of the traditional
line-item appropriations data through which they exert their control of agency affairs also does not appear to be a good way of
making Congressmen desire policy analysis.

Policy analysis must be made relevant to what Congressmen
want. Some legislators desire to sponsor new policies and they are
one clientele for analysis. For other Congressmen, however, policy
is a bargainable product that emerges from their interactions with
their fellows. These members must be appealed to in a different
way. They often have a sense of institutional loyalty and pride.
They know that Congress is a rare institution in this world—a legislative body that actually has some control over public policy. They
are aware that the development of new knowledge and new techniques may freeze them out of many of the more serious decisions.

Policy analysis should be proposed to these men as an enhancement of the power of Congress as an institution. The purpose of analysis would be, in its simplest form, to enable Congressmen to ask good questions and to evaluate answers. Oftentimes it is hardest for a layman to recognize the significant questions implicit in an area of policy. Are there other and better questions to be asked, other and better policies to be pursued?

A Congress that takes seriously its policy role should be encouraged to contract for policy analysis that would stress different views of what the critical questions are in a particular area of policy. Each major committee or subcommittee should be encouraged to hire a man trained in policy analysis for a limited period, perhaps two years. His task would be to solicit policy studies, evaluate presentations made by government agencies, and keep Congressmen informed about what are considered the important questions. In the past, chairmen have not always paid attention to the quality of committee staffs. Following the lead of the Joint Economic Committee, seminars might be held for a couple of weeks before each session. At these seminars discussions would take place between agency personnel, committee staff, and the academics or other experts who have produced the latest policy analysis. If all went well, Congressmen would emerge with a better idea of the range of issues and of somewhat different ways of tackling the problems, and the policy analysts would emerge with a better grasp of the priorities of these legislators.

Suppliers of Policy Analysis

Thus far we have dealt solely with the incentive structure of the consumers who ought to want policy analysis—agency heads, Presidents, Congressmen. Little has been said about the incentive structure of the suppliers who ought to provide it—analysts, consultants, academics. Our premise has been that the supply of policy analysis would be a function of the demand. Now, the relationships between supply and demand have long been troublesome in economics because it is so difficult to sort out the mutual interactions. Upon being asked whether demand created supply or supply created demand, the great economist Marshall was reported to have said that it was like asking which blade of the scissors cuts the paper. There is no doubt, however, that changes in the conditions and quality of supply would have important effects on the demand for policy analysis.

Disengaging policy analysis from PPBS would help build the supply of policy analysis by:

1. Decreasing the rewards for mindless quantification for its own sake. There would be no requests from the Bureau of the Budget for such information and no premium for supplying it.

2. Increasing the rewards for analysts who might try the risky business of tackling a major policy problem that was obviously not going to be considered because everyone was too busy playing with the program structure. Gresham's Law operates here: programmed work drives out unprogrammed activity, make-work drives out analysis.

One way of increasing the supply of policy analysis would be to improve the training of people who work directly in the various areas of policy. Instead of taking people trained in policy analysis and having them learn about a particular policy area, the people in that area would be capable of doing policy analysis. Three-day or three-month courses will not do for that purpose. A year, and possibly two years, would be required. Since it is unlikely that the best people can be made available for so long a period, it is necessary to think in terms of education at an earlier period in their lives. There is a great need for schools of public policy in which technical training is combined with broader views of the social context of public policy. Although no one knows how to teach "creativity," it is possible to expose students to the range of subjects out of which a creative approach to public policy could come.

Another way of increasing the supply of policy analysis would be to locate it in an organizational context in which it has prestige and its practitioners are given time to do good work. Having the policy analysis unit report directly to the secretary or agency head would show that it is meant to be taken seriously.[23] But then it is bound to get involved in day-to-day concerns of the agency head, thus creating a classic dilemma.

Tactics

The effective use of a policy analysis unit cannot be specified in advance for all agencies. There are certain tensions in its functions that may be mitigated on a case-by-case basis but cannot be resolved once and for all. Serious policy analysis requires months, if not years, of effort. A unit that spends its time solely on substantial policy analysis would soon find itself isolated from the operational concerns of the agency. There would be inordinate temptations on the part of its members to go where the action is. Before long, the policy unit might become more immediately relevant at the expense of its long-term impact. The frantic nature of day-to-day emergencies drives out the necessary time and quiet for serious study and reflection. What can be done? One tactic is for the policy unit to consider itself an educational as well as an action group. Its task should be to encourage analysis on the part of other elements of the organization. It should undertake nothing it can get subunits to do. The role of the policy unit would then be one of advising subunits and evaluating their output.

A second tactic would be to contract out for studies that are expected to take the longest period of time. The third tactic is the most difficult, because it calls for a balancing act. Immediate usefulness to top management may be secured by working on problems with short lead times while attempting to retain perhaps half of the available time for genuine policy analysis. To the degree that serious policy analysis enters into the life of the organization and proves its worth, it will be easier to justify its requirements in terms of release from everyday concerns. Yet the demand for services of the analysts is certain to increase. Failures in policy analysis, on the other hand, are likely to give the personnel involved more time for reflection than they would prefer. Like headquarters-field relationships, line and staff responsibilities, and functional versus hierarchical command, the problems of the policy unit are inherent in its situation and can only be temporarily resolved.

These comments on incentives for increasing the supply and demand for policy analysis are plainly inadequate. They are meant merely to suggest that there is a problem and to indicate how one might go about resolving it. We do not really know how to make policy analysis fit in with the career requirements of Congressmen, nor can we contribute much beside proverbial wisdom to the structure and operation of policy analysis units. There are, however, opportunities for learning that have not yet been used. One of the benefits flowing from the experience with PPBS is that it has thrown up a small number of policy analyses that practitioners consider to be good. We need to know what makes some live in the world and others remain unused. Aside from an impressive manuscript by Clay Thomas Whitehead,[24] however, in which two recent policy analyses in defense are studied, there has been no effort to determine what this experience has to teach us. Despite the confident talk about policy analysis (here and elsewhere), a great deal of work remains to be done on what is considered "good" and why. The pioneering work by Charles E. Lindblom should not be wrongly interpreted as being anti-analysis, but as a seminal effort to understand what we do when we try to grapple with social problems.

Reexamination

Critical aspects of policy analysis need to be reexamined. The field cries out for a study of "coordination" as profound and subtle as Martin Landau's forthcoming essay on "Redundancy."[25] That most elemental problem of political theory—the proper role of the government versus that of the individual—should be subject to a radical critique.[26] The fact that cost-benefit analysis began with water resource projects in which the contribution to national income was the key question has guided thought away from other areas of policy for which this criterion would be inappropriate. There are policies for which the willingness of citizens to support the activity should help determine the outcome. There are other policies in which presently unquantifiable benefits, like pleasure in seeing others better off or reduction of anxiety following a visible decrease in social hostility, should be controlling. Although social invention is incredibly difficult, the way is open for new concepts of the role of government to liberate our thoughts and guide our actions.

In many ways the times are propitious for policy analysis. The New Deal era of legislation has ended and has not yet been replaced by a stable structure of issues. People do not know where they stand today in the same way they knew how they felt about Medicare or private versus public electric power. The old welfare state policies have disenchanted former supporters as well as further enraged their opponents. Men have worked for 20 years to get massive education bills through Congress only to discover that the results have not lived up to their expectations; it takes a lot more to improve education for the deprived than anyone had thought. There is now a receptivity to new ideas that did not exist a decade ago. There is a willingness to consider new policies and try new ways. Whether or not there is sufficient creativity in us to devise better policies remains to be seen. If we are serious about improving public policy, we will go beyond the fashionable pretense of PPBS to show others what the best policy analysis can achieve.

NOTES

[1] Robert N. Anthony, *Planning and Control Systems: A Framework for Analysis,* (Boston: Harvard University Press, 1965), p. 16.

[2] Aaron Wildavsky, "The Political Economy of Efficiency," PUBLIC ADMINISTRATION REVIEW, Vol. XXVI, No. 4, December 1966, pp. 298-302.

[3] Yehezkel Dror, "Policy Analysts: A New Professional Role in Government

Service,"PUBLIC ADMINISTRATION REVIEW, Vol. XXVII, No. 3, September 1967, pp. 200-201. See also Dror's major work, *Public Policy-Making Reexamined* (San Francisco: Chandler, 1968).

[4] Aaron Wildavsky, *op. cit.*

[5] See David Novick, "Origin and History of Program Budgeting," The RAND Corporation, October 1966, p. 3427.

[6] I once tried to interest a graduate student who had experience with defense problems in doing research in the City of Oakland. He asked the size of Oakland's budget. "Fifty million dollars," I said. "Why, in the Air Force we used to round to that figure," was his reply.

[7] Aaron Wildavsky, "The Two Presidencies," *Trans-action,* Vol. IV, No. 2, December 1966, pp. 7-14.

[8] For further argument along these lines see my article, "The Practical Consequences of the Theoretical Study of Defense Policy," PUBLIC ADMINISTRATION REVIEW, Vol. XXV, No. 1, March 1965, pp. 90-103.

[9] Thomas C. Schelling, "PPBS and Foreign Affairs," memorandum prepared at the request of the Subcommittee on National Security and International Operations of the Committee on Government Operations, U. S. Senate, 90th Congress, First Session, 1968.

[10] Dr. Alain Enthoven, who played a leading role in introducing systems analysis to the Defense Department, has observed that: "The major changes in strategy, the step-up in production of Minutemen and Polaris and the build-up in our non-nuclear forces including the increase in the Army, the tactical air forces, and the air lift . . . were being phased in at the same time that PPBS was being phased in. . . . We speeded up the Polaris and Minuteman programs because we believed that it was terribly important to have an invulnerable retaliatory force. We built up the Army Land Forces because we believed it was necessary to have more land forces for limited non-nuclear wars. We speeded up the development of anti-guerrilla forces or special forces because we believed that was necessary for counter-insurgency. Those things would have happened with or without PPBS. PPBS does not make the strategy." Subcommittee on National Security and International Operations of the Committee on Government Operations, U. S. Senate, *Hearings, Planning-Programming-Budgeting,* 90th Congress, First Session, Part 2, Sept. 27 and Oct. 18, 1967, p. 141.

[11] *Prospects For Oil Shale Development* (Washington, D.C.: Department of the Interior, May 1968).

[12] The study is presented in *ibid.,*pp. 10-45.

[13] Similar difficulties under similar conditions evidently occur in the business world. It is worth citing Anthony's comments: "Strategic planning [that is, policy analysis] is essentially *irregular*. Problems, opportunities, and 'bright ideas' do not arise according to some set timetable; they have to be dealt with whenever they happen to be perceived. . . . Failure to appreciate the distinction between regular and irregular processes can result in trouble of the following type. A company with a well-developed

budgeting process decides to formalize its strategic planning. It prepares a set of forms and accompanying procedures, and has the operating units submit their long-range plans on these forms on one certain date each year. The plans are then supposed to be reviewed and approved in a meeting similar to a budget review meeting. Such a procedure does not work. . . . There simply is not time enough in an annual review meeting for a careful consideration of a whole batch of strategic proposals. . . . It is important that next year's operating budget be examined and approved as an entity so as to ensure that the several pieces are consonant with one another. . . . Except for very general checklists of essential considerations, the strategic planning process follows no prescribed format or timetable. Each problem is sufficiently different from other problems so that each must be approached differently." *Planning and Control Systems, op. cit.,* pp. 38-39.

[14]Joint Economic Committee, Congress of the Unites States, *Hearings, The Planning, Programming-Budgeting System: Progress and Potentials,* 90th Congress, First Session, September 1967. p. 5.

[15] *Ibid.,* pp. 80-81. One might think that a way out of the dilemma could be had by adopting a number of goals for an area of policy. When Committee Chairman William Proxmire suggested that more goals should be specified, Gorham replied, "I would like to be the one to give the first goal. The first one in is always in the best shape. The more goals you have, essentially the less useful any one is, because the conflict among them becomes so sharp" (p. 83).

[16] *Ibid.,* p. 6.

[17]Anthony again supplies a useful comparison from private firms that makes a similar point: "An increasing number of businesses make profit and balance sheet projections for several years ahead, a process which has come to be known by the name 'long-range planning.' . . . A five-year plan usually is a projection of the costs and revenues that are anticipated under policies and programs *already approved,* rather than a device for consideration of, and decision on, new policies and programs. The five-year plan reflects strategic decisions already taken; it is not the essence of the process of making new decisions. . . . In some companies, the so-called five-year plan is nothing more than a mechanical extrapolation of current data, with no reflection of management decisions and judgment; such an exercise is virtually worthless" *(Planning and Control Systems, op. cit.,* pp. 57-58).

[18]An excellent discussion of different purposes of budgeting and stages of budgetary development is found in Allen Schick, "The Road to PPB: The Stages of Budget Reform," PUBLIC ADMINISTRATION REVIEW, Vol. XXVI, No. 4, December 1966, pp. 243-258.

[19]In another paper ("Toward A Radical Incrementalism," *op. cit.)* I have proposed that policy analysis would be faciliated by abolishing the annual budget cycle. One of the great weaknesses of governmental policy making is that policies are formulated a good two years before funds

become available. Given the difficulties of devising policies in the first place, the time lag wreaks havoc with the best analysis. Since no one seems disposed to consider this alternative seriously, I mention it merely in passing as a change that would fit in with what has been suggested.

[20]Frederick C. Mosher, "Program Budgeting in Foreign Affairs: Some Reflections," memorandum prepared at the request of the Subcommittee on National Security and International Operations of the Committee on Government Operations, U.S. Senate, 90th Congress, Second Session, 1968.

[21] *Hearings, The Planning-Programming-Budgeting System: Progress and Potentials, op. cit.,* pp. 77-78.

[22]"Toward A Radical Incrementalism," *op. cit.,* pp. 27-29.

[23]When Charles Hitch was Controller of the Defense Department, the policy analysis unit reported directly to him, as did the budget unit. One reported result is that the policy unit was able to do its work without being drawn into the daily concerns of the budget men. When policy analysis (called systems analysis) was given separate status, with its own assistant secretary, there was apparently a much greater tendency for its members to insist upon control of immediate budgetary decisions. Hence the distinction between longer-run policy analysis and shorter-run budgeting tended to be obscured. It would be interesting to know whether the participants saw it in this way. Optimal placement of a policy analysis unit is bound to be a source of difficulty and a subject of controversy.

[24]Clay Thomas Whitehead, "Uses and Abuses of Systems Analysis," The RAND Corporation, September 1967.

[25]See Martin Landau, "Redundancy," PUBLIC ADMINISTRATION REVIEW, scheduled for publication in Volume XXIX, No. 4, July/August 1969.

[26]For a fine example of original thought on this question, see Paul Feldman, "Benefits and the Role of Government in a Market Economy," Institute For Defense Analysis, Research Paper, February 1968, p. 477.

14

EDUCATION IN THE PROGRAM BUDGET

by Werner Z. Hirsch

Werner Z. Hirsch makes a venturesome foray into applying PPBS to the Federal education budget. He indicates that the existing budget is tucked away in 42 separate departments and agencies and, consequently, the development of a coherent policy is made extremely difficult. Hirsch raises questions of particular cogency for the 1970's, as for example, whether too much money is spent on defense and not enough on education.

KEY EDUCATION OBJECTIVES AND DECISIONS

The basic education questions calling for decisions by government officials (and citizens) are as follows: What knowledge and skills should be developed; when, where, how, by whom, and for whom? That is to say, in a given year what kind of education should be offered for how many students, by how many teachers (and support personnel), with what background and training, and in what facilities? In addition, there is the issue of who should pay for the education. A proper answer to this last problem requires tax incidence considerations.

Werner Z. Hirsch, "Education in the Program Budget," pp. 180-204. Reprinted by permission of the publishers from David Novick, editor, *Program Budgeting.* Cambridge, Mass.: Harvard University Press, Copyright, 1967, by The RAND Corporation.

In clarifying these questions, it is important to be aware of this nation's traditional heritage. First, in the United States we make free primary and secondary education available to every American, and free higher education to most of those who have the ability to benefit from it. Second, the United States operates under a federated political and fiscal system. Both issues reflect our basic philosophy of life and at the same time provide a setting within which education decisions must be made.

We must now take a look at the nation's main educational objectives. Clearly, the creation of human capital is of great national concern. In this respect, education is an investment designed to produce an enterprising and skilled labor force that can be counted on to contribute to economic growth, prosperity, technological advances, and national security. Education enables people to hold rewarding jobs and in turn provides the nation with economic and military strength. Another important objective is to provide students (and perhaps indirectly their parents) with the joy and satisfaction of learning (current benefits associated with the consumption portion of education). A further objective is to preserve and enlarge the cultural heritage of the country and to strengthen its democratic institutions.

For a theoretical approach, let us consider a hypothetical country with a monolithic government, in which the education ministry can take far-reaching steps affecting education. Although the head of state together with the legislature must decide on the overall investment level of the country, the education ministry makes recommendations about the level of investment in education. Priorities must be established and decisions made about how much money and skilled manpower of different types is to be allocated to primary, secondary, higher, and adult education, respectively. The education industry disseminates accumulated knowledge for the use of individuals, and this knowledge pool must constantly be enlarged with additional knowledge. This is done through fundamental and applied research, which competes with education for personnel and funds. Although the allocation of scarce resources among education and research calls for difficult decisions, further priorities might have to be established among knowledge areas. Under a centralized fiscal system, the major funding issue relates only to the allocation of financial burdens to the various income levels of the population.

In our own federated fiscal system it should be clear that we, too, face all these decisions as well as others. For example, the launching of the first Sputnik persuaded the U.S. government to offer

financial support to education in science and engineering, and to
this day a hot debate is in progress about the wisdom of the step.
The federal government plays only a minor role in directly financing education. Nevertheless, it is in its power to be a catalyst and
bring about adjustments. Federal funds not only must support education but also must induce state and local governments to exert
greater efforts and possibly bring about improvements in their
teaching methods and curricula as well as in financing methods.
Major decisions must be made about the local, state, and federal
role in financing different education programs, and criteria are
necessary to facilitate these decisions. Before purposeful changes
can be discussed, an understanding of educational activities and
the existing budget is needed.

THE EXISTING FEDERAL EDUCATION BUDGET

To review the existing federal education budget, we must examine not only the budget of the U.S. Office of Education but also the
budgets of the other agencies that receive education funds. This
summary will be followed by examples showing how the existing
budget format and budgeting process fail to elucidate key education decisions.

In *The Budget of the United States for the Fiscal Year Ending June
30, 1965*,[1] funds for education are dispersed through more than
forty agencies. The administrative education budget in this document is reproduced in Table 1. It suffers from serious shortcomings,
which will be discussed below in detail.

Although Section VI of the *1965 Budget* contains special analyses
of certain programs (e.g., health, research and development), no
such effort has been made in connection with education. Therefore, we are forced to undertake a separate examination of each
agency.

First let us consider the U.S. Office of Education. Its 1963 expenditure budget is summarized in Table 2. However, it should be
realized that this office's expenditures of $624 million are only
about one-fifth of the total federal education budget.

The Vocational Rehabilitation Administration of the Department
of Health, Education, and Welfare spent in FY 1963 $98 million, of
which $71 million was given for grants to states, $24 million for
research and training in the United States, $2 million for research
and training abroad under a special foreign currency program, and
$2.5 million for salaries and expenses.

The 1165-page *1965 Budget Appendix*[2] provides nine pages of

TABLE 1

Administrative Federal Education Budget: Fiscal Years 1963, 1964, and 1965 (in Millions of Dollars)

Program or Agency	Payments to the Public			Recommended new Obligational Authority for 1965
	1963 Actual	1964 Estimate	1965 Estimate	
Administrative budget funds				
Assistance for elementary and secondary education:				
Schools in federally impacted areas	343	350	395	418
Defense education: science, mathematics, foreign language instruction, guidance and testing	49	61	76	84
Assistance for higher education:				
Construction of academic facilities	—	3	38	464
College housing loans	284	223	208	300
Defense education: student loans, fellowships, language and area centers	116	149	162	165
Land-grant colleges, Howard University, Gallaudet College	28	30	33	28
Assistance to National Science Foundation:				
Basic research and specialized research facilities	106	132	148	224
Grants for institutional science programs	31	37	58	98
Science education	51	70	74	137
Other science activities	18	21	22	29
Other aids to education:				
Vocational education	55	73	127	205
Other defense education assistance	20	24	23	23
Indian education services	78	84	92	97
Library of Congress and Smithsonian Institution	38	48	51	45
Other	27	41	65	79
Proposed education legislation	—	3	118	718
Subtotal, administrative budget	1,244	1,348	1,691	3,115°
Trust funds	2	2	2	2°
Intragovernmental transactions and other adjustments (deduct)	33	48	52	
Total	1,214	1,302	1,641	

Source: *The Budget of the United States Government for the Fiscal Year Ending June 30, 1965*, (Washington, D.C.: U.S. Government Printing Office, 1964), p. 120.

° Compares with new obligational authority for 1963 and 1964 as follows: Administrative budget funds: 1963, $1,420 million; 1964, $1,888 million; Trust funds: 1963, $2 million; 1964, $2 million.

detail on the Office of Education and the Vocational Rehabilitation Administration. For example, Tables 3 and 4 are given in support of item 4 in Table 2, "Payments to school districts." Payments to school districts for the maintenance and operation of schools are made under the Act of September 30, 1950. They are to assist in the maintenance and operation of schools in areas where enrollments are affected by federal activities. Such payments are made principally to school districts; however, where such districts cannot assume responsibility for educating children of parents connected with the federal government, payments are made to other federal agencies for the provision of such education under federal auspices. Also, under certain circumstances the Commissioner of Education can make arrangements for the provision of free public education for children of members of the Armed Forces on active duty who are not residing on federal property.

Payments are made to more than 4000 eligible school districts and federal agencies on account of the attendance of approximately 2 million children of parents connected with the federal government in all states, Puerto Rico, Virgin Islands, Guam, and Wake Island.

Table 3 summarizes payments to school districts by programs (as the term is used in *1965 Budget)* and their financing, and Table 4 presents the data by object classification.

A careful analysis of the rest of the budget of the Department of Health, Education, and Welfare reveals further major education funds in the National Institutes of Health and the Public Health Service. The former agency supports faculty directly through research career awards and indirectly through research grants and facility and equipment grants. It supports students through pre- and post-doctoral fellowships and training grants. The education support of this agency was in excess of a quarter of a billion dollars in FY 1963, while that of the rest of the Public Health Service was about $20 million.

The Department of Defense spent more than $100 million to provide education for military personnel in Defense Department schools. More than $160 million was spent on education in civilian institutions, e.g., Army, Navy, and Air Force ROTC. A further $200 million was granted to universities for the support of research.

The National Science Foundation had a $200 million budget, most of it devoted to the support of education. The Veterans Administration had an education budget of about $150 million for readjustment training, vocational rehabilitation, and war orphan scholarships. Many other federal departments supported education

TABLE 2

FY 1963 Expenditure Budget of the U.S. Office of Education (in Thousands of Dollars)

Category	Amount
General and special funds	
Expansion and improvement of vocational education	34,330
Further endowment of colleges of agriculture and the mechanic arts	11,950
Grants for library services	7,257
Payments to school districts	276,869
Assistance for school construction	66,242
Defense educational activities:	
Assistance for elementary and secondary education	48,690
Assistance for higher education	116,476
Other aids to education	33,169
Expansion of teaching in education of mentally retarded children	960
Expansion of teaching in education of the deaf	1,383
Cooperative research	5,015
Educational research (special foreign currency program)	20
Salaries and expenses	12,041
Colleges of agriculture and the mechanic arts (permanent)	2,550
Promotion of vocational education, Education Act of February 23, 1917	7,144
Intragovernmental fund	— 392
Total	623,705

Source: 1965 Budget, pp. 218-221.

TABLE 3

Payments to School Districts by Programs and Financing (in Thousands of Dollars)

Payments	1963 Actual	1964 Estimate	1965 Estimate
Program by activities			
Payments to local educational agencies	260,477	86,966	339,950
Payments to other federal agencies	17,793	17,500	19,500
Total program costs funded— obligations	274,270	104,466	359,450
Financing			
Unobligated balance brought forward	—367	—217	—
Recovery of prior year obligations	—7,749	—	—
Unobligated balance carried forward	217	—	—
Unobligated balance lapsing	15,951	217	—
New obligational authority (appropriation)	282,322	104,466	359,450

Source: Appendix: The Budget of the United States Government for the Fiscal Year Ending June 30, 1965 (Washington, D. C.: U.S. Government Printing Office, 1964), p. 385.

TABLE 4

Payments to School Districts by Object Classification

Object classification	1963 Actual	1964 Estimate	1965 Estimate
Personnel summary			
Allocation accounts			
Total number of permanent positions	10	11	11
Full-time equivalent of other positions	4	5	5
Average number of all employees	12	15	15
Employees in permanent positions, end of year	9	10	10
Employees in other positions, end of year	5	5	5
Average GS grade	9.0	9.0	9.0
Average GS Salary	7,007	7,184	7,307
Program and Financing			
Program by activities			
Payments to local educational agencies (costs—obligations)	—	216,204	—
Financing			
New obligational authority (proposed supplemental appropriation)	—	216,204	—

Source: 1965 Budget Appendix, p. 386.

in various forms from a few million dollars to around $60 million a year. The latter figure pertains to the Department of Agriculture and the Department of the Interior.

SOME SHORTCOMINGS OF THE EXISTING BUDGET

The existing budget, which incorporates financial support for education in forty-two departments and agencies, makes it difficult to appraise the place of education in the federal government and the role of the government in providing and financing education. In more general terms, the budget neither facilitates the development and implementation of a policy for education nor the examination of the role of education in pursuance of a national education policy. These shortcomings of budget format are perhaps best discussed under the following headings:

1. Intermingling of grant and loan funds.
2. Lack of identification of relevant information, which prevents:
   (a) Coordination of interrelated decisions;
   (b) Consideration of full-cost implications of decisions;
   (c) Consideration of alternatives and their tradeoffs.

Intermingling of Grant and Loan Funds

Until quite recently federal funds for education were made available solely on a grant or contract basis. However, a new development has taken place; loans are made both to students to tide them over the costly years of their training and to colleges to help finance their building programs. In FY 1963 loans reached the half-billion-dollar level—almost the size of the 1963 expenditures of the U.S. Office of Education. The administrative education budget, reproduced in Table 1, intermingles grant and loan funds. In the absence of a careful separation between these two funds, we face problems that are somewhat similar to those encountered by adding tax receipts of school districts to funds raised by them through the sale of bonds.

Lack of Information Preventing Coordination of Interrelated Decisions

Quite a few education activities require budgetary decisions by more than one level of government. In other cases, education activities of different types supplement one another. Therefore, gains can often accrue from presenting information in an orderly, internally consistent manner to facilitate the joint consideration of these activities and their possible coordination.

For example, all three levels of government participate actively in the financing of higher education. Local school districts have assumed major responsibility for the financing of junior colleges, with state governments providing subsidies. The main financial responsibility for colleges and universities rests with the state, while the federal government is providing increasing amounts of direct and indirect financial aid. This aid is made available by numerous federal agencies. For example, student fellowships are offered, among others, by the Office of Education, the National Science Foundation, the National Institutes of Health and other parts of the Public Health Service, the National Aeronautics and Space Administration, the Atomic Energy Commission, and the Department of the Interior. Many more federal agencies make indirect support available.

1965 Budget includes a special analysis of federal aid to state and local governments.[3] This information could be presented in a more useful form. The data follow department lines and much information is concealed, which makes it virtually impossible to take a comprehensive look at the federal support for college students and to integrate it effectively with the financial efforts of the states.

Well-organized information can improve decisions about education activities that supplement one another. In recent years the federal government has provided loan funds for the construction of student housing facilities. Some federal agencies, including the National Science Foundation, the National Aeronautics and Space Administration, and the National Institues of Health under differing conditions, have offered grants for research facilities. State and private funds have also been used to finance the construction of college plants and equipment. These construction projects could be better evaluated and integrated if the budgetary information were more readily available in an explicit and internally consistent end-product oriented form.

Lack of Information Preventing Consideration of Full-Cost Implications

A discussion on the full-cost aspects of a decision should include two somewhat different issues. First, there is the time horizon issue. This full-cost issue is important mainly with regard to financing research and building activities in support of education. Were the federal government to contemplate financing national educational television, for instance, it should consider not only the first-year costs but also the long-term cost implications, perhaps over the next five years.

The second issue related to a full-cost discussion is the need to consider as many of the costs as possible, not just the obvious elements. For example, the cost of instituting a universal junior college system should include not only the junior college expenditures associated with such a proposal but also the implications of further unbalancing of very precarious demand and supply situations for instructional staff in high schools and colleges. One result could be an across-the-board increase in teachers' salaries.

Lack of Information Preventing Consideration of Alternatives and Their Tradeoffs

Our increasing investment in education and in such complementary activities as basic and applied research, both so essential for our future economic and military health, necessitates a systematic consideration of tradeoffs to enable us to make judicious choices. The present budget does not provide organized information that can help estimate the implications, for example, of trading off an additional billion dollars to be spent on higher education for the same amount to obtain more basic research, or applied research. Or should the money be spent to retrain obsolete manpower and help win the war against poverty?

The federal dollar invested in education should do extra duty. It can induce local and state governments to invest more heavily in education, and it can induce them to invest in especially advantageous educational activities. It can have desirable and disadvantageous side effects in terms of economic growth, economic stability, income distribution, etc. These points should be in the minds of those who make education decisions, yet the present budget is of little help to them.

APPLICABILITY OF PROGRAM CONCEPT TO EDUCATION

Let us examine a schematic presentation of the lifetime flow of students through the formal education system. Virtually all individuals attend primary grades and some years of high school. Most high school education is college preparatory, while some is explicitly vocational. From the vocational programs students mainly progress either into the labor force (and the non-working population) or into a junior college system. From the college preparatory courses students enter either regular colleges—including the service academies—or undergraduate divisions of universities, or junior colleges. Part of the junior college students enter four-year colleges to work toward their bachelor's degree; part of the college population continues in graduate and professional schools of universities.

Regardless of whether they have a college education, Americans can participate in a variety of adult education activities, from extension programs to retraining courses. Some federally financed activities are mainly designed to help veterans, others are for government employees, and still others are for farmers.

In short, the educational system assumes a vertical structure, with lower levels of education facilitating and leading into higher levels, and special adult training and retraining programs offering some shortcuts and flexibility.

What are some of the key characteristics of a useful program category in the field of education? Tentatively, an education program should:

1. Directly and effectively relate to the nation's major education objectives, and in this sense it should be end-product-oriented.

2. Lend itself to a meaningful breakdown into program elements that can readily be related to each other.

3. Have administrative relevance and provide for administrative effectiveness.

4. Directly relate to sources of funds and facilitate viable intergovernmental fiscal relations.

With these characteristics in mind, we will next identify the major education programs, remembering that program budgets should have a reasonably long time horizon (e.g., five years) and permit full-cost pricing.

As was pointed out, the education system has a number of components, many of which are vertically related to one another. Thus primary education produces an intermediary output, much of which is preparatory to secondary education, which in turn is preparatory to college attendance.

The identification of key education programs is difficult, partly because of our inability to separate investment and consumption aspects of education, on the one hand, and its research aspects, on the other. Nonetheless, one might recommend the subdivision of the federal education budget into the following main programs: (1) primary education, (2) secondary education, (3) higher education, and (4) adult education.

Each of these four main programs can have significant program elements. For example, in terms of its mission and educational activities, secondary education can be separated into college preparatory and vocational. Except in small rural high schools and private preparatory schools, the two types of education can take place in the same district, which makes expenditure separation into the two groups very difficult, if not impossible.

Similarly, in line with the California experience, it appears desirable to divide higher education into junior college, college, graduate, and postgraduate education. Again, adult education can have a number of program elements. In the abstract we might want to distinguish between continued education and retraining, the first group being further subdivided into general and vocational (or professional) education. Federal participation in these programs stems from a variety of concerns. The most obvious is the desire to educate government employees so that they can better and more efficiently fulfill their responsibilities. Furthermore, we have long-standing training commitments to farmers and veterans and, more recently, to residents of depressed areas in this country.

In addition to these four main programs, it appears useful to single out three further programs: library services, research (and development) in educational institutions and research centers, and international education. The seven programs are summarized in Table 5. Library services provide important support for our categories of higher and adult education as well as research and development. Not unlike library services, research supplements and supports our major educational efforts in that it creates new knowledge that is disseminated by our schools, colleges, and universities. International education falls into a slightly different category in that it enters all levels of education, with the direct beneficiaries being foreigners.

THE EDUCATION PROGRAM BUDGET FOR FY 1963

An effort will now be made to provide data for the main programs of Table 5 in FY 1963. Because no separate data exist, it appears necessary to combine primary with secondary education. We will distinguish between federal grants and federal loans. The FY 1963 data that will be presented are estimates of federal education funds and are not strictly comparable with U.S. education expenditure data.[4]

TABLE 5

Education Programs in an Idealized Federal Budget

Program	1963	1964	1965	1966	1967
Primary education					
Secondary education					
College preparatory					
Vocational					
Higher education					
Junior college					
College					
Graduate					
Postgraduate					
Adult education					
Continued general (liberal)					
Continued vocational					
(professional)					
Government employees					
Nongovernment employees					
Retraining					
Library services					
Research (and development)					
International education					

In Table 6 federal funds for major education programs are presented in terms of their administrative purposes and sources of support. The funds are arranged by the nature of their support in Table 7.[5]

For example, federal support for primary and secondary education is given both directly and indirectly. The indirect support consists mainly of financing such auxiliary school services as lunch and job placement programs. The direct support is mainly across

TABLE 6

Federal Education Program Budget Arranged by Sources of Support FY 1963 (Obligations in Thousands of Dollars)

Source of support	Amount
I. Grants, etc.—Total	3,620,220
A. Primary and secondary education—Total	991,858
1. Federally impacted area support (Public Laws 815 and 874)	332,200
2. Military dependents, schools	45,289
3. Military dependents, bus transportation	550
4. National Defense Education Act	62,622
5. Public lands revenue for schools	44,549
6. Teaching grants (Educational Exchange Program)	6,800
7. Course content improvement group (National Science Foundation)	3,637
8. Science education (National Science Foundation)	3,901
9. Vocational education	26,323
10. Indian education	60,876
11. School aid to District of Columbia and territories	18,021
12. School lunch program	379,258
13. Job placement services for high school seniors	6,900
14. Other	932
B. Higher education—Total	1,242,397
1. Training grants	255,988
2. Fellowships	108,389
3. Institutional grants	38,695
4. Traineeships	23,423
5. Special training programs	9,784
6. Veterans' education	68,446
7. Military academies	51,493
8. Training state and local personnel	5,765
9. Basic research and research facilities in U.S. educational institutions proper	551,376
10. Other, including surplus property transfers	129,038
C. Adult education—Total	209,945
1. Vocational and technical training	67,551
2. Veterans' education	29,007
3. Training federal personnel in nonfederal facilities	31,869
4. Training state and local personnel	3,589
5. Apprenticeship and training programs	4,458
6. Education in federal correctional institutions	2,518
7. Indian education	6,165
8. Cooperative agricultural extension service	63,008
9. Mine safety training	1,400
10. Other	380

TABLE 6 (*Continued*)

D.	Library services—Total	23,896
	1. Library of Congress	12,073
	2. Library Services Act grants	7,406
	3. National Library of Medicine	3,321
	4. National Agricultural Library	1,096
E.	Research (and development)—Total	1,089,124
	1. Applied R&D in educational institutions and research centers	1,089,124
F.	International education—Total	63,000
	1. AID cooperative projects	54,000
	2. Grants for observation and advisory service under the Educational Exchange Program	9,000
II. Loans—Total		481,851
A.	Primary and secondary education—Total	616
	1. Loans to private schools	616
B.	Higher education—Total	481,235
	1. Student loan program	90,692
	2. College housing loans	390,543

Source: Department of Health, Education, and Welfare, Office of Education, *Annual Survey, Federal Funds for Education and Related Activities*, and records.

the board, with all schools eligible to apply for it. In 1963 most of the support was for veterans and war orphans. However, there are some funds earmarked for the support of such special groups as American Indians and residents of the District of Columbia and U.S. territories. In addition, there are funds earmarked for special types of education, e.g., science education and vocational education.

Federal support under Public Laws 815[6] and 874[7] is somewhat different in character from most other support. In many respects it is made available in lieu of taxes to local and state government, and for certain purposes it may not be combined with other federal aid to education. However, we can also take a different view of payments to federally impacted areas. Because a sizable portion of the federal grants are made on behalf of children whose parents work on federal property located outside the school district, parts of the funds can become available without strings and controls. The relevant portion of these funds could then be included in the across-the-board direct support.

Regardless of which view we take of funds made available under

Public Laws 815 and 874, it is revealing that relatively little money is given to schools in terms of across-the-board support, i.e., somewhere between $150 and $350 million in FY 1963.

Federal funds to higher education entail, on the one hand, support on an across-the-board basis and, on the other hand, support for special groups (e.g., veterans, military academies, state and local personnel). During FY 1962 federal grants provided direct support to 182,000 students, full and part time, at all academic levels at a cost of more than a quarter of a billion dollars. Nearly 60 per cent

TABLE 7

Federal Education Program Budget Arranged by Nature
of Support FY 1963[a](Obligations in Thousands of Dollars)

Nature of support	Amount
I. Grants, etc.—Total	3,620,220
A. Primary and secondary education—Total	991,858
1. Across-the-board direct support (4-7, 14)	118,540
2. Support in lieu of taxes[b] (1-3)	378,039
3. Support for special groups (10,11)	78,897
4. Support for special education (8,9)	30,224
5. Indirect support (12, 13)	386,158
B. Higher education—Total	1,242,397
1. Across-the-board direct support (1-5, 10)	565,317
2. Support for special groups (6-8)	125,704
3. Indirect support through R&D (9)	551,376
C. Adult education—Total	209,945
1. Support for special groups (1-10)	209,945
D. Library services—Total	23,896
1. Across-the-board (1-2)	19,479
2. Support for special groups (3, 4)	4,417
E. Research (and development)—Total	1,089,124
F. International education—Total	63,000
II. Loans—Total	481,851
A. Primary and secondary education—Total	616
B. Higher education—Total	481,235

Source: Table 6.
[a]Numbers in parentheses refer to items in Table 6.
[b]For some purposes support in lieu of tax payments may be deducted from federal support of education.

of these funds went to veterans under the readjustment training and rehabilitation programs (both of which are being reduced at a rate of nearly 50 per cent each year) and to war orphans. Eighty-seven per cent of the funds for graduate student support went to students in the sciences and engineering. These figures exclude the military academies.[8] Most of the direct support is directed toward predoctoral work and takes the form of fellowships given directly to the student or the institution or research assistantships as parts of research grants and contracts.

Although some of the federal funds are for direct support of higher education, other funds provide support indirectly through research and development. Support for basic research and research facilities has been increasing rapidly in recent years, from $210 million in FY 1959 to $550 million in FY 1963. About one-third of this total amount comes from the National Institutes of Health and the Department of Defense, respectively. Next in importance are the National Science Foundation, the Atomic Energy Commission, the Department of Agriculture, and the National Aeronautics and Space Administration.

The very fact that major research and training funds are included in the administrative budgets of the agencies mentioned above raises the intriguing question of whether education produces an intermediate or a final output. In terms of legislative intent, many research and training funds are awarded to help specific agencies accomplish their missions. However, the classification in Tables 6 and 7 treats research in educational institutions and research centers and training efforts as purely educational activities. It would be very proper indeed to have a different viewpoint and exclude from the education program budget those research and training funds that directly relate to specific government missions other than education. The excluded items could then be grouped into the program budgets of other departments. Clearly this view would result in a substantially smaller total education budget figure than the $3.6 billion given in Tables 6 and 7—possibly somewhere between $2.6 and $3.0 billion.

APPLYING PROGRAM BUDGETING TO ELUCIDATE EDUCATION DECISIONS

The philosophy underlying this chapter has been that the education budget of the federal government should give expression to the nation's position toward education, and should facilitate long-range projections even though the education demand and supply picture involves major uncertainties. Although different types of education and their output cannot be measured in simple quantitative terms, the program budget, if properly designed, can provide partial quantitative information that elucidates some of the consequences of spending funds of different programs. Fewer difficulties need to be overcome on the input side, where it is often possible to stipulate the requirements for manpower (by types), material, and supplies to support specified activities. These requirements can readily be expressed in money terms. However, it must be kept in mind that much of the nation's investment in education is designed to create human capital. It follows that education decisions relate heavily to the future, and if they turn out to be wrong, they cannot be readily reversed. Thus it is of paramount importance to be aware that today's action or inaction with regard to education can constitute sins of omission or sins of commission whose burdens will fall mainly on future generations.

. . . [Program] budgeting can facilitate the making of decisions on three different levels. For education this means that on the highest level program budgeting can be employed to help select the proper budget size on the basis of information about the preferred mix between education, defense, space, natural resources, etc., and the private sector. On the second level, program budgeting can help in the determination of the best mix of different education programs, often involving judgments about vaguely defined objectives. Finally, there is the relatively low-level decision, which relies on factors for cost and output to determine the most effective way of attaining a given program objective.

It must be remembered that education decisions, unlike defense decisions that are in the hands of a monolithic federal agency, are made by literally tens of thousands of administrative units. Furthermore, three levels of government share in the responsiblity to raise education funds, all in competition with private educational institutions. As was pointed out earlier in this chapter, in terms of funds the federal government is the smallest of the four partners and in recent years provided only slightly more than 10 per cent of the money. Although federal funds are relatively small, they have been increasing and, more important, they can be made available in a way that local and state school officials consider them costless. Local school officials tend to look at state subsidies in a similar way.

Thus the executive branch and Congress ponder not only the question of how much federal aid to education should be made available but also the form it should take. Crucial questions are:

Who should benefit; who should pay; what strings, if any, should be attached; and what are the objectives to be obtained? Elucidation of these questions calls for a benefit-burden analysis that explicitly allows for spatial benefits and cost spillovers. A conceptual framework, developed and implemented in relation to a case study, has been published by the author.[9]

The dispersion of education decisionmaking and complicated intergovernmental fiscal relations must be kept in mind in the preparation of program budgets and in devising applications for them. This admonition holds no less for federal education than for the local school district decisionmaker.

A few samples will next be explored to illustrate possible applications of education program budgets. Only two of the three types of decisions mentioned earlier in this section deal primarily with program budgeting by the federal government. The relatively low-level decision concerned with finding the most effective way of attaining a given subprogram objective basically involves the local school district and therefore will not be considered.

We shall concentrate first on a decision facing the President and his budget advisers. To the extent that the education budget, as well as the budgets of other major federal activities, is end- (or intermediate-) product-oriented, and at least some outputs are in quantitative terms, the tradeoff discussions about an additional billion dollars for education, defense, resources development, or space exploration become sharper and more meaningful. More specifically, on the basis of the 1963 program budget figures the following questions suggest themselves: In the light of a 1963 GNP of about $585 billion, a $93 billion federal budget, and a $25 billion public education budget, is a $3.6 billion federal education budget of optimum size?[10] Or would, for example, an additional billion dollars for education prove more beneficial to the nation than adding $1 billion to NASA's 1963 budget of $3.7 billion for space exploration, or to DOD's 1963 budget of $57.8 billion for defense? Are we putting too much into our defense program and not enough into education? Or vice versa?

Partial answers to these questions would require not only our estimate of contributions that can be expected from a marginal dollar invested in defense space exploration or education, but also the multiplier effects of such contributions. Thus, for example, unlike an additional federal defense or space exploration dollar, an increment of federal contributions to education, depending on the form it takes, could lead to further state and local education funding. In this sense, the additional federal education dollar will carry extra duty, and this increment needs to be estimated and considered in a discussion of whether we would not be better off if the federal government were to increase its education budget.

Another consideration of the desirability of further federal contributions to the financing of education centers around the issue of distributional equity. This issue has a bearing on the allocation of financing responsibility to the three levels of government. If we agree that the federal government is mainly responsible for income redistribution and that large-scale spatial cost and benefit spillovers exist, as well as that they should be either neutralized or made consistent with some norm of distributional equity, greater federal financial participation might be appropriate. Increased federal funds provided through grants (aid), for example, change the distribution of education costs and benefits to different geographic areas and income groups. Because the federal income tax is progressive, larger federal subsidies are likely to improve distributional equity.

Let us turn to another type of decision and ask the question: If the federal education budget is $3.6 billion (or $3.3 billion if we exclude the $0.3 billion aid to federally impacted areas), is a mix of $1 billion (or 0.7 billion if the $0.3 billion is excluded) for primary and secondary education, $1.1 billion for higher education, $0.2 billion for adult education, $0.02 billion for library services, $1.1 billion for research (and development), and $0.06 billion for international education the preferred mix? What is the relative merit of spending an additional given amount of money for each of these programs?

Answers are not easy to come by, but a few simple yardsticks suggest themselves. For example, although the federal budget for primary and secondary education is smaller than that for higher education, many more students attend schools than colleges and universities. The ratio is about 9 to 1.[11] At the same time, adequate higher education per student is not that much more expensive than primary and secondary education,. Because education has a vertical structure, another consideration is that good college education is likely to be much more effective when it is accorded to students with a solid primary and secondary education. Therefore, if there is no immediate crisis that requires a mammoth increase in the supply of scientists and engineers, an orderly long-run program, well balanced on all levels of education, appears to be in order.

On the surface it would appear that since across-the-board direct federal support for primary and secondary education is so small (for example, in FY 1963 it was only slightly more than $100 million), the marginal dollar would yield the highest return. Before we could be confident, however, that primary and secondary education can use additional federal funds better than any other education program, a number of important issues must be investigated. By how much will an additional federal dollar for primary and secondary education increase funds provided for education in general compared with an additional federal dollar for another education program? By how much will an additional dollar for primary and secondary education increase education benefits compared with other education programs?

Although the economist can have only partial answers at best to these resource allocation questions, policy-makers would want to consider them in conjunction with some political "facts of life." For example, the issue of separation of school and church appears to have stymied all congressional efforts to increase the support for public schools. This particular impediment to legislation exists only to a lesser extent in connection with higher education, and it plays almost no role in relation to the other programs. Therefore, major increases in federal support for education may have to be selected from among such programs as adult education, library services, research (and development), and international education.

The question can also be raised whether a 1963 expenditure of $26 million for vocational high school education constitutes an optimum level. In the light of projected demand increases for skilled workers, it may be highly desirable to offer more students schooling in technical high schools, and federal grants for vocational training may be able to induce local governments to take appropriate steps. As a result, marginal returns from such an investment may be high.

Similarly, the question can be raised concerning the heavy emphasis on science. Direct and indirect federal support of institutions of higher learning has no doubt further unbalanced the relative position of the natural sciences, social sciences, and humanities. Although we do not have readily available national statistics, data can be found for specific universities. This leads to the question of whether, for example, $50 million could not be more effectively used if channeled into the humanities rather than into the social or natural sciences.

There is also the issue of adult education, only one aspect of which will be considered here. On June 20, 1964, President Johnson called for an Urban Extension Service in dedicating a new University of California campus at Irvine. No doubt this interest stems, in part, from the exceptional success of our Agricultural Extension Service. With the rural population rapidly declining and urban America growing by leaps and bounds, the President's call appears at first logical and perhaps overdue. Yet much careful work is needed before one can be sure that federal funds for urban extension could be well spent in comparison with other opportunities. For example, the objectives of agricultural extension were clear and almost universally agreed on: make two blades grow where one was growing, and do so efficiently. Also, these objectives were to be achieved with the aid of mechanical and chemical means whose effectiveness had been established in advance, e.g., better ways to cultivate, fertilize, fight diseases, and irrigate crops. However, on the urban scene we have neither agreement on objectives nor tested knowledge to improve urban life and form. Therefore, perhaps we should invest more heavily in urban research before we use federal funds for an urban extension effort.

Application of benefit-cost analysis can elucidate a higher education decision, although it may involve the federal government only indirectly. Early in 1964 the Education Policies Commission proposed universal junior college education, and some suggestions will be made as to how the relative merits of this proposal can be analyzed with the aid of a benefit-cost analysis.[12] There are 908,000 "potential" college students who, according to the proposal at hand, would enter colleges to be educated for a two-year period. For simplicity's sake, it will be assumed that:

1. These 908,000 youngsters will be in college on a full-time basis.

2. Costs will be the same as those of college students presently enrolled in various institutions. (Because junior colleges are less expensive to operate during the freshman and sophomore years, than regular liberal arts colleges or universities, this assumption produces an upward cost bias.)

3. Benefits will be the same as those of college students presently enrolled in various institutions. (Because junior colleges are likely to offer education inferior to that of other institutions of higher learning and, more important, because the caliber of those presently not in college is on the average inferior to that of those attending college, this assumption produces an upward benefit bias.)

4. Marginal cost equals average cost.

Under these assumptions, additional operating costs of $2.8 billion, capital costs of $0.7 billion, foregone earnings of $0.4 billion, and miscellaneous private costs of $0.2 billion, or a total of $4.0 billion a year can be expected. Incremental annual student income benefits (in present-value terms) total $2.5 billion. The resulting benefit-cost ratio would be about 0.63.

Although this ratio does not reflect all the items that are germane to the proposal at hand (a good example is the employment impact of the proposal), it appears to indicate that investment in universal junior college education is likely to produce negative returns. At the same time, under similar assumptions, adding eight-week sessions for five summers following the 7th through the 11th grades would produce a benefit-cost ratio of 2.2. The social cost of the additional sessions would tend to be much smaller than costs associated with the junior college proposal—perhaps only one-third in amount. However, if we are concerned that about 3.5 million teenagers are in the work force today and that of this total 2 million are out of work, placing teenagers in junior colleges is a very attractive way of reducing unemployment in the immediate future.

NOTES

[1] Published in Washington, D.C.: U.S. Government Printing Office, 1964.

[2] *Appendix: The Budget of the United States Government for the Fiscal Year Ending June 30, 1965* (Washington, D.C.: U.S. Government Printing Office, 1964).

[3] *1965 Budget,* pp. 427-435.

[4] The "funds" data are prepared on an obligation rather than an expenditure basis. Federal funds data include the following types of items (for FY 1963) that are not included in the U.S. education expenditure figures: (1) student stipends under federal fellowship and training program (about $200 million); (2) education of military dependents overseas (about $45 million); (3) value of commodities distributed under the school lunch program (about $180 million); and (4) surplus property donations (about $110 million).

[5] In Table 7 funds that appeared in Table 6 as "Other" under primary and secondary education and higher education are grouped together with across-the-board direct support.

[6] *U.S. Statutes . . . 1950—1951,* pp. 967-978.

[7] *Ibid.,* pp. 1100—1109.

[8] *Federal Government and Education,* p. 14.

[9] Werner Z. Hirsch, Elbert W. Segelhorst, and Morton J. Marcus, *Spillover of Public Education Costs and Benefits* (Los Angeles: Institute of Government and Public Affairs, University of California, 1964), p. 465; see also Hirsch, "Regional Accounts for Public School Decisions," paper presented at the Third Regional Accounts Conference, Miami Beach, Fla., November 20, 1964.

[10] *Economic Report to the President, Transmitted to the Congress January 1964,* House Document No. 278, 88th Cong., 2d Sess. (Washington, D.C.: U.S. Government Printing Office, 1964), pp. 207, 274.

[11] *Statistical Abstract of the United States, 1963,* Bureau of the Census, U.S. Department of Commerce (Washington, D.C.: U.S. Government Printing Office, 1963), pp. 127, 136.

[12] The Education Policies Commission, *Universal Opportunity for Education Beyond the High School* (Washington, D.C.: National Education Association, 1964).

SUGGESTIONS FOR FURTHER READING—PART IV

Hirsch, Werner Z. "State and Local Government Program Budgeting." *Regional Science Association Papers,* Vol. 18 (1967), pp. 147-163.

Novick, David, ed. *Program Budgeting.* Cambridge, Mass.: Harvard University Press, 1967.

"Planning-Programming-Budgeting System: A Symposium." *Public Administration Review,* Vol. 26, No. 4 (December 1966), pp. 243-328.

"Planning-Programming-Budgeting System Reexamined: Development, Analysis, and Criticism." *Public Administration Review,* Vol. 29, No. 2 (March/April 1969), pp. 111-202.

The Planning-Programming-Budgeting System: Progress and Potentials. Hearings before the Subcommittee on Economy in Government of the Joint Economic Committee. 90th Congress, 1st Session. Washington, D.C.: Government Printing Office, 1967.

Part V

Social
Indicators

15

TOWARD A SOCIAL REPORT

by U.S. Department of Health, Education, and Welfare

Toward A Social Report *is a pioneering government document, a first attempt to establish a set of social yardsticks
to measure the progress of the society in meeting social
needs. The* Report *was prepared under the direction of
Wilbur Cohen, one of the nation's foremost authorities on
social welfare programs. The excerpt includes some discussion of education and raises a number of basic questions
regarding the lack of adequate data and research in a
nation that is sometimes thought to be overtabulated and
overstudied.*

The Nation has no comprehensive set of statistics reflecting social
progress or retrogression. There is no Government procedure for
periodic stocktaking of the social health of the Nation. The Government makes no Social Report.

We do have an Economic Report, required by statute, in which
the President and his Council of Economic Advisors report to the
Nation on its economic health. We also have a comprehensive set
of economic indicators widely thought to be sensitive and reliable.
Statistics on the National Income and its component parts, on employment and unemployment, on retail and wholesale prices, and
on the balance of payments are collected annually, quarterly,
monthly, sometimes even weekly. These economic indicators are
watched by Government officials and private citizens alike as

Reprinted from *Toward a Social Report,* U.S. Department of Health, Education
and Welfare, Wilbur J. Cohen, Secretary, January 1969, pp. xi-xxii, 95-101.

closely as a surgeon watches a fever chart for indications of a change in the patient's condition.

Although nations got along without economic indicators for centuries, it is hard to imagine doing without them now. It is hard to imagine governments and businesses operating without answers to questions which seem as ordinary as: What is happening to retail prices? Is National Income rising? Is unemployment higher in Chicago than in Detroit? Is our balance of payments improving?

Indeed, economic indicators have become so much a part of our thinking that we have tended to equate a rising National Income with national well-being. Many are surprised to find unrest and discontent growing at a time when National Income is rising so rapidly. It seems paradoxical that the economic indicators are generally registering continued progress—rising income, low unemployment—while the streets and the newspapers are full of evidence of growing discontent—burning and looting in the ghetto, strife on the campus, crime in the street, alienation and defiance among the young.

Why have income and disaffection increased at the same time? One reason is that the recent improvement in standards of living, along with new social legislation, have generated new expectations —expectations that have risen faster than reality could improve. The result has been disappointment and disaffection among a sizeable number of Americans.

It is not misery, but advance, that fosters hope and raises expectations. It has been wisely said that the conservatism of the destitute is as profound as that of the privileged. If the Negro American did not protest as much in earlier periods of history as today, it was not for lack of cause, but for lack of hope. If in earlier periods of history we had few programs to help the poor, it was not for lack of poverty, but because society did not care and was not under pressure to help the poor. If the college students of the fifties did not protest as often as those of today, it was not for lack of evils to condemn, but probably because hope and idealism were weaker then.

The correlation between improvement and disaffection is not new. Alexis de Tocqueville observed such a relationship in eighteenth century France: "The evil which was suffered patiently as inevitable, seems unendurable as soon as the idea of escaping from it crosses men's minds. All the abuses then removed call attention to those that remain, and they now appear more galling. The evil, it is true, has become less, but sensibility to it has become more acute."

Another part of the explanation of the paradox of prosperity and rising discontent is clearly that "money isn't everything." Prosperity itself brings its own problems. Congestion, noise, and pollution are byproducts of economic growth which make the world less livable. The large organizations which are necessary to harness modern technology make the individual feel small and impotent. The concentration on production and profit necessary to economic growth breeds tension, venality, and neglect of "the finer things."

Why a Social Report or Set of Social Indicators?

Curiosity about our social condition would by itself justify an attempt to assess the social health of the Nation. Many people want answers to questions like these: Are we getting healthier? Is pollution increasing? Do children learn more than they used to? Do people have more satisfying jobs than they used to? Is crime increasing? How many people are really alienated? Is the American dream of rags to riches a reality? We are interested in the answers to such questions partly because they would tell us a good deal about our individual and social well-being. Just as we need to measure our incomes, so we need "social indicators," or measures of other dimensions of our welfare to get an idea how well off we really are.

A social report with a set of social indicators could not only satisfy our curiosity about how well we are doing, but it could also improve public policymaking in at least two ways. First, it could give social problems more visibility and thus make possible more informed judgments about national priorities. Second, by providing insight into how different measures of national well-being are changing, it might ultimately make possible a better evaluation of what public programs are accomplishing.

The existing situation in areas with which public policy must deal is often unclear, not only to the citizenry in general, but to officialdom as well. The normal processes of journalism and the observations of daily life do not allow a complete or balanced view of the condition of the society. Different problems have different degrees of visibility.

The visibility of a social problem can depend, for example, upon its "news value" or potential drama. The Nation's progress in the space race and the need for space research get a lot of publicity because of the adventure inherent in manned space exploration. Television and tabloid remind us almost daily of the problems of crime, drugs, riots, and sexual misadventure. The rate of infant mortality may be a good measure of the condition of a society, but this rate is rarely mentioned in the public press, or even perceived as a public problem. The experience of parents (or infants) does not insure that the problem of infant mortality is perceived as a social problem; only when we know that more than a dozen nations have lower rates of infant mortality than the United States can we begin to make a valid judgment about the condition of this aspect of American society.

Moreover, some groups in our society are well organized, but others are not. This means that the problems of some groups are articulated and advertised, whereas the problems of others are not. Public problems also differ in the extent to which they are immediately evident to the "naked eye." A natural disaster or overcrowding of the highways will be immediately obvious. But ineffectiveness of an educational system or the alienation of youth and minority groups is often evident only when it is too late.

Besides developing measures of the social conditions we care about we also need to see how these measures are changing in response to public programs. If we mount a major program to provide prenatal and maternity care for mothers, does infant mortality go down? If we channel new resources into special programs for educating poor children, does their performance in school eventually increase? If we mount a "war on poverty," what happens to the number of poor people? If we enact new regulations against the emission of pollutants, does pollution diminish?

These are not easy questions, since all major social problems are influenced by many things besides governmental action, and it is hard to disentangle the different effects of different causal factors. But at least in the long run evaluation of the effectiveness of public programs will be improved if we have social indicators to tell us how social conditions are changing. . . .

Health and Illness

There have been dramatic increases in health and life expectancy in the twentieth century, but they have been mainly the result of developments whose immediate effect has been on the younger age groups. The expectancy of life at birth in the United States has increased from 47.3 years at the turn of the century to 70.5 years in 1967, or by well over 20 years. The number of expected years of life remaining at age 5 has increased by about 12 years, and that at age 25 about 9 years, but that at age 65 not even 3 years. Modern medicine and standards of living have evidently been able to do a great deal for the young, and especially the very young, but not so much for the old.

This dramatic improvement had slowed down by the early fifties. Since then it has been difficult to say whether our health and life status have been improving or not. Some diseases are becoming less common and others are becoming more common, and life expectancy has changed rather little. We can get some idea whether or not there has been improvement on balance by calculating the "expectancy of *healthy* life" (i.e., life expectancy free of bed-disability and institutionalization). The expectancy of healthy life at birth seems to have improved a trifle since 1957, the first year for which the needed data are available, but certainly not as much as the improvements in medical knowledge and standards of living might have led us to hope.

The American people have almost certainly not exploited all of the potential for better health inherent in existing medical knowledge and standards of living. This is suggested by the fact that Negro Americans have on the average about seven years less expectancy of healthy life than whites, and the fact that at least 15 nations have longer life expectancy at birth than we do.

Why are we not as healthy as we could be? Though our style of life (lack of exercise, smoking, stress, etc.) is partly responsible, there is evidence which strongly suggests that social and economic deprivation and the uneven distribution of medical care are a large part of the problem.

Though the passage of Medicare legislation has assured many older Americans that they can afford the medical care they need, the steps to improve the access to medical care for the young have been much less extensive.

The Nation's system of financing medical care also provides an incentive for the relative underuse of preventive, as opposed to curative and ameliorative, care. Medical insurance may reimburse a patient for the hospital care he gets, but rarely for the checkup that might have kept him well. Our system of relief for the medically indigent, and the fee-for-service method of physician payment, similarly provide no inducements for adequate preventive care.

The emphasis on curative care means that hospitals are sometimes used when some less intensive form of care would do as well. This overuse of hospitals is one of the factors responsible for the extraordinary increases in the price of hospital care.

Between June 1967 and June 1968, hospital daily service charges increased by 12 percent, and in the previous 12 months they increased by almost 22 percent. Physicians' fees have not increased as much—they rose by 5½ percent between June 1967 and June 1968—but they still rose more than the general price level. Medical care prices in the aggregate rose at an annual rate of 6.5 percent during 1965–67.

Social Mobility

The belief that no individual should be denied the opportunity to better his condition because of the circumstances of his birth continues to be one of the foundation stones in the structure of American values. But is the actual degree of opportunity and social mobility as great now as it has been?

It was possible to get a partial answer to this question from a survey which asked a sample of American men about their fathers' usual occupations as well as about their own job characteristics. Estimates based on these data suggest that opportunity to rise to an occupation with a higher relative status has not been declining in recent years, and might even have increased slightly. They also show that by far the largest part of the variation in occupational status was explained by factors other than the occupation of the father.

These encouraging findings, in the face of many factors that everyday observation suggest must limit opportunity, are probably due in part to the expansion of educational opportunities. There is some tendency for the sons of those of high education and status to obtain more education than others (an extra year of schooling for the father means on the average an extra 0.3 or 0.4 of a year of education for the son), and this additional education brings somewhat higher occupational status on the average. However, the variations in education that are not explained by the socioeconomic status of the father, and the effects that these variations have on occupational status, are much larger. Thus, on balance, increased education seems to have increased opportunity and upward mobility.

There is one dramatic exception to the finding that opportunity is generally available. The opportunity of Negroes appears to be restricted to a very great extent by current race discrimination and other factors specifically related to race. Though it is true that the average adult Negro comes from a family with a lower socioeconomic status than the average white and has had fewer years of schooling, and that these and other "background" factors reduce his income, it does not appear to be possible to explain anything like all of the difference in income between blacks and whites in terms of such background factors. After a variety of background factors that impair the qualifications of the average Negro are taken into account, there remains a difference in income of over $1,400 that is difficult to explain without reference to current discrimination. So is the fact that a high status Negro is less likely to be able to pass his status on to his son than is a high status white. A number of other studies tend to add to the evidence that there is continuing discrimination in employment, as does the relationship between Federal employment and contracts (with their equal opportunity provisions) and the above-average proportion of Negroes in high status jobs.

The implication of all this is that the American commitment to opportunity is within sight of being honored in the case of whites, but that it is very far indeed from being honored for the Negro. In addition to the handicaps that arise out of history and past discrimination, the Negro also continues to obtain less reward for his qualifications than he would if he were white.

The Physical Environment

This chapter deals with the pollution of the natural environment, and with the manmade, physical environment provided by our housing and the structure of our cities.

Pollution seems to be many problems in many places—air pollution in some communities, water pollution in others, automobile junk yards and other solid wastes in still other places. These seemingly disparate problems can be tied together by one basic fact: The total weight of materials taken into the economy from nature must equal the total weight of materials ultimately discharged as wastes plus any materials recycled.

This means that, given the level and composition of the resources used by the economy, and the degree of recycling, any reduction in one form of waste discharge must be ultimately accompanied by an increase in the discharge of some other kind of waste. For example, some air pollution can be prevented by washing out the particles—but this can mean water pollution, or alternatively solid wastes.

Since the economy does not destroy the matter it absorbs there will be a tendency for the pollution problem to increase with the growth of population and economic activity. In 1965 the transportation system in the United States produced 76 million tons of five major pollutants. If the transportation technology used does not greatly change, the problem of air pollution may be expected to rise with the growth in the number of automobiles, airplanes, and so on. Similarly, the industrial sector of the economy has been growing at about 4½ percent per year. This suggests that, if this rate of growth were to continue, industrial production would have increased ten-fold by the year 2020, and that in the absence of new methods and policies, industrial wastes would have risen by a like proportion.

The chapter presents some measures of air and water pollution indicating that unsatisfactorily high levels of pollution exist in many places. There can be little doubt that pollution is a significant problem already, and that this is an area in which, at least in the absence of timely reporting and intelligent policy, the condition of society can all too easily deteriorate.

As we shift perspective from the natural environment to the housing that shelters us from it, we see a more encouraging trend. The physical quality of the housing in the country is improving steadily, in city center and suburb alike. In 1960, 84 percent of the dwelling units in the country were described as "structurally sound;" in 1966, this percentage had risen to 90 percent. In center cities the percentage had risen from 80 percent in 1960 to 93 percent in 1966. In 1950, 16 percent of the nation's housing was "overcrowded" in the sense that it contained 1.01 or more persons per room. But by 1960, only 12 percent of the nation's housing supply was overcrowded by this standard.

The principal reason for this improvement was the increased per capita income and demand for housing. About 11½ million new housing units were started in the United States between 1960 and 1967, and the figures on the declining proportions of structurally unsound and overcrowded dwellings, even in central cities, suggest that this new construction increased the supply of housing available to people at all income levels.

Even though the housing stock is improving, racial segregation and other barriers keep many Americans from moving into the housing that is being built or vacated, and deny them a full share in the benefits of the improvement in the Nation's housing supply.

Income and Poverty

The Gross National Product in the United States is about $1,000 higher per person than that of Sweden, the second highest nation. In 1969 our GNP should exceed $900 billion. Personal income has quadrupled in this century, even after allowing for changes in population and the value of money.

Generally speaking, however, the distribution of income in the United States has remained practically unchanged over the last 20 years. Although the distribution of income has been relatively stable, the rise in income levels has meant that the number of persons below the poverty line has declined. The poor numbered 40 million in 1960 and 26 million in 1967.

A continuation of present trends, however, would by no means eliminate poverty. The principal cause of the decline has been an increase in earnings. But some of the poor are unable to work because they are too young, too old, disabled or otherwise prevented from doing so. They would not, therefore, be directly helped by increased levels of wages and earnings in the economy as a whole. Moreover, even the working poor will continue to account for a substantial number of persons by 1974: about 5 million by most recent estimates. This latter group is not now generally eligible for income supplementation.

The Nation's present system of income maintenance is badly in need of reform. It is inadequate to the needs of those who do receive aid and millions of persons are omitted altogether.

This chapter concludes with an analysis of existing programs and a discussion of new proposals which have been put forward in recent years as solutions to the welfare crisis.

Public Order and Safety

The concern about public order and safety in the United States is greater now than it has been in some time.

The compilations of the Federal Bureau of Investigation show an increase in major crimes of 13 percent in 1964, 6 percent in 1965, 11 percent in 1966, and 17 percent in 1967. And studies undertaken for the President's Crime Commission in 1965 indicate that several times as many crimes occur as are reported.

Crime is concentrated among the poor. Both its perpetrators and its victims are more likely to be residents of the poverty areas of central cities than of suburbs and rural areas. Many of those residents in the urban ghettoes are Negroes. Negroes have much higher arrest rates than whites, but it is less widely known that Negroes also have higher rates of victimization than whites of any income group.

Young people commit a disproportionate share of crimes. Part of the recent increase in crime rates can be attributed to the growing proportion of young people in the population. At the same time, the propensity of youth to commit crime appears to be increasing.

Fear of apprehension and punishment undoubtedly deters some crime. The crime rate in a neighborhood drops with much more intensive policing. But crime and disorder tend to center among young people in ghetto areas, where the prospects for legitimate and socially useful activity are poorest. It seems unlikely that harsher punishment, a strengthening of public prosecutors, or more police can, by themselves, prevent either individual crime or civil disorder. The objective opportunities for the poor, and their attitudes toward the police and the law, must also change before the problems can be solved.

Learning, Science, and Art

The state of the Nation depends to a great degree on how much our children learn and on what our scientists and artists create. Learning, discovery, and creativity are not only valued in themselves, but are also resources that are important for the Nation's future.

In view of the importance of education, it might be supposed that there would be many assessments of what or how much American children learn. But this is not in fact the case. The standard sources of educational statistics give us hundreds of pages on the resources used for schooling, but almost no information at all on the extent to which these resources have achieved their purpose.

It is possible to get some insight into whether American children are learning more than children of the same age did earlier from a variety of achievement tests that are given throughout the country, mainly to judge individual students and classes. These tests suggest that there may have been a significant improvement in test score performance of children since the 1950's.

When the chapter turns to the learning and education of the poor and the disadvantaged, the results are less encouraging. Groups that suffer social and economic deprivation systematically learn less than those who have more comfortable backgrounds.

Even when they do as well on achievement tests, they are much less likely to go on to college. Of those high school seniors who are in the top one-fifth in terms of academic ability, 95 percent will ultimately go on to college if their parents are in the top socioeconomic quartile, but only half of the equally able students from the bottom socioeconomic quartile will attend college. Students from the top socioeconomic quartile are five times as likely to go to graduate school as comparably able students from the bottom socioeconomic quartile.

It is more difficult to assess the state of science and art than the learning of American youth. But two factors nonetheless emerge rather clearly. One is that American science is advancing at a most rapid rate, and appears to be doing very well in relation to other countries. The Nation's "technological balance of payments," for example, suggests that we have a considerable lead over other countries in technological know-how.

The other point that emerges with reasonably clarity is that, however vibrant the cultural life of the Nation may be, many of the live or performing arts are in financial difficulty. Since there is essentially no increase in productivity in live performances (it will always take four musicians for a quartet), and increasing productivity in the rest of the economy continually makes earnings in the society rise, the relative cost of live performances tends to go up steadily. This can be a significant public problem, at least in those cases where a large number of live performances is needed to insure that promising artists get the training and opportunity they need to realize their full potential.

Participation and Alienation: What We Need To Learn

Americans are concerned, not only about progress along the dimensions that have so far been described, but also about the special functions that our political and social institutions perform. It matters whether goals have been achieved in a democratic or a totalitarian way, and whether the group relationships in our society are harmonious and satisfying.

Unfortunately, the data on the performance of our political and social institutions are uniquely scanty. The chapter on "Participation and Alienation" cannot even hope to do much more than ask the right questions. But such questioning is also of use, for it can remind us of the range of considerations we should keep in mind when setting public policy, and encourage the collection of the needed data in the future.

Perhaps the most obvious function that we expect our institutions to perform is that of protecting our individual freedom. Individual liberty is not only important in itself, but also necessary to the viability of a democratic political system. Freedom can be abridged not only by government action, but also by the social and economic ostracism and discrimination that results from popular intolerance. There is accordingly a need for survey data that can discern any major changes in the degree of tolerance and in the willingness to state unpopular points of view, as well as information about the legal enforcement of constitutional guarantees.

Though liberty gives us the scope we need to achieve our individual purposes, it does not by itself satisfy the need for congenial social relationships and a sense of belonging. The chapter presents evidence which suggests (but does not prove) that at least many people not only enjoy, but also need, a clear sense of belonging, a feeling of attachment to some social group.

There is evidence for this conjecture in the relationship between family status, health, and death rates. In general, married people have lower age-adjusted death rates, lower rates of usage of facilites for the mentally ill, lower suicide rates, and probably also lower rates of alcoholism than those who have been widowed, divorced, or remained single. It is, of course, possible that those who are physically or mentally ill are less likely to find marriage partners, and that this explains part of the correlation. But the pattern of results, and especially the particularly high rates of those who are widowed, strongly suggest that this could not be the whole story.

There are also fragments of evidence which suggest that those who do not normally belong to voluntary organizations, cohesive neighborhoods, families, or other social groupings probably tend to have somewhat higher levels of "alienation" than other Americans.

Some surveys suggest that Negroes, and whites with high degrees of racial prejudice, are more likely to be alienated than other Americans. This, in turn, suggests that alienation has some importance for the cohesion of American society, and that the extent of group participation and the sense of community are important aspects of the condition of the Nation. If this is true, it follows that we need much more information about these aspects of the life of our society.

It is a basic precept of a democratic society that citizens should have equal rights in the political and organizational life of the society. Thus there is also a need for more and better information about the extent to which all Americans enjoy equality before the law, equal franchise, and fair access to public services and utilities. The growth of large scale, bureaucratic organizations, the difficulties many Americans (especially those with the least education and confidence) have in dealing with such organizations, and the resulting demands for democratic participation make the need for better information on this problem particularly urgent. . . .

HOW CAN WE DO BETTER SOCIAL REPORTING IN THE FUTURE?

Good decisions must be based on a careful evaluation of the facts. This truism is so often the basis for our most mundane behavior that we are seldom aware of its far-reaching significance. Most people do not decide whether to carry an umbrella without first checking the weather forecast or at least glancing out the window to see if it is raining. Yet, those policymakers and citizens who are concerned about the condition of American society often lack the information they need in order to decide what, if anything, should be done about the state of our society. Without the right kind of facts, they are not able to discern emerging problems, or to make informed decisions about national priorities. Nor are they able to choose confidently between alternative solutions to these problems or decide how much money should be allocated to any given program.

Deficiencies of Existing Statistics

Only a small fraction of the existing statistics tell us anything about social conditions, and those that do often point in different directions. Sometimes they do not add up to any meaningful conclusion and thus are not very useful to either the policymaker or the concerned citizen. The Government normally does not publish statistics on whether or not children are learning more than they used to, or on whether social mobility is increasing or decreasing. It does publish statistics on life expectancy and the incidence of disability due to ill health, but some diseases are becoming more common and others less common, and no summary measure indicating whether we could expect more healthy life has been available.

This lack of data would not be surprising if it were simply a result of lack of interest in statistics, or support for statistical collection, in the Government. But at the same time that some bemoan the lack of useful statistics, others are concerned about the supply of government statistics outrunning our capacity to make use of them. One Congressman recently argued that "we may be producing more statistics than we can digest," and argued that the Federal output of statistics may soon leave us "inundated in a sea of paper and ink." A detailed report by a Congressional Committee concluded that in 1967 more than 5,000 forms were approved by the Bureau of the Budget, which were estimated to take almost 110 million man-hours to complete. According to the same study, at the end of 1967 the Federal Government employed 18,902 Federal statistical workers, and spent $88 million on automatic data processing, computer equipment, and statistical studies under contract with private firms.[1] Comments and studies such as these do illustrate the fact that some are concerned about a plethora of statistics at the same time that the lack of particular types of statistical information stands in the way of better policy choices. This paradox suggests that the needed statistics cannot in practice be obtained simply through a general expansion of statistical efforts, but rather require new ideas about what statistics ought to be collected.

The problem does not appear to be unnecessary duplication of statistical efforts, or thoughtless decisions about what statistics should be collected. The Office of Statistical Standards of the Bureau of the Budget guards against any duplication in statistical collection, strives for comparability of different statistical series, and generally coordinates the Federal statistical effort. The Bureau of the Census and other agencies that collect statistics also seek the best advice, both inside and outside the Government, on what statistics ought to be collected. Thus the problem cannot be ascribed to poor management or foolish decisions—it evidently has deeper roots.

One of these roots is the fact that many of our statistics on social problems are merely a by-product of the informational requirements of routine management. This by-product process does not usually produce the information that we most need for policy or scholarly purposes, and it means that our supply of statistics has an accidental and imbalanced character.

Another source of the shortcomings of our statistical system is the *ad hoc* character of the decisions about what statistics should be collected. Numerous and gifted as those who advise us about what statistics we need may be, they cannot be expected to develop a system of data collection which maximizes the value and coverage of the statistics obtained with respect to the cost and number of the statistics gathered. A series of more or less independent decisions, however intelligent, may not provide the most coherent and useful system of statistics.

Social Indicators

A social indicator, as the term is used here, may be defined to be a statistic of direct normative interest which facilitates concise, comprehensive and balanced judgments about the condition of major aspects of a society. It is in all cases a direct measure of welfare and is subject to the interpretation that, if it changes in the "right" direction, while other things remain equal, things have gotten better, or people are "better off." Thus statistics on the number of doctors or policemen could not be social indicators, whereas figures on health or crime rates could be.

A large part of our existing social statistics are thus immediately excluded from the category of social indicators, since they are records of public expenditures on social programs or the quantity of inputs of one kind or another used for socioeconomic purposes. It is not possible to say whether or not things have improved when Government expenditures on a social program, or the quantity of some particular input used, increase.

The phrase "social indicators" evidently emerged in imitation of the title of the publication called *Economic Indicators,* a concise compendium of economic statistics issued by the Council of Economic Advisers.

The National Income statistics are, in fact, one kind of social indicator; they indicate the amount of goods and services at our disposal. But they tell us little about the learning of our children, the quality of our culture, the pollution of the environment, or the toll of illness. Thus other social indicators are needed to supplement the National Income figures. However, the National Income statistics provide a useful model which can help guide the development of other social statistics.

One of the chief virtues of the National Income statistics is their extraordinary aggregativeness. Over any significant period of time, the output of some of the goods produced in a country increases while the output of other goods decreases. In a depression the output of glass jars for home preserves may increase; during a period of rapid growth the consumption of cheaper goods may decline as people switch to substitutes of higher quality. Changing technologies and fashions also insure that the tens of thousands of different types of goods produced in a modern economy do not show the same patterns of growth or decline. The achievement of the National Income and Product Accounts is that they summarize this incredible diversity of developments into a single, meaningful number indicating how much an economy has grown or declined over a period. They summarize this awesome variety of experience so well that we can usually spot even the minirecession, and allow the testing of meaningful hypotheses about the relationship between the National Income, or its major components, and other aggregative variables, such as consumption or investment. Changes in the Nation's health, or in the danger of crime, are in some sense narrower and simpler than changes in the whole economy, yet they have not heretofore been successfully aggregated.

The aggregation involved in the construction of the National Income and Product Accounts is so successful in part because relative prices are used to determine the relative weight or importance to be given to a unit of one kind of output as against a unit of a different type of output. If the number of automobiles produced has gone up by half a million since last year, while the output of potatoes has fallen by half a million bushels, we need to know the relative importance of these two developments before we can begin to make a judgment about the movement of the economy as a whole. It would obviously be arbitrary to determine the relative importance of these two developments by comparing the weight in pounds of an average automobile and a bushel of potatoes. Thus the relative prices of automobiles and potatoes are used to weigh the relative importance of two such developments in the National Income and Product Accounts.

Relative prices at any given moment of time provide weights that are presumably meaningful in welfare or normative terms. This is because a consumer who rationally seeks to maximize the satisfaction he gets from his expenditures, in terms of his own tastes or values, will allocate his expenditures among alternative goods in such a way that he gets the same amount of satisfaction from the last dollar spent on each type of good. If he obtained more benefit from the last dollar spent on apples than from the last dollar spent on oranges, he would obviously be better off if he spent more on apples and less on oranges.

The almost universal reliance on such aggregative measures of a society's income should not, however, obscure the dangers of failing to look behind the aggregates. Imagine these two cases: in one case, the National Income remains constant over a year, and all of the industries have the same level of output over the year; in the other case, the National Income also remains constant, but about half of the industries grow and the other half decline. Obviously, the first economy would be stagnant, whereas the second would be undergoing significant change, including presumably shifts of resources from some industries to others. We would not see the profound differences in these two hypothetical situations simply by looking at the aggregate figures for the National Income: we also have to disaggregate.

But disaggregation is not the enemy of aggregation. Indeed, a consciously constructed aggregate is usually easier to break down into its components than most other statistics. A well-constructed aggregative statistic, like the National Income, can (in principle at least) be compared to a pyramid. At the base are the individual firms, sites of production, and individual income recipients. Just above are the industries and communities, and above them are the major sectors and regions. When the same goods are processed by several firms, double counting is avoided by counting only the "value added." At the top there is the National Income. Such a pyramid can usually exist only when there has been the consistent definition and procedure that aggregation requires, and this systematic approach probably facilitates disaggregation as well as aggregation.

The relevant point that emerges from an examination of the National Income and Product Accounts is that aggregation can be extraordinarily useful, and is compatible with the use of the same data in disaggregated form. The trouble is that the "weights" needed for aggregative indexes of other social statistics are not available, except within particular and limited areas. It would be utopian even to strive for a Gross Social Product, or National Socioeconomic Welfare, figure which aggregated all relevant social and economic variables. There are no objective weights, equivalent to prices, that we can use to compare the importance of an improvement in health with an increase in social mobility. We could in principle have a sample survey of the population, and ask the respondents how important they thought an additional unit of health was in comparison with a marginal unit of social mobility. But the relevant units would be difficult even to define, and the respondents would have no experience in dealing with them, so the results would probably be unreliable. Thus the goal of a grand and cosmic measure of all forms or aspects of welfare must be dismissed as impractical, for the present at any rate.

Examples of Social Indicators

Within particular and limited areas, on the other hand, some modest degree of aggregation is now possible. And even over a limited area, such aggregation can be extremely useful. Some of the possibilities for useful aggregation over a limited span are illustrated in the chapters of this report.

One aggregative index is the expectancy of *healthy* life (strictly, life expectancy free of bed-disability and institutionalization). This index weights each disease or source of disability in proportion to its effect in reducing length of life or in keeping a person in bed or institutionalized. If there is either a reduction in bed-disability due to a reduction in disease, or an increase in life expectancy when bed-disability is unchanged, the index will increase, as it should. Admittedly, this aggregative index is, like the National Income statistics, imperfect in some respects.[2] Yet, its degree of aggregation makes it much easier to do systematic work at a general level on the relationship between health and life and various causal variables, such as medical inputs, income levels, and the like.

Another area in which limited aggregation is possible is that of crime. To determine how much the danger of being victimized by a criminal changes over time, we should weight each type of crime by the extent of harm suffered by the victim. The dollar values lost would provide good weights for larcenies and burglaries, but the loss from personal injury or death would have to be estimated or assumed.

Where changes in the extent of "criminality" (or conversely, "law-abidingness") in a population are at issue, different weights are needed. Though it presumably does not matter to the victim whether he is killed by manslaughter or murder, society put a very different assessment on the two acts. Weights for an index of criminality can be obtained from surveys, which show that respondents of different classes and occupations tend to agree on the relative heinousness of different significant crimes. The results of the best known of these surveys are highly correlated (r=.97) with data on the average length of prison sentences for the same crimes.

Some aggregates do not require the cumulation of qualitatively quite different things. For example, in the Opportunity chapter the operative assumption is that social mobility along some one dimension tends to vary in proportion to social mobility along other dimensions. Thus the correlation coefficient indicating the association between the socioeconomic status of men working now, as measured by the social rank of their usual occupation, and the socioeconomic status of their fathers, measured in the same way, is an aggregative index of social mobility. Its aggregative character derives, not only from the geographic span of the sample, but also from the assumption that changes in occupational status are *representative* of the diverse and manifold changes entailed in any significant intergenerational change in socioeconomic status. The implicit aggregation entailed in using a representative variable is in principle inferior to the more explicit sorts of aggregation discussed earlier, but it is usually easier in practice, and probably more congenial to those who are not familiar with aggregative theories or data constructs.

The Next Step: The Development of Policy Accounts

Although the potential usefulness of several social indicators has been illustrated in this report, this work represents only a beginning. Hopefully, there will be continued studies of social indicators and their method of construction. At the same time we also need to encourage the collection of new and more socially relevant data. If a balanced, organized, and concise set of measures of the condition of our society were available, we should have the information needed to identify emerging problems and to make knowledgeable decisions about national priorities.

The next step in any logical process of policy formation is to choose the most efficient program for dealing with the conditions that have been exposed. Then there must be a decision about how much should be spent on the program to deal with the difficulty. If these two decisions are to be made intelligently, the society needs information on the benefits and costs of alternative programs at alternative levels of funding.

It might seem at first glance that the benefits of an operating program could be obtained directly from the social indicators, which would measure any changes in the relevant social condition and therefore in the output of a program. In fact, it is much more difficult to obtain information on the output of even an existing program than to obtain a social indicator. The condition of an aspect of a nation depends, not only on a particular public program, but also on many other things. Health and life expectancy, for example, depend not only on public health programs, but also on private medical expenditures, the standard of living, the quality of nutrition, the exposure to contagious diseases, and the like. Thus to determine the output of a public program we normally have to solve something like what the econometrician would call the "specification problem"; we have to identify or distinguish those changes in the social indicator due to the changed levels of expenditure on the public program. This is often not a tractable task, but it could contribute much to truly rational decision making.

The fact that rational policy necessitates linking social indicators to program inputs means that social indicators alone do not provide all of the quantitative information needed for effective decision making. Ultimately, we must integrate our social indicators into policy accounts which would allow us to estimate the changes in a social indicator that could be expected to result from alternative levels of expenditure on relevant public programs.

Though an impressive set of social indicators could be developed at modest cost in the near-term future, a complete set of policy accounts is a utopian goal at present. This does not mean that work on a more integrative set of statistics should be postponed. These accounts will never be available unless we start thinking about the statistics we need for rational decision making now, even if this only entails marginal changes in the statistics we already have. The social statistics that we need will almost never be obtained as a by-product of accounting or administrative routine, or as a result of a series of *ad hoc* decisions, however intelligent each of these decisions might be. Only a systematic approach based on the informational requirements of public policy will do.

NOTES

[1]Subcommittee on Census and Statistics, Committee on Post Office and Civil Service, House of Representatives, *1967 Report of Statistical Activities of the Federal Government,* House Report 1071.

[2]It does not deal with the disability which does not force people to bed. Though it weighs the serious disease more heavily than the lesser disease, since the serious disease more often results in death or in longer bed-disability than the minor disease, it makes no allowance for the difference in pain and discomfort per day among various diseases. Finally, it ranks death and permanent bed disability equally, which may not be in accord with our values.

16

EDUCATION AND LEARNING
by Wilbur J. Cohen

Wilbur Cohen's credentials as a student of social indicators are established in his article below. He points to the many indices indicative of substantial progress in expanding the quantity and quality of education, but he raises a series of difficult and thus far unanswered questions regarding the nature of education, its place within an egalitarian society, and the frustrating problem of developing adequate performance indices.

The American people from their beginnings as a nation have set ambitious social and economic goals to improve the quality of life. The evidence of history shows that the nation has made remarkable progress. And further advancement toward these goals continues. But few accurate indicators are available to gauge the rate of progress or to measure the changes in American society that are currently under way and the obstacles that impede attainment of the goals.

PROBLEMS OF ESTABLISHING INDICATORS OF NATIONAL ACHIEVEMENT

The task of enunciating meaningful and relevant national goals is an essential first step for achieving them. Pertinent statistics and other facts are necessary to develop effective programs and plans,

Reprinted from Wilbur J. Cohen, "Education and Learning," *The Annals,* Vol. 373 (September 1967), pp. 80-101. Reprinted by permission of the publisher and author.

to evaluate progress, and to assess resources needed for accomplishing the nation's aims.

Setting up relevant indicators is not an easy undertaking. Not only must they be applicable to complex ideas and concepts, they also are concerned with vital and challenging issues. But the urgency of the task is great. There has already been widespread public discussion of the social changes which are occurring with a rapidity unequaled in history and of the problems concerned with vastly increasing population and mass migration to urban-suburban areas; with substandard education, substandard jobs, and substandard housing for millions of people who do not fully share in the benefits of a prosperous society; with mass communications, rapid travel, mass production, and automation. These discussions have revealed facts related to change. The information, while significant, is only a fraction of the knowledge needed to understand and adjust to life in the twenty-first century.

THE IMPORTANCE OF AN EDUCATED SOCIETY

Not too long ago, education was considered the privilege of only the wealthy—the leisure class. The evolution of the American idea of free public education for all, with public schools locally managed, and largely locally financed, has been closely bound to the development of the nation itself. United States educational history reflects the American commitment to the ideal of education for everyone—the conviction that an educated population is essential to an effective democracy, to freedom, and to economic growth.

The Right to an Education

The national urge to raise the quality of life for all, which—in turn—required providing educational opportunities for all, has produced an addition to the list of basic American rights: the right to an education—or, at least, the right to have an opportunity to acquire an education. Despite a gradually increasing public acceptance of the idea of "full education for every citizen to the limits of his capacity to absorb it," the most casual sampling would reveal thousands of young people who are not accorded this right. From the point of view of the welfare of society—and of the individual as well—this right must be assured.

The Task for Education in the Twenty-first Century

As society becomes increasingly more highly developed and changes occur with ever greater rapidity, not only a person's livelihood, but indeed the very essence of the life he leads—his way of life—will depend upon his education. His ability to discard much that he has learned as it becomes obsolete or irrelevant and to acquire new knowledge—most of it not yet discovered—that will be pertinent to his needs will determine his ability to make the successful transition from life in this decade to a future vastly different in terms of economic and technological achievements.

The development of the nation's schools has been alternately praised and criticized in educational circles, as well as in congressional committees, in industrial conferences, and by the public at large. There is no disagreement, however, that, in its most simple terms, the success of the future will depend to a large degree upon providing more knowledge to more people in less time than is being done today. And this will be a costly enterprise. But perhaps failure to do so would carry an even higher cost.

A NEW ERA IN EDUCATION

This is an era of innovation and change. The methods of gaining new knowledge, transmitting it, and diffusing information and ideas throughout the country must be speeded up. It has become clear that the changes in one area reverberate and indicate new perspectives in others. As an outstanding illustration, the demographic, economic, and social forces fermenting throughout American society are generating significant changes in the nation's educational system. There are new and unprecedented challenges in education, on a national scope, to meet unconventional educational demands —to shift from the traditional school-system emphasis on instruction designed for learning patterns of school-age youth to innovative methods concerned with the learning capabilities of very young children and of adults.

Newly discovered phenomena of early learning capacity and the increasing need for modern adults to have opportunities for "refresher" learning experiences to update and upgrade their knowledge and skills raise provocative questions about restricting the delivery of educational services generally to the "school-age" population. Today's circumscribed educational process, viewed by many as a "preparation for life," is not likely to be applicable and acceptable to people living in an age characterized by space exploration, the crumbling of barriers of time and distance, the rising aspirations of all citizens, the proliferation of knowledge, the advances in technology and computerized methods, high productivity, and growing wealth. Modern man will likely regard the continuation of his learning experience as a normal lifetime activity.

Training Manpower in Relation to Needs

There is wide recognition that the pressures of new technology combined with a growing number of students put a huge burden on education.[1] Increasingly, business leaders are directing their attention to science and technology as they relate to education and the labor market of the present and future, as indicated in the following statement of concern:

It has been predicted that in 1975 some three-fourths of our labor force will be producing goods and services that have not yet been developed. Unless educators—and other public and private policy makers—demonstrate unusually keen foresight, our future economic and technological achievements could be tarnished by a large and growing reserve of inadequately or inappropriately prepared workers.

If the challenges of the future are to be met, business and education must in fact greatly increase their interaction. Corporate giving doesn't complete business' responsibility to the world of study and schooling.[2]

Emerging Patterns in Education

As the public school system developed, intensive efforts have been made to provide better educations and equal educational opportunities for more and more students. Continued interest must now be devoted to assuring that the system will reach out to disadvantaged minority groups which have been largely ignored in the past.

TABLE 1

School Enrollments, United States, 1962-1975 (Millions)

Educational Level	1940	1950	1960	1965	1970°	1974°
	22.9	31.5	46.0	55.4	63.0	68.4
Preschool	.7	1.3	2.7	3.1	5.3	6.8
Elementary School	20.6	21.0	29.7	33.3	34.2	34.7
Secondary School	7.1	6.5	9.6	12.8	15.1	16.4
Higher Education	1.5	2.7	4.0	6.2	8.4	10.5

° Projected.

The formal educational system must be adaptable to the changing role and meaning of education. The line of distinction between the formal education program, ending with a diploma, and informal educational activities continued as a lifelong process is becoming faint and fading rapidly. Education acquired prior to graduation can no longer be relied upon as an adequate preparation for a lifetime career. The acceleration of technological change and new scientific discoveries, which make old jobs obsolete and create entirely new kinds of work, has been much discussed as posing requirements for continuing education and skill-renewal. Indeed, it has been suggested that a worker now entering the labor force may expect to be employed in not one, but probably two, and possibly even three or four entirely different kinds of work over his lifetime.

The Impact of Changing Labor-Force Requirements on the Locus and Modus of Education

The probability that many of today's school children will be working in the twenty-first century— on jobs not yet created— challenges the educational system to foster the art of learning and to provide pupils with the kind of broadly based general education they need in order to adapt to changes that will occur in their lifetimes. In other words, the educational system is charged with offering a student a sound basic education as well as opportunities for continuous learning at all levels of education and throughout his lifetime.

New and different kinds of educational services must be developed for a generation which will become increasingly involved in leisure-time and cultural pursuits. The educational system will have to become increasingly involved in the affairs of the community and of the world as it helps each child, woman, and man to adapt to the revolutionary changes in his life. Education will become a vital process of innovation and interaction—for the students, the teachers, the educational institutions, the local communities, and the nation.

PRESENT EDUCATIONAL TRENDS

The educational system, like many other institutions in American society, is in a state of evolution—some might even say revolution. Beginning with the past decade, a whole continuum of new methods for organization and delivery of educational services is being developed—indeed, *has* to be developed—to cope with the ever larger numbers of students and ever growing mass of knowledge.

The Growing Learning Force

The most significant aspects of change in the American educational system over the past decade have been the explosive increase in school enrollments and the continuing rise in educational attainment. The growth in the number of persons engaged in formal learning activities has been phenomenal.[3]

Regular School Enrollments

School enrollments—kindergarten through college—increased by 9.4 million from 1960 to 1965, an average increase of nearly two million a year.

As reflected in Table 1, elementary and secondary school enrollments are projected to reach 51 million by 1974. The largest enrollment increases over the past decade have been at the high school level, mainly because children born in the years of very high birth rates immediately following World War II are now progressing through high school. Their impact on elementary schools leveled off as they reached high school age and moved up to swell the enrollment rates for secondary schools. Enrollment in grades nine through twelve nearly tripled in the years 1950-1965, and is expected to reach 16.4 million in 1974. Proportionately smaller increases have been projected for elementary school enrollments because the number of five- and six-year-old children entering the school system is approaching a relatively stable figure.

The largest percentage increase in enrollments in recent years has been at the higher education level. Enrollment figures have climbed from 2.7 million in 1950 to 6 million in 1965. By 1974 enrollment may reach 10.5 million.

Vocational, Technical, and Professional Training Activities Outside the Formal Educational Structure

In addition to the growing regular enrollments, there have been dramatic increases in specialized learning activities of a vocational, technical, and professional nature. Although valid statistics have not been compiled on enrollments in correspondence courses or in specialized institutes and commercial schools, reference to city classified directories reveals a large volume and wide variety of such facilities. Recent attempts to determine the extent of participation in such learning activities have produced some rough estimates, which are presented in Table 2.

TABLE 2

**Vocational, Technical, and Professional Training Outside the Formal
Educational Structure, United States, 1940-1974 (Millions)**

Training Institution	1940	1950	1960	1965	1970°	1974°
	11.8	15.3	18.9	25.0	34.0	48.7
Professional and Technical Training	2.5	3.5	4.0	7.8	9.6	18.1
Company Schools	4.7	6.0	6.7	7.2	12.0	17.5
On-the-Job Training	2.4	2.0	3.4	4.5	6.0	6.0
Correspondence Schools	1.0	1.5	2.0	2.4	2.8	3.2
Armed Forces	1.0	2.0	2.4	2.6	3.0	3.0
All Other	.2	.3	.4	.5	.6	.9

° Projected.

Other Formal Education Activities

The hunger of the American people for education is evident in
the great proliferation of formal educational opportunities offered
under a variety of sponsorships. Some courses are conducted as
commercial enterprises, employing high-pressure advertising and
sales techniques to attract customers. Others are provided by institutions (libraries, museums, churches, and charity or other groups)

TABLE 3

**United States Adult Education,
1940-1974 (Millions)**

Form	1940	1950	1960	1965	1970°	1974°
	5.6	6.9	9.6	19.2	24.3	31.1
General	1.5	1.8	3.4	4.5	5.0	6.0
Specialized	2.4	3.0	3.4	4.5	5.5	7.0
Correspondence Courses	1.6	1.9	2.5	2.6	2.9	3.5
All Other	.1	.2	.3	7.6	10.9	14.6

° Projected.

and private instruction of neighborhood or other small groups (for example, Great Books Discussion Groups; literary, poetry, art-appreciation, music, drama, and political and current-events discussion groups; adult leadership training for civilian defense, recreational, or youth work; and first-aid, cooking, home nursing, and other classes conducted by the American Red Cross, Girl Scouts, and other organizations, as well as similar activities offered by industry to employees or members of their families).

Table 3 presents some preliminary estimates based on a study, initiated by Mr. Bertram M. Gross and the author, of adult educational activity and how it is changing in the United States.

Ratio of Learning Force to Labor Force

While the estimates and projections of total educational activity in the United States are still relatively undeveloped, the gross figures on enrollments reflected above are significant. They represent a new area of inquiry into the widely diffused educational function. It must be noted that, because the formal training periods reflected under the various categories vary in duration between two weeks and a two-year or longer period, the number of participants is not equivalent to man-years of training. Indeed, the data limitations suggest further research for more reliable statistics on these largely unidentified—or at least less visible—educational resources and conversion of the participation figures into school-year equivalents.

TABLE 4

Ratio of United States Education
Force to Labor Force, 1940-1974

Learning Force To Labor Force Ratio (Per Cent)	1940	1950	1960	1965	1970°	1974°
	84.2	82.9	101.9	127.0	141.7	159.4
Learning Force (in Millions)	47.3	53.7	74.5	99.6	121.3	148.2
Labor Force (in Millions)	56.2	61.8	73.1	78.4	85.6	93.0

° Projected.

The estimates do not include any assessment of the very considerable volume of education acquired in learning situations represented by basic training in the home, religious instruction in churches, knowledge and skills gained by children in youth-group activities, unorganized individual learning from television, radio, and other informational media, and self-education, including learning from experience. Even with such an omission, the sum of the learning-force components reach a magnitude approaching 100 million participants—a startling total, nearly a quarter of a million higher than the number in the total United States labor force! The fact that today the learning force is greater than the labor force, and by 1974 the ratio—even by conservative estimates—will be considerably higher, emphasizes the great dimension of the pending tasks for the educational complex.

The Increasing Number of Teachers

As noted earlier, the rate of increase in the numbers of school-age children is not so rapid now as it was over the last two decades; nevertheless, the absolute numbers of school children are larger, with the corollary result of increasing demands for teachers.

The teaching force, has, of course, increased. This year, more than two million grade and high school teachers and nearly a half-million college and university instructors were teaching the increasing number of students. The shortage of teachers and staff to supplement and support their work probably poses the single greatest obstacle to general improvement in education programs. As reflected in Table 5, the number of regular school classroom teachers and other instructional staff is projected to reach 3.2 million by 1974.

Rising Educational Expenditures

From time to time, there have been some scattered and unrelated attempts to assess total expenditures for all educational activities. As might be expected, wide variations occur in what has been termed "knowledge industry" expenditures, depending upon the components used in the computations.

In 1958, a figure of $136.4 billion was estimated to cover expenditures for research and development activities, all communication media, and information machines and services, in addition to regular formal educational expenditures.[4] More recently, a $195 billion figure has been used as roughly equivalent to the 1958 estimates, with adjustments for the great expansion in audiovisual materials and educational technology (computers, programmed instruction, and the like) that has occurred.

TABLE 5

United States Teaching Force,
1970-1974 (Millions)

Educational Level	1940	1950	1960	1970°	1974°
	1.0	1.3	2.0	3.0	3.2
Elementary Schools	.6	.7	1.1	1.4	1.4
Secondary Schools	.3	14	.6	1.1	1.2
Higher Education	.1	.2	.3	.5	.6

° Projected.

Although these estimates appear to be extremely high, they may actually be somewhat understated if consideration is given to the increase in total expenditures (both public and private) for formal education, which have been rising steadily by more than 10 per cent a year—a rate greater than the increase in the gross national products (GNP). This year, expenditures for formal education are expected to reach $49 billion, or about 6.5 per cent of the GNP. It has been estimated that they may reach 8 per cent of GNP by 1975.[5]

Spending by all levels of government for education has increased dramatically, from $13 billion in 1956 to $34 billion in 1966; and most of the funds have come consistently from state and local government sources. However, in the last two years the federal share increased from 12 to 16 per cent of the total. Most of the increase in federal funds can be attributed to new support under the Elementary and Secondary Education Act and the Higher Education Act.

Since 1964, federal expenditures for elementary and secondary education have more than doubled, from about 4 per cent to nearly 9 per cent; while the share in higher education rose from 20 per cent to about 22 per cent. However, there has been a shift in the allocation of federal funds; whereas in 1964, 58 per cent of all federal grants for education were made for higher education, the figure dropped to 43 per cent last year, with a resulting increase in support for elementary schools.

For more than a decade, state and local governments have used about 90 per cent of their construction funds to build elementary and secondary schools. From the mid-1950's until about 1962, more than half of the federal government's construction expenditures also went to elementary and secondary schools. Since 1962, however, there have been increasing authorizations for new federal programs for college construction, and last year 93 per cent of federal construction funds went to institutions of higher learning because this is where the great impact of enrollments is, and will be in the future. Because of population trends, elementary and secondary school enrollments will begin to level off, whereas college enrollment will increase dramatically.

The importance that Americans place on education is also reflected in private spending. Since 1955, the amount spent has nearly tripled, due mainly to investments in higher education. In 1955, the private sector was investing $1.3 billion in higher education. By 1966, the outlay was about $3.5 billion.

Changing Methods to Meet New Demands

In addition to the millions of youth in compulsory school attendance, millions of adults also attend classes of one sort or another. Thus, acceptance by a most significant segment of the population of the desirability and real need for a continuous, lifelong process of upgrading and expanding knowledge and skills is an educational phenomenon demanding new ways to satisfy the quest for education. The steadily increasing ratio of the learning force to the labor force indicates that educational services are reaching upward, downward, and throughout the whole age-range of our population.

The institutions that are being developed or vastly expanded in number are of many kinds, including junior colleges and vocational and technical schools. During the past decade, junior-college enrollments multiplied two and one-half times—a growth rate nearly twice that of four-year colleges.

Innovations are also being introduced into the classroom, with experiments involving new concepts of learning, course content, and patterns of teaching. As research and development gain a foothold in the traditional conservative school, old notions of how education should be conducted are questioned and revamped. The pressure of the number of students alone forces change: the introduction of more technology into the classroom; innovations in instruction methods and curricula content at all levels, including graduate schools;[6] more research into learning and motivation; and curriculum research—research into what is taught and how it is taught.

EDUCATIONAL GOALS AND ISSUES

With the outlines of change in economic and social institutions everywhere apparent, the rapid pace of events in the world today demands a closer look at the changes occuring, particularly a critical analysis and evaluation of what is happening in education and the direction it is taking. Difficult questions, at present left unexamined or inadequately explored, must be answered. Is the educational system fulfilling the responsibilities that the American people have assigned to it? Is it meeting the requirements of today, and will it meet them in the future? What is the nature of the learning process? How, precisely, does one human being teach another? What functions can a machine perform better than a human instructor? How could schools and classrooms be organized to make it possible for every student to learn at his own pace? These are questions that educators—in co-operation with a host of other specialists—must ask, and for which they must produce reliable answers. Accurate, meaningful educational indicators are a prerequisite for valid answers and for planning effective remedies when needed.

Qualitative Issues

Whatever indicators are developed must take account of the variety of educational goals and the changes in definitions and emphases of these goals. One kind of indicator, for example, would be used to measure the quality of education: Are students' abilities being developed more fully today than yesterday?Are adequate attention and funds being concentrated on improving the quality of educational services? Are educational programs developing technical competence to meet work-force requirements—a technical competence founded on a good grounding in basic general principles?

Quantitative Issues

A different kind of indicator would be required to measure the quantity of education: Are more people being educated today than yesterday? Are the numbers of young workers who cannot find jobs being reduced as a wider range of vocational education and job-training opportunities are offered?

Education and the Individual

The importance of education to the individual has been elevated to one of the highest values in our democratic society. A primary goal of education is to offer each individual an opportunity to de-

TABLE 6

Gross National Product Related to Total Expenditures[a] for Education: United States 1929-1930 to 1965-1966

Calendar Year	Gross National Product (in Millions)	School Year	Expenditures for Education Total (in Thousands)	Expenditures for Education As a Percent of Gross National Product
1	2	3	4	5
1929	$103,095	1929-30	$3,233,601	3.1
1931	75,820	1931-32	2,966,464	3.9
1933	55,601	1933-34	2,294,896	4.1
1935	72,247	1935-36	2,649,914	3.7
1937	90,446	1937-38	3,014,074	3.3
1939	90,494	1939-40	3,199,593	3.5
1941	124,540	1941-42	3,203,548	2.6
1943	191,592	1943-44	3,522,007	1.8
1945	212,010	1945-46	4,167,597	2.0
1947	231,323	1947-48	6,574,379	2.8
1949	256,484	1949-50	8,795,635	3.4
1951	328,404	1951-52	11,312,446	3.4
1953	364,593	1953-54	13,949,876	3.8
1955	397,960	1955-56	16,811,651	4.2
1957	411,134	1957-58	21,119,565	4.8
1959	483,650	1959-60	24,722,464	5.1
1961	520,109	1961-62	29,366,305	5.6
1963	589,238	1963-64	b36,600,000	6.2
1965	676,300	1965-66	b45,100,000	6.7

[a]Includes expenditures of public and non-public schools at all levels of education (elementary, secondary, and higher education).

Estimated.

Note: Beginning with 1959-60 school year, includes Alaska and Hawaii.

Sources: U.S. Department of Health, Education, and Welfare, Office of Education, "Biennial Survey of Education in the United States"; "Statistics of State School Systems"; "Financial Statistics of Institutions of Higher Education"; and unpublished data. U.S. Department of Commerce, Office of Business Economics, "Survey of Current Business," August 1965 and April 1966.

velop his abilities to the fullest capacity. Education should help him adapt to a rapidly changing world, to think rationally and creatively, to be independent, and to enjoy a rewarding life. Education should provide him with the skills and knowledge he must have to be a productive member of society; it should elevate his economic status as well as enhance his self-confidence, judgment, creativity, and humanity. Education should contribute to his enjoyment of life and widen the range of choices available to him throughout his life.

Education and Society (Public Policy)

The great basic goals of education are to foster individual fulfillment and to nurture the free, rational, and responsible men and women without whom our kind of society cannot endure. Educated citizens are essential to an effective democracy and a healthy economy. They are politically active, responsible citizens, less subject than others to corruption and less easily influenced by demagoguery. The related problems of poverty and racial injustice are closely linked to the restricted educational opportunities of the disadvantaged. Yet, too often, schooling offered to children in depressed areas is ill-suited to their needs, and public educational programs have not coped adequately with the special educational problems of disadvantaged children.

Education and Economic Productivity

Educated citizens are productive citizens, whose efforts and abilities and increased demands will add to the nation's economic growth. Economist Theodore Schultz, for example, has estimated that:

As a source of economic growth, the additional schooling of the labor force would appear to account for about one-fifth of the rise in real national income in the United States.[7]

Education is expected to help break the vicious cycle of poverty, which is often perpetuated from generation to generation. Low educational attainment is a product—and in turn a producer—of poverty, unemployment, and discrimination. Investment in education is expected to pay off in still other gains to the economy: in research and development of new products and in economic efficiencies that result when the labor force has high literacy and higher educational attainment.

Defining Goals

In addition to the broader, basic goals of education mentioned above, there are other—more narrowly defined—goals within the educational system that lead to attainment of the broader aims:

1. to provide equality of educational opportunities to all of the nation's citizens, and
2. to improve the quality of education for all.

To achieve goal number one, action is needed, for example, to:
• increase the quantity of education,
• provide continuous learning opportunities, and
• improve the efficiency and economy of the delivery of educational services.
To achieve goal number two, the system will have to:
• revise and improve curricula,
• improve the quality of teaching,
• stimulate research and development, and
• adopt innovations.

It can be clearly seen that these goals are complementary, each contributing to the other. Both are concerned with the conservation and development of individuals. And both will produce the benefits that result from strengthening the individual through education: not only will the manpower resources of the nation be improved, but, at the same time, the quality of life for the individual will be enhanced.

EDUCATIONAL INDICATORS

Much discussion, debate, and ferment are going on today about the attainment of national goals. Probably never before in history has there been a period when greater attention was focused on education. Surely there never has been a time when so much money has been spent on education. But much of the discussion, debate, and spending proceeds without basic knowledge of what is happening.

When we survey the voluminous, yet unsuitable, data now available for assessing the products of education, we must conclude that practically none of it measures the output of our educational system in terms that really matter (that is, in terms of what students have learned). Amazement at the revelation of the tremendous lack of suitable indicators is almost overshadowed by the incredible fact that the nation has, year after year, been spending billions of state and local tax dollars on an enterprise without knowing how effective the expenditures are, or even if they are being directed to stated goals. Indicators would provide an insight into changes taking place in education and into existing and potential problems. They would also offer a means of evaluating progress toward defined goals.

It is generally acknowledged that effective plans for achieving educational objectives and the execution of those plans depend upon the availability of continuing, regularly collected, comprehensive information pertinent to the status of education. But what are the data that are pertinent? What information will reflect where we are today, and what must we know to measure the changes that will take place in the future?

Present Indicators

Although, as already indicated, there is an urgent need for new indicators, a preliminary examination of those that exist is appropriate.

More than one hundred years ago, the United State Office of Education was directed by the Congress, when it established the Office, to collect "such statistics and facts as shall show the condition and progress" of American education. Thus, the Office has counted the numbers of pupils, teachers, classrooms, equipment, and other relevant items such as the kinds and numbers of degrees awarded.

In co-operation with the Bureau of the Census, the Office of Education has developed some national historical series showing illiteracy rates of the population, percentage of school-age groups enrolled, retention rates of school population, educational attainment of the population by specific age groups, the median years of school completed by the labor force, the correlation of income and years of school completed, sources of educational revenues, and other quantitative data related to formal education.

But the gaps between what is known and what needs to be known are great.

In addition, there is a critical need to develop new data—through either simple counting procedures, longitudinal studies, or more limited case studies.

But perhaps most important is the need for basic research in education. There are still great gaps in knowledge about learning, motivation, and other aspects of human behavior—the foundations upon which an educational system should be built.

Educational Opportunity

To some extent, available data are indicators of how well the goal of providing equal educational opportunities to all is being met. At least it is known that 25 million more students are enrolled in formal education today than were in school 25 years ago. The data also enable projections of future needs. In addition, they permit some comparisons among states and regions of educational inputs—pupil-teacher ratios, pupils per classroom, average salaries, and expenditures per pupil.

Much of the support for federal assistance to education grew from the realization that local support varies widely and that when education is inadequate in any one section of the country, the entire nation suffers. Comparisons showing state expenditures per student in 1966–1967—ranging from $335 in Mississippi to $912 in New York—sharply point up the vast disparities and resulting inequities in educational input. Recognition that poor states, though often spending relatively more of their personal income per capita on education, are still not able to provide satisfactory education helped to bring about federal legislation designed to eliminate the disparities in the amount of education offered students in different sections of the nation and from different segments of the population.

Quantity of Education

Statistics now compiled also are indicators of quantitative output of the educational system. There is, for example, an indicator of the increasing level of educational attainment in the United States, which can be correlated with indicators of variations in the financial support given the schools by different states and regions. In 1960, 30 per cent of the adults in Mississippi were high school graduates, compared with 41 per cent in the entire country. Also, some already existing indicators show educational output by race; for example, the average years of schooling for the nonwhite population over age 25 in 1965 was 9.0 years, compared with 11.8 years for total population over age 25. Among those aged 25-29, nationwide, some 12.4 per cent of total population had completed four or more years of college, but only 8.3 per cent of nonwhites had done so (Table 7).

Quality of Education

Although there is a considerable amount of quantitative data, little of it reveals information about the quality of the educational system or its products. Practically none of the data measures output

TABLE 7

Level of School Completed by Persons 25 Years Old and Over and 25 to 29 Years Old, by Color: United States, 1940 to 1965

Date, Age, and Color	Per Cent by Level of School Completed			Median School Years Completed
	Less Than 5 Years of Elementary School	4 Years of High School or More	4 or More Years of College	
1	2	3	4	5
White and Nonwhite				
25 years and over				
March 1965	6.8	49.0	9.4	11.8
March 1964	7.1	48.0	9.1	11.7
March 1962	7.8	46.3	8.9	11.4
March 1959	8.0	42.9	7.9	11.0
March 1957	9.0	40.8	7.5	10.6
October 1952	9.1	38.4	6.9	10.1
April 1950	10.8	33.4	6.0	9.3
April 1947	10.4	32.6	5.4	9.0
April 1940	13.5	24.1	4.6	8.4
25 to 29 years:				
March 1965	2.0	70.3	12.4	12.4
March 1964	2.1	69.2	12.8	12.4
March 1962	2.4	65.9	13.1	12.4
March 1959	3.0	63.3	11.0	12.3
October 1952	3.8	56.7	10.0	12.2
April 1950	4.6	51.7	7.7	12.1
April 1940	5.9	37.8	5.8	10.4
Nonwhite				
25 years and over:				
March 1965	18.4	28.6	5.5	9.0
March 1964	18.6	27.5	4.7	8.9
March 1962	22.1	24.8	4.0	8.6
March 1959	23.5	20.0	3.2	8.1
March 1957	26.9	17.8	2.8	7.7
October 1952	30.3	14.7	2.4	7.1
April 1950	31.5	13.2	2.2	6.8
April 1947	31.4	13.2	2.4	6.9
April 1940	41.1	7.5	1.3	5.8
25 to 29 years:				
March 1965	4.8	52.2	8.3	12.1
March 1964	5.3	48.0	7.0	11.8
March 1962	6.1	41.6	4.2	11.2
March 1959	7.8	39.1	4.6	10.9
October 1952	15.2	27.8	4.6	9.3
April 1950	15.6	22.9	2.8	8.7
April 1940	26.7	12.1	1.6	7.1

Note: Beginning in 1962, includes Alaska and Hawaii, Statistics for 1962 and subsequent years are not strictly comparable with earlier data.

Source: U. S. Deqartment of Commerce, Bureau of the Census, "Current Population Reports," Series P-20, Nos. 99, 121, and 138; Series P-19, No. 4; and unpublished data.

of the system in terms of what students have learned, or inputs in terms of how good the teaching is that is provided for students.

Only very recently have efforts been started to develop and analyze statistics that may furnish some clues as to geographical or racial variations in the quality of the educational output.

The adverse effects of unequal facilities, staff, and services, reinforced by handicaps brought to the school by many minority-group children, are reflected in these recent studies of educational attainment. The effects are clearly apparent in the mental scores of the Armed Forces Qualification Test (AFQT)—about as close a national indicator of educational strengths and weaknesses as now exists— and in a more limited survey conducted by the Office of Education on equality of educational opportunity.[8]

The AFQT shows that:

Southern Negroes are behind Southern whites, who are behind whites in all other regions of the country; Southern Negroes are behind Negroes in other parts of the country;

In every State, test performance is significantly higher for whites than for Negroes;

Negroes who fail the AFQT have, on the average, one more year of schooling than whites who fail the test.[9]

The Office of Education survey showed that Negro students at each grade level tested (grades 1, 3, 6, 9, and 12) scored distinctly lower than white students in the same grades; by the twelfth-grade level, the differences were still greater. Negroes were 10.7 points below white children in nonverbal scores; for example, at the first-grade level, on tests with an average of 50 and a standard deviation of 10, by the twelfth grade, the gap had grown to 11.1 points.[10]

The Office of Education study revealed further that Negroes generally are offered fewer of the facilities assumed to contribute to academic achievement, such as laboratories, libraries, textbooks, and audio-visual aids.[11] (However, the results of the survey also implied that differences in family background account for more variations in achievements of white and Negro children than do differences in school facilities.)[12] The study, which contains much valuable information, emphasizes the need for further inquiry into the problem of equal educational opportunities. To gain insight into the problems raised by the report requires the development of a number of indicators dealing with unequal opportunities for education.

Tests—Usefulness and Limitations

Over the years, a considerable amount of testing activity has been undertaken in individual schools in attempts to measure Intelligence Quotient (IQ), attainment levels in subject matter, and other student characteristics. However, the test results have not been compiled in any meaningful way or in a way that permits analyses on broad comparative bases. Furthermore, the primary purpose of IQ testing has been to locate an individual child on a scale—not to determine the range of knowledge of a group of children at a given grade or age level.

In addition, there is considerable controversy over the use of IQ tests. Some educators contend that the tests have been misused by teachers who use the test results to limit the opportunities available to a child by placing him in a rigid mold that determines the way he is treated in the school system and hampers him from accomplishing much that he, perhaps, has the ability to do.

Others question exactly what it is that IQ or attainment tests measure. What, for example, is meant by "intelligence"? Would not a test that measures creativity be just as useful? Certainly, today's IQ tests take little account of creativity. But this line of inquiry leads to still a further problem: how to measure creativity.

Needed Indicators
To Extend Educational Opportunities

In spite of the existing multitude of quantitative statistics, additional quantitative as well as qualitative data are needed to measure progress in extending equal educational opportunities. The present series fail to distinguish between rural and urban schools or to show variations among the schools within a community. There is no accurate picture of inputs—in terms of money, students, or resources—for rural schools, or what the output is in levels of student attainment. Similarly, there are no accurate statistics on the input-output of urban slum schools, compared with middle-class suburban schools. On a national basis, it is not known how many children fail at each grade level and repeat the grade, or how many skip a grade, let alone why.

Data are almost completely lacking on the very important matter of the distribution of dropouts by geographic areas, socioeconomic levels, and degrees of urbanization of their communities. The proportion of dropouts who would have completed high school with adequate financial support or other incentives is not known; nor is there information, on any systematic basis, about what happens to dropouts, although it is clear that many fall into the ranks of the unemployed. An equal lack of information exists about college dropouts. [It is known that for every 10 pupils in the 5th grade in 1957-58, 9.4 entered the 9th grade in 1961-62; 8.1 entered the 11th grade in 1963-64; 7.1 graduated from high school in 1965; 3.8 entered college in fall 1965; and 1.9 are likely to earn 4-year degrees in 1969.]

Accurate national data on school segregation—actual or *de facto* —are not yet available. And a whole new area for research could be devoted to the effects of segregation on the child.

Indicators related to staffing are also needed. No information has been compiled to show the numbers of teachers and professors who leave the profession each year, why they leave, or what subsequently happens to them. How many go to better-paying jobs? Are those who do so among the most experienced teachers? Is there a pattern of returning to teaching, say, for women who quit to raise a family? What is the flow of personnel back and forth among college teaching and business organizations and government agencies? What are the migration patterns of teachers within school districts and from lower-paying districts to higher-paying districts?

Although great emphasis is placed on the need for continuing education, very little accurate data exists about learning activities outside the usual classroom setting.

Although many people say that learning activities are expanding, almost no data have been collected to back up such a conclusion. And only very rough estimates have been made about the back-and-forth interchange or duplication that exists between the labor force and the learning force. Likewise, little is known about the extent to which employers conduct in-service training or management-improvement courses or provide other opportunities for employees to upgrade their skills and knowledges.

Nor are there any valid measures of the extent of educational activities of social clubs, labor unions, or fraternal organizations. No count has been made of those who engage in self-education with the help of libraries, museums, and cultural facilities, or of those who take advantage of the vast new opportunities through educational television programs.

Without basic quantitative data, it is almost impossible to analyze some of the problems involved in education today. And, clearly, in this age of computers with almost limitless capabilities, it is feasible to begin collecting the data—although that beginning could be on a somewhat limited basis. Perhaps a case-study approach in certain areas would eventually develop into statistical series that could serve as indicators, and any other promising possibilities for developing meaningful indicators should be explored.

To Improve the Quality of Education

When measurement of progress toward the second goal—to improve the quality of education—is attempted, it becomes clear that few significant indicators exist. First, few measures show the output of the system in terms of what students learn, even at the point where formal instruction is given.

A nationwide assessment of educational progress would be of great value not only for allocating public funds to the educational enterprise, but also to the educational community, as well as to educational policy-makers at all levels.

One project concerned with devising testing instruments to assess learning in several subjects is being developed under the leadership of Ralph W. Tyler, Director for the Center for Advanced Study in the Social Sciences. This study, supported by the Carnegie Corporation and the Ford Foundation, represents the first attempt to get nationwide indices of educational output. It is expected to provide greatly needed insights into the strengths and weaknesses of the present educational system.

The problems involved in trying to measure the quality of teaching are as complex as those concerned with measuring student ability. Today there are few, if indeed any, indicators available. Of course, there never has been a nationwide assessment of teaching, and it is doubtful that there ever will be. Although educational statistics reveal that the proportion of public school teachers with substandard certification is higher today than it has been during the last three years, this does not necessarily indicate that the *quality* of teaching has deteriorated. In fact, it is possible that the infusion of "new blood"—Peace Corps veterans, retired persons, and other normally nonteaching, professional workers who were recruited last year to help ease the teacher shortage—could have improved the quality of teaching. It is by no means certain that present accreditation qualifications are necessary for high-quality teaching. Teacher-licensing by state governments affects the entry of persons into the profession. The certification process, clearly, should be looked into, and changes and revisions made, where necessary.

The need for basic research into what constitutes high-quality teaching is urgent. What are the characteristics of a good teacher? How are such characteristics developed? What improvements could be made in recruiting and training teachers? Can measures be developed to show the relative value of in-service training? What would be the effects of new ways to encourage in-training and upgrading of teachers' skills? Can old standards and concepts of professional training be discarded? Could people without teacher training be used effectively in new methods of teaching? Would the injection of a large number of teacher aides or assistants improve the quality of teaching by allowing the instructor to concentrate on important subject matter and individual students?

The development of yardsticks to evaluate the quality of teaching would be important not only for a social inventory—but also as the key to put teaching back into the center of education, particularly higher education. Rewards in terms of salaries, for example, could be more accurately related to measures of the quality of the teaching. Very little is known about the effect of salary levels on high-quality teaching or whether present salary levels attract and retain highly qualified teachers. Likewise, it is not known whether the prestige attached to certain teaching positions is a measurable factor in high-quality teaching.

To Improve the Organization and Direction of the System

Similarly, very few attempts have been made to assess the efficiency and economy of the operation of the formal educational system. The long-term trend toward consolidation of school districts may be cited as an indicator of improved efficiency. Ten years ago there were 55,000 local school districts; today, only 23,500—a reduction of nearly 60 per cent. Last year alone, more than 3,500 school districts were eliminated.

Nevertheless, the impression is widely held that the educational system is slow to adopt new ideas and techniques. How can this impediment to change be overcome?

To Assure Appropriate Emphasis and Future Orientation of Content of the Educational System

Traditionally, the educational system has been both conservative and innovative, transmitting the wisdom of the past and attempting to equip man to cope creatively with an unknown future. Too often, however, emphasis has been on acquiring knowledge of the past. Frequently, there has been neglect for building into the individual a respect for learning in the present, a hope for the future, and a sense of purpose and direction in sharing the problems, challenges, rewards, and responsibilities of society.

In deferring to tradition and continuity, there has—perhaps naturally—too often been resistance to imaginative departures from conventional methods of education. New concepts of what should be taught, as well as *how* and *when* it should be taught have failed to gain wide acceptance.

Clearly, more attention must be given to building a future-oriented educational system. The importance of doing so becomes even more evident if the extension of man's knowledge during this century is contemplated. While it was reasonable, in the eighteenth century, to expect the well-educated man both to have absorbed most of the knowledge from the past and also to keep abreast of new trends, such expectations are not realistic in the twentieth century. In the wake of the information explosion produced by advances in this era, the knowledge problem has become one of collecting, storing, transmitting, and retrieving the multitude of complex facts being produced almost daily.

Since today's youth needs broadly based knowledge and skills to equip him for life in a world vastly more complex than any visionary imagined a generation ago, the educational system is challenged to change methods that, although successful in the past, are no longer enough. What was accepted and fitting in another era may be inadequate for today. Nevertheless, change must be carefully accepted and evaluated. It is necessary to assess the value for the future of present plans for the organization and content of the educational system. Most planning has been confined narrowly to the outlines of ongoing institutions, and has not moved into the new dimension of what is possible for the present and necessary for the future—a new conception of where, and how, and when, and to whom educational services will be provided.

To Assure Application of Experimentation and Innovation Results to the School System

As the results of research and development efforts become available to help to reorganize the schools and what is taught in them, hard questions must be asked about alternative and better uses of technology in bringing about the comprehensive changes needed in education today. Recent federal legislative support for research and innovation in education reflects growing national concern for improving curricula, methods of teaching, individualized instruction, and experimentation in new patterns for the delivery of services.

It is a truism that the way to excellence in education is through research, which leads to innovation, and then into generally applied practice. But the United States has lagged in applying this principle to education. While financial support for educational research and development has increased in the past few years as a result of federal legislation, the amount is still small when compared with spending by other basic industries. Less than one-half of one per cent of the nation's total outlay for education is spent on research and development, compared with 10 per cent of total outlay in other major industries—nearly twenty times as much is spent on health research and sixty times as much, on defense research.

Not only are the amount and quality of research in education low, but there is relatively little feedback—even from good research—to the local school system. Unpublicized innovations—however successful in experimental application—are far too often not adopted simply because they are unknown. Thus, the results of research in education are too long delayed in application, or lost. It has been estimated that, over-all, there is a thirty-year lag between development of an innovation in education and its widespread adoption. It is fifteen years before 3 per cent of the school districts have made the change. The twenty experimental regional educational laboratories established under federal legislation in 1965 are designed to close this gap by speeding up dissemination of research findings and making research results operative.

It would be fallacious, of course, to assume that all research findings and resulting innovations will be productive. More intensive evaluations are needed of the relative costs and benefits of much high-priced technology, teaching machines, use of television, new teaching methods, and changes in organizational structure before they are widely instituted. Some evaluations may require long-term study, and the results cannot be immediately applied.

Lack of Feasible Indicators—Implications for Educational Research

The more readily apparent areas inviting inquiry already noted leave largely unphrased an almost infinite number of questions about education. And as answers for some questions are found, they stimulate still further inquiry. Many separate efforts will be necessary to develop the wide-ranging variety of indicators needed for measuring progress toward the diverse goals in education.

Behavioral Indicators

First, and of great importance, fundamental research into human behavior is needed. Should children with the highest learning abilities be grouped in classes with children of lowest learning abilities? Should children be grouped according to their parents'

earning abilities or some other home factors? What are the effects
of different groupings on individual children? What are the effects
of racial discrimination on learning? What are the reactions of
teachers to desegregation policies?

Can potential dropouts be identified at any early age? What are
the characteristics of school dropouts? Answers could point the way
for action to reduce the dropout rate. Present data show that although the percentage of students entering college has increased
tremendously, the college dropout rate has remained about the
same over the past twenty years. Why has the system failed to
retain a progressively larger number of students? Outside of a great
deal of discussion, relatively little has been done to find valid answers.

Learning and Education

There is also urgent need for research into the learning process
itself. Do we know what really constitutes "intelligence?" How
people learn? The factors that motivate them? How knowledge or
"learned experience" is retained? What test scores indicate? How
to relate early test scores to achievements in later life? Can valid
indicators of learning rates be developed? What are the optimum
situations for learning by children?

It may be that computers will help to uncover many secrets of
learning, may, in fact, offer more promise of learning about learning
that any other approach. Studies by Patrick Suppes and Richard C.
Atkinson, of the Institute for Mathematical Studies in the Social
Sciences at Stanford University, may provide some further answers.
They point out that computers keep a minute record of a child's
progress so that the point at which learning may falter or stop can
be immediately determined.[13]

John Gardner also pointed out that self-teaching machines seem
certain to have an impressive impact on the teaching process: "The
self-teaching device can individualize instruction in ways that are
not now possible—and the student is always an active participant."[14]

Other recent studies have been concerned with the importance
of early education.[15] According to Benjamin Bloom, half the growth
in intelligence takes place between birth and age 4; a 30 per cent
increase, from age 4 to age 8; and only about a 20 per cent gain is
made between age 8 and age 17. Such findings suggest that our
entire philosophy of education should be re-examined and our present expenditure pattern for education should be reassessed.

Additional experience with Headstart projects, which emphasize the importance of early education and the value of parent involvement, may substantiate some of the research conclusions. Some significant conclusions have already been drawn from Headstart results—the importance of teacher aides and assistants for individual attention to children and the value of follow-through programs in the early school years. Potential effects of the innovative program are far-reaching. Indicators could be developed quite simply to measure changes attributable to Headstart. Longitudinal studies of enrollees in the program could show what happens to them in elementary school, in high school, and beyond. The extent to which local school districts adopt Headstart techniques—parent involvement, use of teacher aides, regular classes for three- and four-year olds—might also be measured.

Education and Human Behavior

Other interesting questions could be explored by researchers in the educational field. For example: How does the level of a person's education relate to his personal adjustment, happiness, or fulfillment? Are there correlations between various levels of educational attainment and rates of different types of mental illness?

The answers to some questions of this type would depend upon information which could be obtained only from longitudinal studies. And few such studies have been attempted so far, primarily because the price-tag on them is high. However, unless data cover a significant period to permit assessment of results and causative factors, educational policy decisions will be made on the basis of shaky conclusions reached in the light of only fragmented knowledge.

Correlation Between Educational Level and Political Participation

Another area for inquiry concerns the effects of education on political behavior. Political scientists could examine whether a correlation exists between levels of education and political participation rates. Further study of voting behavior, related to educational level, might produce indicators of how well the educational system is producing politically responsible citizens. Case studies of political leaders could give further insights into the attributes that are associated with leadership ability, and how these characteristics are related to various educational factors.

Economic Indicators

Recently expressed interest by economists in human-resources investment opens up an entirely new area of research. Theodore Schultz, for example, when he became President of the American

Economic Association, chose this as the subject of his address.[16] Original work could develop indicators of progress toward educational goals, stated in terms of the relationships between education and economics.

Further study of the relationship of education to earnings levels would also be helpful. What is the relationship of his educational level to an individual's lifetime earnings? Where does the greatest payback come, in terms of educational input at different levels? Is it at the preschool, elementary school, high school, or graduate school level? (See Table 8.)

An interesting study was made of postcollege careers of June 1958 college graduates—their further studies, work activities, and continuity between studies and work.[17] Longitudinal studies correlating education, experience, and earning levels of diverse occupational groups could furnish valuable insights into whether people use skills they acquire in college, and into a number of other questions.

Further studies of the payback to employers who upgrade their employees through in-service training and management-improvement courses would reveal information about optimum investment return from training expenditures. Studies to ascertain short-term and long-term manpower needs would provide meaningful guides to education-expenditures allocations. Indicators of trends in occupational requirements could be matched with indicators of educational output. Are schools training people today for the jobs that are now available and for jobs that may be available in the next century? Most likely, the three-year-old child of today will be living in the year 2020. Will his educational experience prepare him for that world?

Education is a long, lead-time operation. A college graduate has normally spent sixteen years in school. Since curricula planning and development require perhaps four years, educators should be developing school curricula today for those who are going to be entering the work force from high school in 1982 or college in 1986. Failure to plan or poor planning for the future by this generation will penalize the next generation.

Provision in the short run of an appropriate mix of skills in the labor force requires not only projection of future manpower requirements but also knowledge of the present mix of skills and how the mix is changing through death or retirement. The schools must fill the gap between the pool of existing manpower, what will exist in the future, and what will be required. To do this, the school system needs information for projecting future requirements to fill

TABLE 8

**Estimated Lifetime Income for Males, by Years of School Completed:
United States, 1949, 1956, and 1961**

Years of School Completed	1949	1956	1961
1	2	3	4
	Income, age 18 to death		
Elementary:			
Total	$113,330	$154,593	$176,008
Less than 8 years	98,222	132,736	151,348
8 years	132,683	180,857	204,530
High School:			
1 to 3 years	152,068	205,277	234,960
4 years	185,279	253,631	272,629
College:			
1 to 3 years	209,282	291,581	333,581
4 years or more	296,377	405,698	452,518
	Income, age 25 to 64		
Elementary:			
Total	$ 91,932	$127,047	$145,519
Less than 8 years	79,654	108,310	124,930
8 years	106,889	148,033	168,810
High School:			
1 to 3 years	121,943	169,501	193,082
4 years	148,649	208,322	224,417
College:			
1 to 3 years	173,166	243,611	273,049
4 years or more	244,427	340,131	360,604

Source: U. S. Department of Commerce, Bureau of the Census, *Statistical Abstract of the United States*, and unpublished data.

demands for trained manpower. And there is little information about the composition by age levels of various groups of skilled and professional workers—for example, physicians, engineers, and teachers. A study by Frederick Harbison and Charles Myers[18] of high-level manpower available and potentially available in individual countries is an example of the inquiries that are needed.

RELEVANT INDICATORS: POWERFUL FORCES FOR CHANGE AND MODERNIZATION IN THE EDUCATIONAL SYSTEM

Looking again at the multiple and diverse goals set for education confirms the importance of developing more than the traditional yardsticks to measure progress. There can be no confidence that decisions *are* the best possible without more data than are now available. The need to educate greater numbers of the population and to open up educational opportunities for those who have not had them in the past also underscores the need to make high-quality educational services available to the entire population.

New measures of educational activities and achievement must be developed and old measures revised to present a composite picture of the status and direction of the American educational system. The urgency of doing so cannot be overstated. The high purpose of American education places this task in a rank of high priority; its accomplishment must proceed without delay. Developing the needed indicators is the joint responsibility of both public and private interests—government, business, educators, labor unions, and civic and community groups.

As noted earlier, some of the data needed for meaningful indicators already exist, but are scattered and fragmented. There are gaps to be filled, new data to be developed. And, most importantly, the data must be presented in an orderly, comprehensive fashion; they must by analyzed and interpreted in a way that will contribute to effective planning and revision of plans for achieving national goals in education.

NOTES

[1] For further discussion of problems and issues concerning education, see James D. Finn and Gabriel D. Ofiesh, "The Emerging Technology of Education," *Educational Implications of Technological Change*, Vol. IV, Appendix: *Technology and the American Economy: The Report of the Commission*, February 1966, p. 34.

[2] Excerpt from a speech by M. A. Wright, President of the U.S. Chamber of Commerce, at Shaw University in Raleigh, North Carolina, on February 13, 1967.

[3] In discussions with the author in late 1965 and early 1966, Bertram M. Gross, Professor of Political Science, Syracuse University, first used the term "learning force" to express a broad concept of all of the people involved in some kind of organized group-learning process. He later defined the term "learning force" as embracing "the total number of people developing their capacities through systematic education—that

is, where learning is aided by teaching and there are formal, organized efforts to impart knowledge through instruction," and subsequently referred to the term in his article on the State of the Union Message, published in the May/June 1966 issue of *Challenge—The Magazine of Economic Affairs*, Vol. 14, No. 5.

[4]Fritz Machlup, *The Production and Distribution of Knowledge in the United States* (Princeton, N.J.: Princeton University Press, 1962).

[5]Leonard A. Lecht, *Goals, Priorities and Dollars: The Next Decade* (New York: Free Press, 1966), p. 160.

[6]For changes in curriculum in recent years, see James B. Conant, *The Comprehensive High School* (New York: McGraw-Hill, 1967).

[7]Theodore W. Schultz, *The Economic Value of Education* (New York: Columbia University Press, 1963), p. 11.

[8]Section 402, Civil Rights Act, 1964 (P. L. 88-352), directed the Commissioner of Education to carry out a survey on equality of educational opportunity. The survey was conducted, under contract, for the Commissioner by James S. Coleman, Johns Hopkins University.

[9]Richard de Neufville and Caryl Conner, "How Good Are Our Schools?", *American Education* (October 1966), p. 4.

[10]*Ibid.*, p. 6.

[11]*Ibid.*, p. 7.

[12]James Coleman, "Equal Schools or Equal Students," *The Public Interest* (July 1966), p. 73.

[13]Patrick Suppes, "The Uses of Computers in Education," *Scientific American* (September 1966) p. 9.

[14]John W. Gardner, "National Goals in Education," *Goals for Americans* (New York: American Assembly, Columbia University, 1960), p. 90.

[15]Benjamin Bloom, *Stability and Change in Human Characteristics* (New York: John Wiley, 1964).

[16]Theodore W. Schultz, "Investment in Human Capital," *American Economic Review*, 51: 1-17 (March 1961).

[17]Bureau of Social Science Research, *Two Years after the College Degree* (Washington, D.C.: U.S. Government Printing Office, for the National Science Foundation, 1963).

[18]Frederick Harbison and Charles Myers, *Education, Manpower, and Economic Growth* (New York: McGraw-Hill, 1964).

SUGGESTIONS FOR FURTHER READING—PART V

Bauer, Raymond A., ed. *Social Indicators.* Cambridge, Mass.: The M.I.T. Press, 1966.

Bell, Daniel. "The Idea of a Social Report." *The Public Interest,* No. 15 (Spring 1969), pp. 72-84.

Levin, Melvin R. *Community and Regional Planning: Issues in Public Policy.* New York: Frederick A. Praeger, Publishers, 1969. Chapter 3, "Costs, Benefits, and Social Indicators," pp. 64-82.

Olson, Mancur. "The Plan and Purpose of a Social Report." *The Public Interest,* No. 15 (Spring 1969), pp. 85-97.

"Social Goals and Indicators for American Society," Volume I. *The Annals,* Vol. 371 (May 1967).

"Social Goals and Indicators for American Society," Volume II. *The Annals,* Vol. 373 (September 1967).

Part VI

Cost-Benefit
in Action

17

FEDERAL TRAINING AND WORK
PROGRAMS IN THE SIXTIES

by Sar A. Levitan and Garth L. Mangum

*Sar Levitan and Garth Mangum are two of the nation's
leading authorities in the field of manpower. Levitan's
searching evaluation of cost-benefit analysis for the Job
Corps may well serve as a model for similar hard-boiled
analyses of other types of education and training programs. He concludes that although the Office of Economic
Opportunity probably overestimated the benefits of this
relatively costly training program, the evidence seems to
show that Corpsmen who stayed more than six months did
benefit significantly from their training. (Most, however,
remained less than six months.)*

The Job Corps was created as part of the Economic Opportunity
Act in order to prepare youths, aged 16 through 21, "for the
responsibility of citizenship and to increase (their) employability
. . . by providing them in rural and urban residential centers with
education, vocational education, useful work directed toward conservation of natural resources, and other appropriate activities"
(Section 101). The assumption underlying this mission was that
many youths from impoverished homes should be removed from
their home environment before they could be rehabilitated
through training and education.

Reprinted from Sar A. Levitan and Garth L. Mangum, *Federal Training and
Work Programs in the Sixties,* Institute of Labor and Industrial Relations, The University of Michigan, Wayne State University, 1969, pp. 163-5, 179-80, 182-6, 189-
90, 192-203, 205-8. Reprinted by permission of the publisher and authors.

385

Although the antecedents of the Job Corps may be traced back to the Civilian Conservation Corps of the thirties, the contrasts between the two institutions are more significant than the similarities. The CCC was a product of the Great Depression, when deprivation and need were widespread, and the 1.5 million enrollees represented a broad cross-section of the population. It was terminated when the Armed Forces absorbed the bulk of its clients and acute labor shortages developed from wartime conditions. The Job Corps, on the other hand, focuses upon the special needs of a small minority of youths who because of educational deficiency and debilitating environment, are at a competitive disadvantage in the labor market. The CCC was essentially a job creation program (although the term did not come into vogue until three decades later) which emphasized conservation work. The Job Corps stresses the needs of the individual corps-members—though the work experience of enrollees in conservation centers is also devoted to "useful social work."

The idea of reviving residential centers for disadvantaged youth was advanced by then Senator Hubert H. Humphrey in 1957. Although a bill authorizing conservation camps for youth passed the Senate two years later, the bill was not even taken up by the appropriate House Committee and attracted scant support. By 1963, however, youth unemployment was recognized as a pressing national problem which was not responding to overall improvements in economic conditions. In that year, a coalition of conservationists and welfare organizations expanded the rural conservation bill proposed earlier to include federally-supported job creation programs in urban areas. The expanded bill, which included the basic features of the Job Corps and the Neighborhood Youth Corps, was again approved by the Senate. In the House, the Education and Labor Committee approved the measure, but the Committee on Rules prevented it from reaching the floor. The opposition included segregationists as well as opponents of welfare legislation—the two were not, of course, mutually exclusive groups—but the fact that the proposed camps were to be racially integrated added force to the coalition.

In January 1964, the publication of *One-Third of a Nation* by the President's Task Force on Manpower Conservation confirmed that the Armed Forces annually rejected one of three potential draftees because of mental and physical deficiencies. Most of the rejectees came from impoverished homes. This gave impetus to the proposed program, which was incuded as part of the Administration's antipoverty bill.

The 1964 Administration proposal differed substantially from the 1963 bill. While the earlier bill emphasized conservation work, the antipoverty bill stressed the establishment of residential centers where youth could receive educational and vocational training. Although the 1964 bill did not preclude conservation centers, in deference to the conservation interests, it was intentionally vague to permit maximum flexibility in administration. Under pressure from the conservation groups, Administration witnesses testifying on the Economic Opportunity bill indicated they would establish two types of camps: urban centers emphasizing vocational training for youth with a reading achievement of sixth grade level or better; and conservation centers emphasizing basic education and work experience for enrollees with more acute educational deficiencies. Sargent Shriver distinguished between the two types of centers as follows:

Let us say after six months or a year in the conservation corps [the] boy had reached the levels [of education] indicated . . . he then could be transferred into the educational centers . . . and get further training so that he could get a skill [1]

The expressed objective of the Job Corps has been that of "taking people where they are and advancing them as far as they can go in the time allotted."[2]

The main opposition the Job Corps was directed against the establishment of conservation centers. It was argued that conservation work would add little to the employability of the youth, and that whatever conservation work might be performed at the centers would not justify the high costs of maintaining the centers. The conservation lobbyists were, needless to say, not persuaded. Unwilling to leave the size of the conservation component to the discretion of program administrators, they succeeded in persuading Congress to specify that 40 percent of male Job Corps enrollees be assigned to conservation centers.

Although the Job Corps did have its disciplinary problems—including fights, stabbings, and even riots—most of the incidents hardly merited national publicity. Part of the unfavorable publicity resulted from the failure of the Job Corps and its contractors to prepare communities for their newly-acquired neighbors. This oversight was understandable during the early days when there was little time to do this kind of groundwork. As the Job Corps matured it tried to overcome these initial difficulties, and in 1967 OEO sponsored an amendment which gave statutory recognition to these efforts. The amendment required OEO "to establish a mutually beneficial relationship between Job Corps centers and surrounding or nearby communities."

COSTS

Underlying much of the discontent over the Job Corps was the undeniably high cost of the experiment. The total funds allocated to the Job Corps during the first four years of operation amounted to $989 million, divided as follows: fiscal 1965, $183 million; fiscal 1966, $310 million; fiscal 1967, $211 million; and fiscal 1968, $285 million.

The total annual cost per enrollee was more $8,000 in 1967. Opponents were quick and persistent in exploiting this fact, stressing that the cost to the taxpayer of supporting a corpsman was higher than the cost to parents supporting their children at the best American colleges. Pundits and Congressmen entered into the debate; and the Congressional Record carried a detailed analysis of the cost of supporting a student for a year at Harvard University compared to that of an enrollee in a Job Corps center. The fascination with this subject might deserve the close study of social psychologists, but it was as useful as the debates about the number of angels that can stand on the head of a pin. Few raised questions about the relevancy of the comparison. Dr. Otis Singletary, former Director of the Job Corps, when confronted with the unfavorable comparison of costs between the Job Corps and Harvard University, offered to pay personally for any Job Corps enrollee accepted by Harvard. The offer, to no one's surprise, was not taken up.

Regrettably, the Job Corps added to the confusion over costs by being less than candid with the public and with Congress. Their failure to explain the reasons for the high costs added to the impression that there were grounds for the charge that the centers were "country clubs for juvenile delinquents." Most cases where the Job Corps spent public funds on "frill" activities were attributable to inexperience or errors of judgment on the part of some center personnel. Providing enrollees with occasional bus transportation to attend a dance several hundred miles from their center may be classified in this category. There was also room to question some of the continuing practices, such as the payment of corpsmen's transportation costs for home visits during the Christmas season, or the payment of legal fees on behalf of corpsmen who encountered brushes with the law. The Armed Forces are not as generous with their enlisted men.

Conscious of the widespread attacks upon the cost of maintaining the Job Corps, OEO has trimmed its costs to the point where further belt tightening could not be effected without damaging the training and education of enrollees. The maintenance of residential centers which provide education and training is a costly affair and the program, if it is to continue, must be judged on its merits and not on the hopes that the expenditures per enrollee will decline. In response to public criticisms of the high cost of operating Job Corps centers and sniping by officials of competing federally-supported programs, Congress in 1966 imposed a ceiling on Job Corps expenditures of $7,500 for fiscal year 1967 for each Job Corps enrollee. The annual ceiling was further reduced to $6,900 for the subsequent year. Though Congress may get credit for cutting the costs, the action was unnecessary since the Job Corps had already taken steps to eliminate some of the more expensive training programs, reduce the number of training occupations, and eliminate most of the "frills."

. . . Total average annual costs per enrollee of established centers (those in operation more than nine months) average $8,100, ranging from $7,400 for conservation centers to $9,600 for women's centers. Although the average cost in 1967 exceeded the statutory limitation by nearly $600 per year, the Job Corps did not ignore the limitation imposed by Congress. The law excluded from the $7,500 limitation overhead costs—enrollee recruitment, screening, placement, Job Corps headquarters, and regional expenses—which averaged $600 a year per enrollee; the cost of amortizing the $141-million capital investment ($600 per enrollee); and the cost of materials expended on conservation work ($854 per conservation center enrollee).

The rationale for excluding the last item is persuasive. The materials were utilized on useful public works and therefore do not represent a real training cost. Indeed a case could be made, as the Job Corps did, for subtracting the value of the work performed on public projects from conservation center enrollee expenditures. The rationale for the exclusion of the overhead and amortization costs is less convincing and appears to be an arbitrary decision on the part of Congress. A calculation of true costs cannot ignore these expenditures.

Many difficult considerations obscure the true cost per enrollee of operating the Job Corps. The dropout rate during the first 30 days, though decreasing, still stood at 20 percent in the first quarter of fiscal 1968. It could be argued that for those who stay such a short time, the Job Corps experience has little positive impact, and may actually represent a setback. Early studies of wage earnings showed that those staying less than three months actually earned less six months after termination than a control group who did not join the Job Corps and had been in the labor force an equal time.

Spokesmen for the Job Corps, however, insist that even a short stay in the Job Corps is not a total loss since the enrollees receive counseling, medical treatment, and are fed and housed. Job Corps officials also maintain that average annual costs exaggerate the true investment per enrollee because most corpsmen complete their course of study in less than a year. This claim that the prescribed curriculum can be mastered by deficiently educated youth in less than a year, however, raises questions about the quality and quantity of education and training offered at the centers.

However the costs may be measured, there are limits to further belt tightening. The 1967 amendment requiring equal representation of the sexes will raise costs. In fiscal 1967, women's centers had a statutory cost of $8,400 compared to the men's average of $6,900. The higher cost of operating centers for women did not reflect higher living standards. Almost a third of the total annual differential between female and male urban centers was accounted for by lease costs since no rental was paid for the male centers located on government property. Economies of size accounted for most of the balance. At any rate, increasing the percentage of women in the Corps will put upward pressures on average annual costs per enrollee.

The higher average costs of female urban centers have important policy implications. Some advocates of residential centers opposed the Job Corps because of its policy of sending youths far from home, frequently to isolated areas. According to this view, it would be better to place the youths in small residential centers, preferably in the communities in which they live. If such a policy is adopted, however, the cost of male Job Corps centers is likely to rise significantly since many such centers must be leased from private concerns and would be too small for economical operation.

SCREENING OF CANDIDATES

The cost per Job Corps enrollee could be justified if enrollment were limited to youths whose needs could not be met by a less costly alternative program and if the enrollees remained long enough to benefit from their experience. The evidence on both points is not conclusive.

The record of the Job Corps is clear—at no time was there an attempt to "cream" applicants, a common feature of other federally-supported training programs. The Job Corp extended the welcome mat to all youths from impoverished families. The agency was even willing to take chances with youths convicted of a felony, if an appropriate review board decided that an applicant was willing to conform to Job Corps standards. It does not follow, however, that Job Corps enrollees were carefully screened or that adequate care was taken to offer alternative programs for applicants when appropriate. At first the screening of enrollees was necessarily haphazard and chaotic. Although improved, it still leaves much to be desired. Pressures to meet quotas result in the occasional "pushing" of the Job Corps reminiscent of "specials" offered in department stores.

A great many of the difficulties were caused by the Office of Economic Opportunity. Even before opening its first center, the Job Corps embarked on an extensive national advertising campaign to interest young people. Concerned that the Job Corps could not attract an adequate number of enrollees and that the potential clientele would have to be sold on the idea, interested youths were invited to complete "opportunity cards" indicating an interest. The response of about a quarter of a million was better than the most enthusiastic advocates had hoped. Though many of those who responded were neither qualified nor really interested in the Job Corps, a large proportion were potential candidates. It took the Job Corps months to respond to the deluge of inquiries, some of which were never acknowledged. When the campaign started, the Job Corps had facilities for only a few hundred.

Under the circumstances, it is hard to understand the need for the extensive advance publicity. Indeed, knowledgeable advisors cautioned Shriver not to embark upon the campaign. In this manner the Job Corps disappointed many potential clients even before it opened for business. The performance also antagonized some of the program's best friends. For example, Congressman William F. Ryan of New York, a consistent advocate of the antipoverty war, complained publicly that as of June 1, 1965, 1,600 New York youths had applied but only two had been selected for the Job Corps.[3]

To screen applicants, the Job Corps turned to several agencies. Most of the screening of men was delegated to the United States Employment Service and its affiliated state agencies. In addition, 14 Community Action Agencies were designated to undertake the job in their communities. The task of screening women was turned over to WICS (Women in Community Service) a volunteer agency whose members were the National Council of Catholic Women, the National Council of Negro Women, the National Council of Jewish Women, and the United Church Women. As the recruitment of girls was stepped up to meet the statutory requirement, WICS could not meet its quota and the USES was asked to provide half of the female enrollees. In addition, the Job Corps expanded its contracts for outreach and screening with Community Action Agencies, Urban Leagues, and the AFL-CIO Appalachian Council. During fiscal 1967, the USES accounted for almost three-fourths of the 96,000 youths who were screened and referred, and the proportion was about the same for the first half of fiscal 1968. Earlier plans to rely upon other sources than USES for screening did not materialize, and the USES accounted for a slightly higher proportion of all Job Corps screening and referral during fiscal 1967 and 1968 than in the first two years.

The agencies were reimbursed for the cost of screening applicants, which averaged $73 per qualified youth screened and referred to the Job Corps in fiscal 1967. The costs ranged from $83 per person for USES to less than half of that amount for WICS— whose members not only screened the candidates for women's centers but also provided numerous volunteer service for the selectees, including clothing and other needs.

Having little previous contact with such youth, most of the local employment services were poorly prepared to screen Job Corps enrollees. Some counselors oversold the Job Corps in order to fulfill their quotas. A study of former Job Corps enrollees showed that half felt that they had not been given a true picture of "what the Job Corps would be like."[4] The major complaint was that they didn't receive the training or money promised by the counselors. Although there was considerable room for misunderstanding about the former, disappointments concerning Job Corps allowances are more difficult to explain and would suggest that applicants were misinformed by the screeners.

During the first two years, the Job Corps experienced difficulty in filling its available capacity. By the spring of 1967, with expanded recruitment activities, OEO expressed confidence that it had licked this problem. Diverse factors contributed to the difficulty in recruiting enrollees. OEO underestimated the rate of enrollee turnover and consequently planned for a lower level of recruitment than the needs indicated. Aside from the initial ineffectiveness of local employment offices, extraneous factors complicated the job of recruiting. Expanding job opportunities and increases in military manpower needs provided alternative opportunities. Congressional action, or more precisely inaction, further complicated recruitment plans. During the summer of 1966, OEO was prevented from planning the future size of the Job Corps pending Congressional approval regarding the authorized enrollment level. When passed the law allowed the Job Corps to expand to a capacity of 45,000. Finally, continued attacks on the Job Corps marred its image and probably discouraged potential applicants.

Altogether, one of every seven youths interviewed by the screening agencies ended up in the Job Corps. The vast majority of those interviewed either showed no interest in enrolling, were referred to other programs, or received no help at all. Of those who indicated interest in joining a center and who qualified on the basis of income and age, nearly one of every eight was rejected during 1966. Previous behavior patterns accounted for the bulk of the rejections. About three of every ten who were selected never reached a center, having lost interest between the time of the interview and notification of acceptance; a few were never assigned to a center. With experience, the Job Corps has succeeded in reducing the elapsed time between the initial interview and final acceptance from an average of six weeks to less than half that time. Another two or three weeks normally elapsed before the youth was assigned and scheduled to arrive at the center.

EDUCATIONAL GAINS

Since the average beginning corpsman has a level of math and verbal achievement roughly equivalent to the fifth grade norm and about one of every five attained a reading level below that of third grade prior to enrollment in the Job Corps, improvement of the corpsman's basic education is vital if he is to improve his employability, and at times it is necessary before he can even begin to receive vocational training. The question of educational gains is at the heart of any analysis of the benefits to the Job Corps experience.

The Job Corps claimed that:

"the average Corpsmember progressed in arithmetic one and three-fourths times faster than the school norm, and in reading one and one-fourth times the average public school rate."[5]

The Job Corps study indicated that the educational progress of corpsmen varied widely by type of center. Men in urban centers made the highest progress, followed by men in conservation centers. Women showed the least achievement. The explanation for the smaller gains made by the girls was that "many of the girls had higher entry scores and were not kept in programs all the time they were in a center." There were also wide variations among individual centers. The Job Corps found that the median educational gains of enrollees in five high performance conservation centers was "nearly three times the public school norm in reading and exactly three times the norm in arithmetic. These rates of gain are nearly twice as great as the Job Corps average."[6]

OEO was quick to publicize the results of this study and to pronounce the educational attainments of the Job Corps success. Three reservations or comments are in order. First, as Job Corps officials themselves admit, "Some of the 'gain' is simply the recovery of skills once possessed but lost through disuse."[7] Second, the gap between the best and worst centers of each type, and between the types themselves, indicate that optimal educational programs have yet to be adopted in the greater majority of centers. And third, educational programs apparently do not continue past a basic level, yielding the longer-term or initially better-trained corpsman little benefit.

In the absence of any reliable standards for comparison, it is difficult to appraise the educational gains claimed by the Job Corps. However, a more recent set of data generated by the Job Corps and not yet released yields a much less favorable picture. These data ... are a compilation of the mean gains measured in terms of school years completed for corpsmen over varying lengths of training.

By weighting the mean gains in each training-time category by the percentage of terminees in each category since the beginning of the Corps, the average gain should be represented by the sum of the weighted means. Since data were not available as to the percentage of terminees in each training-time category over the history of the Corps, percentages were calculated from records of terminees in the first quarter of fiscal 1968. These results suggest that the average corpsman raised his reading ability by about one-third grade. For men's centers the gains indicated in the published studies were more than twice those shown [elsewhere]. Women's progress at the centers was lower than that of male enrollees according to both studies.

The Job Corps has maintained that the unpublished data contained some technical flaws and are not as reliable as the publicized data. Careful evaluation of these arguments suggest that the actual achievements of corpsmen are somewhere in between the two estimates. What seems the most valid conclusion to draw is that Job Corps educational gains are probably not greater than public school norms, but that they are probably better than the gain rates corpsmen maintained in public school.

VOCATIONAL EDUCATION

It is even more difficult to assess the quality of vocational training received in centers. In the absence of standards, the impressions and views of former enrollees and their employers must suffice. According to a survey by Patricia A. Goldman, prepared for the Chamber of Commerce of the United States, employers thought that four of every five former corpsmen in their employ received satisfactory to excellent training in centers. The views of the employers were corroborated by 90 percent of the former corpsmen who, according to the survey, found that the training was "excellent" or "good." And nearly the same proportion considered the entire program "great" or "good." "I had only one chance in life," was a typical response, "and found it was in the Job Corps." Nevertheless nearly half of the corpsmen felt that the skill training they received was of no help to them in obtaining a job skill.[8]

The duration of training, rather than its quality, explains in part why many corpsmen found the training no help in obtaining a job. A survey by Louis Harris and Associates of enrollees who left the Job Corps in August 1966 found that the longer a youth stayed in the Job Corps, the more likely he was to use the training he received at the center: 42 percent of those who stayed longer than six months used their Job Corps training, compared with only five percent of those who stayed less than three months.[9]

A serious weakness of the Job Corps has been that from the beginning it has decided to "go it alone" without involving the vocational education establishment and state vocational education institutions, even though a number of states had previously operated vocational residential centers. Spokesmen for the Job Corps have recognized that closer cooperation with state vocational authorities could have broadened support for the program and added to its available professional capability. Involvement of state institutions might have ameliorated some of the tensions between centers and their neighboring communities. State operated centers could also have provided vehicles for experimenting with new and different program approaches. According to an unpublished report submitted by the Office of Economic Opportunity to the Senate Committee on Labor and Public Welfare:

There is great flexibility for innovation and experimental approaches in program content and in management. If this flexibility is properly exploited, many valuable lessons of potentially wide application throughout Job Corps and other similar programs may result.

Nevertheless, the Job Corps has done little to achieve a rapprochement with state vocational authorities: less than three percent of the Job Corps enrollment were in state related conservation centers by mid-1967.

Proposals to place the Job Corps in the Vocational Education Division in the Office of Education present inherent problems, despite the indicated advantages. Since the residential centers would be operated by state vocational authorities, it is likely that some would not acquiesce to establishing racially integrated residential centers. While few Job Corps centers were located in the southeastern states, where the problem is most acute, youths from these areas can enroll in centers outside their state or region. State operation of residential centers would intensify problems of integration and probably preclude some youths from enrolling. Past experience has shown that federal proscription of racial discrimination does not solve the problem.

The vocational education establishment might also lack experience in handling the special problems of operating residential centers for disadvantaged youth. The Job Corps has gained considerable expertise in this area.

Although there is a need to expand the base of support for the Job Corps and to involve more vocational educators in its operations, transferring the Job Corps to HEW is a doubtful solution. On the other hand, ignoring the capability of state and local vocational authorities in the operation of the centers has been a serious shortcoming of the Job Corps. The issue is not a new one. In the spring of 1966 the Advisory Commission on Intergovernmental Relations recommended that OEO "take positive steps to interest states in acting as prime or supporting contractors for Job Corps facilities."[10] The Commission's recommendations were ignored by OEO. It was left to Congress to force in 1967 closer cooperation between the Job Corps and related state institutions.

DURATION OF STAY

The benefits of vocational and basic education are directly related to length of training, and the retention rate of the Job Corps is thus crucial to the success of the institution. A study conducted for the Job Corps by Harris and Associates found that six months after they left, 56 percent of the former corpsmen thought that they were better off as a result of their Job Corps experience, 16 percent thought they were worse off, and the balance either were not sure about the impact of the experience or thought it had made no difference (Table 1). Significantly, those who remained in the Corps for longer periods of time gave a more favorable evaluation. Three of every four corpsmen who stayed in the Job Corps for more than six months thought they were "better off," compared with 44 percent of those who stayed in the center for less than three months. This study concluded:

There is clear evidence that a successful stay in the Job Corps can improve a youth's chances. The graduates and those in centers over six months have not only improved their employment situation and their pay rate more than the other groups, but they also sensed this improvement. Whether these groups will maintain their advantage in the future is a question that, at this point, cannot be answered.[11]

There is additional discussion later on about the correlation between length of stay and wage and employment levels. While the answer to Harris' above question is by no means definitively answered, it does appear from subsequent data that the advantage over the short-stayers tends to narrow.

The record of the Job Corps leaves much to be desired when judged on its ability to retain enrollees. The law authorized a two-year enrollment, giving the OEO Director discretionary power to allow a youth to remain at a center even longer. Experience clearly indicates either that the authorized length of stay in the Job Corps was excessive, or that centers failed to hold youths for a sufficient length of time. Only one of every nine corpsmembers remained in the center for as long as one year. Indeed, the Job Corps curriculum was designed to allow a youth to complete his course of training in nine months or less.

The decision to "graduate" youths from the Job Corps in this short a period was based on pragmatic considerations: few enrollees apparently indicated an interest in staying longer, and the Job Corps has even had difficulty retaining them long enough to complete the abbreviated course of study and training. Thus, the "quickie graduation" served a double purpose: while it established a reachable goal for some enrollees, it also provided the Job Corps with a justification for calculating costs per enrollee on less than an annual basis in response to widespread criticism of the high cost.

Job Corps spokesmen have argued that low retention rates were largely because of lack of experience of center staffs. This was true. While half of the enrollees departed within two months during fiscal 1966, the median length of stay doubled the following year and continued to improve during fiscal 1968. But retention rates are still low. The mean length of stay for terminees in fiscal 1967

TABLE 1

Labor Force Status of August 1966 Job Corps Terminees:
Before Entering and Upon Leaving Job Corps and Six and Twelve Months After Termination

Percent[1]

	Working				Unemployed				In School and Other[2]			
	Before Entering Job Corps	Upon Leaving Job Corps	Six Months Later	Twelve Months Later	Before Entering Job Corps	Upon Leaving Job Corps	Six Months Later	Twelve Months Later	Before Entering Job Corps	Upon Leaving Job Corps	Six Months Later	Twelve Months Later
Total	58	60	57	58	32	27	36	37	10	15	12	7
Graduates	61	59	66	62	29	26	28	32	10	16	9	8
Dropouts	56	61	52	56	34	27	40	39	10	14	13	7
Discharges	56	51	55	54	30	36	37	39	14	16	10	8
Sex												
Men	59	61	57	58	31	26	37	36	10	15	11	8
Women	38	43	51	56	50	40	29	45	12	18	23	5
Race												
Negro	61	62	58	53	29	27	35	40	10	13	9	8
White	52	57	54	63	37	28	39	33	11	17	14	8
Length of time in Job Corps												
Less than 3 months	50	59	49	52	38	27	43	43	12	17	15	6
3 to 6 months	61	61	56	56	28	25	36	38	11	17	12	9
more than 6 months	58	60	69	66	34	32	27	28	8	10	8	7
Age												
Under 18 years	44	48	44	44	38	28	45	50	18	26	17	10
18-19 years	56	62	60	50	33	26	34	33	11	14	10	10
20 and over	68	65	61	61	28	33	34	36	4	3	9	4

[1]Figures may add up to more than 100 per cent because some were both in school and working.

[2]Most were in school. Data do not include former corpsmen who entered military service. If, in the follow-ups, those in the military were included, the overall figures would be for the six months and twelve months respectively: working 53% and 50%, in school 10% and 3%; in military 7% and 15%; unemployed 34% and 32%; and other 1% and 2%.

Source: Louis Harris and Associates, A Study of August 1966 Termination from the Job Corps, March 1967, and A Study of the Status of August 1966 Job Corps Terminees—12 Months After Termination, October 1967 (Revision).

was 5.3 months, but 22 percent terminated within the first month, 43 percent within the first three months, and only 34 percent stayed longer than six months (Table 2). For the first quarter of fiscal 1968, both the median and average lengths of stay had further improved to 4.2 and 5.6 months respectively.

TABLE 2

Length of Time Spent in the Job Corps, Fiscal 1966 and 1967

Duration in Months	Fiscal 1966	Fiscal 1967
Median	2.0 months	3.9 months
Average	3.3 months	5.3 months
	Percent	
Less than 1	33	22
1 to 1.9	17	11
2 to 2.9	13	10
3 to 5.9	18	24
6 to 8.9	12	15
9 to 11.9	5	8
12 to 17.9	2	10
18 and over	—	1

Source: Job Corps, Office of Economic Opportunity.

A particular retention problem is found among younger corpsmen. For 16- and 17-year-old terminees in 1967, average stay was only 3.9 and 4.4 months respectively compared to 5.3 and 5.4 months for 19- and 20 year-olds. While the on-board percentage of 16- and 17-year-olds was 40 percent in the first quarter of fiscal 1968, they constituted 57 percent of all arrivals. Not only do the younger enrollees tend to drop out more quickly, but child labor laws and arbitrary age restrictions prevent them from securing employment in many of the trades for which they were trained. This is reflected in the higher percentages of unplaced terminees among 16- and 17-year-olds, and the lower starting wages of younger terminees. (Table 3).

To provide incentives for enrollees to extend their stay, the Director of OEO exercised discretionary authority to raise the basic monthly allowance from $30 to $50. Relatively few enrollees received the maximum authorized rates, though an increasing proportion received increases above the minimum (Table 4).

Two measures were introduced in the EOA amendments of 1967 to encourage longer duration of stay. Personal allowances were limited to $35 per month during the first six months of enrollment, and to $50 per month thereafter. Enrollees had also received readjustment allowances of up to $50 per month upon termination from the Job Corps. According to the amendments, this allowance should only be paid to enrollees who had served at least 90 days in the Job Corps.

TABLE 3

Selected Data of 1967 Job Corps Terminees by Age

	Age at Termination						
	16	17	18	19	20	21	22
30 day Terminees (%)	19.1	17.8	16.1	16.0	15.9	15.6	5.0
Length of Stay (Months)	3.9	4.4	4.9	5.3	5.4	6.0	8.0
Unemployed Terminees (%)	60.1	54.7	50.5	49.1	47.8	47.4	41.7
Starting Wage (Dollars)	1.41	1.50	1.57	1.57	1.61	1.62	1.82

Source: Job Corps, Office of Economic Opportunity.

In the final analysis, the effectiveness of the Job Corps will be measured in terms of the education and the training it provides enrollees and the lasting impact of the experience. No doubt the Job Corps experience may yield other benefits to enrollees. These may include social development and the family stability resulting from higher income and additional education achieved by enrollees.[12] Unfortunately, these benefits cannot be measured at this time; and, in fact, studies over many years would be required to gain insights about the extent of these additional effects.

TABLE 4

Allowance Distribution Among Job Corps Enrollees
Percent of Enrollees

Monthly Pay	May 1967	Jan. 1968
$30	74	64
$35	11	18
$40	8	11
$45	4	4
$50	3	3
Mean Monthly Pay	$32.60	$33.20

Source: Job Corps, Office of Economic Opportunity.

As of October 1, 1967, nearly 110,000 youths had enrolled in and left the Job Corps. In an attempt to fulfill the congressional requirement to gather follow-up information concerning employment and earnings records of former corpsmembers, OEO contracted with Louis Harris and Associates to conduct periodic sample follow-up studies. As a result of information collected under these contracts, data are now available for terminees who left centers around August 1966, about their status prior to enrolling in the Job Corps and similar data upon leaving centers and at six month intervals during the succeeding 18 months.[13] Another series was for November 1966 terminees with data prior to their enrollment at termination, and six and 12 months later.[14] An attempt was also made to design a control group for the August 1966 terminees by studying "no-shows"—applicants who had been accepted but never actually entered the program.[15] In addition, a special study was devoted to dropouts.[16]

Based on the early sample studies, OEO estimated that 70 percent were either working, in the military, or enrolled in school, and the balance were "not placed." (Characteristically, OEO does not use the term "unemployed" in connection with former corpsmembers.)[17] Also typically, the OEO claim was far too sweeping and generalized. Of more importance than aggregate figures are the specific details which the sample studies yielded on various aspects of the Job Corps placement record, offering possibly the most comprehensive follow-up data on any federally-supported manpower program (Table 1).

Despite this comprehensiveness, however, the data from these studies must be used with caution. There are shortcomings in the original sample as well as in the follow-up ones which make it reasonable to conclude that the findings may not only tend to overestimate the total Job Corps achievements but also that the findings from the later follow-up data may be particularly "iffy." The problem with the 12- and 18-month follow-ups is mainly that of a shrinking sample which became less and less reliable because so many interviewees were lost—from 868 interviewed for the 6-month follow-up down to 430 for the 18-month. Use of the 18-month follow-up data is further hampered because they are not completely comparable with the information obtained in earlier surveys.

A major finding (for the August 1966 terminees), as suggested earlier, appears to be a positive correlation between the employment status of former corpsmembers and the time they spent in the Job Corps—although the advantage of the long-stayers over the short-stayers seems to have narrowed considerably with the passage of time. Harris observed in his 6-month follow-up:

The longer a corpsman stays in the Job Corps, the more likely he is to have worked since leaving the center and the less likely he is to have changed jobs. Longer exposure to the Job Corps thus leads to higher employment and greater job stability.[18]

Job Corps graduates and those who stayed longer than six months—as contrasted with those who stayed less—usually displayed advantages in securing employment after leaving the Corps, although the advantage was not manifested immediately upon leaving the Corps. Six months after termination, over two-thirds of those who remained more than six months were employed; in contrast, less than half of those who remained under three months had jobs, and only a little over half of those staying three to six months. In addition, the rate of employment for the long-stayers was higher than before they entered the Corps.

That the immediate effect of a longer stay in the Job Corps upon securing employment was not greater probably reflected the limited assistance that centers offered to youths upon completion of their Job Corps career. Only six percent of the youths who obtained jobs immediately upon leaving the centers in August 1966 reported that they secured employment through the Job Corps—though, as might be expected, the Job Corps exerted a greater effort for those with longer stays. State employment agencies also exerted greater efforts for these, placing 28 percent of those who were in centers more than six months but only 12 percent of those who stayed less than three months.[19]

While both the level of and amount of increase in employment of those who remained for more than six months became more pronounced six months after they left the Job Corps—up 11 percentage points over pre-entry as contrasted with only two points up immediately after leaving the Corps, the employment rate of corps members who stayed less than three months declined six months later, even though it had temporarily gone up immediately after leaving the Corps. Apparently, a short stay in the Job Corps had little lasting effect, and these corps members lost ground a short time after returning to their old environment. Therefore, it would appear that enrollment of less than three months brought limited advantage to the corpsmen, if any.

With the passage of time, however, the picture apparently changed. While the long-stayers continued to have a higher rate of employment than the short-stayers, the difference narrowed so that by 18 months after leaving the Corps, it appeared insignificant—only three percentage points higher. (The shortcomings, however, of the 18-months data must be remembered here.)

Differences in the employment record of ex-corps members were also noticeable for other categories besides length of stay. Age showed a major difference. Those who were under 18 years when entering the Job Corps tended to find less employment than those who were over 18, both prior to Job Corps entry and in the months after their stay. This could be expected, of course, in view of the higher unemployment rate of younger workers and the operation of the "aging vat" process. A longer stay in the Corps, however, could offset the handicap of the younger age: 16- and 17-year-old enrollees who remained in centers long enough to graduate had an unemployment level of 34 percent compared with a 45 percent unemployment rate of younger trainees who stayed less than three months.[20]

Women showed greater employment gains than men but lost their early momentum within 18 months after leaving centers when less than half were employed. The drop is apparently accounted for by a temporary or permanent departure from the job because of pregnancy and marriage. Negroes did not do as well as whites; the proportion employed fell to about half at 18 months while the whites rose to over two-thirds employed. Harris feels this reflects "the pervasiveness of the national problem of discrimination." As might be expected, the percentage of ex-trainees going into the military continued to rise as an increasing proportion reached draft age. Six months after termination seven percent went into the military; by 12 months it rose to fifteen, and by 18 months it was almost a fifth.

The hourly rates of the former corps members are another aspect of assessing the Job Corps. Again, graduates and those who stayed longer than six months in centers had higher wage levels and made much greater gains than dropouts or discharges (Table 5). Although prior to enrollment the graduates and dropouts had similar wage rates, the average hourly wage gain of the men with the longer stay was 88 cents after 18 months, compared with 59 cents for dropouts. Women showed less improvement than men, possibly reflecting discrimination against the fairer sex in the labor market rather than Job Corps performance. Whites improved more than Negroes. A special breakdown by age showed that length of stay did outweigh the lower age handicap: the younger graduates earned 19 cents an hour more after 18 months than did either the younger or the older corpsmen who stayed for the shorter time.[21]

TABLE 5

Average Hourly Wage Rates for August 1966 Job Corps Terminees

	Pre-Job Corps	After Termination		Net Improvement From Pre-Job Corps
		12 months	18 months	
Men	$1.23	$1.80	$1.90	$ .67
Graduates	1.24	1.92	2.12	.88
Dropouts[1]	1.21	1.69	1.80	.59
Discharges	1.19	1.79	1.84	.65
Negro	1.23	1.82	1.85	.62
White	1.23	1.82	1.98	.75
Conservation Center	1.21	1.72	1.86	.65
Urban Center	1.26	1.91	1.94	.68
Women	1.14	1.37	1.67	.53

[1]Defined here as those in Job Corps less than 3 months.

Source: Harris, "A Study of the Status of August 1966 Job Corps Terminees 18 Months after Termination," op. cit., p. 3.

This analysis of Job Corps achievements has been largely based on the data gathered by the surveys of Louis Harris and Associates, particularly those for the August 1966 terminees. The August 1966 terminees were used here rather than the November 1966 terminees because a longer series of follow-up data was available. There are, however, substantial differences in the trends shown between the two groups. No attempt has been made here to summarize or track down the reasons for the discrepancies between the two sets of data. Assuming that the information supplied by the former trainees is accurate, the overall results would still be subject to reservations because of the previously mentioned shortcomings in both the original and follow-up samples.

In further assessing the achievements of the Job Corps, it does not follow that the improved employment and wage levels of former trainees were necessarily the result of Job Corps training and education. Improvement could be the result of other factors—a changing labor market, increased military demand, and especially the aging process inasmuch as the employability of youths increases as they mature.

There is evidence for the importance of exogenous factors in the survey of "no-shows" mentioned earlier.[22] Since the "no-shows" displayed characteristics similar to those of youths who actually entered the Job Corps, it is reasonable to consider them an appropriate control group.

Both groups increased their level and amount of employment, but these were higher for the "no-shows" than for corps members: 60 percent were employed and 27 percent unemployed six months after failure to enter the Job Corps, while the August 1966 terminees had only 57 percent working and 36 percent unemployed six months later.[23] This would seem to indicate that, relatively, employability was not increased by the Job Corps.

As for wages, the differences between the "no-shows" and ex-corps members (August 1966 terminees) was quite small. Table 6

TABLE 6

Average Hourly Wage for August 1966 Job Corps Terminees and "No-Shows" from 1966

	Graduates	Dropouts	"No-Shows"
Pre-Job Corps Wage	$1.14	$1.19	$1.17
Wage 6 Months after Termination	1.48	1.40	1.42
Wage Gain	.34	.21	.25
Net Improvement Compared With "No-Shows"	+.09	-.04	
Weighted Average Improvement		+.01	

Source: Louis Harris and Associates, "A Study of August 1966 Terminations from the Job Corps," March 1967, and "A Study of Job Corps 'No-Shows': Accepted Applicants Who Did Not Go to a Training Center," February 1967.

shows that the average improvement of corps members' wages over pre-entry levels compared with the improvement of the "no-shows" was only nine cents more an hour for graduates and four cents less an hour for dropouts with a weighted average hourly advantage of one cent for both categories. Dropouts were thus comparatively worse off after the program. Job Corps "results" on wages can thus be questioned on the basis of the six month later wage gain.

It would be a mistake, however, to conclude from these "no-show" data that the Job Corps had no impact. When the record is analyzed in terms of length of stay—namely, for those staying more than six months—the value of the Job Corps experience itself does appear significant, and it would be a grievous mistake to underestimate it. Those remaining in the Job Corps for more than six months did do better than the "no-shows"—and were the

only group to do so. They earned more than the "no-shows"—
$1.50 per hour compared with $1.42, and a greater proportion
found jobs—69 percent versus 60 percent.[24]

There were many other instances—already discussed—in which
those staying six months or more usually did better than those staying
a shorter time. Apparently, six months represented the crucial cut-off
period needed to make the Job Corps experience a "success"—even
though the most recent data seem to indicate that those with shorter
stays tend to "catch up" with the passage of time. Unfortunately, as
has already been pointed out, a major problem of the Job Corps has
been its inability to keep enrollees in the centers for an adequate
time to affect their future employability.

Some observers have argued upon an examination of the pre-
employment record of former corpsmen that youths who remained in
the Job Corps for six months or longer could possibly have made it on
their own, without the aid of the Job Corps. Fifty-eight percent of
this group was employed prior to entering the Job Corps and 34
percent were unemployed; while of those who stayed less than three
months, 50 percent were employed prior to entering the Job Corps,
and 38 percent were unemployed. The group that stayed the longest
thus demonstrated increased employability from the very start.

The argument is not persuasive. It can be argued that boys who
qualify for Harvard (or Muddy Gulch University) could also make it
on their own. The need is to establish institutional arrangements
which would help eligible candidates of the Job Corps to acquire a
basic education and rudiments of a trade, help them to gain employment and to advance at a pace commensurate with their ability and
motivation.

NOTES

[1]U.S. Congress. Senate. Committee on Labor and Public Welfare, *Hearings on the Economic Opportunity Act of 1964*, 88th Cong., 2nd Sess., (Washington: U.S. Government Printing Office, 1964), Part 1, p. 147.

[2] *Ibid.*, p. 148.

[3]"Lag in Job Corps Assailed by Ryan," *The New York Times*, June 2, 1965.

[4]Louis Harris and Associates, "A Study of Job Corps Non-Graduate Termina-
tions," January 1967. Printed in *Hearings on Economic Opportunity Amendments of 1967*, 90th Cong., 1st Sess. (Washington: U.S. Government Printing Office, 1967), Part 1, p. 155; and "A Study of August 1966 Terminations from the Job Corps," March 1967, in U. S. Congress, House Committee on Education and Labor, *Hearings on Economic Opportunity Amendments of 1967*, 90th Cong., 1st Sess. (Washington: U. S. Government Printing Office, 1967). Part 1, p. 364.

[5]Job Corps, Office of Economic Opportunity, "Educational Gains," (Assessment and Research Reports, No. 5), January 1967, p. 4, (mimeographed).

[6]*Ibid.*

[7]Job Corps, Office of Economic Opportunity, "Status Report No. 3: The Job Corps Evaluation," May 15, 1967, p. 4, (mimeographed).

[8]The Chamber of Commerce of the United States, *Youth and the War on Poverty,* (Washington: The Chamber of Commerce), 1966, pp. 46-48.

[9]Harris, "A Study of August 1966 Terminations from the Job Corps," March 1967, *op. cit.,* p. 419.

[10]Advisory Commission on Intergovernmental Relations, *Intergovernmental Relations in the Poverty Program,* (Washington: U. S. Government Printing Office), April 1966, p. 187.

[11]Harris, "A Study of August 1966 Terminations from the Job Corps," March 1967, *op. cit.,* p. 435.

[12]Glen G. Cain, "Benefit-Cost Estimate of Job Corps," Office of Economic Opportunity, May 22, 1967, pp. 13-14, (mimeographed).

[13]Louis Harris and Associates, "A Study of August 1966 Terminations from the Job Corps," March 1967, *op. cit.,* pp. 337-469; Louis Harris and Associates, "A Study of the Status of August 1966 Job Corps Terminees 12 Months after Termination," October 1967, (mimeographed); and Louis Harris and Associates, "A Study of the Status of August 1966 Job Corps Terminees 18 Months after Termination," March 1968, (mimeographed).

[14]Louis Harris and Associates, "A Continuing Study of Job Corps Terminations: WAVE II—Initial Interview with Terminations from August 15, 1966, to December 15, 1966," May 1967; printed in *Hearings on Economic Opportunity Amendments of 1967,* 90th Cong., 1st Sess., (Washington: U.S. Government Printing Office, 1967), Part 1, pp. 471-500; and Louis Harris and Associates, "A Study of the Status of November 1966 Job Corps Terminees—12 Months after Termination," January 1968, (mimeographed).

[15]Louis Harris and Associates, "A Study of Job Corps 'No-Shows': Accepted Applicants Who Did Not Go to a Training Center," February 1967; printed in *Hearings on Economic Opportunity Amendments of 1967,* 90th Cong., 1st Sess., (Washington: U.S. Government Printing Office, 1967), Part 1, pp. 241-336.

[16]Louis Harris and Associates, "A Study of Job Corps Non-Graduate Terminations," January 1967; printed in *Hearings on Economic Opportunity Amendments of 1967,* 90th Cong., 1st Sess., Washington: U. S. Government Printing Office, 1967, Part 1, pp. 123-239.

[17]Office of Economic Opportunity, "Progress Report by Job Corps Director," Press Release, June 11, 1967.

[18]Harris, "A Study of August 1966 Terminations from the Job Corps," March 1967, *op. cit.,* p. 411.

[19]Harris, "A Study of August 1966 Terminations from the Job Corps," *op. cit.,* p. 420.

[20]Harris, "A Study of the Status of August 1966 Job Corps Terminees 18 Months after Termination," *op. cit.,* p. 5.

[21] *Ibid.,* p. 6.

[22]Harris, "A Study of Job Corps 'No-Shows': Accepted Applicants Who Did Not Go to a Training Center," *loc. cit.*

[23]Harris, "A Study of Job Corps 'No-Shows': Accepted Applicants Who Did Not Go to a Training Center," *op. cit.,* p. 296; and Harris, "A Study of August 1966 Terminations from the Job Corps," *op. cit.,* p. 412.

[24]Harris, "A Study of the Status of August 1966 Job Corps Terminees 18 Months After Termination," *op. cit.,* pp. 412 and 424; and Harris, "A Study of Job Corps 'No-Shows': Accepted Applicants Who Did Not Go to a Training Center," *op. cit.,* pp. 296 and 301.

18

VOCATIONAL VERSUS ACADEMIC EDUCATION IN SECONDARY SCHOOLS

by Jacob J. Kaufman, *et al.*

Kaufman and his colleagues discuss the returns from vocational high schools compared to the returns from standard academic high schools. Their conclusion is that vocational education graduates enjoy a transitory edge in earnings over academic school graduates. As with all of the other authors, they issue a cautionary warning concerning cost-benefit techniques. They suggest that the technique is less valid for human resource programs than for allocating investments for public works projects.

The Vocational Education Act of 1963 (Public Law 88-210) authorized the appropriation of $60 million for the fiscal year 1963-1964, $118.5 million for the fiscal year 1964-1965, $177.5 million for the fiscal year 1965-1966, and $225 million for each successive fiscal year.

This substantial investment of federal funds in vocational education was designed "to maintain, extend, and improve existing programs of vocational education" and "to develop new programs of vocational education."

Reprinted from Jacob Kaufman and others, *Analysis of the Comparative Costs and Benefits of Vocational Versus Academic Education in Secondary Schools*, Chapters VII and VIII, Institute for Research on Human Resources. Pennsylvania State University, October 1967, pp. 1-2, 149-156.

In the Report of the Panel of Consultants on Vocational Education, which appeared in 1963 under the title of *Education for a Changing World of Work*, it was noted that a "*Lack of data and tangible evidence* . . . make it difficult for laymen and professionals to fully evaluate the vocational program of vocational education." (Emphasis in original). The report further stated that "Objectives and standards are quite valueless if, as criteria of appraisal, they cannot be compared with the data that indicate whether, or *how efficiently*, purposes are being achieved." (Emphasis added).[1]

The Report also stated that "Research of an evaluative type, which is fundamental to sound development, has been also very limited. Little or no evidence has been gathered regarding the results or effectiveness of the instruction given. . . ."[2]

It should be noted that the Panel expressed a concern over *efficiency* with respect to the investment of resources in vocational education. What does efficiency mean to the economist? To understand this concept it is essential to recognize that human wants are unlimited and resources are scarce (not in the sense of "few" or "rare", but only in the sense that they are not unlimited). Thus, the economist is concerned with "doing the best with what we have". Since all wants cannot be satisfied, society must concern itself with obtaining the "greatest possible satisfaction of these wants." In this respect economics is "a science of efficiency."[3]

If society is to concern itself with efficiency it must automatically concern itself with inputs and outputs. Too often in the evaluation of educational programs consideration is given only to outputs. This is only half of the task, for one cannot evaluate "benefits" or outputs without taking into account "cost" or inputs. Similarly, one cannot evaluate costs without taking into account benefits.

It can be further asserted that society is at its most efficient if the *ratios* of benefits to costs of all investments are equal. Any other condition would call for a shift in resources from that investment which has a lower ratio to one which has a higher ratio until a point of equality is reached.

This, in its simplest form, is the basis for the current study on the analysis of the costs and benefits of vocational education. The word "preliminary" is to be emphasized, since it is anticipated that the final report will base its conclusions on a more detailed analysis of the data, some of which will be further expanded and refined.

. . .

Before considering any implications of the theoretical and empirical results contained in this report, it is useful to recapitulate the essence of the above presentations.

A. RECAPITULATION

Cost-effectiveness analysis is a technique which concerns itself with the optimum allocation of resources. To evaluate the alternative courses of action in government educational programs, it is necessary to discuss the fundamental theory of public expenditures for education. [Our discussion of] public expenditures theory has discussed the rationale for governmental agencies in spending a large share of revenue for education; it has discussed the determinants of public expenditures for education; and it has discussed the sources of public expenditures for education. Since there is a limitation on the supply of public expenditures for education, while the demand for public expenditures for education is virtually unlimited, then, given the total amount of resources available for public education, it is relevant to determine the optimum allocation of expenditures on various educational programs. The optimum amount of public expenditures for vocational and academic education is at the point where the additional benefits from additional dollar spent on these alternative educational programs would be equal.

[We have previously examined] conceptual problems in the application of cost-benefit techniques to education. It was pointed out that education, as a component in the production, distribution, and consumption of private goods and services, is not comparable with private goods and services. In other words, education is a precondition for the existence and continuation of a given society. Taxation is a means to provide this education. Because of this, adjustment procedures, such as imputations of tax loss on property and sales tax differentials on current government purchases, are unwarranted.

It was also emphasized that cost-benefit analysis was first developed for application in the area of public investment projects. Economists have attempted to apply this evaluation technique to problems in education without looking into the distinctive nature of education in contrast to other public investment projects. Because of this, until enormous efforts are made to refine the conceptual and measurement problems in costs and benefits of education, analysis of only limited meaning can result from cost-benefit analysis of education. . . .

[The] actual study data on sample composition costs and benefits . . . indicated that, while benefits are conceptually more difficult to measure than costs, the indices of benefits in this preliminary report, as measured, are of a more reliable nature than the indices of costs. Wide cost variations occur but these variations are not indications of relative "costliness" or "quality." Employment and earnings benefits to vocational-technical curriculum graduates are shown to be generally higher than those to academic curriculum graduates.

The empirical results of costs and benefits for vocational and academic high school education have been estimated. . . . For City A, marginal costs of vocational-technical high school during the study period (1954-60) were higher than nonvocational senior high schools by $105 to $226 per additional student. However, at this stage of analysis only current and not capital costs are available. Therefore, no final conclusion can be drawn regarding the actual amount of difference in costs between vocational and nonvocational education. In the final report, it is anticipated that more satisfactory data, including measures of capital costs and costs by different programs, as well as structural data such as quality of teachers, which affect these cost variables, will be obtained.

The statistical analysis of benefits gained by vocational and academic graduates relies on two important indices of labor market performance, the percent of time employed after graduation and average monthly earnings after graduation. The statistical results indicate that over the six year period following graduation, the vocational-technical graduates have, on the average, earned $2,880 more than the non-college academic graduate, given that the two sets of graduates have the same socio-economic background. In terms of employment, the vocational-technical graduates were employed 5 months more in the six years than the non-college academic graduates. The differences between the two kinds of graduates are statistically significant at the one percent level. However, it should be noted that although the differences between these two sets of graduates were significant during the first year after their graduation, the differences are not statistically significant during the sixth year. These results suggest that as time after graduation passes the labor market performance (in terms of earnings and employment) between vocational and academic graduates tends to narrow and ultimately shows no statistically significant difference.

In investment terms, . . . for City A the monetary marginal costs of the vocational-technical curriculum are higher than the monetary marginal costs of the nonvocational-technical curriculum. However, for the study sample of non-college attending graduates from City A, the monetary marginal benefits to the graduates of the vocational-technical curriculum are also higher than the monetary marginal benefits to the graduates of the nonvocational-technical curricula, in particular, the academic curriculum. For the vocational-technical curriculum of City A, deflated marginal costs range from $528 to $573 over the relevant years of this study (fiscal years 1956-57 through 1959-60). The range of marginal cost for the nonvocational-technical curriculum is from $337 to $386. The average of these marginal costs for the vocational-technical curriculum is $553 and $374 for the nonvocational-technical curriculum. Graduates from the vocational-technical curriculum in City A earned $644 more (undeflated) per year over the six year period after graduation than did their academic curriculum counterparts.

Given the assumptions used to compute the ratio of the difference in marginal benefits to the difference in marginal costs, this ratio is 5.2, discounting at a six percent interest rate, and 4.4 at a 10 percent interest rate.

Given the assumptions used to compute the net present value, the benefit-cost ratio, and the internal rate of return, net present values of the vocational-technical curriculum are $1,013 and $590 per graduate, discounting at six and ten percent, respectively; the ratios of discounted marginal benefits to discounted marginal costs for the graduates of the vocational-technical curriculum are 1.7 and 1.4, discounting at six and ten percent respectively; and finally, the marginal internal rate of return is estimated at 20 percent for the graduates of the vocational-technical curriculum.

B. COMPARISON WITH PREVIOUS STUDIES

In recapitulating the presentation of this report, it is evident that this comparative study of vocational education versus academic high school education differs from the studies of Arthur Corazzini and Michael Taussig,[4] not only in empirical results, but also in methodology and conceptual framework. The methodology and conceptual work of Corazzini and Taussig which tend to limit the usefulness of their studies are briefly described as follows:

First, the benefit data used in Corazzini and Taussig studies pertained only to the period immediately following graduation. The uncertain state of affairs confronting a person during this period casts doubt on the reliability of such benefit data. In addition, Corazzini made the unrealistic assumption that the differential in starting wage rates between vocational and academic graduates would persist over a life time. Needless to say, Corazzini was aware of the shortcomings of such an assumption.

Second, both Corazzini and Taussig compared wage rates of vocational graduates with that of academic graduates instead of earnings. This comparison precludes a consideration of the employment factor and, therefore, gives an incomplete picture of benefits.

Third, Corazzini and Taussig studied the performance of vocational and academic graduates without properly controlling for the socio-economic factors which significantly affect earnings and employment. That is, the indicated differences in the performance of vocational and non-vocational graduates in the Corazzini and Taussig studies might have been due to differences in background of students instead of the effects of educational programs.

Fourth, in making a cost-benefit comparison of vocational and academic education, Corazzini and Taussig also implicitly assumed that these two types of educational programs are different means to the same end. Corazzini and Taussig did not consider the organic nature of the society where combinations of diversified skills are required. Vocational and academic education can conceivably service quite different functions. Vocational education and academic education are really different means to different ends. Without rigorously clarifying the circumstances under which meaningful comparison between the two curricula can be made, the studies can yield misleading implications.

Fifth, Corazzini and Taussig conducted their studies under the implicit assumption that economic variables or quantities are additive. In fact, however, perhaps more than any other type of economic or social activity, the effects of education have a high degree of interdependency. Thus, any change or difference in demand, supply, or any other economic variables would significantly affect the existing earnings and employment quite apart from the influence of education. Furthermore, earnings, employment, and monetary costs are not necessarily an appropriate index for decision making in education.

Sixth, in their studies of vocational versus academic education, Corazzini and Taussig apply cost-benefit analysis techniques without looking into the fundamental differences in the nature of education from that of other public investment projects. For example, the application of investment concepts to education and the use of discounting may not be appropriate because the perpetuation of the society requires that certain resources be used on education regardless of any strictly monetary efficiency measure.

Seventh, Corazzini and Taussig discussed the cost-benefit comparison of vocational versus academic education as if society was static. For example, both Corazzini and Taussig estimate that it costs more to provide vocational training than on-the-job training. They, therefore, suggested that it was cheaper for the society to subsidize employers so that they would provide on-the-job training for vocational students. However, these recommendations did not concern themselves with a consideration of economies of scale with respect to those employers providing training for workers. If employers were to provide all workers in the economy with on-the-job training, production or training facilities might have to be greatly expanded. The result may be that the employers would have to set up training programs which may cost society as much or more than vocational training programs within the public school system would have cost.

Finally, but fundamentally, both the Corazzini and Taussig studies cannot answer whether or not vocational education is worthwhile or desirable in an economic efficiency sense. To answer this question, one has to assume that the existing programs are already efficiently operated. This, in fact, is the implicit assumption contained in the Corazzini and Taussig studies. The fact is, however, that vocational and other educational programs may be inefficiently operated and that an assumption of efficiency is simply not valid. Without investigating the cost and production functions of the educational programs to determine the economies of scale, Corazzini and Taussig made inferences on the desirability of vocational education from an improper basis. Their conclusion that vocational education is not worthwhile may be interpreted to mean that vocational programs were merely inefficiently operated, and not that investment in them should be cut back either in absolute or relative terms.

C. CONCLUSIONS

1. Cost-effectiveness and cost-benefit analysis indicate the optimum allocation among alternative educational investments.
2. As a corollary, given that investment in education must occur, the proper technique for making comparisons between alternative educational programs is the comparison of marginal, or extra, benefits with marginal, or extra, costs among the competing programs. Neither costs nor benefits should be considered in isolation.
3. Public and private goods, especially when public goods are direct expenditures on the human agent, are not strictly comparable in economic efficiency terms.
4. The application of cost-effectiveness or cost-benefit analysis is less valid for those public investments or expenditures occur-

ring directly on the human agent, than, it is for public investments in goods, such as dams or highways.

5. Before cost-effectiveness and cost-benefit analysis can be used effectively, considerable refinement must be done with respect to the relationship between economic concepts and theory and the institutional (e.g., human, political, and social patterns of behavior) framework surrounding education.

6. The intent of cost-effectiveness or cost-benefit analysis must be to maximize the present value of net benefits, regardless of the particular criterion used in the investment decision-making process.

7. There is no universally correct criterion in either theoretical or practical terms.

8. Social and private costs and benefits do not necessarily coincide.

9. Social and private costs and benefits do not necessarily coincide with monetary or accounting costs and benefits.

10. Joint costs should not be distributed. Where two or more programs share costs jointly, the marginal costs and benefits of each program should be assessed independently of joint costs. The inclusion of joint costs in cost-effectiveness or cost-benefit analysis requires that the total benefits of the sharing programs should be compared with the total costs of the sharing programs, both joint and marginal.

11. If cost-effectiveness or cost-benefit analysis is to be performed, educational institutions must begin keeping adequate cost records as well as other information which relate to the production of education. This requires the maintenance of historical data in consistent and meaningful classifications. This data must be kept at the school level, and, even, at the curriculum and course level.

12. If monetary indices are accepted as a measure of benefit and cost, then, given the study sample of non-college attending high school graduates of City A, extra public funds allocated to secondary education should be distributed toward vocational-technical education to maximize the total monetary benefits to secondary education.

13. The immediately preceding finding assumes that the various curricula are already being efficiently operated. Such may not be the case. Therefore, a recommendation of this study is that efforts should be made to determine the degree to which various educational programs are being efficiently operated, independent of the question as to the optimum allocation of

resources between alternative educational programs. This implies that the cost functions of various educational programs should be analyzed.

D. IMPLICATIONS

The conclusion of this study is clear, namely, that vocational-technical education when compared with other curricula has a "pay-off" in terms of earnings and employment, recognizing at the same time the methodological and statistical limitations which have been discussed in this report.

Does this mean, however, that investment in vocational-technical education along traditional lines is desirable? Although this report was not directly concerned with this question, a brief discussion is in order.

There is evidence that vocational-technical education has not penetrated the student body, limiting its enrollment to a small percentage of students who not only must meet certain ability and aptitude requirements, but also are confronted with the teaching of related subjects in the more traditional manner.[5] To a large number of students in both the academic and vocational curricula the requirements are too rigid and the courses are not relevant to their needs.

Thus, vocational education, which has the potential to train youth for broad occupational skills, should be encouraged to expand in this direction. Many innovative curricula have been developed to accomplish this objective. Naturally, these experimental programs should be subjected to an appropriate evaluation along the lines followed in this report.

In effect, what is being suggested is that training youth for jobs should be expanded if we are to be concerned with earnings and employment. This expansion should include an investment either by re-allocating existing educational resources or by additional expenditures in training youth in broad occupational programs as well as in traditional vocational programs.

NOTES

[1] *Education for a Changing World of Work,* U.S. Department of Health, Education, and Welfare, Office of Education (Washington: U.S. Government Printing Office, 1963), p. 207.

[2] *Ibid.,* p. 213.

[3] C.R. McConnell, *Economics,* 3rd Edition (New York: McGraw Hill, 1966), p. 26.

[4] Arthur Corazzini, *Vocational Education, A Study of Benefits and Costs* (A

Case Study of Worchester, Mass.), submitted to the Office of Education, Department of Health, Education, and Welfare, August, 1966; and Michael Taussig, *An Economic Analysis of Vocational Education In The New York City High Schools,* A Paper Prepared for the Conference on Vocational Education, The Brookings Institution, Washington, D.C., April 17-18, 1967.

[5]See Kaufman, Jacob J. *et al., The Role of the Secondary Schools in the Preparation of Youth for Employment.* The Pennsylvania State University, Institute for Research on Human Resources, 1967. See also forthcoming report on vocational education in Pennsylvania.

SUGGESTIONS FOR FURTHER READING—PART VI

Borus, Michael E. "A Benefit-Cost Analysis of the Economic Effectiveness of Retraining the Unemployed." *Yale Economic Essays,* Vol. 4, No. 2 (Fall 1964), pp. 371-430.

Corazzini, Arthur J. "Prevention of High School Dropouts: An Analysis of Costs and Benefits." Mimeographed. Princeton University, 1965.

"Cost-Effectiveness Analysis of Manpower Programs." In *Manpower Report of the President.* Washington, D.C.: Government Printing Office, January 1969, pp. 219-224.

Harbison, Frederick and C. A. Myers. *Education, Manpower, and Economic Growth* (Strategies of Human Resource Development). New York: McGraw Hill Book Co., 1964.

Lichfield, Nathaniel. "Cost Benefit Analysis in Urban Development—A Case Study: Swanley." *Regional Science Association Papers,* Vol. 16 (1966), pp. 129-153.

Page, David A. "Retraining Under the Manpower Development Act: A Cost-Benefit Analysis." *Public Policy,* Vol. 13 (1964), pp. 257-267.

Somers, Gerald G. and Graeme H. McKechnie. "Vocational Retraining Programs for the Unemployed." In Gerald G. Somers, ed., *Proceedings of the Twentieth Annual Meeting,* Industrial Relations Research Association. Madison, Wisconsin, 1967, pp. 25-35.

Somers, Gerald G. and Ernst W. Stromsdorfer. "A Benefit-Cost Analysis of Manpower Retraining." In Gerald G. Somers, ed., *Proceedings of the Seventeenth Annual Meeting,* Industrial Relations Research Association. Madison, Wisconsin, 1965, pp. 172-185.

A NOTE ABOUT THE PRODUCTION OF THIS BOOK

Typesetting, page makeup, and indexing of this book were done by computer, using a program especially developed for TEACHERS COLLEGE PRESS, and set on an RCA Videocomp by Publication Services, North Bergen, N.J.

Printing and binding were done at Port City Press, Baltimore, Maryland, who also set some of the display type.